A Study of
Early Christianity

A Study of Early Christianity

Joseph B. Tyson

Southern Methodist University

MACMILLAN PUBLISHING CO., INC.
New York

COLLIER MACMILLAN PUBLISHERS
London

MACMILLAN PUBLISHING CO., INC.
866 THIRD AVENUE, NEW YORK, NEW YORK 10022
COLLIER-MACMILLAN CANADA, LTD., TORONTO, ONTARIO

Library of Congress catalog card number: 74-190674

Printing: 2 3 4 5 6 7 8 9   Year: 4 5 6 7 8 9

To My Mother;
To My Aunt Jo;
To My Wife, Peggy, and
To My Daughter, Linda

Preface

Although I did not begin to work actively on this book until 1968, I believe that the germinal idea for it came on the evening of October 20, 1966. At the invitation of Professors Albert C. Outler and William R. Farmer, both of the Perkins School of Theology at Southern Methodist University, a "somewhat motley crew of historians" gathered in Dallas for the first session of a Seminar on the Development of Catholic Christianity.* In the first paper of the seminar, Professor Outler challenged the traditional separation of New Testament and patristic studies. He claimed that neither constituted an intelligible field of inquiry and insisted that studies in early Christianity should draw on both. It was under this kind of conviction that I undertook to write an introductory textbook.

Textbooks in this field have traditionally been introductions to the New Testament. The general quality of these books has been high, but the approach has failed to do justice to the fullness of Christianity, which, in the early period, produced many more documents than those in the New Testament. The approach has reduced Christianity to that which was acceptable to later generations and has ignored many of those ideas that were not incorporated into later orthodox Christianity. My purpose in this book is to bore a small hole in the wall that separates the New Testament from early church history. The Introduction attempts to show, in greater detail, the reasons for the present approach. Part One reviews the historical and cultural heritage of Christianity in Hellenism and Judaism. Part Two introduces the relevant literature of early Christianity and includes treatments of canonical and noncanonical documents up through Irenaeus. Part Three focuses attention on various versions of Christianity in the first two centuries and attempts to show that Christians had not, at that time, developed a precise distinction between the orthodox and the heretical. The final section treats the early

---

* Designed as an ecumenical interdisciplinary seminar, it has been meeting for over five years. Four of the papers for the first year, including that of Professor Outler, are published in *Anglican Theological Review* 50 (April 1968).

Christian understanding of the historical Jesus. The book is designed chiefly for use in college-level courses which introduce students to the beginnings of Christianity, but may also be useful in other contexts. It should be used in connection with the primary material to which it refers. It will be best to read the relevant documents along with the section on the literature of early Christianity. In working through the later sections of this book, frequent reference should be made to the primary material. In appropriate footnotes, I call attention to available editions and English translations of the primary documents.

I wish to thank the faculty of the Department of Religion and the Provost of Southern Methodist University, H. Neill McFarland, for the help provided by a faculty fellowship in 1968. In that year I was able to explore the idea of this book for a term at the University of Cambridge. There I enjoyed the hospitality of the Reverend Principal Alan G. MacLeod and other faculty members at Westminster and Fitzwilliam Colleges. The assistance of two excellent typists, Mrs. Barbara Harper and Miss Teresa Gundy, has been invaluable. The interest, encouragement, and support of Mr. Charles E. Smith, formerly religion editor at The Macmillan Company, is greatly appreciated. I also wish to thank my own students, who, for the past three years, have been the unwitting victims of many of the ideas in this book. Their response has helped put these materials in final shape. I could not have completed this project without the support of my wife and daughter. They both assisted in reading proofs, and my wife, Peggy, devoted a great deal of time and care to the preparation of the index.

Joseph B. Tyson
Southern Methodist University
Dallas, Texas

Acknowledgments

Except where otherwise noted, Biblical quotations are from *The New English Bible.* © the Delegates of the Oxford University Press and the Syndics of the Cambridge University Press 1961, 1970. Reprinted by permission.

Where noted, the Scripture quotations in this publication are from the Revised Standard Version of the Bible, copyrighted 1946 and 1952 by the division of Christian Education of the National Council of the Churches of Christ in the U.S.A., and used by permission.

Contents

Part One: *The Heritage of Early Christianity*

Chapter One *The Historical Background*   33

Chapter Two *The Heritage from Hellenism*   67

Chapter Three *The Heritage from Judaism*   87

[xi]

Contents

Contents

Chapter Thirteen *The Tradition and Jesus* 385

List of Maps

[xv]

St. Gregory and the three scribes, book cover, ninth century. (Courtesy Kunsthistorisches Museum, Vienna.)

Introduction

Although this is a book about a religion, it is not a religious book. It is a history book which deals with the origin and formative events in Christianity. A study of early Christianity is essentially a study of the historical factors behind and within the movement in its initial stages. It should enlighten us on the chief personalities whose words and deeds impressed their contemporaries. It should bring us up against ideas on the nature of reality and on human existence. It should give us some knowledge of the course of events through which the movement gained acceptance.

How to Study Early Christianity

In order to proceed with the study, it is necessary to have a clear understanding of the boundaries within which it is to take place and the method by which it is to be pursued.

The Boundaries

The boundaries of a historical study are set by the object of study and by the period to be studied. To give a definition of Christianity at this point would be premature and misleading. It is possible to say, however, that the object of our study is a religious movement that took various names and exhibited diverse characteristics but that came generally to be called Christianity. The surprising thing about the movement is that, in its early stages, several quite different groups could call themselves Christian.

We shall find that there were deep rifts dividing these groups and that hostility sometimes existed between them. We shall not, in advance, attempt to distinguish between them by referring to one as true or orthodox and to all the rest as false or heretical. If we simply let the material speak to us, we find that the various groups that thought of themselves as Christian can be distinguished only by their leadership, their writings, and their characteristic emphases. Thus, we shall be able to speak of Pauline Christianity, Jewish Christianity, and Gnostic Christianity, as well as of other Christian groups. It is clear that out of this amalgam a more unified kind of religion eventually emerged, but it is equally clear that we cannot assume the latter to be identical with one of the earlier forms or that there was a single thread leading from the origin to the developed form. Our object of study, therefore, will be the movement called Christianity in the chief known forms in which it was presented in its early period.

Closely connected with a definition of the object of study is a limitation of the period to be covered. Any historical study must be limited in order to be manageable. A comprehensive study of the history of the world from the beginning of historical records to the present, although noble in its ambition, is essentially impossible.[1] For this reason, a historian specializes in a relatively brief period of time. Although he may have a general working knowledge of broad stretches of past time, he never considers himself at home in anything more than a brief period.

The temporal boundary of a historical study must be set not only in terms of its manageability but also in terms of its meaningfulness. The period must be set off by events which bring certain forces into operation at the beginning and by other events which alter conditions at the end. To study early Christianity, we must devote our attention to a period of time which starts with some originating event or series of events and concludes with a time when one can say that there is a fundamental change.

The originating event in Christianity is not hard to find. Although we may discuss the question of the precise beginning of the Christian church—whether with Jesus, the earliest disciples, or Paul—there is no doubt that the originating event for the Christian movement is somehow connected with Jesus. This is not to presuppose that he intentionally started the movement or founded a church, but only to say that the groups which thought of themselves as Christian, to a greater or lesser degree, found their origin in Jesus.

To set the concluding point for early Christianity is much more difficult, and one's choice is almost altogether a matter of judgment. Although most studies of this subject confine their attention to the books of the New Testament, this is not to mark out a meaningful history. In this case, the limiting of the period is determined by the quality of the literature rather than by historical conditions. It may be more defensible to mark the end of the

---

[1] Works such as Arnold Toynbee's *Study of History* are no exception. Toynbee is in search of principles for the operation of civilizations. He does not attempt to write a full history of the world.

period to coincide with the writing of the last New Testament book—that is, about A.D. 150. But in this case the historian must give his attention not only to the canonical literature but also to other writings by Christians of the same period. In no case can we confine ourselves to the books of the New Testament and claim that we are studying early Christianity.[2]

The application of good historical principles to our problem would seem to favor a date of about A.D. 320. At this time, the emperor Constantine acceded to the Roman throne, and the character of Christianity was dramatically changed. The religion which had been persecuted now became the religion of the emperor and, in a short time, the state religion of the Roman Empire. A history marked off by Jesus on one side and Constantine on the other would appear meaningful.

Another alternative is to set the concluding date shortly before the beginning of the third century. By that time, the chief groups that constituted the whole range of Christianity were in existence. From about that time on, a single form of Christianity began to dominate, a single universal organization began to emerge, and Christians began to attempt to agree on creedal statements. Anyone acquainted with Christianity in these and subsequent centuries knows that the process by which this absolutism was worked out went on for several centuries even beyond the time of Constantine. But once the church began to develop a procedure for discerning the difference between "true" and "false" Christianity, a new set of forces was introduced.

It is the conviction of the present author that the earlier date is somewhat more meaningful than the later one. The introduction of absolutist factors prepared the way for the imperial state church after the accession of Constantine. The earlier date also creates an obviously more manageable period than does the later. For these reasons, our time period will extend from Jesus to the end of the second century.

The Method

The claims of a religion are not limited to history, but they are made within history. A religion produces institutions that are phenomena of history. Its course of development includes a series of events relating to human beings, and it participates in events which have meanings of a human quality. It is, therefore, appropriate that a historical method be used in the study of a religion, for history is the study of human activities locatable in time and space. There is, however, no single, universally accepted historical method.

[2] This subject will be pursued in greater detail later in this chapter; see pp. 27 ff.

The fact is that historians have not all studied history in the same way, and we need to speak of "proposed methods" rather than of "method."

In his well-known book entitled *The Idea of History*,[3] R. G. Collingwood analyzed various approaches to the study of history as they made their appearance in the past. He maintained that in most studies done before the Enlightenment of the eighteenth century the common way of writing history was by the "scissors-and-paste" method. This phrase is particularly descriptive, for it pictures the historian as first using his scissors to excerpt writings from the past and then using his paste to put them together, editing them in such a way as to produce balance, perspective, and comprehensiveness. This method, says Collingwood, calls for little critical work on the historian's part beyond his exercising judgment in the selection and editing of materials. Such a historian raises few questions about the accuracy of the materials he uses. Through most of the pre-Enlightenment period, no method was available for such sophisticated criticism, although the work of Herodotus stood as a significant exception. In general, scissors-and-paste histories simply repeated the opinions of past writers with no reflection on the value of the material.

With the Enlightenment there arose a new approach to the study of history, which we may call a "testimonial method." In this, the documents of the past are treated as possible sources for ascertaining what really happened in the past—that is, they are allowed to give testimony about the past. This approach is different from the scissors-and-paste approach in that Enlightenment and post-Enlightenment historians recognized that the documents must be questioned as a lawyer questions a witness giving testimony. The historian must know just when a document is telling the truth, and in order to do this, he must know something about the author and his purpose in writing. A historian will not expect to read the truth in a document which is essentially propagandistic, for these documents may distort the past in order to prove a point. The historian's job is the difficult one of ascertaining the conditions under which he can expect to find the truth and of sifting his documents in search of it.

Although the Enlightenment produced a significant change in the study of history, Collingwood was convinced that the testimonial method did not make it possible for historians to approach their subject most profitably. He felt that post-Enlightenment historians were obsessed with the pursuit of factual data of minute proportions and that this did not permit them to get on with their task of ascertaining the intention and meaning of past events.

[3] (New York: Oxford University Press, 1956). The first edition appeared in 1946.

At a deeper level we may also question the concentration of this method on the past in terms of raw events. Indeed, we may ask, Is a raw event a part of history, and is it available to the historian?

A rather simple illustration may help us answer this question. Let us suppose that we want to discover the whereabouts of a man named George on a certain evening. In particular, we want to know whether he attended a certain party on that evening, a party attended by a relatively large number of people. Our only possible sources for this information would be people who had been present at the party, and their presence must be established. We could not, at any rate, accept the testimony of a person known not to be there, for his testimony would be hearsay at best. Even if George's wife said that he went, but without her, her testimony would not be conclusive. George may have stopped at a bar or at a friend's house, or he may have met with an accident which prevented him from going on to the party. Our witnesses to the event in question, therefore, are solely the people at the party. But not all of them would qualify, for some may not know the answer to our question. If George happened to be a particularly mousy individual, he could have been there and not been noticed. In this case, however, let us suppose that at least two witnesses could testify to George's presence at the party. One witness is Max, an outspoken political conservative who was able to engage in conversation with George for a brief period of time. In the conversation George expressed some doubt about American values—"I'm not so sure about this whole theory of planned obsolescence." Max would, in this case, remember George's presence at the party, but he would have a much stronger memory that George was "some kind of fuzzy-headed radical." The other person who can give testimony is Belinda, a young girl who takes a very negative view of the American establishment. She finds American values highly questionable and American life restrictive and generally oppressive. Like Max, she too had a brief conversation with George at the party. In the conversation George shocked Belinda by suggesting that he might someday like to have a Cadillac. Belinda, thus, will remember George's presence at the party, because she remembers him as a "crass defender of the American establishment."

This illustration has been drawn broadly on purpose so that we can extract from it several principles. The testimonial approach to history, which attempts to establish facts of the past by treating documents as testimony, has a basic problem: it must deal with the nature of human memory. In the above illustration we can establish George's presence only by consulting memory. Even if a photograph could be produced showing George and others at the party, we would require a qualified witness to identify the photograph. Human memory is our only source of testimony in history, but the nature of human memory is such as to make it quite deficient for our purposes. What are some of the drawbacks?

1. Not everything is remembered. We all know that no human being can remember everything which he has experienced and that there are some things which no one remembers. A perfectly good event may have escaped human memory altogether, because it carried with it no significance for the people who saw it. A mousy, untalkative George might not be remembered as present at an otherwise lively party.

2. What is remembered is remembered as having meaning. Max and Belinda both remember George because of their reaction to him. If we ask what they remember, we must say that they remember the complex of event plus meaning. They do not remember event alone. This habit of mind complicates the task of the historian, because the fact he is in search of is not precisely what is remembered.

3. After a time, the memory of meaning tends to obliterate the memory of event. Long after Max has forgotten the party and George's presence at it, he will remember that George is a "fuzzy-headed radical." Belinda also will remember George as a "crass defender of the American establishment." The fact that what Max and Belinda remember is contradictory further complicates the task of one in search of a raw event. It is only a slight exaggeration to say that the one thing human beings do not remember is raw events. It is an exaggeration, because events do form a part of human memory. But it is only a slight exaggeration, because people remember only significant events, and, when they remember them, the significance is attached to the event.

4. In the passage of time, events of a public nature gather traditional significance. This principle cannot be illustrated by reference to George at the party, for with public events we are dealing with those which have significance for groups of people. Such events are first remembered because of the significance they have for the participants or observers. But as generations pass, these events either accrue meanings relevant for each succeeding generation, or they cease to be remembered. The deeper in the past an event lies, the more it is subject to various interpretations. This process can be understood from Figure 1, where E represents the raw event and S represents

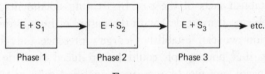

| Phase 1 | Phase 2 | Phase 3 |

FIGURE 1

the meaning of the event as ascertained in various phases. Phase 1 represents the event as it was seen by a group of observers. Even at this stage the event is observed with meaning, for if it had no meaning to the observer, it would not be noticed, let alone remembered. Phase 2 represents the event as remembered by the observers. Notice at this point that the event may have gathered a different meaning. Phase 3 represents the event as remembered by persons who were not observers but who heard of it from them. At this stage the significance of the event has been changed into something meaningful to later people who hold it in memory. The historian comes into this situation, usually, at a late stage. The historian in search of a raw fact must be able to discern the difference between E and S at every phase. His chances of working back to a point where he has only the raw event, E, are quite slim.

There are, to be sure, some things to be said on the other side. In the first place, it is not always necessary for the historian to begin his investigation at the latest possible point. Ideally, he may be able to look back from Phase 2. He can do this where an observer has made a record of the event and its meaning for him. In the second place, we cannot assume that all people lack an interest in separating event from meaning. If historians have some interest in doing this, chances are that others do also. In the third place, we can spot times and customs in which people unconsciously separate event from significance or where a custom is retained without specific meaning for the present generation. We must acknowledge the conservative nature of human institutions and observances, many of which are retained without relevant meaning for the present.

These three factors may guard us against a wholesale indictment of the testimonial method. But, by and large, it is not well suited to its purpose of understanding the past. This is so because it pursues the raw event, which is not directly a part of human memory. Furthermore, in its pursuit of the raw event, it proceeds by attempting to establish the veracity or mendacity of witnesses. The analysis above should show that, to some extent, almost every witness has a degree of falsehood, if one is simply after the truth about a raw event. A raw event does not have intrinsic meaning, but it is not remembered without some meaning. The historian who begins by accrediting some documents as testimony should end by discrediting almost all documents. This is the doom of the testimonial approach: there are so few to bear witness.

The scissors-and-paste approach to history has little contribution to make toward an understanding of the past, and the use of documents as testimony has serious defects. Collingwood suggests a third kind of historical method that he believes to be adequate to the task. In describing this method he continues the legal analogy of the post-Enlightenment approach, but he suggests that we use documents not as testimony but as evidence. The difference is not so subtle as the terms might imply. To treat a document as testimony means to ascertain the truth or falsity in it and then to accept only the true parts. To treat a document as evidence, however, means to allow it to shed whatever light it can on the problem at hand. In the following statement Collingwood uses the term *scientific historian* to refer to the ideal historian who works in the way he describes:

> Confronted with a ready-made statement about the subject he is studying, the scientific historian never asks himself: "Is this statement true or false?" ... The question he asks himself is: "What does this statement mean?" And this is not equivalent to the question "What did the person who made it mean by it?," although that is doubtless a question that the historian must ask, and must be able to answer. It is equivalent, rather, to the question "What light is thrown on the subject in which I am interested by the fact that this person made this statement, meaning by it what he did mean?"[4]

The general aim of Collingwood's evidential approach to history is clear enough from this statement. Now we must ask how one goes about this. There are three aspects to this method: the use of historical imagination, the use of questions and inferences, and the use of historical argument.[5]

HISTORICAL IMAGINATION

This is Collingwood's term for the central act of the historian. By means of imagination the historian attempts to re-enact the intention present in the mind of an actor in the past. To concentrate on intention is to move beyond the problem of the testimonial approach, for in his use of historical imagination the historian is not simply searching for a raw event. Collingwood says that a part of any event is its inside, namely, the intention of the actor who performed it, and that this inside can be described only in terms of thought. Thus, "for history, the object to be discovered is not the mere event, but the thought expressed in it."[6] The historian, therefore, attempts to duplicate the thinking of his object of study. Collingwood can even say, "All history is the history of thought."[7] This is really the only way to know the past, according to Collingwood, who says: "To know someone else's activity of thinking is

---

[4] Ibid., p. 275.
[5] Collingwood himself speaks only of the first two aspects. The analysis of historical argument is the work of Van A. Harvey, *The Historian and the Believer* (New York: The Macmillan Company, 1966).
[6] Collingwood, op. cit., p. 214.
[7] Ibid., p. 215.

possible only on the assumption that this same activity can be re-enacted in one's own mind."[8] The use of historical imagination means simply that we attempt to put ourselves back into a past situation, to judge alternative responses which might be made to the situation, and to discover what an actor meant by a deed he performed.[9]

QUESTIONS AND INFERENCES

Such rethinking is done by asking questions of past documents and artifacts and by drawing inferences. This procedure adds an objective ingredient, and Collingwood believes that public verifiability is possible, that everyone who rethinks a historical intention will draw the same inferences. To illustrate the process of inference making, he cites the analogy of the detective story. In a good detective story, the hero will evaluate any evidence he receives not simply in terms of truth or falsehood but in terms of the possible inferences it enables him to make. In the familiar situation where an unlikely suspect in a murder case confesses to the murder, the detective must not only decide whether the witness is telling the truth or not, but he must also ask why this person made this statement. The latter question is essential even if the person is lying. Is he covering up for someone else? Does he suspect that his wife is the murderer, and, if he does, why does he? Does he have some information he is trying to keep hidden, or to uncover indirectly? In other words, the detective does not just treat a statement as testimony which may be either true or false. He treats it as a basis of inference, as something which may have a bearing on the case. The detective must always ask himself: What may I *infer* from the fact that this person made this statement? The questions he asks cannot be formulated in advance. They will all spring from his basic question: What light does this shed on the case? His subsidiary questions will be guided by his basic one and will be related to the material with which he deals. Thus he will probe away at the case by asking questions and drawing inferences. The historian, by the use of historical imagination, will do the same.

THE HISTORICAL ARGUMENT

It is too imprecise to say simply that the historian makes inferences from the artifacts and documents at his disposal. We also need to know the grounds on which he can make these inferences, for surely there are both legitimate and illegitimate grounds. Are there not some rules he must follow

[8] Ibid., p. 288.
[9] The problem of a change in perspective is dealt with later in this chapter; see pp. 22 ff.

in making legitimate inferences? Van A. Harvey[10] has recently made an analysis of the process by which historical arguments are made. He does not cite the formal rules of logic but describes the process of historical argumentation in much less formal terms. The reason for this is that he conceives of history as a "field-encompassing field." It is not a field in itself such as mathematics or sociology. It is, rather, interested in human affairs, which are partly mathematical, partly political, partly sociological. Since it encompasses these fields, it has no uniquely historical method but uses whatever is appropriate in each field under discussion. Although there is a recognizable form for any historical argument, it is not really very different from any other kind of statement made in ordinary discourse. Any assertion made can be regarded as a conclusion (C). Behind this assertion stand certain data (D). Ordinarily, the data are not cited unless someone challenges the conclusion, by asking, "What have you got to go on?" But it is also possible for someone to challenge the transition between data and conclusion, and to answer this challenge we hold in abeyance certain warrants (W). The difference between data and warrants may appear subtle, but it is not negligible. The data are the indisputable facts which call for some conclusion. The warrants are the facts which give legitimacy to the step taken between data and conclusion. Moreover, warrants "confer *differing degrees of force on a conclusion*. They permit us not merely to assent to a claim but they justify a certain texture of assent."[11] There are some warrants which call for heavy assent and some which do not. Our assent can range from the admission of a possibility to an acknowledgment of certainty. So Harvey suggests that before every conclusion we place a qualifier (Q), that is, one of the following: possibly, presumably, probably, necessarily. He diagrams this situation in Figure 2.

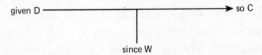

given D ————————————→ so C

since W

FIGURE 2 The Historical Argument. (Reprinted with permission of The Macmillan Company and SCM Press, Ltd. from *The Historian and the Believer* by Van A. Harvey. © Van A. Harvey, 1966.)

The data lead to certain conclusions, which call for a certain quality of assent, since there are warrants for the conclusions.

But there are various grounds on which an objection can be raised. Harvey

---

[10] Op. cit., pp. 38–67. In his analysis, Harvey depends heavily upon Stephen Toulmin, *The Uses of Argument* (New York: Cambridge University Press, 1958).

[11] Harvey, op. cit., p. 53.

calls attention to two kinds of objections: "(1) One may insist that the warrant does not apply in the particular case under discussion, that it has, for some reason, no authority, or (2) one may challenge the truth of the warrant itself."[12] If the first objection is made, a rebuttal (R) has been entered. If it is the second, the argument must now be beefed up by providing a backing (B) for the warrant. The complete diagram of a historical argument would look like Figure 3.[13]

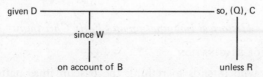

FIGURE 3 (Reprinted with permission of The Macmillan Company and SCM Press, Ltd. from *The Historian and the Believer* by Van A. Harvey. © Van A. Harvey, 1966.)

Harvey illustrates the method by the use of an argument about the crucifixion of Jesus in which a rebuttal is entered:[14]

D—Jesus was crucified.
C—So Jesus was judged to have been a political enemy.
Q—Presumably.
W—Since crucifixion was reserved by the Romans for political enemies.
R—Unless, in this particular case, an exception was made to please the Jewish authorities.

If, instead of a rebuttal, we had a challenge of the truth of W, then B would be provided, such as—Josephus and other contemporaries record only political crucifixions.

This is a complex structure of argument, but it is clear that it is, in form, a kind of common sense used in familiar speech. If we should analyze it closely, we might find that it draws on various patterns known in classical logic. But this is not the basic point. What is basic to this structure is the principle that conclusions must have data, and arguments must have warrants, and warrants must have backing. A secondary point is that assent to conclusions may be called for in varying degrees. The familiarity of this pattern of argument should not make it contemptible but should, instead, make it more useful as a description of the process of making inferences.

12 Ibid.
13 Ibid., p. 54.
14 Ibid., p. 53.

Of the various historical methods open to us, that proposed by Collingwood (with amendments by Harvey) seems to offer the best possibilities for
study. At this point it would be possible to present a number of criticisms of
this method. It seems better, however, to move on to an analysis of the way
in which it might be used for our particular study. Such an analysis should
show up the strengths and weaknesses as well as bring to light any problems
inherent in the method.

Historical Imagination and Early Christianity

A FRAMEWORK FOR IMAGINATION

A historian who intends to rethink the past in imagination must do so
within a certain framework. In order to approach potential evidence with
some sophistication, a detective must have a certain amount of information
to begin with—specifically, he must have a framework within which he can
ask questions, evaluate answers, and draw inferences. To the detective working on a current case, the framework is part of the available data, for it is the
environment in which he himself lives. The detective is quite familiar with
his framework and takes it for granted. This is an advantage which the
historian usually does not have.

Because people generally assume their historical framework without question or comment, the documents that a historian consults usually contain
little direct information about the environment of the author. Yet the historian must know his framework, for he is aware that it has an unconscious
influence on the persons who produce the documents. A Persian living in
the fourth century B.C. does not question the fact that he lives at that particular time and place. But the fact that he does so live deeply affects his
attitude toward himself, his life, and his world. His attitude is affected by his
own past and that of his people, as well as by the past of his neighbors, by
social, political, and religious institutions, by technology and education, and,
above all, by world view. Not only must the historian know these factors,
he must imagine himself embraced by this framework as he studies history.

In our study of early Christianity we must become aware of the historical
environment under which the documentary evidence has been produced.
The first three chapters of this book constitute an attempt to describe those
factors that seem to form a framework for early Christianity. We shall there
ask: What has been going on just prior to the opening of this period? What
cultural factors influenced life in the first and second centuries? What institutions did men take for granted? What intellectual forces were at work? How
did men at this time account for their world? It will be essential for us not

only to have this information but also to be able to see how it could fit together into a framework within which men did their working, thinking, worshiping, and writing. We must somehow be able to see how such a framework could dominate men at that time and place.

HOW TO TREAT THE EVIDENCE

Not only is it necessary for the historian to imagine himself as existing within the framework of that past which concerns him, but he must also know how to treat the evidence. There are preliminary questions which he must ask before he is able to make any inferences from the evidence. In general, he must be able to evaluate the material at his disposal for the evidence that might be contained in it. Since most of the material useful to the student of early Christianity is written material, there are certain questions he will ask before he can begin to use it as part of a historical argument. The historian needs to know: Where did this document come from? When was it written? Who wrote it? What was the specific background of its writing, and why was it written? Do we possess the original text of the document or must the text be reconstructed? If the document is written in a foreign language, can it be translated? All these are preliminary questions, and in order to answer them we must use some of the tools of literary scholarship. These must now be described in some detail.

Provenance. We know that Christianity during the period under discussion covered areas of Palestine, Syria, Greece, Macedonia, North Africa, Egypt, Italy, and Gaul. As we would expect to find some local variations in the religion of these areas, it is important for us to know the provenance of a document, that is, the geographical location of the author who wrote it.

How can this be determined? In rare instances the author may tell us where he is. If he gives us no information about his origin, we may be able to determine something about him from other sources. Some other document or documents may tell us that this author was associated with a particular city at a certain time, or we may discover that this is a generally known fact. If we have no such direct information, it is still possible to have indirect indications of origin. The document in question may display knowledge of other documents, or people, or events which are associated with a particular area. It may have linguistic, stylistic, or ideological traits which are similar to those characteristic of a certain geographical area. It may share ideas with a movement known to be located in a certain part of the world. Finally, we can find out where the document was originally known by examining references or allusions to it in other writings and can assume that it was known first in its own home country. No exactitude can be claimed for the inferences made upon indirect evidence of this sort, but we can determine where the cumulative weight of all such evidence falls. We might examine several alternative locations for a piece of writing and see for which one we can muster the greatest weight of evidence. In most cases, only the probable location of a document can be determined.

Chronology. Chronology is an essential part of history. To be sure, anyone who believes that the study of history is solely a matter of chronology, only the process of cataloguing events and people along a time line, should by now be disabused of this erroneous opinion. At the same time, however, history cannot proceed without reference to chronology, for history is the study of human affairs set in time and place. The proper setting of these affairs in time is what chronology is all about. Proper chronology is essential in evaluating documents as evidence. Without it we would be able to say nothing about the framework within which a document was composed. And unless we are able to say something of the historical environment of a document, we are not able to ascertain its evidential value.

But how does one judge the date at which a document was written? In general, there are two kinds of evidence for chronology: external and internal. External evidence is that evidence outside of the document which has a bearing on its date. It is frequently possible to set the date of a document by reference to another writing which mentions it. It is fortunate that some documents contain direct information about others, such as authorship, provenance, and date. Although a historian cannot simply take information at face value, he can make inferences from it. If we want to establish a date for Document A, and we know the date of Document B, which mentions A, we can conclude that A was written before B. Not all documents contain this direct kind of information. More frequently, we find that one document quotes from an earlier one or makes an allusion to something contained in it. Still more frequently, we may be able to find some way in which an earlier document has influenced a later one. All of these bits of external evidence—specific references, quotations, allusions, and influences—are helpful in the process of chronology.

Internal evidence for chronology is that which is found within the document in question. When one is looking for this, he simply reverses the procedure used in the search for external evidence, and now he looks for references, quotations, allusions, and influences within the document which can be traced to earlier writings. He may also look for traces of events whose dates are known. In some cases even the lack of such a trace may be an aid in chronology. If a document makes no reference to some event of crucial significance where it would be appropriate to expect some reference, it is probable that the document was written before the event. In somewhat more nebulous ways, the literary scholar and historian may try to set the time of a document by studying the relationship of its ideas to the general thought forms of possible periods. This kind of study is by no means precise, but one ought to be able to determine the century within which a certain book was written by examining the thought forms represented in it. Not only may thought forms be examined for purposes of dating, but also language patterns may throw some light on date. It is not difficult, for example, to ascertain that Chaucer's language does not come from the same period as Steinbeck's.

When one has collected all the relevant evidence, both external and internal, on the dating of a document, he may then attempt to infer a specific date for a document in question. In doing this he will first set up a pair of extreme dates: the *terminus a quo* is the earliest possible date for the writing of a document; the *terminus ad quem* is the latest, the date after which the document could not possibly have been written. These extreme dates must be rigidly determined. The *terminus a quo* may be set by a reference in the document to an event of known date. The *terminus ad quem* may be set by a datable quotation from the document in question. In other words, the terminal dates must be matters of universal agreement. After the extreme dates have been set, the attempt may then be made to narrow their range by the use of somewhat less rigid evidence. It is rare, in the study of early Christianity, that relatively certain dates for documents can be set, and frequently the student will meet with a range of dates of a decade, or a half century, or a century. But even this is of genuine value, for this kind of dating can eventually produce a chronology which, although not absolutely precise, enables the historian to see the proper relationships of priority and subsequence between several documents, between several events, or between documents and events.

Authorship. The knowledge of an author's name is of little intrinsic value. It is a different matter, however, if we know something about an author. If, for example, we know a name and can associate it with a person who held a high administrative post in Rome or commanded a legion in Gaul, that knowledge may add significant clues to the meaning of a document. Or, if we know that the author was a member of a certain philosophical school or religious group, or best of all, if we find that he wrote other books, we have discovered a great deal. With that information we are able not only to solve some chronological problems, but also to use one book as an aid in the interpretation of another.

How does one discover authorship? This can be done only by the evaluation of clues. Clues can come from anywhere, but the most likely places are the document itself and the writings that share its historical environment. We must admit, however, that success is quite illusory on this aspect of the study of early Christianity. We are rarely able to identify the authors of our earliest literature. The most we can hope for is to be able to identify the historical characteristics of the author or the group he represents.

Two special problems plague the efforts of historians of early Christianity. One is the tendency toward anonymous authorship. Many of our documents contain no statement on authorship. The four gospels of the canon—Matthew, Mark, Luke, and John—nowhere contain the names of these or any other authors.[15] We suspect that in these cases we are dealing with material which is not "authored," that is, not written by a creative writer. It is more likely to be traditional material, material which belongs to the community and has been passed down by it through the years. In these cases our efforts to identify an author will be frustrated. We shall go into this problem in greater detail later.[16]

The other problem is created by the special place assigned by the church to the writings of the apostles of Jesus. The church more highly revered books it thought were written by a select group of men and regarded others as having only a secondary value. But the church did not have the critical facilities to enable it to determine which books were indeed apostolic. Ultimately, it drew up a list of documents which it regarded as of primary validity, and one requirement for inclusion on the list was apostolic authorship. Since, in the process of canonicity, some books would have vigorous sponsorship from individual churches, we suspect that the claim of apostolic authorship was invoked in a number of historically dubious cases. It may be very helpful for us to know that a certain book was not written by an apostle, even when we are not able to say positively who the author was.[17]

Occasions and Purposes. The general historical environment of a document provides us with some knowledge of the occasion for its composition But most documents have a more specific occasion. Something has happened

---

[15] These names do not appear in the earliest manuscripts of the gospels, which must have circulated without titles. The familiar titles, "The Gospel According to Matthew," etc., appear only in later manuscripts. See the section on textual studies later in this chapter, pp. 17 ff.

[16] See chaps. 4 through 8.

[17] See pp. 27 ff., where the problem of canonicity is pursued further.

which causes the author to feel that his writing is necessary. It is helpful for us to know this occasion, for it frequently turns out that certain remarks in the document will be directed to the occasion and may be explicable only by reference to it.

More directly to the point is the purpose of the writing. Whereas occasion refers to the situation which prompted the author to write, the purpose is the end he has in view. When we ask his purpose, we ask: What did the author hope to accomplish by this writing? The relationship between the purpose of a document and its evidential value should be apparent, for we should know why an author said what he did. Such knowledge puts us one step closer to a proper evaluation of the document as evidence.

In rare cases, an author may tell his readers of the occasion or purpose of his writing. In most cases, however, the historian must resort to his usual method of inferring these matters from an examination of the clues provided in the document itself.

Text. The detective is usually able to confront his evidence directly, and the documents he consults are originals. This is also the case with most

Rylands Greek Pap. 457. A papyrus fragment of the Gospel of John, dating from the second century. The photograph shows both the front and back of a single leaf. (*Courtesy* The John Rylands Library, Manchester, England.)

historians whose area of study is in the Western world of the past three hundred years. But the historian who concentrates on a more remote past is rarely so fortunate. For the study of early Christianity, we have on hand today no document which is assuredly original. In almost every case, the original document has been copied and recopied and has finally disappeared.

Some of the documents relating to early Christianity were produced to be used in public; none of them was produced to be kept as a museum piece, or to be completely protected from harm. Many items, such as the letters of Paul, which were intended to circulate only in limited areas, were used by Christians in their services and were circulated widely. These documents, though revered, were subject to the fortunes of repeated use. Reverence is no guarantee of protection. In St. Peter's Cathedral in Vatican City, pilgrims for centuries have revered the statue of St. Peter and have expressed their reverence by kissing the right foot of the statue. Today, the foot is worn so smooth that it no longer resembles a foot. In manuscripts, use alone would have a disastrous effect. Some of our documents were written on scrolls and rolled up. In time, their outer edges would become worn and would perhaps fall off. Other documents were produced as codices, i.e., in the form of modern books with the text appearing on sequential pages. These were usually quite bulky, and repeated use would cause damage, especially to the first and last pages.

In addition, the text of documents relating to early Christianity was preserved for a long period without benefit of printing. The gospels of the New Testament, for example, were copied by hand for almost fourteen hundred years before they were produced in printed form. In the earlier centuries, copies of documents would be produced quite haphazardly, as occasion demanded, by an individual who would copy by sight. Anyone who has ever attempted to do this will recognize the difficulties. Such a scribe would find it very easy to omit a word, a phrase, or an entire line, to substitute one word for another, to write words in an incorrect order, to misspell words, or to duplicate a word, a phrase, or an entire line. Some scribes might intentionally correct what they took to be a mistake in the manuscript they were copying. Some people who had private access to manuscripts and studied them made marginal notes, a common practice of many students. But when a scribe copied a manuscript with marginal notes, he would have no way of knowing which marks were added and which were there already. So he might transfer a note from the margin to the body of a manuscript. In this way a pious remark of a student of the ninth century could end up in a later manuscript as a saying of Jesus.

A page from Codex Sinaiticus, fourth century. Note the marginal additions. (*Courtesy* the Trustees of the British Museum, London.)

In the medieval monasteries, the copying of manuscripts became better organized, but the hazards of copying were not overcome. In these institutions one monk would read from a manuscript, and the others would write down what they heard. This practice would perpetuate errors of the old system and would add some of its own. A scribe might not have heard a word that was read, or he might have heard it incorrectly. This possibility becomes a probability when we recognize that most of the documents were written in Greek and many of the monks knew only Latin. At one stage, the reader began to pronounce all vowels with one sound, that of the Greek iota, in a phenomenon known as iotacism. The poor scribe would have a most difficult time knowing what to write down. The result is that we now have a multitude of manuscripts, all defective, and no original documents.

The historian has not been defeated by the lack of original manuscripts. Using the methods and tools of literary scholarship, the historian of early

Christianity attempts to reconstruct these originals. This is a form of detective work in itself, and it is too highly technical to be treated at length here. Nevertheless, we can cite a few of the basic principles used by textual scholars.

The first thing that must be done with a manuscript is to date it. We must be able to ascertain the approximate time the copy was made before we can do anything else with it. This dating can be done by a study of calligraphy, for we know that letters had different shapes at different times. Another aid is the carbon-14 test, which can determine the approximate age of the material on which the manuscript was written. In general, the earlier manuscripts are to be preferred, but this is not a universal rule, as we shall see. A second step in the process is to try to place the manuscripts into families. The relationships of manuscripts to one another can be expressed in familial terms as shown in Figure 4.

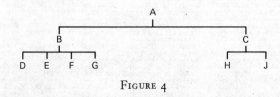

FIGURE 4

In this diagram, A represents the original document, which is the ancestor of all the copies but is no longer extant. In this case only two copies, B and C, were made from the original. The third step in the study of the text is to attempt a reconstruction of the original, using the family relationships of available manuscripts. If we have B and C and know the precise family relationships in the group, then our job is relatively simple. We could reconstruct A by comparing B and C, and we need pay no attention to the more recent descendants, D through J. But if B or C or both are missing along with A, then B and C must be reconstructed by a close examination of their descendants. This process can be carried on down the line without limit. If we can place each manuscript within the family structure, painstaking labor should produce a fairly accurate reconstruction of each ancestor up to and including the original.

Certain implications can easily be drawn from this procedure. For one thing it is apparent that a reconstruction of the original cannot be accomplished by seeing how many manuscripts carry one reading and how many another. Let us suppose that at a certain point in our reconstruction we are not sure whether the verb should be *was* or *will be*, since in Greek these two are more similar in form than they are in English. We would not be able to decide this question by saying that the majority of manuscripts must be correct. For if A contained *was*, it may be that C copied it correctly and B did not. If so, five of the manuscripts in our diagram would have an incorrect reading, and only three would be correct (assuming that each descendant, D through J, copied its ancestor correctly). A second implication is that we cannot rely exclusively on the date of a manuscript. It is true that the older a manuscript is the less the chance of compounding inaccuracies and that within family groups the older manuscripts are preferable. But age in no way guarantees accuracy. Indeed, we may have a relatively young manuscript with fewer errors than a more venerable one, simply because the younger had a more accurate ancestor. It is the family relationship that provides the clue to a reconstruction of a lost original. Without this reconstruction, we do not really know what the original author wrote.

Language. The detective usually shares the language of those involved in his case, and so do many historians. But the historian of early Christianity must become fully acquainted with the language of his documents.[18] The knowledge of language is not simply that of a word-for-word equivalency. The historian must be familiar with the inner workings of the language, aware of the way in which mental concepts are expressed in language, and aware of the effect that language has on mental concepts. Not only is there a possible barrier of language due to different historical environments, but barriers can be created because language may differ with the use to which it is put. Common words may have quite different meanings as they are used in different kinds of language. The chief difficulty we shall have to face is the peculiarity of religious language. It is increasingly recognized not only that religious language has its own technical terms, such as *heaven, angels,* and *God*; but also that it uses quite common words with uncommon, though analogous, meanings. Terms like *father, son,* and *kingdom* may have both common and religious meanings; and it is very important for the historian to distinguish them.

These preliminary matters are essential for establishing the evidential value of documents. Once the historian is satisfied about the nature of the documents, he may proceed to the more specifically historical task of making

[18] In the case of most of the early Christian literature the language is a form of Greek known as *Koine*. This was related to classical Greek, but it was altered in the Hellenistic period. It is now possible to study the use of this language in commercial documents and private correspondence from the period. A few of the documents relevant for our study were originally composed in Coptic, the language of Egypt during this time. It is possible that some of our documents may have been written originally in Syriac, Aramaic, or Hebrew.

inferences. We shall face this task in the latter part of this book. Once we have collected all the documents we deem to be pertinent, set their historical environment, and determined their literary history, our task becomes one of using historical imagination to infer meaning. We shall address our authors with this question: In view of the fact that you, living within a certain historical nexus, have written this document in response to this situation and for this purpose, what light does this shed on an understanding of early Christianity? As soon as we frame this question, we recognize that it cannot be addressed to the author but only to ourselves. We are really asking: What can I infer from this? This is not, however, a purely subjective question, although the subject asks it of himself. For we must remember the nature of historical argument, which includes the use of data, warrants, and backings, and hangs its conclusions on these harder nails. When we say that we infer, we mean that our conclusions are based on data and must be backed up by warrants which can be publicly cited.

Some Questions

Before we can move on to a direct application of this method to the study of early Christianity, there are certain questions which must be faced, some of which are directed to the method generally and others which arise because of the character of the object of study. These are crucial questions for our study, and they demand our serious attention.

DOES MY PERSPECTIVE AFFECT MY UNDERSTANDING OF THE MATERIAL?

This is one of the chief questions of historical study, and it is the virtue of twentieth-century historiography that it has recognized the part played by the historian's perspective in his study. Any historian neglects the question of perspective to his own detriment. An affirmative answer to this question means that every historian is a child of his own times and sees all things from the point of view he occupies. The modern historian cannot feel that the pre-Copernican view of the universe is as good as the one he holds. He cannot maintain that demon possession is an adequate explanation of human behavior, nor can he feel that magic formulas will protect him against harm. This is what it means to live in the twentieth century. If our perspective so profoundly affects our understanding, how can anyone pretend to be a historian, when being a historian means entering imaginatively into the thought of men who do not share our perspective? Perhaps this question can be answered by saying that no one person is the ideal historian. But in addition there are some positive observations which can be made.

For one thing, the historian who understands his own perspective is in a good position to understand another. This form of self-understanding is among the first steps that a historian ought to take. If a person can understand his own perspective, it ceases to be a completely determinative condition of his existence, for by understanding he can look *at* it and not solely *through* it. He can see why he acts in certain ways, why he accepts some things and rejects others. If he can see what his own perspective is, he may be able to push it to the side long enough to try on a different one.

In the second place, the understanding of a different perspective does not involve the adoption of it. It is possible for the historian to understand that people once accepted a belief in demon possession, but it is not necessary for him to use that belief as an explanation of the activities he observes. He cannot jump out of his skin and become what he is not, but he must *imaginatively* set himself in a position where he can see the world through another perspective. He does not need to become an ancient Egyptian in order to understand ancient Egypt any more than a detective needs to become a criminal in order to understand the criminal mind. We cannot overemphasize the need for sympathy and even empathy in the imaginative process. Without these there is lacking the quality of openness, which the historian must have. But this does not require the historian to identify with the object of his study. Thus a maxim for our study is: it is not necessary for the student to be an early Christian in order to study early Christianity, although he must be open to its perspective and sympathetic to the alternatives it presents.[19]

[19] An implication of this argument is that it is not necessary for the student to be a Christian in order to undertake this study. This is, however, a hotly debated question, for some feel that only the Christian is able to have the necessary sympathy toward the alternatives presented by this religion. Perhaps this question can be studied empirically, but at the outset two observations are in order. In the first place, the continuity between early Christianity and modern Christianity appears to be highly questionable. It is difficult to see that modern Christians have retained enough from the past to give them an advantage in the process of understanding. Secondly, it is difficult to arrive at any inelastic definition of the modern Christian. We do not seem to be at all sure of what it means to be a Christian. Anyone can see a number of Christian elements in various churches. But it is also possible to see Christian elements in groups which seem hostile to the churches. On the grounds of lack of continuity and lack of precise definition, it seems impossible to require the student or historian of early Christianity to be a Christian. In addition, however, there is a fatal flaw in the contrary argument. To suggest that only Christians can make this study is to close the subject to public examination. We maintain that historical arguments must be based upon data, warrants, and backings which are publicly available, and this means available to the Christian and the non-Christian. In summary, the present writer suggests that the historian of early Christianity must set himself *imaginatively* within the historical environment of early Christianity and must be open to its perspective. We have no evidence to show that the modern Christian is able to do this better than anyone else.

Introduction

Although this seems to be another form of the same question, it is necessary for us to face it because of the special problems it raises for our study. The historian who works with western materials produced after the Enlightenment has a great deal more in common with those materials than does the student of early Christianity with his. The scientific revolution forms a watershed for the historian, for it stands behind the profound ideological changes that define the modern world. This revolution means that we now think of our world in ways that would be incomprehensible to the ancient mind. Or, to put the problem where it belongs, the prescientific view of the world appears to be incomprehensible to the mind of the twentieth century.

It was a scholar of early Christianity, Rudolf Bultmann, who did the most to call attention to this problem.[20] He did it by talking quite directly of the presence of mythology in the New Testament. Mythology is not just a set of views which goes against some specific scientific discovery, for within the framework of scientific methodology it is possible to hold contrary views at different times. Mythology is "the use of imagery to express the other wordly in terms of this world and the divine in terms of human life, the other side in terms of this side."[21] Bultmann describes the mythology of early Christianity as having a cosmological view which assumes the existence of three stories in our universe with the earth in the center, the heaven above, and the underworld beneath. This is not simply a prescientific cosmology born of ignorance; it is really an attempt to express certain theological conceptions in physical terms, or to express other-worldly ideas in this-worldly terms. The ancient man thought of his life as a battleground in the struggle between the forces of good and evil. He would objectify this by thinking of these forces as locatable in the physical world; thus good spirits are in heaven, and evil ones in the underworld. Because he could do this, he could also imagine that the spirits travel back and forth and cause visible events on earth. If an inhabitant of the lower world influences man, we have a case of demon possession. The only way to get rid of such a demon is for a superior power to eradicate him, and thus we have an exorcism. If an inhabitant of the world above wishes to create an effect on earth, we have what we call a miracle. We must be careful to note that *miracle* is our term and not one which could be used by the ancients. It designates a phenomenon which challenges the

[20] See his article, "New Testament and Mythology," in H. W. Bartsch, *Kerygma and Myth*, trans. R. H. Fuller (New York: Harper-Row, 1961), Vol. 1, pp. 1–44. This article was actually written in Germany during the Second World War.
[21] Bultmann, in op. cit., p. 10, note 2.

regularities of nature; thus, by definition, a *miracle* is an impossible phenomenon, for, to speak scientifically, there are only regularities in nature.
Miracle is that which cannot happen; that is the meaning of the word. But
such a concept would not occur to the ancient mind, which would not grasp
the meaning of impossibility in nature. To be sure, men in the first century
knew the meaning of the usual, and they counted on certain natural functions. But, in these circumstances, the word *natural* did not mean *invariable*.
Although ancient man may not expect exceptions to usual patterns, he is
always ready for them. This readiness means that he has at hand an explanation for anything which appears strange to him: it is caused by a being from
heaven.

The problem for the modern historian is that he cannot think in terms of
miracle and demon possession. Yet the historian of early Christianity must
somehow set himself in a position where he can imaginatively reconstruct
ideas which are set within a mythological context. As Bultmann says, we
cannot simply adopt a world view; it is part of the inheritance we have as
citizens of the world at a particular time, and the mythological view of the
world is obsolete. Bultmann's solution to this problem is that of "demythologization." This process must not be confused with that tendency of
nineteenth-century scholarship to identify and then delete mythical elements.
That procedure bore close similarity to what Collingwood called testimonial
methodology in history, for it simply took each statement in the literature
and decided whether it was true or false. Bultmann's proposal is that we
attempt to understand the nature of myth. He says: "The real purpose of
myth is not to present an objective picture of the world as it is,
but to express man's understanding of himself in the world in which he lives.
Myth should be interpreted not cosmologically, but anthropologically, or
better still, existentially."[22] Bultmann continues in this article to illustrate the
method by proposing existential interpretations of the cross and resurrection
of Jesus. We need not follow this line of thought at present, but we must
understand that Bultmann is insisting on the interpretation of myth rather
than the discarding of it. He means that we must ask: What does it mean
that this myth is used? Why do men view the world this way? In the case of
a report of what we call miracle, we do not ask whether it happened, nor
do we ask what event caused men to think it happened. Rather we ask:
What kind of world is presupposed in this report? What light is shed upon
early Christian beliefs by acknowledging that men reported this miracle?

The similarities between the procedure of demythologization and the
evidential method in history should be obvious. It simply involves the applica-

[22] Ibid., p. 10.

tion of the question of evidential value to the special problem of mythology. In the case of a reported miracle we do not simply say: "This did not happen." Although we shall not be able to entertain the possibility that such a report factually records a raw event, still we are vitally interested in the value of the report as evidence for our basic question: What was early Christianity like? It is hoped that in this way a modern person can understand an ancient mind, despite the wide gulf which separates the two.

DOES THE NATURE OF RELIGIOUS MATERIAL INHIBIT ITS USE FOR HISTORICAL PURPOSES?

This is a particularly relevant question for our study, for the material we deal with is largely religious. But religious literature is not all of a kind, and it does not have a single character. When we speak of religious literature, we are speaking of various kinds of writings, each kind with its own purpose. Some may be liturgical, to be used formally by the religious community in a service of worship. Some may be devotional, designed for use in individual prayers. Or some may be homiletical, designed to exhort the faithful to greater devotion to the Lord of the cult. Other religious literature may be evangelistic, designed to convert the unbeliever to Christ. Or it may be prophetic material, which attempts to give some religious explanation to events in time. All of these types of literature may be called religious. Our question then is: Does the fact that our literature has these purposes mean that it cannot be used for an understanding of the movement it represents?

The historian's response to this question is an immediate one: There is no material which can be excluded as a possible clue to history solely on the basis of its character or purpose. To put it another way, simply because the material does not intend to make straightforward, historical statements does not mean that it cannot be used as evidence for the past. Certainly a criminal may not intend to give a straightforward account of a crime in which he was involved. But this does not keep the detective from taking his statements as evidence which might constitute a case against him. Any man may speak of his own guilt without so intending, and the fact that he intended to speak on a different subject does not diminish the value of his statement.

The fact that we are dealing with material with religious intentions simply presents a special form of the historian's general task of understanding the relationship of the purpose of a document to its evidential value. But one complication should be noted before we leave this question. Although our material has certain religious intentions, it contains sections which smack of straight historical reporting. We shall see that this creates a serious problem in those documents which seem to report facts about the life of Jesus. Here we have several rather long books which appear to be biographical as well as some, relating to the earliest Christian communities, which appear to be historical. What can we do with these? In general, we must treat them as we do any other documents. We address them with the question of purpose, and we must treat this problem sharply. In the case of our gospels, canonical and uncanonical, it will be essential to know whether the purpose is religious or whether the authors have some other intentions. It is crucial for us to make a correct decision at this point, and this decision cannot be made simply on the basis of the appearance of the material. A good detective is not fooled when his suspect goes into a long narrative which appears to be a factual report. He still asks: Why is this man telling me this? This must also be our attitude when we read a narrative which sounds like a historical report. We do not simply ask about its truth or falsehood, although we shall eventually need to determine it. But first we need to know why the document records this material.

The question about the relation of religious material to historical study must be answered as follows: The historian must determine the author's purpose in the case of all documents he approaches, and he must gauge the effect of this purpose on the material itself. An awareness of the religious nature of our documents should guard us against a premature acceptance of some material as if it were strictly historical.

WHAT EFFECT DOES CANONICITY HAVE ON A STUDY OF EARLY CHRISTIANITY?

During the first centuries of its existence, the general Christian community found it necessary to make a distinction between the various documents used in individual communities. It was recognized that the church would be in a better position vis-à-vis the rest of the world if it were unified in its religious point of view. We shall see as we proceed that an important element in the thought of early Christianity was the concept of authority. This concept emerges to overcome individual differences. Most Christians believed that religious truth was a matter of revelation. God disclosed truth to man; man did not discover truth by his own power. If so, one does not look toward man for religious truth, and truth will not result from the corporate agreements of groups of men or from majority decisions of the populace. The source of religious truth is God, but how does he disclose this truth? We shall not pursue this question fully here except to say that the Christian church ultimately came to the view that certain documents formed one source of truth. The churches, however, were using a multiplicity of books. It is apparent that truth cannot be present in books that contain diverse points of view, so some choice must be exercised. God must say specifically which books contain his truth. Thus, in forming a canon, the church was saying that a specific group of books contains God's truth and that this group may be read in public.

This demand for a canon had been building since before A.D. 200. From about that time we have the Muratorian Canon, a list of books that were authorized for public reading apparently in the Church at Rome.[23] The final solution to this problem is represented by a letter of Bishop Athanasius to his pastors, written at Easter, A.D. 367.[24] The verdict in this letter does not seem to rest upon a decree of some church council but rather upon a consensus in the church. The books included in the list may be referred to as canonical, and the full Christian canon is composed of three basic parts: Old Testament, Apocrypha, and New Testament.[25]

There are several principles which went into the making of a canon. The books of the Old Testament, including the Apocrypha, were not questioned.[26] In the case of the New Testament, we have already mentioned the desire for apostolic authorship. It was felt that, because the apostles were close to the historical Jesus and chosen by him, they formed a direct link in the chain of God's revelation. Another principle of canonicity was age. A book of recent date would not be likely to be revelatory, for it would present ideas unknown to more primitive Christians and would imply that they, and even the apostles, were not fully Christian. A third principle was that of widespread usage. No book could be considered canonical unless it had been used in various Christian churches, especially in the great Christian centers such as Rome, Constantinople, Antioch, and Alexandria. One may observe that the effect of this principle is that the canon largely represents ideas acceptable at the time of canonization, because a book would not be used in a

[23] We do not possess a complete manuscript of this canon, but only a fragment, which was discovered in 1740. It accepts Mark, Luke, and John, calling Luke the third and John the fourth gospel. The original probably included Matthew as the first gospel. It also accepts Acts and seven letters of Paul to churches, together with four to individuals (Philemon, I, II Timothy, Titus), as well as Jude, I, II John, the Wisdom of Solomon, the Apocalypse of John, and the Apocalypse of Peter. There is no mention of I, II Peter, James, Hebrews, or III John.

[24] The New Testament section is identical with that accepted today.

[25] It seems best to divide the writings this way, although the term *Apocrypha* needs some explanation. In Athanasius' letter there is only the distinction between the Old and New Testaments, and this distinction prevailed until the time of the Protestant Reformation. At that time, the reformers questioned the canonicity of several Old Testament books. This group of books came to be called Apocryphal. In the present situation, Roman Catholic Christians accept the Apocrypha as part of the Old Testment. Protestants reject it. Incidentally, the Protestant Old Testament is identical to the Hebrew Bible.

[26] We shall see later that Gnostic Christians had serious questions about the Old Testament. At the time of canonization, however, their objections were not heard.

church if it were not liked. It may also seem as if this is another version of majority decision making. To demand widespread usage is to make the practices of the majority of Christians determinative. Although this was the effect, it was not the intention. For no one stopped to count the number of Christians in each of the churches or even to count the churches, and the individual Christian was not asked for his views. The church felt that God would lead it into a correct decision in any perplexity and that he spoke to the church itself, which meant that he spoke to the leaders.

Our question is: What effect does canonicity have on the study of early Christianity? If we are to answer this question empirically, we must observe that it has had a profound effect. In general, the study of early Christianity has been carried on in two distinct disciplines: One is the study of the New Testament, which has made use of historical methodology but has been mainly a literary study. By concentrating on the canonical materials, this study silently grants to these materials an authority which its critical methodology would find unpalatable. The other discipline is the history of Christianity, basically a historical study, starting near the end of the first century and omitting a study of the New Testament itself. This fact is symbolized by the existence in most theological schools of two departments: the department of New Testament and the department of church history.

Not only does this separation imply an authority to the canonical documents, but it also means that a great deal of documentary evidence is either overlooked or examined as a kind of curiosity. It has been assumed that the documents of the New Testament, though they may not present an exhaustive picture of Christianity, do at least represent its main lines of development. But it should be apparent that those lines of development are, in part, the lines preferred by the fourth-century church, for the use of these books in the churches of that time was a key factor in their selection. After the fourth century, noncanonical books lost whatever popularity they once had. Many, perhaps most, of them are no longer extant. To proceed with a study of early Christianity and neglect those documents that are still available is to make a premature decision about the nature of the subject.

Although we must say that empirically the fact of canonicity has had a profound and detrimental effect on the study of early Christianity, we must also say that it need not continue to have this effect. A historian must be willing to look at any document which might contain a clue about his subject matter. For the historian of early Christianity, this will include all that material written during the first two centuries by people who considered themselves Christians. It will, of course, be necessary to classify this material and to use some for one purpose and some for another. It will not all be equally worthwhile. But for a historian to decide in advance that the basic or sole source of his information consists of a group of books canonized in a period subsequent to the time he is studying is for him to abdicate his position as historian.

A Summary of Principles

It is possible to state now the principles which can guide our study of early Christianity along the lines of an evidential historical method.

STEP I: ENTER IMAGINATIVELY INTO THE PERIOD TO BE STUDIED.

For us this is the first and second centuries. The scene will be the Mediterranean world. To enter this world imaginatively it will be necessary for us to know its past, its traditions, its institutions, and its world view. We must understand these factors as forming the framework in which our subjects lived, and we must understand what it means to see the world as they did. In Chapters One through Three, it will be our task to describe this framework.

STEP 2: COLLECT AND EXAMINE THE RELEVANT DOCUMENTS.

To speak of documents at this point is not to exclude other sources of information, such as art, architecture, and artifacts. But it is clear that the bulk of our information will come from written materials. In collecting these documents we must be open to all materials written by people who called themselves Christian or who wrote about Christians or addressed themselves to some topic relevant for Christianity. After collecting these documents it will be necessary to subject them to a rigorous examination to determine their provenance, date, authorship, occasion, and purpose. A proper text and a correct translation must then be provided. This book will not deal directly with the matters of text and languages, but Chapters Four through Eight will attempt to deal with the other matters for the chief relevant writings.[27]

STEP 3: BY HISTORICAL ARGUMENT USE THE DOCUMENTS AS EVIDENCE FOR THE NATURE OF EARLY CHRISTIANITY.

This step is unique to the study of history and crucial to evidential methodology. Chapters Nine through Thirteen will attempt to show how we can use the documents to understand the nature of first- and second-century Christianity and its memory of Jesus.

[27] For the canonical material, the Revised Standard Version or the New English Bible both present good, readable translations based on the best textual scholarship. For the noncanonical material, reference will be made at the appropriate points to available translations.

Part One

— ·◆·◆· —

The Heritage of Early Christianity

The cross of Lothar, reverse side. (*Courtesy* Ann Münchow, Aachen, Germany.)

Chapter One

The Historical Background

Although some phenomena appear to burst on the historical scene unannounced and without antecedents, the historian cannot pretend to understand them without first analyzing the nature of the world in which they made their appearance. In many cases he will find that the phenomena which so appeared had unheeded announcers and unrecognized antecedents. In this chapter it will be our task to do two things: *first, to analyze the political and social situation of the world at the birth of Christianity,* as it manifests itself in terms of historical events; *second, to give a thumbnail sketch of the history of early Christianity.* In the following two chapters, we shall analyze certain aspects of the intellectual and religious heritage of early Christianity.

Many writers used to speak of the *preparatio evangelii,* preparation for the gospel. They were speaking of the character of the world in the last few centuries before the birth of Jesus, a time in which they saw God working to get the world ready for the appearance of his son. To be sure, the representation of the world as controlled by the Divine Being is one which goes beyond the range of historical study, but we may still speak of a preparation for the gospel if we understand by it the complex of events, institutions, people, and ideas which formed the world in which Christianity first appeared. We are inevitably interested in what was going on in the world just prior to the appearance of Christianity and during the early period of the new religion. It was in the language and ideology of this world that the Christian message was first proclaimed. We are chiefly interested in the three centuries preceding the birth of Jesus and the two centuries afterward. We shall focus our attention on the eastern Mediterranean world—in particular, on Palestine, Egypt, Asia Minor, Greece, and Italy.

THE HELLENISTIC PERIOD

The historical period in which Christianity made its appearance and grew up is called the Hellenistic period. Since information on the basic history is easily accessible, no attempt will be made to duplicate it here. However, to refresh the minds of some and guide the reading of others, an outline of the period is presented.[1] It seems best to follow the suggestion of F. C. Grant[2] and divide the Hellenistic period into two parts: Alexandrian Hellenism from 336–31 B.C., and Roman Hellenism from 31 B.C. to the end of our period.

It was Alexander the Great who stood at the beginning of that period named for him. His father, Philip, king of Macedonia, had defeated a league of Greek cities headed by Athens and Thebes and created a political union of Greece and Macedonia. After the assassination of Philip, Alexander fell heir to this new arrangement and ruled from 336–323 B.C. The unification of Macedonia and Greece was preparatory to a much larger task, that of freeing both these areas from Persian interference, which had plagued this part of the world for two hundred years. To this task Alexander quickly turned. The defeat of Persia in 331 B.C. found him in possession of those lands which Persia formerly held, and the extent of this territory still baffles the imagination. Never before had so much territory, containing so many people and such diverse lands, changed hands so rapidly. Alexander could claim control not only of Greece, Macedonia, and Asia Minor, but also of that land around the Nile, Jordan, Orontes, Tigris, Euphrates, and even the Indus rivers.

Alexander was not only a superb military man; he was also something of a missionary. Perhaps because he had been tutored by Aristotle, he came to recognize the values of Greek or Hellenic culture, and he attempted to introduce some of its aspects in the lands he conquered. He settled certain of the eastern areas with his veterans and opened others for general colonization. From these outposts it was assumed that Hellenic culture would radiate into and ultimately permeate the older ones. But Alexander did not attempt to abolish the institutions of conquered nations. In fact, many of them survived, and what we have after Alexander is a mixture of Oriental and Hellenic culture, a mixture for which the word *Hellenistic* (meaning Greek-like) is quite appropriate.

Alexander's premature death in 323 B.C. left his dream unfulfilled. Politically, the reins of government fell to his generals. No single successor to Alexander was ever strong enough to exercise political control over this

---

[1] The basic history of the period may be found in any of the standard textbooks such as *A History of Civilization* by Crane Brinton, John B. Christopher, and Robert L. Wolff (Englewood Cliffs, N.J.: Prentice-Hall, 1967). See especially chaps. 2 and 3, on the Greeks and the Romans, and the bibliographies on pp. 92 ff. and 138 ff.

[2] *Roman Hellenism and the New Testament* (New York: Scribner, 1962), p. 83.

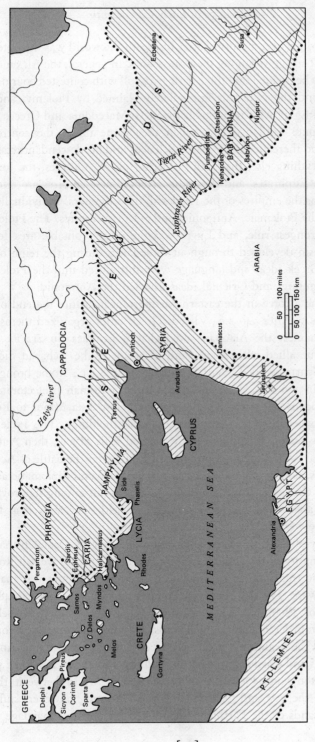

FIGURE 5 The Hellenistic Empires, c. 275 B.C. (Adapted with permission of The Macmillan Company from *The Macmillan Bible Atlas* by Y. Aharoni and Michael Avi-Yonah. Copyright © 1968 by Carta, Jerusalem. © Copyright 1964 by Carta, Jerusalem. © Copyright 1966 by Carta, Jerusalem.

whole area, and for over a century after his death the world was disrupted by almost constant struggles among these successors. In general, the Alexandrian empire came to be divided into three basic parts, all with contested boundaries. The area around the Nile was immediately claimed by Ptolemy, and his successors held Egypt with remarkable firmness. Macedonia and Greece were subject to dispute until 279 B.C., when they came under the control of Antigonus I and thereafter by his heirs. Seleucus and his descendants claimed just about everything else, that area bordering on the Orontes, the Jordan, the Tigris, the Euphrates, and the Indus rivers. These empires are referred to collectively as the empires of the Diadochi, the successors. Individually we may speak of the Ptolemaic, Antigonid, and Seleucid empires. The Ptolemies enjoyed the strongest rule, and Egypt was the most profitable area for its rulers. Hellenism developed throughout these lands during the reign of the Diadochi, as Greek ideas and language were introduced into the Ptolemaic and Seleucid empires and Oriental ideas invaded the Antigonid.

Rome became a force in the eastern Mediterranean before the end of the third century B.C. After 240 B.C., various Greek cities organized themselves into leagues, namely the Aetolian and Achaean Leagues. In 212 B.C., the Aetolian League allied with Rome, and in 196 B.C., the Achaean did the same. When Sparta seceded from the alliance in 148 B.C., Rome brought it back in and, in 146 B.C., declared Greece to be a Roman protectorate. In 188 B.C., Antiochus III, a successor to Seleucus, lost Asia Minor to Rome, and in the next century the Seleucids lost other holdings. The Ptolemaic empire stood a bit longer. Julius Caesar claimed it in 48 B.C., then Antony, but finally Octavian declared it a province of Rome after the battle of Actium in 31 B.C. Thus, not by any blitzkrieg but by military and diplomatic action of a piecemeal character, Rome could, by 31 B.C., count among its provinces most of those areas over which Alexander had held sway as well as those lands far to the west, in Gaul, Spain, and Britain.

It is precisely at the time of the annexation of Egypt by Octavian that we count the beginning of the Roman Empire and of the period we call Roman Hellenism. The transition from republican to imperial Rome was marked by three civil wars. The first, between Pompey and Caesar, ended in 48 B.C. at the battle of Pharsalia. The victorious Caesar proclaimed himself as dictator. The murder of Caesar by Brutus, Cassius, and other senators in 44 B.C. marked the beginning of the second civil war. Octavian and Antony defeated Brutus and Cassius at the battle of Philippi in 42 B.C. For some years thereafter, Antony and Octavian split the Roman world between them, Antony ruling the east and Octavian the west. Antony, however, suffered defeat at the hands of the Parthians, repudiated his previous marriage with

Octavian's sister, and settled with Cleopatra VII in Egypt. These actions brought about the third civil war, which concluded with Octavian's defeat of Antony at the battle of Actium in 31 B.C. Thereafter Octavian was the sole ruler of the Roman world, both east and west.

For a brief period it appeared that Octavian had not only rid the world of his enemies but that he had established blessed peace. A grateful Senate and citizenry bestowed on him the titles and powers which enabled him to function as emperor. He was, in fact, the creator of the Roman Empire. His most notable achievements were in the areas of political and military control. In respect to the former, he retained the forms of the Republic but, with the cooperation of the Senate, arranged them around his own person. He was *princeps*, or first citizen. The Senate gave him the title which became his name, Augustus, and thereby caused him to be regarded as semidivine. He had proconsular authority, which gave him ultimate power in the government of Spain, Gaul, Syria, and Egypt. His power as tribune carried with it the right to call the Senate into session and the right to veto any action. In 12 B.C., he was named *pontifex maximus,* chief priest of the state religion. At one point the Senate granted him an all-encompassing power to do "whatever he may deem to serve the interest of the Republic."[3]

Augustus' military control was exercised through the various Roman legions. At full strength a legion consisted of 6,000 men, although most were never full. At Augustus' death there were twenty-five such legions, mostly concentrated in the imperial provinces. This army of fewer than 150,000 men was called upon to put down a number of conflicts during Augustus' reign, and it performed effectively. The emperor made two significant military decisions. First, he concluded that the extent of effective control was limited. The boundary of the Empire in the west was the Rhine-Danube line, and in the east the Parthian frontier (see Figure 6). Although the Romans could probably have extended their borders, Augustus recognized that the value of any newly acquired territories to the Empire was not commensurate with the problems of governing them. Augustus' second military decision was a rejection of the republican policy of raising a force for a particular command. Instead, he created a standing army and placed various legions in the frontier areas, reserving only a small contingent, the Praetorian Guard, in Rome. Each garrison was responsible for the defense of its own outpost. The arrangement was based on the assumptions that Rome's enemies were those outside the borders and that within the Empire security could be guaranteed. The policy worked well in Augustus'

---

[3] See *Lex de Imperio Vespasiani.*

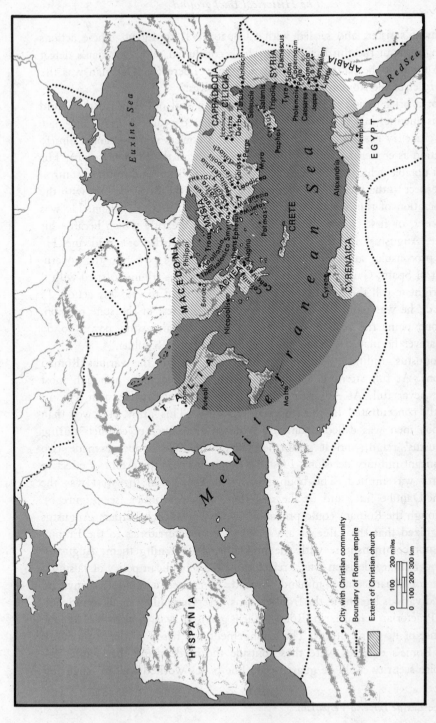

Figure 6   The Roman Empire. (Adapted with permission of The Macmillan Company from *The Macmillan Bible Atlas* by Y. Aharoni and Michael Avi-Yonah. Copyright © 1968 by Carta, Jerusalem. © Copyright 1964 by Carta, Jerusalem. © Copyright 1966 by Carta, Jerusalem.

time, so well that he could look upon his reign as a time of peace. Actually, it has been observed that there was more fighting during Augustus' reign than during that of any other emperor of the first two centuries.[4] Most of the fighting, however, was limited to border skirmishes, and the inner core of the Empire was relatively secure.

```
┌─────────────────────────────────────────┐
│                                         │
│   The Earlier Roman Emperors            │
│                                         │
│   Augustus, 31 B.C.–A.D. 14             │
│   Tiberius, 14–37                       │
│   Gaius, 37–41                          │
│   Claudius, 41–54                       │
│   Nero, 54–68                           │
│   Galba, 68–69                          │
│   Otho, 69                              │
│   Vitellius, 69                         │
│   Vespasian, 69–79                      │
│   Titus, 79–81                          │
│   Domitian, 81–96                       │
│   Nerva, 96–98                          │
│   Trajan, 98–117                        │
│   Hadrian, 117–138                      │
│   Antoninus Pius, 138–161               │
│   Marcus Aurelius, 161–180              │
│                                         │
└─────────────────────────────────────────┘
```

FIGURE 7   The Earlier Roman Emperors

No constitutional measure was devised for determining succession to the principate. It was, however, generally assumed that an emperor should have a say in the choice of his successor and that the Senate should have the right of confirmation. The reality of the situation dictated that the army also had a strong voice in such selections. In an ideal situation the three elements would agree, but this was rarely the case. Emperors would normally designate their successors from within their families or would adopt them as sons and heirs. As a result, dynasties were formed in several cases. The Julio-Claudian dynasty includes the first five emperors—Augustus, Tiberius, Gaius, Claudius, and Nero. Augustus had chosen his stepson, Tiberius, as successor, and his choice was ratified by the Senate. The Senate, however, voided the will of Tiberius on the grounds of his insanity and elected a grandson, Gaius. Nero was proclaimed emperor by the Praetorian Guard, and the

[4] See Stephen Benko, "The History of the Early Roman Empire," in *The Catacombs and the Colosseum*, ed. Stephen Benko and John J. O'Rourke (Valley Forge, Pa.: Judson Press, 1971), p. 43.

Senate confirmed him. The Guard and the Senate later turned against him, and he committed suicide before he could be captured. During the civil war which followed Nero's death, three emperors served in the space of one year. The Flavian dynasty (Vespasian, Titus, and Domitian) brought a temporary end to internal hostilities. Toward the end of Domitian's reign, however, there were several plots to overthrow him. He became increasingly suspicious; his last days were marked by tension and distrust, and he was assassinated by partisans of Nerva. Nerva was not popular with the army, and he was forced to accept as coemperor Trajan, who was acceptable to both army and Senate. It was alleged that on his deathbed Trajan adopted his nephew, Hadrian, and he was proclaimed emperor by the legions in Syria and accepted by the Senate. Hadrian adopted Antoninus Pius, a senator from Gaul, who adopted Marcus Aurelius, a Spanish nephew of Hadrian's wife.

Aside from the civil war at the death of Nero and the disputes which brought an end to the Flavian dynasty, the city of Rome was at peace. The borders, however, were frequently threatened, and unsettled conditions prevailed in the frontier provinces. Parthia, in the east, was always a thorn in the side of the Empire. After a number of conflicts during the rule of the Julio-Claudian dynasty, Nero established peace on the eastern frontier. Trajan extended Roman control temporarily into Parthia, but he was compelled to withdraw. His annexation of Armenia stood up, however, until it was consciously abandoned by Hadrian. A victory over Parthia by Marcus Aurelius brought Armenia back as a client kingdom of Rome. Augustus' establishment of the imperial boundaries generally stood up. Britain was added under Claudius, and the northern frontier was pushed farther into Germany under Domitian. Trajan conquered and settled Dacia and annexed Arabia and Armenia. His reign proved to be the high point of Roman expansion, for his successor, Hadrian, followed a policy of retraction. He felt that the Empire had overtaxed itself and needed consolidation. His wall in Britain is a symbol of his effort simply to defend his holdings. The boundaries changed little after Hadrian's rule.

The personal character of Augustus' successors cannot be simply summarized. Some, such as Trajan, were men of judicious temperament; some, such as Hadrian, possessed remarkable talents for administration; and some, such as Nerva, had a sincere concern for public welfare. But Tiberius was thought to be insane, Gaius became a tyrannical monarch, Nero was blamed for a disastrous fire in Rome, and Domitian's reign became a debilitating witch-hunt. In general, the second-century emperors are looked upon as better than the first, and it is a common judgment that Marcus Aurelius was the last great emperor.

The Jordan River near the southern end of the Sea of Galilee. (*Courtesy* Israel Government Tourist Office, Atlanta, Georgia.)

THE HELLENISTIC PERIOD IN JUDAEA

A study of the political events in Judaea during this period is a good exercise in determining the specific effect of these general patterns. Moreover, Judaea holds a singular importance for us as the originating location of Christianity.

Judaea, like Macedonia, had been under the control of Persia for two centuries when Alexander came to power. The fact that the people of Judaea enjoyed a higher degree of personal freedom under the Persians than they had under their former overlords, the Babylonians, does not mask the fact that they passionately desired political independence to match their religious uniqueness. But such independence was something they had not known for some time, not in fact since 586 B.C. Most of them seemed happy to see Alexander, for he appeared to be a liberator when he wrested Palestine from Persian control in 331 B.C. In the period of the Diadochi, Judaea was under Ptolemaic rule until about 200 B.C. The process of Hellenization was not vigorously promoted by these rulers, although Ptolemy IV (221–c. 203 B.C.) attempted to establish the worship of Dionysus throughout his empire. But at the conclusion of the Fifth Syrian War in 200 B.C., Antiochus III annexed Judaea to the cumbersome Seleucid empire, and almost immediately the Jews became subject to greater Hellenizing pressure.

Antiochus IV of Seleucia (175–163 B.C.)[5] was a worthy successor to his father, for he intended to press the advantage of the victory of 200 B.C. by invading Egypt itself. He initiated the invasion in 169 B.C. and laid siege to Alexandria in 168. But at this point Rome entered the picture and forced Antiochus to leave Egypt. On his way back north, he sent one of his generals to occupy Judaea's sacred city, the city of Jerusalem, and he entered the Temple, removed the high altar, and replaced it with an altar to Zeus Olympias. Subsequently Antiochus ordered Judaeans to offer sacrifices to Zeus either in their home towns or at the Temple.

In a small town near Jerusalem, an incident occurred which sparked one of the most memorable resistance movements in Jewish history. The Seleucid authorities felt that their new policy on religion would be more readily acceptable if the native leadership showed its support. One of these leaders in Modein was a priest by the name of Mattathias bar John bar Simeon bar

---

[5] It was customary for Hellenistic kings to add a designating title to their names, and Antiochus IV chose the title Epiphanes, meaning revelation. He believed himself to be a revelation of Zeus, although some of his contemporaries preferred to call him Epimanes, or mad. The name is written "Antiochus IV Epiphanes."

Hasmoneus.[6] It was felt that if Mattathias were to show his public support of Antiochus' policy, it would be difficult for another leader to gain support as a reactionary. Perhaps the Seleucids did not expect a great deal of resistance from the priests, for of all Jewish groups the priests had shown themselves to be most friendly to Hellenization. They had accepted the gymnasium and participated in Greek sports in Jerusalem. As recently as 170 B.C., Antiochus IV had entered a dispute between two priestly parties and named Menelaus, of the Tobiad family, as high priest of the Jews. When Jason, of the Oniad family, rebelled, Antiochus put him down. The Seleucids must have felt that the priesthood was theirs and was subject to their demands. It is possible that Mattathias had been a supporter of the defeated Oniads, although we have no direct information on this. At any rate, Mattathias was not their man. He appeared at an altar set up to Zeus in Modein, killed the royal commissioner and a fellow Jew who was about to make his sacrifice, destroyed the altar, and ran for the hills, calling all loyal Jews to support him. The book called I Maccabees dates this incident in December, 167 B.C.[7]

Mattathias was soon joined by his five sons and hundreds of fellow supporters. The resistance movement which now began is known as the Hasmonean or Maccabean War. Hasmoneus was the great-grandfather of Mattathias, and this became a family name for the leaders. The name Maccabeus was first given to Mattathias' son Judas; it seems to mean "the hammerer" and was probably applied to Judas out of respect for his military ability.

After the initial act of resistance by Mattathias, real leadership fell to Judas, whose untrained troops were outnumbered at one point by as much as six to one, according to I Maccabees.[8] But Judas met the enemy in four instances, which turned into remarkable victories for the Jews. Under his leadership the Jerusalem Temple was restored to its original purpose—according to I Maccabees exactly three years after its desecration, that is, in 164 B.C. Jews still remember this in the festival of Hanukkah (or festival of lights), which occurs annually in December. The people of Judaea were now free to follow the dictates of their religion.

Although religious freedom had been attained, it could be secured only

---

[6] The word *bar* is the Aramaic equivalent of the Hebrew *ben*. Both words may be translated *son of*, and they are used to designate family names.

[7] I Maccabees 1:54 ff. I Maccabees is one of our two primary sources for this period, probably written before 100 B.C. The other is Josephus' pair of works, *The Antiquities of the Jews* and *The Jewish Wars*, written about A.D. 90.

[8] I Maccabees 4:28–29.

The Three Hebrews in the Fiery Furnace, fresco, early fourth century, Catacomb of Priscilla, Rome. The painting was inspired by the Book of Daniel, which was probably written during the Maccabean revolt. (*Courtesy* Pontifical Commission for Sacred Archives, Rome.)

by a comparable political independence, and this the Maccabean warriors continued to seek. Antiochus IV died in 163 B.C., but, during the reign of his son, Antiochus V, the general Lysias recaptured Jerusalem for the Seleucids. In spite of his success, he could not press his advantage, because he found it necessary to return to Antioch to defend it against a challenger to the throne. The next Seleucid king, Demetrius I, attempted to interfere with Jewish religion by making an appointment to the high priesthood. Judas challenged this appointment and, in 161 B.C., defeated another Seleucid general, Nicanor. From about this time Judas himself began to assume the high priesthood, a position which the later Maccabees retained. Judas also entered into a treaty of friendship with the Romans, in which the Jews agreed to aid the Romans in case of war and the Romans agreed to treat the Jews as their allies. Notice of this treaty was sent to the Seleucid king, Demetrius I, but he acted speedily in sending another contingent into Judaea. In this encounter Judas himself was killed.

The leadership of the Jewish cause now fell to Judas' brother, Jonathan,

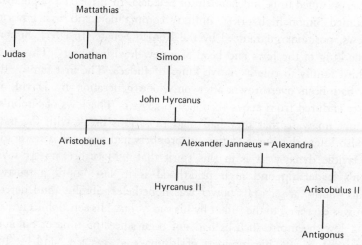

The Hasmonean Family

FIGURE 8   The Hasmonean Family

leadership which he held from 161–143 B.C. Our sources are less detailed on this period, but we can gather that Jonathan was able to consolidate divergent forces among the Jews. Moreover, during this time conditions in Antioch were quite unsettled, with the succession to the throne being constantly questioned. This not only limited opportunities for Seleucid generals to make forays into Judaea, but it also meant that Jews could play some part in the succession by supporting one pretender against another. At one particular point Jonathan was able to win important concessions from rivals to the throne. Alexander Balas, son of Antiochus IV, actually appointed Jonathan as high priest, and his rival, Demetrius I, offered to remit tribute which Jews had paid, to enlarge Jewish territory, to give presents and privileges to the Temple, and to rebuild the walls of Jerusalem, which had been destroyed by Antiochus IV. Jonathan agreed to support Alexander Balas, who killed Demetrius in 150 B.C. When Balas was married to Cleopatra, the daughter of Ptolemy Philometer of Egypt, Jonathan was dressed in regal attire and seated beside the bridegroom. Jonathan's influence in the international arena continued to increase. He used his own troops to suppress revolts in Antioch, in Askelon, and in Gaza. He conquered Galilee for the Jews, renewed the covenant with the Romans, and even opened negotiations with Sparta. Eventually, however, the Seleucid king Trypho became suspicious of Jewish power and led Jonathan into a situation where he was captured and ultimately murdered.

[45]

Simon bar Mattathias completed the work of his brother Jonathan, and Judaea continued to be independent of Seleucia. In 141 B.C., a popular decree proclaimed Simon high priest, military commander, and civil governor of the Jews, positions guaranteed by the Roman Senate. In effect, Simon had become king of the Jews and head of a new Jewish dynasty. This was only the third family to rule as native kings of Judaea. The first family, that of Saul, had been overthrown after only one generation by David, whose dynasty endured from about 1000 B.C. to 587 B.C. The Jews of Simon's time were not unaware that they had made a serious break with the past, for they also knew that some of the old prophets had expected a restoration of the Davidic dynasty. It is in this spirit that I Maccabees 14:41 says that Simon's leadership and high priesthood is to last "until a trustworthy prophet should arise." His power was nonetheless absolute and hereditary, and it was exercised to the fullest by his successors. His son, John Hyrcanus I, built a Jewish empire such as had not been since the time of Solomon. A fateful venture was his conquest of Idumaea, c. 125 B.C., and his forcible assimilation of these people into Jewish society.

The reigns of the later Hasmoneans were marked by family disputes. Aristobulus I had to imprison his mother in order to secure the throne for himself.[9] The reign of Alexander Jannaeus (104–78 B.C.) was notable for a war with Egypt and for internal conflict. Josephus reports that the king was once pelted by opponents at the altar of the Temple, that he massacred six hundred Jews, and that he had to call on the Seleucid king to help him put down a general rebellion.

The earlier part of the reign of Alexandra was fairly peaceful, but civil war between two of her sons was brewing during the latter years of her life. This civil war proved to be the undoing of Jewish independence, and Rome was able to make the most of it. The war broke out in 69 B.C., between Aristobulus II and Hyrcanus II. The former was victorious that year in a battle near Jericho and settled himself on the Jewish throne. But Hyrcanus, supported by the Idumaeans and the Arabians, was not yet ready to admit defeat. In 63 B.C., Pompey was advancing toward Damascus in his conquest of the east, when he was met by both contenders, who asked for his help, and by another embassy of Jews, who asked for a "restoration" of the theocracy. Pompey immediately perceived a personal advantage in the situation and delayed a decision. Aristobulus accompanied Pompey in a campaign against the Nabataeans but later deserted. Pompey captured and imprisoned

[9] Josephus, *Antiquities* XIII, 11:1, says that Aristobulus, in 105 B.C., was the first to use the royal title, but this seems to be only a nominal change, for Simon had effectively functioned as king.

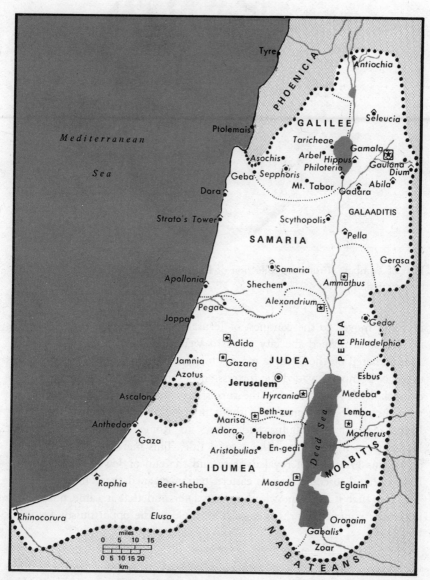

FIGURE 9 The Kingdom of Alexander Jannaeus, 104–78 B.C. (Adapted with permission of The Macmillan Company from *The Macmillan Bible Atlas* by Y. Aharoni and Michael Avi-Yonah. Copyright © 1968 by Carta, Jerusalem. © Copyright 1964 by Carta, Jerusalem. © Copyright 1966 by Carta, Jerusalem.)

Bust of Pompey. (From the collection of Professor Frank E. Brown, Rome. Used by permission.)

him and moved to the conquest of Jerusalem. The supporters of Hyrcanus in Jerusalem opened the city gates to welcome Pompey, but Aristobulus' men gathered on the Temple mound to offer resistance. After three months of siege, Pompey invaded the fortress and even entered the most sacred precints of the Temple, leaving the furnishings undisturbed and allowing the religious services to continue without interruption. He claimed Judaea for Rome, carried Aristobulus and others to Rome as prisoners, and left Hyrcanus as high priest without royal title. This marks the end of the independent Hasmonean royal dynasty and the end of Jewish independence. It was bound to come, for no eastern nation escaped the control of Rome. The fact that it came now rather than later and that it came under such unfortunate circumstances is a good example of the opportunistic tactics of the Romans.

The Seleucid monarchy was also over, and Pompey exercised control over the entire area through governors subject to his appointment, as Julius Caesar and Cassius did later. This was the case until 41 B.C., when Mark Antony gained control of the east, and thereafter it was Antony's men who governed the province the Romans called Syria. After the battle of Actium, Octavian continued the practice of appointing governors to Syria. Technically, Judaea was a part of this province throughout our period, but, in fact, it always presented a special problem. Although the Syrian governor attempted to keep order in Judaea, the historic events of these years are those which bring together Hyrcanus II, the Idumaean Antipater, and Julius Caesar. The Idumaeans had been incorporated into the Jewish empire of John Hyrcanus I in 125 B.C.; three quarters of a century later Antipater had become the representative of dynastic power in Idumaea. In 48 B.C., when Caesar moved against Pompey at the battle of Pharsalia, both Hyrcanus II and Antipater were on his side and contributed to his victory. As a reward, Caesar appointed Hyrcanus as ethnarch of the Jews and Antipater as procurator. The word *ethnarch* means ruler. It invests its holder with political power subject only to the oversight of Caesar himself. It might or might not be granted for life, and, although usually nonhereditary, Caesar made an exception in the case of Hyrcanus. Procuratorship, at this point, seems to designate a financial officer who has the duty of collecting Roman taxes. He too is directly responsible to Caesar; he does not hold his job for life, and the title is nonhereditary. Antipater was, however, one to take every advantage open to him, and, as procurator, he appointed his son Phasael as governor of Jerusalem and another son, Herod, as governor of Galilee. Antipater died before Antony came to power in 42 B.C. But the two had been friends in earlier years, and Antony did not forget this friendship. In 41 B.C., he stripped Hyrcanus of all political authority and made Phasael and Herod tetrarchs of the Jews.[10]

Things were still in a most fluid state, however, for in the year 40 B.C. Jerusalem witnessed a terrifying invasion of Parthians from the east. Antony had not been able to exercise control over these people or to protect his holdings against them. During negotiations for peace, Phasael and Hyrcanus were both captured, but Herod fled to the city of Rome. The victorious Parthians set up Antigonus, a son of Aristobulus II, as puppet king of Jerusalem. As it turned out, Antigonus was the last of the Hasmoneans to rule in Judaea.

While in Rome, Herod obtained from the Senate a declaration making him king of the Jews. With the help of Antony and the governor of Syria, he fought his way back to Jerusalem, which he captured in 37 B.C. Antigonus was arrested by the Romans and executed at Antioch. When the dust settled in Jerusalem, the Parthians had been defeated, the Roman troops had been withdrawn, and the Idumaean Herod was, in both name and fact, king of the Jews. He is known as Herod the Great, and his reign lasted from 37–4 B.C.

[10] *Tetrarch* literally means a ruler of one-fourth of a kingdom or province.

```
The Hasmonean Rulers

Mattathias, 168-165 B.C.
Judas, 165-161
Jonathan, 161-143
Simon, 143-135
Hyrcanus I, 135-105
Aristobulus I, 105-104
Alexander Jannaeus, 104-78
Alexandra, 78-69
Aristobulus II, 69-63
Hyrcanus II, 63-41
Antigonus, 40-37
```

FIGURE 10   The Hasmonean Rulers

```
Political Control of Judaea

Ptolemaic Empire, 323-200 B.C.
Seleucid Empire, 200-141
Hasmoneans, 141-63
Pompey, 63-48
Julius Caesar, 48-44
Cassius, 44-42
Mark Antony, 41-40
Parthians, 40-37
Mark Antony, 37-31
Augustus, 31 B.C.-A.D. 14
```

FIGURE 11   Political Control of Judaea

The character of Herod the Great has always been a fascinating object of study. Our sources do not allow us to picture him other than as a tyrant who knew the meaning of power politics. He was careful to retain every ounce of power due to him, brutal in executing his will, and insensitive to the feelings and needs of his subjects.

Throughout his reign he was fearful of any challenge to his regal right. He married, among others, Mariamne, the granddaughter of Hyrcanus II, and through her he could legitimize his reign. But her brother, Aristobulus, was drowned at Jericho, probably by assassins paid by Herod; Hyrcanus II was executed in 31 B.C., probably on a charge of conspiracy; and Mariamne herself was executed on a charge of attempted murder in 29 B.C. Alexandra, Mariamne's mother, was put to death in c. 28 B.C., as were two distant male

Hasmoneans, for conspiracy, in 25 B.C. In short, Herod left no one alive who could pretend to the throne on the ground of having Hasmonean blood.

Herod's relations with Rome demonstrate his political ability. His original appointment as king came from Mark Antony and the Roman Senate. But when Augustus defeated Antony and established the empire, Herod was found on the winning side. In 30 B.C. he met with Augustus, who confirmed his royal title and even increased his territory. He could legitimately claim the title *rex socius*, or client king of the Romans. This was a title conferred by the emperor on a ruler of a fairly extensive territory. It was not hereditary, it did not carry with it the right to wage war without imperial consent or to conclude treaties, and it granted only a limited right to coin money. Internally, the client king had unlimited power of life and death over his subjects, unquestioned power to impose taxes, and complete control of the police force. In general, Rome favored the policy of using native rulers in this capacity as long as they proved their ability to govern and raise the Roman taxes, and as long as they could put down rebellion. Herod worked well in this capacity. Though there are hints that some courts met for the purpose of deciding capital cases, it is clear that they were completely under Herod's control. Although the Mishnah granted the power of capital punishment to the Jewish Sanhedrin, that body does not appear to have met during his reign. Many of the executions in his career are due to rebellions attempted against himself and against Rome. In sum, whatever else may be said about Herod, he fulfilled Rome's requirements for a *rex socius*: he put down rebellion; he raised taxes; he was loyal to Rome.

Physically, the face of Judaea was changed during Herod's reign. He is noted for great building enterprises: temples, theaters, amphitheaters, race tracks, and even reconstruction of entire cities, including Samaria, and the building of new cities, such as Caesarea. In Jerusalem itself he built a theater an amphitheater, a fort, and a magnificent royal palace. Nor were his buildings confined to Judaea; they were to be found in Arabia, Rhodes, Athens, Tyre, Sidon, and Damascus. His most magnificent enterprise, however, was the enlargement and renovation of the Jerusalem Temple. This was the second Temple, built c. 515 B.C. on the site of Solomon's Temple, but the renovations Herod made were so extensive that the building was often referred to as Herod's Temple. The extent of the work can be seen from the fact that it was begun in 20 B.C. and was not completed until about A.D. 64. The building enterprises demonstrate Herod's desire to bring Judaea into line with the dominant culture of the world. The Hellenization which Jews had successfully resisted in the time of Antiochus IV now had come back with a vengeance.

A view of the city of Jerusalem, showing the Dome of the Rock, center. (*Courtesy* Israel Government Tourist Office, Atlanta, Georgia.)

The latter years of Herod's reign were beset with family difficulties. He suspected three of his sons of conspiracy, two of whom were executed in 7 B.C. and one in 4 B.C. But it was a time of suspicion and intrigue, and no one was really safe. Herod died in 4 B.C., shortly after the execution of his son Antipater, leaving in a will the amazing order that, at his death, several men of prominence should be killed so that there would be mourning. This order was not carried out.

For several months after Herod's death, the situation in Judaea was turbulent and explosive. Both Antipas and Archelaus claimed to have a will of their father which gave them the royal title. Archelaus was, however, more forceful in making his claim, and he attempted to secure power immediately upon his father's death. But at Passover time of that year a popular rebellion broke out against him, a rebellion which could be quelled only if Archelaus were willing to execute some of his father's advisors. It took his entire police force to restore a temporary order.

A will of Herod the Great would carry a good deal of weight, but no one forgot that it was the Roman emperor who selected provincial rulers. Thus, Archelaus and Antipas both headed for Rome, while a third brother, Philip, held the fort at home for Archelaus. When the two Herodian contenders reached Rome, they found that other members of their family were already there. They requested that Augustus put Judaea under direct Roman rule, but they were willing to accept Antipas if a Herodian must be appointed. Augustus listened to all claims and proposals but made no formal decision, although it was clear that he leaned heavily toward Archelaus. Pending a final settlement, he sent a Roman, Sabinus, as procurator. Upon his arrival in Judaea, further revolts broke out, this time apparently directed at securing freedom from Rome. These uprisings were dealt with by the use of troops assigned to the governor of Syria, who dealt brutally with the revolutionaries. Josephus says that two thousand of them were crucified. Next, another popular assemblage went to Rome to request that no Herodian be made king, and Philip also went to press his own claim. Finally, Augustus made his decision: Archelaus was to be ethnarch of Judaea, Samaria, and Idumaea; Antipas was made tetrarch of Galilee and Peraea; and Philip became tetrarch of Batanea, Trachonitis, and Auranitis. The extent of territory assigned to each is misleading. But it is clear from the title that Archelaus had precedence over his two brothers; Augustus also promised to give him the royal title if he governed well. In addition, the annual income received by the three reveals something of their responsibilities: Antipas' was double that of Philip, and Archelaus' was three times that of Antipas.

The difficulty in Archelaus' territory is also symbolized by the brevity of his rule, from 4 B.C. to A.D. 6. In that latter year a deputation of Jews complained to Augustus, who banished Archelaus and put Judaea under the rule of a procurator. Philip and Antipas seem to have had a more peaceful rule, the former retaining his position until A.D. 34 and the latter until A.D. 39. What little we know of these two indicates that they were fairly good rulers. Philip was responsible for a good deal of building, and his loyalty to the Romans was unquestioned. His authority continued to his death. Antipas seems to be of a piece with his father so far as ambition is concerned. After Philip's death the emperor, Tiberius, turned his territory over to another Herodian, Agrippa, and gave him the title "king." Antipas felt that he should also have a royal title and went to Rome to plead his case. But Agrippa's representatives opposed him; he was deposed and banished, and his territory was turned over to Agrippa.

The deposition of Archelaus in A.D. 6 amounted to a significant political shift. From this point on (with a brief break from A.D. 41–44), procurators were appointed by the emperors to rule Judaea, Idumaea, and Samaria.

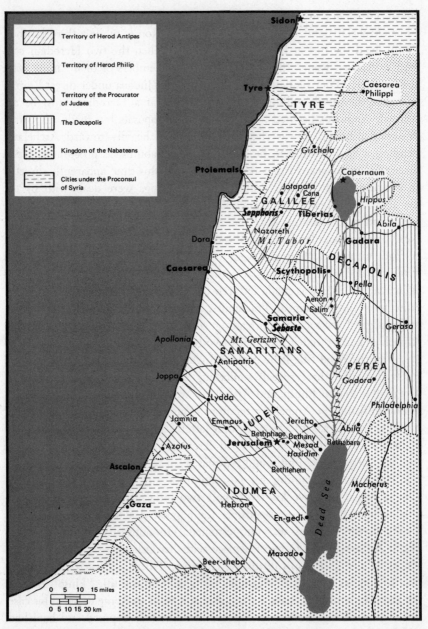

FIGURE 12 The Divisions of Herod's Kingdom. (Adapted with permission of The Macmillan Company from *The Macmillan Bible Atlas* by Y. Aharoni and Michael Avi-Yonah. Copyright © 1968 by Carta, Jerusalem. © Copyright 1964 by Carta, Jerusalem. © Copyright 1966 by Carta, Jerusalem.)

Originally procurators were financial officers, but in imperial days they were used to administer recently acquired, frontier, or particularly difficult provinces. In general, procurators had supreme judicial authority, but they left many matters to native courts. They had the right of capital punishment over all persons in their provinces, even over Roman citizens, who could, nevertheless, appeal the verdict. We do not know if the native courts retained their right of capital punishment, and this creates a particular difficulty in the study of the death of Jesus. The procurators also had complete financial and legislative control in their areas. Certain concessions were made for Jews because of their unique religion: in general they were not compelled to worship the emperor (except that certain emperors demanded it), but they were required to hold a sacrifice twice daily in the Temple "for Caesar and the Roman people." They were not usually required to revere the image of the emperor, which was always odious to Jews not only because it represented foreign domination but also because images were forbidden in the Torah. So Roman troops in Jerusalem generally carried no image of the emperor, and Romans permitted the minting of copper coins without the image. The strangest concession was that Rome did not bring a murder charge against a Jew who killed a Gentile within the sacred precincts of the Temple, even when the victim might be a Roman citizen.

Among the earlier procurators the only one worthy of note is Pontius Pilate, who bears a special relationship to early Christianity. Josephus probably knows nothing of this relationship, but he records several incidents

---

The Procurators

Coponius, A.D. 6–9
Marcus Ambivius, 9–12
Annius Rufus, 12–15
Valerius Gratus, 15–26
Pontius Pilate, 26–36
Marcellus, 36–37
Marullus, 37–41
Cuspius Fadus, 44–c. 46
Tiberius Alexander, c. 46–48
Ventidius Cumanus, 48–52
Felix, 52–60
Porcius Festus, 60–62
Albinus, 62–64
Gessius Florus, 64–66

FIGURE 13   The Procurators

involving Pilate and gives some insight into his administration. On one occasion he ordered his soldiers to display the emperor's image in Jerusalem. He diverted certain Temple funds to the building of an aqueduct. He imprisoned a prophet, who gathered a crowd in Samaria by displaying objects associated with Moses; and for this he was recalled to Rome. Philo records Agrippa I as saying that Pilate was recklessly arbitrary and that during his administration there was "corruptibility, violence, robberies, ill-treatment of people, grievances, continuous executions without even the form of a trial."[11]

The later procurators seemed particularly lacking in administrative skills and in understanding of the people they governed. They ruled with a heavy hand, attempting to suppress every sign of revolt but inadvertently creating the conditions which led to rebellion. From A.D. 40–66, groups of Jewish revolutionists became more and more prominent. These groups represent a basic Jewish desire for independence. Many people desire to control their own affairs, but with the Jews this desire was reinforced by their memory of recent independence under the Hasmoneans, by Roman attempts to interfere with religious rites and taboos which they little understood, and by the peculiarity of their monotheism. The understanding of the covenant, combined with a universal monotheism, amounted to a claim of religious sovereignty. There were two revolutionary groups: Zealots and Sicarii. The Zealots made clear the implications of basic Jewish affirmations: If we are God's people, God is not pleased by this Roman challenge, and his people must not allow it to go unanswered. We have no king but God, and his kingdom must come. The Sicarii would agree with this argument, but they seemed more prone to action than argument. A member of this group carried a *sicarius*, or short dagger, and he was prepared for the assassination of any Roman official or sympathizer.

Not all Jews were prepared to go so far as the Sicarii or Zealots. Many wealthier ones were able to adjust to Roman rule, and the great middle group seemed to be willing to wait for God to bring in his own kingdom. By A.D. 66, however, the whole nation seemed ripe for rebellion. This attitude was certainly inflamed by the ineptitude and downright dishonesty of the last few procurators. Josephus reports that Albinus operated by bribery and that Florus was in league with robber bands, which plundered whole cities.

The disastrous war broke out in May, 66, and before it was over two Romans destined for the imperial throne did battle with the Jews. Vespasian was military commander from the summer of 67 to the summer of 69, when he was proclaimed emperor. Titus took over in 69 and concluded the war

---

[11] Philo, *Embassy to Gaius*, 38.

in 73. The climax came in 70, with Titus' conquest of Jerusalem and burning of the Temple. Effectively the war was over in that year, and the widespread effects of the burning of the Temple will be noted later.

Another rebellion broke out in A.D. 132, against the emperor Hadrian. The probable reason for it was that Hadrian had announced plans for rebuilding Jerusalem as a non-Jewish city, with a temple to Jupiter on the site of the old Jewish Temple. In addition, this rebellion could claim the leadership of one who was widely regarded as Messiah, Bar Cochba. Bar Cochba was supported by a priest, Eleazar, and a rabbi, Akiba. But in the end the leaders were captured, and Jerusalem was converted into a Gentile city with its temple to Jupiter and a sanctuary to Aphrodite. After A.D. 135, Romans drove Jews out of Jerusalem and issued a decree forbidding them entrance to the city.

Judaea's turbulent history, which is marked by a religiously based demand for independence from foreign control, forms a dramatic backdrop for the appearance of Christianity and constitutes a significant part of its heritage. Before we can move on to sketch the rise of this new religion, however, it will be necessary for us to take note of certain sociological factors which affected the eastern Mediterranean world.

Social Conditions in Imperial Rome

Here we must briefly consider some of the more important aspects of Roman life—political, social, and economic. It is essential to have at least a general idea of these aspects of culture in order to understand the response to the Christian message and the social contributions to it. Since it is not possible to present an exhaustive treatment of social conditions throughout the Mediterranean world, our attention will be focused on Rome in the first two centuries.

Cultural Unity

The most serious internal problem for the Empire was the creation of unity among diverse nationalities. The emperors attacked the problem politically, by superimposing Roman government on top of native government in the provinces or by recognizing a client king. In either case, the Roman presence was clear to all. Governors and procurators in the imperial provinces were appointed by the emperor and were responsible to him. Taxation was a constant reminder of Roman authority. Armed garrisons in the provinces frequently functioned as cultural influences. The Empire committed itself to maintain peace within and between provinces and to protect them from non-Roman invasion. The guarantee of peace was, however, not always effective, for peoples such as Parthians frequently disrupted it. Nevertheless, borders in most areas were fairly secure for the first two centuries. The price that the provinces paid for the pax Romana consisted of accepting Roman political institutions and paying the taxes. It was a high price, but it was not without its benefits. Aside from sheer political control, Rome made few incursions into the social and religious life of the provinces. Most of the native institutions continued to function as long as they did not interfere with the governing process. Language served as an important tool of unification. To be sure, native languages continued to be used within each province, but in international affairs, commerce, and literature, Koine Greek was the language. The use of Greek was not a Roman demand on the provincials; it was a natural development during the period of Alexandrian Hellenism. Latin was used in legal circles, in Italy, and in some western provinces, but it did not replace Greek until after the second century. The use of Greek in the provinces opened minds to the classics of Hellenic literature, philosophy, and religion, and probably contributed greatly to cultural unification. Nevertheless, there was little feeling of such unity in the east, and there were numerous conflicts of culture. In Augustus' time, large numbers of people migrated into Italy from the east, and they generally considered Italian culture to be inferior. Cultural unity was more nearly a reality in the west than in the east. Hugh Last observed that "The time was to come when Gauls and Illyrians would show themselves more zealous Romans than the inhabitants of Italy itself."[12]

Social Classes[13]

The social class system among the Romans was far more definite and visible than are those in modern western countries. The system was not a product of the Empire but was inherited from republican times, and in fact it remained constant in the shift from Republic to Empire. In republican times, birth and legal status defined the social classes, but under the Empire,

[12] In *Cambridge Ancient History* (New York: The Macmillan Company, 1934), Vol. 10, p. 427.

[13] In the section which follows, the author is heavily dependent on John G. Gager, "Religion and Social Class in the Early Roman Empire," in Benko and O'Rourke, op. cit., pp. 99–120.

money and talent were beginning to carry some weight. Furthermore, an upward mobility was a characteristic of the system in imperial times.

The top class was the senatorial aristocracy. This was originally a nobility of blood, but Augustus imposed an additional capital requirement of 1 million sesterces (about $50,000). It was generally felt that a senator needed the income from this much capital in order to perform his public duties. The most notable feature of the aristocratic class during the first two centuries was the decline in its numbers. As a result of deliberate purges by the Julio-Claudian dynasty and a declining birth rate, the number of the old senatorial families shrank until only one was left by A.D. 130. Senatorial positions were consequently filled from the lower social ranks, from among persons who possessed the necessary capital. The chief source of capital for the older families was land; the newer ones engaged in commerce. The satirists Martial and Juvenal are devastating in their portrayal of the morality of the nobility. Samuel Dill attributes the immorality to imperial despotism: "The reign of such men as Caligula [Gaius], Nero, and Domitian not only stimulated the grossness of self-indulgence, but superadded the treachery and servility of cowardice."[14] It is also true that family loyalty was not the respected virtue it had once been, but the more serious problems were in the area of public morality. In speaking of Seneca's criticisms, Dill says: "The vices which Seneca treats as most prevalent and deadly are not so much those of sexual impurity, although they were rife enough in his day, as those of greed, gross luxury, treacherous and envious cruelty, the weariness of jaded nerves and exhausted capacities of indulgence."[15]

The equestrian order ranked next below that of the senatorial nobility. The emperor could admit into the order any free-born citizen who could supply a capital of 400,000 sesterces ($20,000). No limit was placed on the number of families in the order, and the titles were not restricted by heredity. Procurators and provincial governors were drawn from this class, and many became capitalists in business and commerce and acquired considerable wealth.

The class of freedmen, or emancipated slaves, was perhaps the most aggressive in Rome. They owed a kind of allegiance to their former masters, and many remained in their service. Others were able to acquire significant wealth and occupy positions of power. They were to be found in commerce, banking, and government service. Those in the employ of the emperor, the

---

[14] Samuel Dill, *Roman Society from Nero to Marcus Aurelius* (New York: Meridian, 1956), p. 7.
[15] Ibid., p. 11.

imperial freedmen, managed the major administrative departments of the government, and some served as public secretaries and controlled access to the emperor. Rome protected the rights of freedmen, both in their attempts to work for wages and in their assimilation to the body politic.

In terms of class, the plebs ranked ahead of the freedmen, but in terms of the benefits they derived from the class structure they must be regarded as occupying a position just above that of slaves. Although the plebs were free-born citizens, they were poor, and many were on public relief. They served as artisans, farm hands, and construction workers. Their wages were low, for they had to compete with slaves for jobs.

Slaves formed the bottom rung of the social ladder. Slavery was an accepted institution throughout the Mediterranean world, and the ranks were filled with Rome's conquered people. The problems of dehumanization and of relations between master and slave are endemic to the institution. In addition, slavery created an economic situation which restricted possibilities for a genuinely free labor market. If one looks at labor as a commodity which may be bought and sold, it is apparent that if the market is filled with cheap or free labor, there is little place for the wage earner. Thus, the price of labor was kept down by slavery, and both pleb and slave were victims. A reversal began to take place in late republican and early imperial times, however, as many masters found it too expensive to maintain large numbers of slaves. Manumissions became increasingly numerous, so much so that they had to be controlled.

Provincial foreigners were generally regarded as being outside the class system and irrelevant to it. Most were on a par with slaves, because they were not Roman citizens. Such citizenship was a birthright for children of recognized Roman marriages, and it carried with it the right to vote in certain local matters and the right to appeal an unfavorable legal decision to the emperor or his designate. Citizenship was usually granted by the emperor to native political leaders in the provinces and frequently to persons who made some outstanding contribution to the Empire. Such persons had all the rights of citizenship, including the right to hold a position as an equestrian, a senator, or even emperor (witness Antoninus Pius and Marcus Aurelius). Citizenship was finally granted to all free provincials by Caracalla in A.D. 212.

Women's rights were increasingly recognized and protected in imperial times. Free-born Roman women enjoyed the rights of citizenship. By the second century, women were not compelled to marry against their will; the absolute authority of husband over wife had disappeared; and divorce was permitted on the request of either partner. Juvenal writes of women who attempt to rival men in law, international affairs, sports, and drinking.

Education

Although Rome never aspired to universal education, schools were available for a wide range of men and women. They were not exclusively for the wealthy. There were three levels: primary, secondary, and advanced. Children could start school at age seven, where the primary curriculum included the Greek and Latin classical writers, music, and mathematics. In the secondary schools, students were taught to write in the classical style. Advanced education was available for the professions of law, rhetoric, philosophy, and medicine, and was concluded at about age twenty. The study of philosophy involved a commitment to a particular philosophy or philosophical school. Jewish education was structurally parallel to Roman, but the curriculum consisted almost entirely of the Scriptures.[16]

Living Conditions

The population of the Empire under Augustus is usually set at about fifty million, of whom about five million were citizens. The population of the city of Rome has been variously estimated, but Carcopino's calculation of about one million at the time of Augustus and 1,200,000 under the Antonines must be nearly right.[17] These figures may not surprise the modern reader until he realizes that urban transportation did not allow ancient cities to expand to a size comparable with modern ones. Consequently, imperial Rome housed a large population in a relatively small area. Although there were many private dwellings, most Romans were crowded into apartment houses. These houses were built in multiple stories to a height sometimes exceeding sixty-five feet. In most the base was inadequate to support the height, and many of them collapsed. Furthermore, the wooden structures frequently burned. They were built close to the streets, which were crowded, twisting, and unmarked. Public latrines, which were scrupulously clean, were available, but most people carted sewage to dung heaps or turned alleyways into cesspools.

[16] See John T. Townsend, "Ancient Education in the Time of the Early Roman Empire," in Benko and O'Rourke, op. cit., pp. 139–163.

[17] See Jerome Carcopino, *Daily Life in Ancient Rome*, ed. Henry T. Rowell, trans. E. O. Lorimer (New Haven, Conn.: Yale University Press, 1940).

Standards of living varied considerably. Cities fared better than towns and rural areas, and Italy was more prosperous than the provinces. But even within the city of Rome, which appeared to those outside as a glamorous paradise, the situation was one of contrasts. By the end of the second century, about half the inhabitants lived on public charity, and most of the rest were slaves. Carcopino estimates that only about 150,000 families could live independently.[18] The range in the cost of living is indicated by the fact that a minimum annual wage was 20,000 sesterces ($1,000) and that no one with less than 20 million sesterces ($1 million) could consider himself wealthy. The government also took a large bite out of income. Every adult paid a poll tax and a 1-per cent sales tax. In addition there was a 5-per cent inheritance tax, a 4-per cent tax on the sale of slaves, a 5-per cent tax on manumissions, and a 2½-per cent tax on the transportation of goods.[19] In a province such as Judaea, the situation was extreme. Jews in Palestine paid all of these taxes plus a number of religious dues—a tithe on income, a Temple tax, redemption money required for a first-born son, a tax on an annual harvest, and a tax on early spring fruit. The good Jew was also expected to make a contribution for the support of the Temple, for the poor, and for the building of local synagogues. After A.D. 70, Vespasian required a special poll tax of a half shekel on every Jew between the ages of three and sixty. F. C. Grant estimates that for the Jewish family in the first century, a staggering 30 to 40 per cent of the income went to support Roman and religious taxes.[20]

There was social unrest in the first two centuries but no significant reform movement. The aristocratic class, frustrated at the loss of ascendancy, came closer to revolt than did the other classes. Small farmers felt that they were being exploited by absentee landlords, and they developed a deep hostility toward the cities. Others, such as the plebs, were not happy with their lot, but they felt the social disadvantages more keenly than the economic. Freedmen were working within the system for their own betterment, and slaves, who could look forward to manumission, felt that the system worked on their behalf. Although it had weaknesses which were to become apparent, it worked as a tolerable system in the first two centuries.[21]

[18] Ibid., p. 65.

[19] See John J. O'Rourke, "Roman Law and the Early Church," in Benko and O'Rourke, op. cit., p. 183.

[20] See F. C. Grant, *The Economic Background of the Gospels* (London: Oxford University Press, 1926), p. 105.

[21] See Clarence L. Lee, "Social Unrest and Primitive Christianity," in Benko and O'Rourke, op. cit., pp. 121–138.

A Preview of Early Christian History

Although we cannot here anticipate the results of our study of early Christianity, it is essential to have in mind a basic historical context, which can be filled in as we proceed. The purpose of this sketch is only to locate in place and time the key people and movements which will form a focus for our study.

Many early Christian writers affirm that John the Baptist had something to do with the foundation of the movement. John is presented as a desert preacher who called Jews to repentance in preparation for the coming kingdom of God. He used baptism as a rite of initiation into the movement and as a protective seal against the holocaust to come. Probably because he was critical of the marital life of Herod Antipas, that ruler had him beheaded. The movement he initiated seems to run parallel to Christianity for a period, but, as time passed, competition and even hostility developed between the two groups. John's activity seems to be located in Peraea, on the east bank of the Jordan River, and probably centered on the years A.D. 27–28.

It is, of course, to Jesus that all Christians look for the initiation of the movement. The precise date of his birth is not known; his public preaching would be just after that of John the Baptist, and his death occurred between A.D. 28 and 30. The initial scene of his activity was in Galilee, but his ministry reached its climax in Jerusalem. His preaching was cast in terms of Jewish thought forms and concepts and, in its emphasis on the imminence of the kingdom of God, was quite similar to that of John. He drew around himself a group of students, or disciples, many of whom were with him both in Galilee and Jerusalem. Most of the details of his life are subject to a great deal of debate, and some will be investigated at the appropriate time. Even the cause of his death is unclear, although it is certainly the result of litigation involving Jewish and Roman authorities.

After his execution, some of Jesus' former disciples began to preach that he had been raised from the dead. They regarded his resurrection as a signal that the Messianic kingdom was about to come, and they preached that Jesus was soon to return as Messiah to initiate the events of the end time. Their mission seems to have been confined to Palestine, and their preaching had a Jewish cast to it. Many Jews who accepted their message met together in Jerusalem, where they continued to participate in the Jewish cult but also formed a community around specifically Christian practices. The head of this congregation was James, known as the brother of Jesus and intended as the head of a family dynasty.[22] Communities of Jewish Christians in Palestine attempted to keep alive the memory of Jesus' life and teaching but apparently did not write down this information.

Although the Christian movement started in Palestine, it soon moved out into the wider Graeco-Roman world, where it found a reception among both Jews and Gentiles. Precisely when the Judaean Christians began to feel that Gentiles should have a part in their new religion, we cannot be sure. We do know that there were some even in the Jerusalem congregation who urged a Gentile mission. There were Christian communities in Damascus and Antioch in the early days and in Alexandria and Rome only a short time later. We know most about the work of a single missionary to the Gentiles— Paul, who at various times was associated with men of a like mind, such as Barnabas. Paul had been a diaspora Jew and a persecutor of the Christian movement. After his conversion, he came to the recognition that Christianity could not be confined to Jews, and he spent a number of years (between A.D. 40 and A.D. 60) preaching the news of Christ in Asia Minor, Macedonia, and Greece. He finally came to Rome and was probably executed there in A.D. 62 or 64. By the end of his career, Christian meeting houses were established in many important centers, such as Ephesus, Thessalonica, and Corinth.

We have little information on Christian participation in the Jewish rebellion against Rome, but the end of the war almost certainly brought with it the end of Judaean Christianity. There is an old tradition that the Christians in Jerusalem escaped before the fall of the city in A.D. 70 and reassembled in Pella, to the east of the Jordan River. Little is known of this community but Jewish Christianity continued in a number of places, especially in Syria.

After A.D. 70, a number of Christian writings appear which focus attention on the initiating emphasis given the movement by Jesus. These books, called gospels, appear to be compilations of material, some of which originated among the earliest Christians and circulated for several decades in oral form. Each one represented the viewpoint of its own Christian community: Matthew probably came out of Syria, while Mark seems to come from Rome

---

[22] James is usually identified as the *adelphos* of the Lord. The Greek customarily designates a brother. Mark 6:3 and Matthew 13:55 list James and three others as brothers of Jesus, and they also mention sisters. Jerome seems to be the first Christian to claim that *adelphos* should be translated as cousin rather than brother. In support of this view, see Genesis 13:8, where Lot and Abraham are called *adelphoi* but are described as nephew and uncle. Since the Greek had a different word to designate a cousin or other distant relative, we should probably translate *adelphos* in the usual way. The Book of James claims that Jesus and James were half brothers. See pp. 223 ff. On James' position in primitive Christianity, see p. 278 f.

and John from Ephesus. Only slightly later we have gospels from Egypt and Asia Minor.

In the last decades of the first century and throughout the second, the Christian movement was attempting to consolidate itself. The different communities had used a number of patterns for their organization. The earliest was probably a structure which functioned with charismatic leadership, in which people were spontaneously elevated because of their special abilities. Local groups met in homes and, until Christianity achieved a sense of its own identity, in synagogues. At first there was only minimal contact among local communities, but the growth of the movement brought with it a corresponding need to unite separate communities. Just after the turn of the century, we have evidence of a developing episcopacy.[23] Ignatius, for example, was the bishop of Antioch, who stood as the unifying figure for Christian churches in Syria. In the latter part of the second century, this pattern became the dominant one, and we can point to bishops in most important centers of the Roman world. There seems to be no effort to unite the episcopacy by means of a chief bishop during this period, but by A.D. 180 Irenaeus was pointing to Rome as the center of the Christian movement.

The consolidation of Christianity in the second century faced the problem of theological diversity. This century witnessed a multitude of quite different interpretations of the meaning of Christianity. The geographical separation of Christian settlements and the lack of overall doctrinal supervision made this situation possible. During this period we can point not only to Jewish Christianity and Pauline Christianity, but also to Gnostic versions, as well as to a growing attempt to solidify Christian theology in terms of an orthodoxy.[24] The latter attempt will be symbolized in Irenaeus. One of the chief methods used to combat diversity was that of canonization. The Old Testament had been used as sacred Scripture from the beginning; but as the volume of Christian writing increased, the need for selecting certain documents as authoritative and of eliminating divergent works came to be recognized. The first known canon is that of Marcion, in c. 150; a second is that of Rome in c. 200. During our period, however, no decision binding on the whole church was reached.

In addition to the problems of organizing a spreading movement and of consolidating theological diversity, Christianity faced problems with political authorities. Persecutions broke out from time to time. In the early days there

---

[23] From the Greek *episcopos*, meaning bishop.

[24] Orthodoxy literally means thinking which is straight. One who uses the term assumes that only one kind of thinking can be straight; thus it designates a single form of thought or teaching to which all Christians should subscribe.

was persecution from Jews in Palestine and from Gentiles in Asia Minor, but most of these were localized and short-lived. In some cases persecution involved physical torture and death, while in other cases its methods were more subtle. Christians were frequently tried on charges of cannibalism and orgiastic practices. In the sixties, Christians in Rome were persecuted by Nero on suspicion of arson; and toward the end of the first century, many in Asia Minor were persecuted for failure to make the required sacrifice to the emperor Domitian. In 117, there is evidence that people were convicted simply for being Christians. In 177, a particularly severe persecution broke out in two cities in France, where Christians faced unbelievable tortures. The most effective defense Christians had was the pen, and a group of apologists[25] wrote tracts which attempted to explain Christianity in terms acceptable to the intellectuals of the day. Many of these found it useful to compare Christianity with Hellenistic religions and philosophies to show that it was not alien.

By the end of the second century, Christianity could be found in most important centers of the Roman world, including Syria, Asia Minor, Greece, Egypt, North Africa, Italy, and France. Although most churches were in the east, there was a decided thrust toward the west. It was not yet a church with headquarters in Rome, but Rome was moving toward a more weighty authority. Its importance as the seat of imperial government and crossroads of the world gave it a significance that no other city could attain. Even before the second century was over, a bishop from France, Irenaeus, was suggesting that Rome should symbolize the theological unity of the entire church.

[25] An apologist is one who attempts to provide an intellectual defense of a movement or doctrine. As used here it refers to a specific group of writers who performed this function for Christianity in the second century. See pp. 260 ff.

Chapter Two

The Heritage from Hellenism

Although the intellectual and religious forces of an age are those which shape its basic character, they are generally intangible and elusive. We need to know how people did their thinking and what they expected of their world. In respect to the intellectual forces, the age of Roman Hellenism presents us with a more tangible phenomenon than we might have expected, for it inherited something of the Greek taste for philosophy. This taste led to the creation of several significant philosophical schools, which attempted in a systematic way to raise the basic questions of life. Any attempt to understand these forces must wrestle with the stated philosophies as well as with the religious and political institutions; but it must also look into the general culture to discover the ideals that men held. Certain general characteristics played a large role in the formation of the intellectual and religious forces of Roman Hellenism. These characteristics presented the problems that philosophy and religion tried to solve and created the context in which men thought and believed.

Paul Wendland[1] suggests that cosmopolitanism and individualism were two of the fundamental features of Hellenistic culture. Cosmopolitanism began with Alexander the Great, who felt that the culture he had known would benefit all men. It subsequently became manifest by the large-scale adoption of eastern practices in the west and the acceptance of western institutions in the east. The broadening geographic and political horizon led to a lively interest in people beyond one's national borders. Dialectical distinctions became less pronounced, and shortly after Alexander's time Koine Greek came to be used throughout the east. In imperial times, the old nations became provinces of Rome and accepted her political institutions. The status of Roman citizenship was highly prized by provincial leaders and local magistrates. The new political structures allowed men and women of the provinces to think of themselves as citizens of the world.

[1] *Die hellenistisch-römische Kultur* (Tübingen: Mohr, 1912).

Individualism was an equally important characteristic of Hellenistic culture. Its significance is exemplified in the fact that biography, as an indication of interest in individual life, first made its appearance in this era, with the work of Polybius, Sallust, and Tacitus. Mass movements and institutions were de-emphasized in the interpretation of history, and great events of the past were understood as the deeds of great men. Virgil's *Aeneid,* for example, presented the founding of Rome as an act of the brave Aeneas and attributed present bliss to the genius of Caesar Augustus. In Roman society, mobility was a characteristic of the early Empire. Slaves could become freedmen, senators could become paupers, and much depended upon individual initiative. Cosmopolitanism and individualism went hand in hand, for, as national and racial distinctions gave way, a man could be judged on the basis of his individual qualities rather than his social relationships.

These features formed the context in which Romans and provincials lived their lives. But they also created human problems to which the philosophies and the religions were obligated to speak. The alteration of political structures, social class mobility, and the movement from nationalism to cosmopolitanism created a certain insecurity. A citizen of pre-Hellenistic Antioch may have been dissatisfied with his status, but he knew what it was. He had learned that he belonged to a certain family and nation and had a specific relation to divinity. The more fluid situation in Hellenistic times meant for many a loss of the accustomed context. As a result, men and women in the provinces were unsure of their place in the universe. Even Roman citizens were threatened with a feeling of insecurity, because of the social changes. People were raising agonizing questions about their relationship to God, nature, and human society. The insecurity brought with it a lack of confidence in the forces which controlled human destiny. People were fearful of the unknown and generally skeptical about life after death. The changing patterns demanded new duties, and moral insecurity resulted. When one is faced with a changing moral demand and is perplexed about what is expected of him, he usually feels an undefined guilt. He thinks that he has, somehow or other, not met the demands placed upon him. It is true that the new forces could lead the individual to feel significant. Emancipated slaves who were climbing the social ladder surely appreciated this fact. But in far more cases, it appears that individuals felt isolated rather than important. Even in Rome, some persons were looking for ways to compensate for their loss of status.

Cosmopolitanism and individualism created new opportunities, but they brought the problems of insecurity, fear, moral perplexity, guilt, and isolation. The philosophies and the religions addressed themselves to these problems, and they enjoyed popularity in rough proportion to their success in solving them.

HELLENISTIC PHILOSOPHIES

The chief philosophical schools of the Roman world owe their origin to the Greeks of the fourth century B.C. F. C. Grant says that Greek philosophy contrasts with modern in that the former was popular and was widely discussed in the market place.[2] To be sure, there were people who could be called philosophers in a more technical sense, but the main impression we get is that of a much more vigorous discussion of ideas then than is usual now. Grant adds: "The pooling of influence, the exchange of terminology, the mutual attraction and the modification of one school of ancient philosophy by another is a conspicuous feature of the early Roman period."[3] The popularity of the various philosophies was partly due to their practical purposes. In the background lie the Platonic and Aristotelian emphases on a life of contemplation and on a god undisturbed by human events, and these emphases are still found in the Roman period; but the newer philosophies seem more attuned to the life of the individual. They seem to be aware of the need to give guidance in perplexing times, and they exhibit a greater tendency to address themselves to the concrete questions men ask about life, death, and duty.

In Cynicism we have one of the more direct approaches to human problems. This movement was founded by Diogenes (412?–323 B.C.), whose lamplit search for an honest man is well known. Fundamental to Diogenes' view is an anthropology—a view of man. To a Cynic, man is essentially a product of nature, and he must attune himself to nature. He must so order his life that it becomes as natural to him as the dog's life is to the dog. Diogenes himself advocated that the dog should be a model for man, and thus his movement came to be called "Cynic" (meaning *canine*, from the Greek word for dog). Diogenes' own life was one that shunned human society and the things of civilization, and his intention was to avoid fear, desire, and possessions.

Cynicism might be admired but was not widely imitated. Far greater popularity attached to Stoicism and Epicureanism. With the former we associate the names of Zeno (c. 334–262/261 B.C.), Cleanthes, the ex-slave Epictetus, and Marcus Aurelius, Roman emperor, A.D. 161–180. The Stoics

[2] *Roman Hellenism and the New Testament* (New York: Scribner's, 1962).
[3] Ibid., p. 54.

agreed with the Cynics that man must live according to nature. But, whereas the Cynics understood nature in terms of animal life, Stoics understood it as a principle of life uniquely appropriate for man himself. When the Stoic says that man must live according to nature, he does not mean that man must take the dog as his model. He means that there is a particular kind of life that is natural for man and that man will find his happiness in accepting this life with enthusiasm. To say that there is a life appropriate for man is to say something quite positive about the universe. A Stoic would say that the cosmos has a purpose for man and for men. This means that there is a kind of harmony between man and the universe, a harmony expressed in the word *logos*. This Greek word is difficult to translate. It stands for the substance which is the structure of the universe, but it is also present in all men. The usual translation of *logos* in Stoic writings is *reason*. But one should not understand this in terms of eighteenth-century rationalism but rather in terms of that which constitutes the universe and man.

The *logos*-harmony of universe and man has a very definite moral implication: man has a purpose as part of the universe. The duty of each man is to discover this purpose and then to govern his life in accordance with it. This ethical theory presents a strange combination of fate and free will. Although it is clear that man's destiny is set, he is called upon to exercise his will in accepting this fate. He has the freedom either to accept his destiny or to reject it but not to change it. According to Epictetus, this is where real freedom lies: in the freedom of the will. There are certain things that are obviously not within the power of man. For example, a man may not be free to accrue and retain certain possessions, for he is limited by their availability, their present ownership, the conditions of obtaining them, and by his own abilities and financial circumstances. Any one of these factors may so affect a man and his possessions as to limit his freedom to have and to hold. If freedom is not present in having and holding, where is it to be found? Only in the will. Man is not free to have or not have; but he is free to will to get, or to will to avoid. He can intend the getting or intend not getting. Thus Epictetus can say: "That man is free, who lives as he wishes, who is proof against compulsion and hindrance and violence, whose impulses are untrammelled, who gets what he wills to get and avoids what he wills to avoid."[4] But since one has control only over the will, we should say that the happy life is the one in which one wills to get what he does in fact get and wills to avoid what he does in fact avoid. One should first see

[4] Epictetus, *Discourses* IV, 1. A good edition of the works of Stoics and Epicureans is that by Whitney J. Oates, *The Stoic and Epicurean Philosophers* (New York: Modern Library, 1940).

Bronze statue of Marcus Aurelius, Rome. (*Courtesy* Alinari-Art Reference Bureau.)

what he gets and then will it. More broadly, man must discover the essence of what it means to be human, what is under his control and what is not. When he does this, he will find that there are certain characteristics appropriate to man. Epictetus says that among these characteristics are will and reason. This means that man is intended to command (as an act of will) but to command with interest for the whole of mankind (as an act of reason). Thus, if a man finds himself to be a father, his duty is to issue commands for the benefit of the family; if he is a son, his duty is to obey the commands of the father. And when man discovers what is really under his control, he discovers his will. Nothing else belongs to a man—not his body, his soul, his children, or time.

Stoic ethics, therefore, revolve around the concept of duty, the obligation to be what one is, to discover the purpose of his life, and to govern his life in such a way that he is always in harmony with this purpose. The nobility of this ethic has usually been recognized, but it has been understood as a cold severity. We should recognize, however, that basic to Stoic ethics is a feeling of harmony between the universe and human values. Although these values do not include creature comforts, they are such as to enable man to feel at home in the universe. This is given clear expression in the *Meditations* of Marcus Aurelius. The *logos*, which is the harmony between the universe and man, is itself a deity; thus, there is a deity in all men. Moreover, the presence of *logos* in all men creates a community of intelligence among humans, and there is a kinship between each man and the whole human race. Man's place in the universe is clear; he has a home and a family, and, as in all families, each man has certain duties. The Cynic philosophy must have appeared much colder in its assertion of the estrangement from the universe of characteristically human values.

The Epicurean philosophy was basically an attempt to understand nature, although, like Stoicism, it had a number of ethical implications. Epicurus (341–270 B.C.) largely addressed himself to the analysis of natural phenomena, but his purpose in doing so was in large measure a moral or even religious one. He intended to free people from needless superstition, and he felt that if all things could be explained there would be no need to fear the gods. People fear gods because they experience inexplicable events and catastrophes. If people can understand that these things are not products of some whimsical or mischievous deity or effects of displeasing the gods, then they will be able to live their lives without fear of the unknown. Today, we are familiar with the understanding that a fear of the unknown may be a basis of religion. But Epicurus did not intend to be antireligious, and he certainly was no atheist.[5] To him God was real but was not to be feared. On the other hand, Epicurus was no systematic theologian, for, although he attempted to bring all natural phenomena under a unified science, he did not suggest that gods were responsible for them or that nature was the description of divine activity. In short, gods may have reality but not relevance.

The world view which Epicurus sets forth is a scientific one in the sense that it attempts to explain all phenomena from within the natural system and to set forth a consistency. He assumes that nothing is created out of that which does not exist; thus he understands the universe as a self-contained entity. It always was as it is now, and it is boundless. It is composed of space and bodies, and bodies are compounds of indivisible atoms. The atoms, which form the irreducible part of each body, are infinite in number and of an unlimited variety in respect to shape. They are continually in motion —falling, swerving, colliding, and recoiling. The atoms are also different from one another in texture. Some, of unsurpassable fineness, produce the sensations of sight, sound, and smell. Bodies formed by these atoms are similar in shape to solid bodies, but their fine texture means that they are images and not solid bodies. This distinction conveniently allows Epicurus to distinguish between a body and its image, and it allows him to account for both without introducing a second kind of nature. The same is true of man's soul. The soul is a body of very fine particles, distributed throughout the entire structure of the human body. Its primary function is sensation: it receives the sight, sound, and smell atoms, which travel at an unsurpassable rate of speed.

Epicurus' system has been called a materialistic monism. This is correct, except that we must be cautious in our understanding of these terms. The Epicurean system is a monism in the sense that all bodies are reducible to atoms. Although atoms vary in texture, shape, and speed, they do not vary in kind. This means that at its base the universe is of a single kind. It is this monism which allows the Epicurean to give a consistent explanation to all natural phenomena and to use the knowledge of these phenomena as a guide in discovering the secrets of stars and planets.[6] To say that Epicureanism is materialistic is to describe the quality that is common to the atoms. Yet this kind of description may be misleading, because it implies its opposite. It suggests that there is a "spiritual" realm which is ignored in Epicureanism. It would be better to speak simply of a monism, for the quality predicated of the basic atom is not such as to exclude those things we think of as spiritual. Still, it is true that, at its base, man's soul is not

[5] In his letter to Menoeceus, Epicurus refers to God as blessed and immortal.
[6] See especially Lucretius, *On the Nature of Things*.

different from his body, and there is no suggestion that man really transcends the body. Epicureanism lacks anything corresponding to the Stoic concept of the *logos*.

Perhaps the major consequence of Epicurean monism is the belief in human mortality. Although nothing comes from nothing and nothing that is can become nothing, nevertheless the change from life to death is irreversible. This is so because Epicurus defines death as the deprivation of sensation. Since the soul is the seat of sensation, it is not immortal. At times, in Epicurean writing, the soul appears to be a function of various parts of the body. Lucretius says that man does not experience the soul as a complete entity, nor does one experience death as the loss of a thing called soul: "For no one when dying appears to feel the soul go forth entire from his whole body or first mount up the throat and gullet, but all feel it fail in that part which lies in a particular quarter; just as they know that the senses all will suffer dissolution each in its own place."[7] Thus we can say that death means that the ear no longer hears, the eyes no longer see, and the fingers no longer touch. And in this sense death is of no real concern to man. In a letter to Menoeceus, Epicurus says: "So long as we exist, death is not with us, but when death comes, then we do not exist. It does not then concern either the living or the dead, since for the former it is not, and the latter are no more."[8]

The greatest injustice has been done Epicureanism by the popular aphorism: "Eat, drink, and be merry, for tomorrow we die." It is true that death is irreversible in Epicurean thought and that the gods do not interfere with man's life in terms of rewards and punishments. It is also true that those things the Stoics called virtues played a secondary role in Epicureanism and that the goal of life is happiness. But Epicurus does not advise men to pursue happiness directly. Rather happiness results from a life of virtue, the chief feature of which is affection (*philia*) for one's fellow man, and from an absence of fear. Epicurean ethics would, then, be characterized by affection on the one side and study of nature on the other. A far better summary of Epicurean ethical thought is that given by Diogenes of Oenoanda in c. A.D. 200:

> There is nothing to fear in God;
> There is nothing to feel in death;
> Evil can be endured;
> Good can be achieved.[9]

[7] Lucretius, *On the Nature of Things*, III.
[8] Epicurus, *Letter to Menoeceus*, Oates edition, p. 31.
[9] Quoted in Grant, op. cit., p. 71.

These two most popular philosophical schools had an impact upon the intellect of Roman Hellenism of significant proportions. Together they brought religion into question, for the gods of Olympus could no longer be taken seriously. Divinity could be thought of in impersonal pantheistic terms, as in Stoicism; or it could be relegated to an irrelevant position, as in Epicureanism. Ethically, the two had a joint impact in focusing attention on the inner self. Both philosophies would lead men away from a concentration on their outward circumstances to a nurture of their attitudes. Both would call men from fear. Stoicism could assure man that he had a place in the universe; Epicureanism could show him that the government of the universe was not by some strange mystery. The great lack in both was that they could not guarantee man a personal immortality. In Stoicism, of course, the *logos* is divine and immortal, but it is not individually differentiated. In Epicureanism, immortality is specifically denied. In the section on Hellenistic religions, which follows, we shall see that the mystery religions were profoundly successful precisely because they could answer this need.

Hellenistic Religions

Many of the religions and religious institutions in the Hellenistic world have an origin deep in the past. Religion in Italy, Greece, and Asia Minor goes back to obscure beginnings perhaps as early as the second millennium before Christ. It is not appropriate to trace these beginnings here, but the student who wishes to do so may consult any number of works on the origin of Graeco-Roman religions.[10] Although it may be necessary to refer to practices and beliefs prior to our period, the focus of attention will be on those aspects in the Hellenistic period itself, and we can concentrate on private religions, the state cult, and mystery religions.

Private Religions

Although no religion is ever purely private, there are some which are practiced by individuals in isolation or in small groups or which concentrate their attention on strictly individual needs. In the Graeco-Roman world there were certain religious practices that were closely tied to the home. This seems to be particularly important in Italy, where the religions of the home had an

---

[10] E.g., H. J. Rose, *Religion in Greece and Rome* (New York: Harper, 1959); Gilbert Murray, *Five Stages of Greek Religion* (Boston: Beacon Press, 1951).

ancient history. It consisted in the worship of household deities, who were expected to protect the family from disaster and each member of the family from illness. These gods were also expected to concern themselves with the economic welfare of the family. Harold R. Willoughby believes that home religion was the original essence of religion in Italy and the surviving heart of it in imperial days. He says: "In its primitive development Roman piety was the cult of a household living in a rural environment and engaged in ritual practices intended to placate the powers on which the welfare of the family was chiefly dependent."[11] Even in the imperial period, these religions would include the veneration of a small statue of the deity or deities, sacrifices of grain or meat, and certain family observances centered on the hearth.

Another kind of private religion was astrology. This was Persian in origin but was widely practiced in the Graeco-Roman world. It consisted in the belief that stars determine the fates of individual men. A man's fate was inexorable, but the practice of astrology was intended to provide a way by which he could discover it. He could gain insight into this by finding out which star was his, what particular kind of configuration of stars he was born under, and what kind of stellar arrangement prevailed from day to day. Anyone who follows a horoscope in one of our daily newspapers can understand how this kind of religion worked and can recognize the pervasive appeal it has. Although astrology produced community scholars who would prepare guidebooks for its adherents, the practices of the religion would be carried on in private by the individual.

The hero cult is a private religion only in the sense that its concerns were with the individual. In outward respects it would not differ from a public religion, for it had shrines, which were often well staffed. But the private aspect of these religions was their interest in human concerns, even the most minute. People would go to shrines of heroes to ask not only for general financial aid, but also for good luck at the race track or victory in a dispute or success in a business venture. In the main, however, the hero shrines were devoted to healing. The healing ability of the hero is attributable to his divinity, for he possesses divine birth. In general, one parent was divine and the other human. Asclepius, for example, was the son of Apollo, by the unfaithful Coronis. The general belief was that he lived in Epidaurus, which was the chief seat of his worship, and that during his lifetime he cured the sick and raised the dead. To keep men from attempting to avoid death altogether, Zeus killed Asclepius with a thunderbolt but placed him among

---

[11] Harold R. Willoughby, *Pagan Regeneration* (Chicago: University of Chicago Press, 1929), pp. 9 f.

the stars at the request of Apollo. In Hellenistic times, Asclepius was worshiped not only in Epidarus but also in Rome and elsewhere.

The State Cult

Harold R. Willoughby once wrote: "It was a characteristic Roman conviction that the primary function of religion was to serve the interests of the state and that as a guaranty of political prosperity the rites of religion were potent in the extreme."[12] Rome did not invent state religion, for it roots in the oriental deification of the monarch. The Greeks had come in contact with this when Alexander conquered the east. To most citizens and subjects of Rome, imperial worship seemed the most natural thing in the world, for it was clear to them that the emperor was the most powerful person alive and that he had in his hands the ultimate destiny of all within the realm. Thus, the association of power with divinity was reasonable. Specifically, imperial worship included reverence to the person of the emperor and to his image. In many places it also included making a sacrifice to him.[13] There was some tendency for the state cult to displace the Olympian. In some imperial statues, Augustus is identified as Apollo, Nero as Zeus, and Hadrian as Zeus Olympias.[14]

One can readily see that Jews would have serious problems with these requirements, which conflicted with their religious duties at fundamental points. Moreover, Roman officials found it difficult to be flexible in respect to the demands of the imperial cult, for to them it was the very basis of the state, that without which the state could not exist. On the few occasions when Roman standards, topped by images of the emperor, were displayed on parade in Jerusalem, Roman demands for political loyalty and Jewish demands for religious duty came into face-to-face confrontation.

Mystery Religions

The mystery religions constitute the most popular form of Hellenistic religion. Shirley Jackson Case estimated the importance of these religions

---

[12] Ibid., p. 15.

[13] Not every Roman emperor required the sacrifice. Note the exception usually granted to Jews (see p. 55). Augustus expected to become divine at death but did not encourage worship in his lifetime. Gaius, Nero, and Domitian demanded it during their reigns.

[14] See John Ferguson, *The Religions of the Roman Empire* (Ithaca, N.Y.: Cornell University Press, 1970), pp. 88-98.

A priestess of Isis, Capitoline Museum, Rome. (*Courtesy* Alinari-Art Reference Bureau.)

[78]

highly: "It would not be a mere rhetorical figure if one were to designate the religious history of the Mediterranean world in the early imperial period as the age of the mysteries."[15]

Although there were many religions which can be called mysteries, there are certain characteristics which can be found in each of them. The designation *mystery* indicates one of the common qualities. At the heart of each of these religions there is a mystery, a secret which the devotees are pledged to keep. In general, the secret is the myth which lies behind the ritualistic practices of the religious community, but in some religions the rituals themselves are secret. This fact is, of course, tremendously inhibiting to our understanding, for most of the devotees honored their pledge of secrecy, feeling that they were in possession of a reality which elevated them above the common man. To be sure, several Greek and Roman writers were deeply interested in the mystery religions and wished to describe them. But these men were not members of the cult. Apuleius is perhaps the only exception. This second-century (A.D.) writer once was an initiate of mystery religions, and he pictured his hero Lucius as one who could observe human activities undetected because he had been transformed into an ass. Lucius, in fact, obtained release from this through the religion of Osiris. In the process Apuleius was able to give us glimpses of the mysteries.[16] In a few other cases the rituals of the religion were public, and some have been described by contemporary writers. From these descriptions we can infer the myth which was hidden within them.

A second quality common to mystery religions is that of apotheosis, a process by which an initiate becomes divine. This divinization seems to be open to any devotee who accepts the initiatory rite; it guarantees him the right to be worshiped by his contemporaries; and it grants him the assurance of a blessed immortality.

Apotheosis is closely related to the sacramental aspect of the mystery religions, for it is by a sacrament that the devotee participates in the life of the god. In most cases the sacrament was understood in quite a realistic way. Ancient sacraments were generally associated with eating and drinking. Even in ancient Semitic religion we meet the idea of sharing a meal with the deity. In other forms of religion the idea of eating the deity is uppermost. This latter practice is described by Prudentius,[17] who narrates the consecration of a priest into the service of the Great Mother, through the

---

[15] Case, *The Social Origins of Christianity* (Chicago, Ill.: Chicago University Press, 1923), p. 113.

[16] See Apuleius, *Metamorphoses* or *The Golden Ass*.

[17] *Peristephanon* X, 1011–1050. See the translation of this below, p. 84 f.

Detail of a scene from the Villa of the Mysteries, Pompeii. The fresco portrays an act from one of the mystery religions. (*Courtesy* Anderson-Art Reference Bureau.)

rite of the taurobolium. In this sacrament the priest washes himself in the blood of a bull, covers himself thoroughly with it, and even breathes and drinks it. The blood of the bull is divine life, and the priest who partakes of it imbibes the life of the god.

The quality of redemption is also common to the mysteries. The individual could look to these religious practices for assurance, but assurance of a nonmaterial kind. They provided a redemption from the evils of this life as well as an expectation of eternal life itself, and this of a blissful quality. They attacked the issues men faced at the ultimate level of life itself, and in this is to be found their chief distinctiveness and their widespread appeal.

The moral value of the mysteries is by no means clear, but apparently for many the experience of initiation and sacrament reinforced the individual's interest in nonmaterial things and even resulted in an elevation of his present life. Aristophanes, Cicero, and even Epictetus speak of the moral value of these religions.

The origin of the mysteries can be traced to diverse locales, and one suspects that certain similarities in their mythology may have resulted from cultural assimilation. The Dionysian and Orphic religions come from Thrace (roughly equivalent to modern Bulgaria); the Eleusinian mysteries originated in Eleusis, near Athens; the religion of the Great Mother arose in Anatolia, in Central Asia Minor. The religion of Mithras came from Iran, and that of Isis and Osiris came from Egypt. It is notable that all of these religions originated in the eastern part of the Roman Empire and that many are identified by names familiar to readers of Homer.

Scenes from the Villa of the Mysteries, Pompeii. (*Courtesy* Alinari-Art Reference Bureau.)

The similarities in the various myths are striking.[18] In the Eleusinian mystery, the myth tells of the kidnaping of Demeter's daughter, Persephone,

[18] For the information in this and the following paragraphs, the author is dependent on H. R. Willoughby, op. cit.

by Pluto, in retaliation for which Demeter caused a grave famine. In the myth of Dionysus, the mortal Semele gave birth to Dionysus by the divine Zeus. Zeus then destroyed her with lightning but saved Dionysus, who is frequently called "twice-born." The Orphic religion is often looked upon as a reformation of the Dionysian, and the myth gives evidence of this. Zeus and Persephone gave birth to Dionysus Zagreus, who was captured and eaten by Titans. But Athena captured Dionysus' heart and brought it to Zeus, who ate it. Finally, Zeus and Semele gave birth to Dionysus, who is looked upon as Zagreus reborn. In the Egyptian religion of Isis and Osiris, the latter had been an Egyptian king who was killed by one Typhon. Isis found his body, and with help from other deities she brought him back to life and made him "Lord of the Underworld and Ruler of the Dead." In all of these we see the dominant themes of birth, life, death, resurrection, and apotheosis. At some points the myths give indications of their origins in fertility cults, which attended to the death of nature in the winter and its resurrection in the spring. Many scholars consider the seasonal rituals which dramatized these changes to be the original form of all mystery religions and believe that the mythological formulations came along at a later date. This thesis rests upon the understanding that the original needs of men in the Mediterranean were those which centered in the raising of crops. In the Hellenistic period these needs were not so prominent, although the religions of the home persisted in some areas. The great international mystery religions, however, answer to the needs of this period, for they center in the problems of birth, life, guilt, and death, which are posed by individual needs. The durability of these religions was due to their adaptability to changing circumstances and needs.

The religion of the Great Mother can serve as an illustration of the general phenomenon of mystery religions. Fortunately, many of the rituals of this religion were public, and our information about it is relatively full. Although there are several myths associated with the religion and, therefore, some resulting confusion, the general lines of its mythology are clear. The Great Mother, usually called Cybele, is the mother of all gods and men. Her companion is Attis, a semidivine hero, who was born of a virgin and was associated with vegetation. Cybele loved Attis, who later was unfaithful to her. Out of guilt, Attis castrated himself and died. Cybele was so grieved over her loss that she restored Attis to life, deified him, and made him immortal. The motifs of life, death, sexuality, and seasonal change are profoundly intermixed in the myth. The association of Attis with vegetable life would call to mind the death of nature in the winter and its resurrection in the spring.

Dionysus on a Panther, mosaic, House of Masks, Delos. The religion of Dionysus was a widely practiced mystery religion in Hellenistic times. (*Courtesy* École Française d'Archéologie, Athens.)

The rituals of this religion are, on the one side, the dramatic presentations of the myth and, on the other, the sacramental participation of the devotee in the life of the god. There were two basic rituals; both were public and are well known. The spring festival of Attis began on March 15. On the sixteenth, a pine tree was brought into the temple of Cybele, and this tree was regarded as the corpse of Attis. On the seventeenth, we have a day of fasting from vegetables and cereal. The climax of the spring festival came on March 24, the day of blood. The day was marked by a frenzied dance accompanied by noisy music. While dancing, people would wag their heads to the point of dizziness, lacerate their flesh, and sprinkle the Attis tree with blood. At the high point of the dance, some of the men would emasculate

[83]

themselves and run through the streets, demonstrating evidence of the deed. In this act a young man would become a priest of Cybele and, indeed, a god. He became the counterpart of Attis, for he had done for Cybele what Attis had done.[19] The following days must have appeared anticlimactic: on March 25, the resurrection of Attis was celebrated; March 26 was a day of rest; and on March 27 the statue of Cybele was washed in a nearby river. This last act is probably thought of as signifying a new birth for the religious community.

The second major ritual in the religion of the Great Mother was that of the taurobolium, or bathing in the blood of the bull. This could apparently be performed at any time. The bull represents the dying Attis, whose blood cleanses the bather from his past guilt and signifies his entry into a new life. The idea of deification is not absent, however; for the believer, in drinking the blood, is partaking of the life of the deity. The description of Prudentius is an eye-witness account of the ritual, in this case the ordination of a priest. It is brief enough to be quoted in full:

The high priest who is to be consecrated is brought down under ground in a pit dug deep, marvellously adorned with a fillet binding his festive temples with chaplets, his hair combed back under a golden crown, and wearing a silken toga caught up with Gabine girding.

Over this they make a wooden floor with wide spaces, woven of planks with an open mesh; they then divide or bore the area and repeatedly pierce the wood with a pointed tool that it may appear full of small holes.

Hither a huge bull, fierce and shaggy in appearance, is led, bound with flowery garlands about its flanks, and with its horns sheathed; yea, the forehead of the victim sparkles with gold, and the flash of metal plates colours its hair.

Here, as is ordained, the beast is to be slain, and they pierce its breast with a sacred spear; the gaping wound emits a wave of hot blood, and the smoking river flows into the woven structure beneath it and surges wide.

Then by the many paths of the thousand openings in the lattice the falling shower rains down a foul dew, which the priest buried within catches, putting his shameful head under all the drops, defiled both in his clothing and in all his body.

Yea, he throws back his face, he puts his cheeks in the way of the blood, he puts under it his ears and lips, he interposes his nostrils, he washes his very eyes with the fluid, nor does he even spare his throat but moistens his tongue, until he actually drinks the dark gore.

[19] It is also possible that the new priest now thought of himself as the male counterpart of the goddess, for he would put on feminine dress and begin to wear long hair.

Afterwards, the flamens draw the corpse, stiffening now that the blood has gone forth, off the lattice, and the pontiff, horrible in appearance, comes forth, and shows his wet head, his beard heavy with blood, his dripping fillets and sodden garments.

This man, defiled with such contagions and foul with the gore of the recent sacrifice, all hail and worship at a distance, because profane blood and a dead ox have washed him while concealed in a filthy cave.[20]

In addition to these major rituals, there were certain private rites which must have included a marriage of Cybele with an emasculated priest and a ceremony of eating and drinking with the deity.

Several general features of mystery religions can be abstracted from the description of this one example. We must keep in mind the fact that many of the religions were quite old. The religion of the Great Mother goes back to the sixth century B.C. Their antiquity means that we are dealing with a changing phenomenon and that the result is a mixture of Olympian myths, vegetation cults, and regenerative rituals. Nevertheless, the chief features of mystery religions in Roman days illuminate the yearnings of men as well as their beliefs on how their needs can be satisfied. Feelings of human *guilt* play a major role in these religions. Although the nature of sin is ill defined, it characteristically relates to the body. Matter itself is evil and must be overcome. The practice of emasculation in the religion of Cybele signifies not only the act of Attis but also the devotee's attempt to expiate for sexual acts, which are acts of infidelity to the divine mother. These feelings of guilt move the devotee toward the need for *regeneration*. One feels that his guilt is so great that he cannot expiate for it as he is. He must have a new birth and become a new man. The bathing in bull's blood is the washing away of one's past, and the creation of a new person. Regeneration means that the person is no longer what he was. As a new man he has the right of *participation* in the life of the deity. He takes divine life within himself as he drinks the blood of the bull, or the blood of the god. The culmination of his religious progress is *apotheosis*, the act in which the devotee himself becomes divine. In this way he has completely overcome evil and the temptation to do evil. He may now be the object of worship and devotion. Since a happy immortality is essentially associated with the gods, a man's divinization is his own guarantee of such *immortality*. The popularity of the mystery religions can be understood in terms of the needs they attempt to satisfy—

[20] Prudentius, *Peristephanon* X, 1011–1050. This translation is from C. K. Barrett, *The New Testament Background: Selected Documents* (London: S.P.C.K., 1958), pp. 96 f.

the needs for expiation, regeneration, participation, divinization, and immortality. These needs are characteristic of men in the age of Roman Hellenism, and any religion will have to speak to them if there is to be any hope of success.

Chapter Three

---◆◇◆---

The Heritage from Judaism

When we come to look at Judaism as a religious institution, we must acknowledge that we are dealing with something which cannot be isolated from its wider context in culture and history. Judaism is the religion and culture of a people with a very long history. It is a religion which is communicated in terms of particular thought forms, and it has produced a voluminous body of literature. Although it is our concern now to investigate the nature of this religion at the time of the birth of Christianity, it will be necessary to make some reference to the whole body of Jewish literature and to some ideas far older than the period of Roman Hellenism.

THE LITERATURE

Where do we get our information about Judaism? There are six major collections of literature which bear directly on the subject. In addition, two individual writers of the first Christian century must be consulted.

The first major collection of writings is variously called the Holy Scriptures, the Hebrew Bible, and the Old Testament. These names are used by modern Jews and Protestant Christians to designate a group of thirty-nine books, the earliest written perhaps about 1000 B.C. and the latest about 165 B.C. This was a fundamental collection for the Jews of Jesus' day, although it was not officially canonized until A.D. 90. It was traditionally divided into three parts: the Torah; the prophets; and the writings.

The canonization of these thirty-nine books in A.D. 90 was probably effective only for Palestinian Judaism. In Alexandria, and probably in other centers of diaspora Judaism, the canon must have included some thirteen additional books. Even Christians adhered to the larger canon until the sixteenth century, and Roman Catholic Christians still accept it. Jews and Protestant Christians now refer to these additional books as the Apocrypha, and this designation will be used here for convenience. Some of the books

A passage from one of the Dead Sea Scrolls (1 Q Isaiah 49:12). (*Courtesy* The Israel Museum, Jerusalem.)

in this collection appear to have been written as early as 200 B.C., and the latest comes from around A.D. 100.

The third collection is that of the Dead Sea Scrolls. This is the most recent set of writings to come to light. The story of their accidental discovery in 1947 is by now well known, and the reader may consult Millar Burrows' *The Dead Sea Scrolls*[1] for an account of it. The scrolls appear to have belonged to a group of Jews, called Essenes, who had established a religious community near the northwest shore of the Dead Sea in the vicinity of the modern village of Khirbet Qumran. They were written during the last two centuries before the time of Jesus. Many of the scrolls are manuscripts of Old Testament books, and every Old Testament book except Esther is represented in the collection. In addition, there are several scrolls produced especially for the Qumran community, which contain information on the beliefs and practices of the group.

A fourth collection of writings is known as the pseudepigrapha, a group of books produced approximately between 200 B.C. and A.D. 200. The word *pseudepigrapha* means false writings. These books are false in the sense that, although they were written at a relatively late date, they claim ancient authorship. Some of the books claim to have been written by Eve, Moses, Enoch, Solomon, and Baruch. In each case it is clear that the document was not known prior to the Hellenistic period. It is equally evident that certain ones represent the character of Judaism in the period of our chief interest and that some have had a marked effect on early Christianity.

The Mishnah constitutes a fifth major collection of Jewish writings. It is a group of commentaries on the Pentateuch and was codified about A.D. 200.[2] Even so, it represents the deposit of a far older oral commentary, much of which would have been in circulation in the time of Jesus.

In addition to these major collections, which in varying degrees were considered sacred, there are two Jewish writers, Philo and Josephus, whose work is relevant for our study. Philo (20 B.C.–A.D. 50) was a leader in the Jewish community of Alexandria, and his works shed a great deal of light on diaspora Judaism. His writing manifests an attempt to resolve the intellectual conflict between Hellenism and Judaism, and Philo is a philosopher in his own right. He does not neglect the characteristic Jewish veneration for Moses, but he understands Moses in terms of Hellenistic philosophy.

---

[1] (New York: Viking Press, 1955).
[2] The word *Pentateuch* designates the five books traditionally ascribed to Moses—Genesis, Exodus, Leviticus, Numbers, and Deuteronomy.

Josephus was a Palestinian Jew who was active in the rebellion against the Romans in the war of A.D. 66–73, when he was in charge of the Jewish forces in Galilee. From his own account we can determine that he put up only a slight struggle before surrendering. He was taken to Rome, where he spent the rest of his life (until c. A.D. 110) in the care of the Flavian household, writing for Romans an interpretation of the Jewish character and history. His two largest works, *The Antiquities of the Jews* and *The Jewish Wars*, are invaluable for an understanding of Palestinian Judaism during the Hellenistic period.

THOUGHT FORMS

Although the literature cited above displays a great deal of diversity, due to different temporal and geographical origins and individual biases, it is possible to sketch a basic picture of Judaism in the early days of the Roman Empire. We must first give our attention to certain fundamental ways of thinking which seem distinctive to Jews. When we reflect upon such thought forms, we are not concentrating upon overt or conscious ideas but rather upon the intellectual context out of which ideas are formed. Historically, thought forms are older than ideas and may serve as the groundwork of developed thought. In what follows we shall concentrate on four major areas, and ask: How did Jews approach the understanding of God, society, man, and history?

The question of God seems easy enough: Judaism was monotheistic. But this had not always been the case, and even in the first century there were some signs of amendment. Although Jews in Jesus' day customarily looked back to Moses for the origin of monotheism, it is probable that Mosaic religion only made Yahweh the god of the people of Israel. There is no sign in the early covenant formulations that the existence of other national deities was denied, and even in the prophetic literature of the eighth century we often have the figure of Yahweh in combat with the gods of other nations. Technically, we should describe the religion which sprang from Moses as monolatrous rather than monotheistic. It stood for the worship of one god, but it stopped short of claiming the universal sovereignty of that god. It did not claim that Yahweh was the god of other nations, although some writers believed that he could dominate other gods and make use of other nations. Moreover, the ideal of national monolatry was not always realized. The Book of Judges makes it clear that Yahweh was then thought of primarily as a war god and that in times of peace Israelites worshiped Canaanite deities. The existence of shrines called "high places" and their use at least through the time of Jeremiah is a sign of the worship of gods other than Yahweh. The great architect of Jewish monotheism was II Isaiah, the unknown prophet during the Babylonian exile and author of the later chapters of the Book of Isaiah. His is a manifestly creative effort to proclaim the universal sovereignty of Yahweh over against the claims of Babylonian astral religion. Nevertheless, this was done about 540 B.C., far enough back from the Roman period to form a fundamental and unexamined premise for Jewish thought. By Jesus' time, the sole existence of Yahweh was proclaimed in unequivocal terms, and his lordship over all of life and all nations was affirmed. The claims about the gods of the Greeks and Romans seemed to Jews as hollow and meaningless. In this respect Jewish religion could join with much Hellenistic philosophy in laughing at polytheism.

An illustration of the profundity of Jewish monotheism can be seen in the use of the names for deity. The Hebrew name Yahweh is used in most of the earlier parts of the Old Testament to designate the national deity. In Exodus 3 it is said to be the personal name of the god who revealed himself to Moses. After the time of II Isaiah, the name almost disappeared from literature and was generally replaced by the generic word *Elohim*, a word formerly used to designate any divine being. By the time of Jesus it had come to be regarded as the sacred name, too sacred to be pronounced. Only the high priest was allowed to speak the name, and he only once a year in a voice too low to be heard.

The Jewish insistence on monotheism was a notable exception to the general tone of religious life in the Hellenistic period. Even so, we must take note of two examples of modification. One is the understanding of Wisdom in Proverbs 8. Most scholars regard Proverbs as a post-exilic book, possibly written during the Hellenistic period. It is obviously later than Genesis 1 and shows signs of acquaintance with it.[3] Proverbs 8 may be regarded as a later version of the creation story. It speaks of the presence of Wisdom at creation and of God's using it as his agent. It stretches the meaning of the text to regard Wisdom as simply an attribute of God or as some part of his character. Wisdom is, in fact, a personification—that is, a person distinguishable from God. Although this is a significant modification of pure monotheism, it is clear that the author of Proverbs is not constructing a systematic ditheism in any sense of the word.

The second possible softening of monotheism is seen in the angelology of

---

[3] Genesis 1 is usually dated during the exilic or postexilic period, i.e., 550 B.C. or later.

Judaism. Angels had been present in the earliest strands of Old Testament literature, where they were spoken of as divine messengers.[4] Generally speaking, these beings had no real personality in that literature, where they had no names. The first time an angel is named is in Daniel, the latest book in the Old Testament canon. In the Apocryphal books, the appearance of named angels is a commonplace, and with the names come personal functions: Gabriel is the angel of revelation; Michael and Raphael are the champions of the Jews. George Foot Moore describes this popular belief:

> God's will in the world was executed by a multitude of such deputies. Not only is his revelation communicated through them, not only are they his instruments in providence and history, but the realm of nature is administered by them. The movements of the heavenly bodies are regulated by an angel who is appointed over all the luminaries of heaven. There are regents of the seasons, of months, and of days, who ensure the regularity of the calendar; the sea is controlled by a mighty prince; rain and dew, frost and snow and hail, thunder and lightning, have their own presiding spirits. There are angel warders of hell and tormentors of the damned [e.g. Satan]; champions of nations and guardians of individuals, recording angels—in short, angels for everything.[5]

One may even say that the angels have wills, sometimes wills which conflict: the angel of the Jews may contend with those of other nations. Angels are wiser than men, and they are immortal. Although we must regard this as a movement away from pure monotheism, it does not function as a polytheistic structure. No literature suggests that any angel is equal to God, and, although some angels operate by their own wills, God's will is never thwarted. At most, the activity of the angels is a reflection of activity on earth and a means of attributing a metaphysical dimension to history. It does not appear to detract from the worship of the one God.

The Jewish approach to society is closely related to the understanding of God. One of the fundamental Jewish memories is that of a covenant. The basic covenant is associated with Moses and consists very simply in Yahweh's adoption of a people. The earliest written formulation of it is in Exodus 20:2 f.: "I am Yahweh your God, who brought you out of the land of Egypt, out of the house of bondage. You shall have no other gods before me." In context, these verses form a preface to the Ten Commandments and the first commandment of the ten. But verse 3 has the fundamental force

---

[4] The Hebrew word can be translated either as angel or messenger.

[5] George Foot Moore, *Judaism* (Cambridge, Mass.: Harvard University Press, 1927), Vol. 1, pp. 403 f.

of the religion associated with Moses, for the covenant is the establishment of a relationship between a god and his people.

In its historical context, the covenant was not unusual, for it was only to be expected that a god would have a people. This arrangement was typical among ancient Near Eastern peoples: the Assyrians had Assur; the Babylonians had Marduk; the Canaanites had Baal. Since none of these cultures was monotheistic at the time, the situation was a relatively tolerant one in religious matters. The gods of other nations can be looked upon as competing gods, perhaps inferior to Yahweh, but gods nonetheless. But when monotheism develops within the Yahweh faith, the situation becomes totally different. Monotheism means that Yahweh is the sole and universal deity and that the claims of all other nations are only false claims. The gods of other nations can no longer be looked upon as competing gods; now they are no gods at all.

Even after monotheism becomes an unquestioned assumption among the Jews, the covenant is looked upon as the heart of their relationship to God. It is the combination of the covenant understanding with the affirmation of monotheism which creates the fundamental Jewish position: there is only one God, and we are his people. The practical issue which comes from this understanding is Jewish exclusivism, which determines some of the basic patterns of Jewish life and affects the conception of other nations. Exclusivism was potentially a part of Judaism all along, but the strictest formulation of it came with Ezra in the fourth century. At this time we have a thoroughgoing effort to eliminate from Judaism all foreign influences. It was Ezra who published a list of the men of Judaea who had taken foreign wives, and he compelled them to divorce these women and send them and their children back home. The observance of the Sabbath, although antedating Ezra, was emphasized as a visible sign of the distinction between those who are God's people and those who are not. Circumcision was also a physical mark which was intended to demonstrate this difference. Such signs were taken very seriously in Jesus' day, and we must understand them as parts of the general effort to exclude from God's people all those who were not born as Jews and those who did not engage in basic Jewish practices. Thus we have the fundamental Jewish approach to society: all men fall into two groups—Jews and Gentiles.

We cannot leave this subject without noting a trend in the opposite direction. It appears that some Jews, notably Pharisees, were willing and perhaps anxious to incorporate foreign-born people into the Jewish community. There was a standard form employed for this purpose. One who wished to become a part of this people would be baptized and circumcised and then would offer a sacrifice in the Temple. Moreover, Gentiles were welcome to attend services in synagogues, and those who were particularly interested formed a special group called God-fearers. Nevertheless, there were certain areas in synagogues and in the Temple which were off limits for all Gentiles. And, when all is said and done, the basic exclusivism in Judaism shines through. For when a proselyte had gone through the process of baptism, circumcision, and sacrifice, he was no longer a Gentile; he had become a Jew. There is no exception to the rule that society is formed of two groups of people—Jews and Gentiles.

The basic Jewish understanding of man is that which is fundamental to the Old Testament. Any genuine significance which might attach to the individual is lacking in most of the books, and there is little emphasis on the immaterial in man. The stress on corporateness is a characteristic feature of ancient Near Eastern thought forms. The important events are those which involve tribes or nations, not individuals. Even when the book of Genesis tells the story of one such as Abraham, who appears to be an individual, it is apparent that the actions and events surrounding him are really those of a group and that Abraham himself is representative of the Hebrew people. When Yahweh makes his covenant, it is not with each Israelite but with Israel. Participation in the covenant is never a matter of individual voluntarism. The group accepts the covenant in the person of Moses; no vote of the people is taken. The punishment for the sins of one generation may be meted out on subsequent generations. The sin of Adam, whose name means mankind, is the sin of all men, and all men suffer the punishment thereof. Although there are some signs of a growing interest in the individual in later Judaism (notably in Jeremiah), Jews in the Roman period did not exhibit that emphasis so notable in Hellenistic religions and philosophies. Whereas the latter attempted to answer the needs of individual men for security and redemption, Judaism retained its emphasis on group significance, thought mainly in terms of national life, and continued to divide men into two classes—Jews and Gentiles.

The other aspect of Jewish thinking about man relates to his make-up. Hellenistic thought characteristically affirmed both a material and an immaterial side to man, although Epicureanism would not allow such a distinction. In Judaism, the emphasis is on the functional integrity of man. Although Jews may speak of various parts of man's make-up, there is never a suggestion that these parts war against one another. When a man does well, his whole being is involved; and when he does ill, the whole man sins. This does not mean that Jews had no understanding of intangible human functions such as love, hate, desire, or thought. But it does mean that they did not separate these functions from the body. They thought of the body as the seat of all such activities: the heart is the place of reason, the bowels the location for love and hate. Although Hebrew has a word which may be translated *spirit*, in the use of that word, the emphasis is on the unity of man. There is no attempt to contrast body and spirit, no attempt to identify personality with one rather than the other, no suggestion that one is material and the other immaterial, and no feeling that the spirit is immortal. Wheeler Robinson made famous the Jewish description of man as "an animated body, and not an incarnated soul."[6]

A major consequence of this kind of understanding is that it leaves little room for belief in life after death. The absence of such a belief is clearly exhibited in the Old Testament literature, which takes death seriously. The absence of immortality is partly due to the emphasis on the group, which made a theory of individual significance irrelevant; but it was also due to the tendency to identify life with the body. Even at so late a time as the Book of Job, there is no suggestion of life after death, although there is a desire for it.[7] The severity of his complaint could be softened if Job could have had some basis for belief in life after death.

> For there is hope for a tree,
>   if it be cut down, that it will sprout again,
>   and that its shoots will not cease.
> Though its root grow old in the earth,
>   and its stump die in the ground,
> yet at the scent of water it will bud
>   and put forth branches like a young plant.
> But man dies, and is laid low;
>   man breathes his last, and where is he?
> As waters fail from a lake,
>   and a river wastes away and dries up,
> So man lies down and rises not again;
>   till the heavens are no more he will not awake,
>   or be roused out of his sleep.
> Oh that thou wouldest hide me in Sheol,
>   that thou wouldest conceal me until thy wrath be past,
>   that thou wouldest appoint me a set time and remember me!
> If a man dies, shall he live again?
>   All the days of my service I would wait,
>   till my release should come.

[6] In A. S. Peake, *The People and the Book* (Oxford: The Clarendon Press, 1946), p. 362; cf. also J. A. T. Robinson, *The Body* (London: S.C.M. Press, 1952), pp. 11–16.
[7] The Book of Job is certainly postexilic and may be as late as the Hellenistic period.

Thou wouldest call, and I would answer thee;
    thou wouldest long for the work of thy hands.
For then thou wouldest number my steps,
    thou wouldest not keep watch over my sin;
my transgression would be sealed up in a bag,
    and thou wouldest cover over my iniquity.[8]

Job might even find his fate tolerable if it were not permanent, but he sees no ground for hope. The earliest Jewish expectation of life after death is in the book of Daniel (12:2–3). Here a resurrection of many is expected at the end of things. Some are to be raised to everlasting reward and some to everlasting punishment. II Maccabees also expects the resurrection of those who gave their lives in the war against the Seleucids.[9] In other Apocryphal and pseudepigraphical writings this idea becomes more common, but in every case the resurrection is postponed to the last days. The predominant view remains one of resurrection of the body, although a few passages speak of a separation of body and soul.[10] By the time of Jesus and Paul, resurrection was a bone of contention between two major Jewish groups—Pharisees and Sadducees.[11] Pharisees accepted the resurrection of the body as a standard event relating to the last days, all of which Sadducees denied. It is notable, however, that, even in this "modernistic" aspect of Pharisaic thought, there was no speculation about individual immortality. Man is naturally mortal, and only by an act of God at the end of time is the mortality of some overcome. The contrast between this and most Hellenistic thought (save only Epicureanism) is dramatic, and it illustrates the profundity of the Jewish emphasis on man's integrity and on the identification of life with the body.

One final thought form which plays a very important role in Judaism is that which relates to history. The deep interest in history illustrates the Hebraic assumption that there is a dimension of reality in the arena of human affairs. We must keep in mind the Semitic tendency to think in corporate rather than individualistic terms and to think of history as that which occurs between tribes, nations, and empires. It includes the rise and fall of kings, military conquests and defeats, and political affairs. The Jew assumed that this is where Yahweh was active. It was on this level that the divine made himself known, rather than in nature or in thought. In short, history belongs to God. He controls what happens, and he controls the duration of an era. This is what is meant by an eschatological understanding.

---

[8] Job 14:7–17, Revised Standard Version translation.
[9] See II Maccabees 7:11; 7:22 f.; 14:46.
[10] E.g., Wisdom of Solomon 3:1 ff.
[11] See Acts 23:8; 26:8; Josephus, *Antiquities* XVIII, 1:4; *Wars* II, 8:14.

History is not a self-perpetuating series of events set in motion either by strong individuals or by natural or sociological forces. It is simply the area in which God works. Moreover, time belongs to God; it is his to give and his to withhold. For this reason, the Jew of Jesus' day could look upon his own era as about to end or look forward to a new age or to a final judgment. We shall see these forms of thought operative in the Messianic expectation of the Jews.

Having looked at the basic ways in which Jews thought in reference to God, society, man, and history, we can now move on to some fundamental expressions of Judaism in Jesus' day: the Torah, the Temple and the synagogues, and Messianism. After this, two final words about Judaism will be in order: first, on Jewish sectarianism; and second, on diaspora Judaism.

THE TORAH

Most readers automatically translate the Hebrew word *Torah* as law and then proceed to interpret it in line with their own understanding of the translation. In fact, however, *law* is only one facet of the meaning of Torah and not even the chief one. The basic meaning of the word is *teaching* or *direction*. It can stand for any teaching, but, when applied to God's instruction, it effectively signifies revelation. It is the revealed teaching of God.

When we ask where this teaching may be found, we come upon one of the fundamental points of dispute in first-century Judaism. All Jews agreed that the teaching was originally given to Moses and that it was recorded in the Pentateuch. All could, therefore, call the Pentateuch Torah. But Sadducees limited the concept to the written words, while the Pharisees understood it as the sum total of God's revelation, all that God had made known to his people throughout their history. Josephus makes the distinctive interpretations of these groups clear:

> The Pharisees have delivered to the people a great many observances by succession from their fathers, which are not written in the laws of Moses; and for that reason it is that the Sadducees reject them, and say that we are to esteem those observances to be obligatory which are in the written word, but are not to observe what are derived from the tradition of our forefathers.[12]

In their development of oral tradition, Pharisees did not look upon themselves as innovators. They felt that the written revelation was stated in such

[12] *Antiquities* XIII, 10:6.

a general way that it always needed more specific explanation. They were also aware that changing circumstances may bring about a tendency to neglect words which are cast in an ancient context. If one reads that he is not to muzzle an ox which is treading out the grain, he may assume that the words are inapplicable if he owns no ox. But Pharisees felt that the words had eternal significance and must not be limited to simplistically literal meanings. Their oral tradition made it clear that the words were valid for a man who employed human workers rather than animals. To them this was not a matter of making new laws but of discovering the contemporary applications of the eternally valid written teaching.

Pharisees also emphasized the continuity between written and oral Torah. They did not regard the oral tradition as human interpretation of a divine word. The entire Torah, written and oral, is God's revelation of his will. A late Jewish tractate speaks of the whole tradition as sacred and affirms that the whole of it was revealed to Moses on Sinai: "At the time when the Holy One, blessed be He, revealed Himself on Sinai, to give the Torah to Israel, He delivered it to Moses in order—Scripture, Mishnah, Talmud, and Haggadah."[13] Or, there is this startling statement: "Even that which a distinguished disciple was destined to teach in the presence of his master was already said to Moses on Sinai."[14]

In their distinction from Sadducees, Pharisees must be regarded as the more modernistic group, for they attempted to make Torah applicable to their own and succeeding generations. They would, on occasion, ignore the letter of a law which they felt went against the more basic revelation of God. The law in Exodus 21:24–25, which calls for an eye to be given for an eye taken (the *lex talionis*), was interpreted as requiring financial compensation rather than physical retaliation. Jacob Lauterbach says that the Pharisees "could not believe that these laws were ever meant to be taken literally."[15] For the Pharisees, therefore, the Torah was a divine revelation continually being made known. Their effort was to allow Torah to be what it should be —a perennial guide to man's daily life. Travers Herford sees the impact of the Pharisaic view as a breaking of "the fetters which were cramping the religious life of the people, and [setting] its spirit free to receive fresh inspiration from God."[16]

[13] Midrash Rabbah, Exodus 47:1. Midrash Rabbah is a Jewish commentary on the Pentateuch, compiled in the eleventh or twelfth century.

[14] Palestinian Talmud, Peah 17a.

[15] Lauterbach, *Rabbinic Essays* (Cincinnati, Ohio: KTAV Publishing House, 1951), p. 120.

[16] Herford, *The Pharisees* (New York: The Macmillan Company, 1924), pp. 65 f.

There is an inescapable tendency toward casuistry in the development of the oral tradition. Whenever the attempt is made to apply general rules to specific situations, this danger is present, and Pharisees seem intent on explicating the general rules, frequently to a fine point. The development of laws on the Sabbath may illustrate this tendency. The written Torah says that the Sabbath must be kept holy and that one must avoid work on that day. In the application of this principle it became necessary to define the precise limits of the Sabbath (from sundown on Friday to sundown on Saturday) and to provide a signal for its beginning and end (the blowing of a trumpet). Moreover, since work may be defined in diverse ways, it was necessary to make its meaning more precise. If one should consider work to be anything which involves motion, only complete rigidity would be permitted on the Sabbath. The Pharisees recognized that certain human functions could not be restricted and attempted to make provision for them. One could, therefore, eat food which had been prepared earlier, and he could move about so long as he traveled no more than two thirds of a mile. The Mishnah lists thirty-nine kinds of activity prohibited on the Sabbath, and one rabbi enumerated 1,521 varieties, listing thirty-nine examples for each of the Mishnaic thirty-nine. Pharisees also recognized that certain activities might be necessary in the case of imminent danger. In the Jewish war against Antiochus IV, Mattathias and his men decided that they would defend themselves if attacked on the Sabbath. In general, anything necessary for saving a life was permitted on the Sabbath, and many such activities are enumerated in the literature. Although this procedure produced a large number of minute regulations, it must be remembered that the purpose was to allow for essential functions while not avoiding the obligation to keep the Sabbath holy. Moore says, "The general principle is: The Sabbath was committed to you, not you to the Sabbath."[17]

The Pharisees seem to be aware of the danger of formalism in their position, and they seek to counteract it by emphasizing intention. The Rabbinic literature makes it abundantly clear that, by itself, the most careful observance of commandments does not constitute actual obedience. In the reciting of the Shema, which is a required duty, it is not just the recitation that is important but the recitation with the intention to fulfill duty. Even prohibited acts may escape condemnation if the perpetrator did not intend to disobey. Work which is prohibited on the Sabbath may be permitted if the worker did not intend to do the work at that time. In the trial of murder

[17] Moore, op. cit., II, 31; see Mark 2:27 and Mekilta on Exodus 31:13. The Mekilta is a Jewish commentary on Exodus. The core of it may go back to the second century, but most of it is medieval.

cases, the intention is of paramount importance, and accidental killing does not render a man culpable. Martin Buber calls attention to the fact that the Pharisees were aware of the possibility of fulfilling Torah without the intention to surrender oneself to God. Those who acted in this way were called "tinged ones," "i.e., those whose inwardness is a pretense."[18] Buber says further: "The project of sin and the reflecting upon it and not its execution is the real guilt."[19] He quotes a Talmudic passage to this effect: "The sin for God's sake is greater than the fulfilling of a commandment not for God's sake."[20]

The manner in which Torah stood as the measure of men may also have the danger of producing certain undesirable attitudes. The man who performs well may be boastful, while the one who does not may have a feeling of utter failure. The former attitude may be reinforced by a concept of merit. Such a concept is found in Jewish writings and may lead to the feeling that one obtains righteousness by obeying certain commands. Although an obedient act gives merit to the actor, the Jew is frequently warned against obeying for the purpose of being rewarded. Still greater emphasis lies on the concept of corporate merit. Such an emphasis is to be expected among those who think in terms of the solidarity of the people of God. Most passages do not refer to an individual's building up merit for himself but to his drawing on the merit of the Patriarchs or other worthy persons of the past, present, or future. There is less emphasis on individual accomplishment than might have been expected, and the sheer individuality of a man standing before the Torah is not the key to Jewish understanding at this point. Furthermore, the Pharisees and later rabbis do not feel that a person who has completely obeyed Torah has anything to boast of. There is a more desirable kind of person—a saint—who really rises above the Torah. This is the teaching behind the concept of a "fence around the Torah." The Jew is advised not only to obey the commands but also to do more than the Torah requires. "Sanctify thyself even in that which is permitted thee."[21] Sanctification includes not only acts but also intentions and thoughts. The saint does not disobey Torah, but this is quite incidental to his character. Such positions would not prohibit the boasting of an individual such as the Pharisee cited in Luke 18:9 ff., but it would indicate that Pharisaism did not intentionally promote it.

[18] Buber, *Two Types of Faith*, trans. Norman P. Goldhawk (New York: Harper & Row, 1961), p. 58.

[19] Ibid., p. 64.

[20] Ibid., p. 65; the Talmudic passage is Nazir 23.

[21] Midrash Sifre, 95a, a Jewish commentary on Numbers and Deuteronomy, possibly dating from the second century.

The feeling of failure may be partially overcome by two concepts. The first is the principle that one is not required to perform every duty in the Torah. The great quantity of commands is looked upon as beneficial rather than burdensome—the more commands, the more the opportunity to obey. Solomon Schechter says that every Jew has many chances to obey at least one command.[22] He quotes Rabbinic statements which say that a person who has accomplished one duty is as valuable as he who has done all things and that the only person who will not escape punishment is he who has not fulfilled a single duty.[23] Other statements in the Rabbinic literature say that a man is judged by the majority of his deeds, but even these statements do not imply that God takes a mechanical approach by adding up the number of obedient and disobedient deeds. In any case, a man who has not done all the required duties need not think of himself as an utter failure.

The second aid in avoiding the attitude of failure is the concept of repentance and forgiveness. According to Schechter, the general Rabbinic rule on repentance is "that there is nothing which can stand in the way of the penitent, be the sin ever so great."[24] "Thus neither the quantity of sins, nor the quality of sins, need make man hesitate to follow the Divine call to repentance. He has only to approach, so to speak, the 'door' with the determination of repentance, and it will be widely opened for his admittance."[25] Even here the intention is of fundamental importance. The Mishnah says: "If a man said, 'I will sin and repent, I will sin and repent;' he will be given no chance to repent. [If he said] 'I will sin and the Day of Atonement will effect atonement,' then the Day of Atonement effects no atonement."[26] Just as the intention to love God must be present for an obedient act to fulfill Torah, just so must it be present for repentance to effect forgiveness.

In summary, the Jewish understanding of Torah, particularly in its Pharisaic emphases, presents an approach to the religious life which is definite but not mechanical. It produces a religion in which it is possible for a man to know precisely what God expects of him and in which it is possible for him to do what is expected and even more than is required. Man must make every effort to do what God requires and to do it out of love for God. He must do it not for reward, but because it is God's will. If he fails to do it, he may repent and be forgiven, but all must be done with sincerity.

[22] Schechter, *Aspects of Rabbinic Theology* (New York: Schocken, 1961), p. 164.
[23] Ibid., pp. 164 f.
[24] Ibid., p. 333.
[25] Ibid., p. 326.
[26] Mishnah, Yoma 8 :9.

A model of Herodian Jerusalem. (*Courtesy* Israel Government Tourist Office, Atlanta, Georgia.)

THE TEMPLE AND THE SYNAGOGUES

The Temple and its ritual have roots deep in Israel's past. The original building was erected in the tenth century B.C. by Solomon. It was probably regarded from the beginning as a royal shrine and so took precedence over other centers in Israel. In the mid-seventh century B.C., there was a strong movement toward the elimination of all other shrines in Judaea. This was accomplished by King Josiah in 621 B.C., after the discovery of a book claiming the authorship of Moses. That book was probably a large part of what we now call Deuteronomy. Josiah made every effort to abolish the so-called high places, some of which had been associated with Canaanite deities, and he made it illegal to perform a sacrifice to Yahweh anywhere but in the Jerusalem Temple. The building was destroyed by Babylonians in 587 B.C., and many Jews were exiled to Babylonia, where they formed a subculture. Even during their exile, they did not modify the conception that sacrifice was permitted only in the Temple in Jerusalem. After the return of some Jews in 540 B.C., the second Temple was built in Jerusalem, and sacrifices were resumed. We have previously observed the significance of the Temple in the war against the Seleucids and the renovating work of Herod the Great. The Temple was finally destroyed by the Romans in A.D. 70 and has not been rebuilt to date.

The primary function of the Temple was to serve as the place where the sacrifices were to be performed. These are sacrifices, required in the Torah, of animals or grains, and the literature carefully restricts the kind and condition of both. A sacrifice is basically a gift, and some would be of things owed to God, while others would be offered as expressions of gratitude. Still others carried expiatory significance. There were also daily offerings of animals, cereal, and bread, which were thought of as the daily food for God. The sacrifices were presided over by priests, who must be in a condition of purity—that is, having no physical defect and having no uncleansed contact with death.

The Temple was also the scene of certain special observances. The Day of Atonement was the annual recognition of the need to atone for guilt. Most of the other festivals celebrated events in Israel's past: Passover was a reminder of the Exodus from Egypt; Pentecost probably signified the giving of Torah on Mount Sinai; Hanukkah celebrated the restoration of the Temple by the Maccabees; Tabernacles was a reminder of the nomadic period of Hebrew history. These festivals drew great crowds of Jews into Jerusalem from all parts of the world. Josephus certainly exaggerated when he estimated some three million visitors in Jerusalem for Passover of A.D. 66, but he could not have made any such statement unless great crowds had swarmed into the city.[27] The international character of such a festival as Pentecost is illustrated in Acts 2:5.

The priesthood of the Temple fell into three classes: the high priesthood; the priesthood; and the Levitical priesthood. The high priest was not only the head of the entire body of priests; he was regarded by most as the spiritual head of the Jewish nation. It was such an important office that, in the days before the Maccabean war, one man purchased it and another murdered for it. The Hasmoneans enjoyed the privileges of the high priesthood, and

[27] Josephus, *Wars* II, 14:3; in *Wars* VI, 9:3, the number is 2,700,000.

The wailing wall in Jerusalem contains a portion of Herod's Temple. (*Courtesy* Israel Government Tourist Office, Atlanta, Georgia.)

the later ones combined this office with that of king. Normally, the high priesthood was hereditary from Eleazar, the son of Moses' brother Aaron, and it was held for life. The high priest was the chief mediator between God and his people; he performed the sacrifice on the Day of Atonement and presided at sessions of the Sanhedrin.[28] The second class of the priesthood was simply called the priests. These were drawn from twenty-four families, sixteen from Zadok ben Eleazar ben Aaron, and eight from Ithamar ben Aaron. Each family served in the Temple on two separate weeks each year, and all families were called upon for the festal days. In addition to their supervision of the daily sacrifices, priests were charged with administering justice, giving medical advice, and teaching.[29] The third priestly order was composed of the Levites—that is, Levitical families not included in the order of priests. These assisted the priests and were responsible for the care of the building and its furnishings. They too served in rotation at appointed times.

The origin of the synagogue is obscure, although it is obviously a younger institution than the Temple. Philo and Josephus both claim that it started with Moses, but there is no reference to it in the Old Testament. Because of its character and function, most scholars look to the period of the Babylonian exile as providing the conditions under which such an institution could originate. Those Jews who were exiled to Babylonia in 587 B.C. had only recently been persuaded that sacrifices to Yahweh could be offered only in Jerusalem. Yet those Jews managed to retain the character of a community and remembered many of their traditions. This would not have happened without some institution, and the synagogue is well suited to perform this function. It would have served as a place of assembly, for reading the Scriptures, and for prayer. Even though its origin may have been as early as this, its development and consolidation must have come during the time of Ezra in the fourth century B.C. After his time, synagogues served as supplements to the Temple. They were not places of sacrifice, so there was no restriction on their number or location. They served as gathering places for local communities of Jews who could seldom travel to Jerusalem, and they were to be found all over the eastern Mediterranean world and in Mesopotamia—wherever Jews were to be found. There was even one synagogue located in the precincts of the Jerusalem Temple.

The chief officials in a synagogue were the scribes, who were originally

[28] According to the Mishnah, the Sanhedrin in Jerusalem was the supreme judicial body for Jews. There were probably local courts of an inferior level also known as Sanhedrim.

[29] The job of teaching was increasingly taken over by lay scribes.

Ruins of a third-century synagogue in Capernaum. (*Courtesy* Israel Government Tourist Office, Atlanta, Georgia.)

copyists of Scripture but who developed into interpreters. This fact points to the chief character of the synagogue as a place of instruction. To be sure, many religious functions not specifically restricted to the Temple were carried on in the synagogues; and synagogues performed many secular functions of a political and judicial nature. But their educational services were, far and away, their chief contribution. Here the learned would gather to pore over the Scriptures, to teach those who wished to learn, to solve problems brought to them, and to expound on the meaning of Torah in public gatherings. Indeed, we may identify the development of the oral Torah with the synagogue, for it is precisely under the conditions presented by this institution that such interpretation could take place.

It is no overstatement to assert that the synagogue was the institution that saved Judaism from total oblivion after the destruction of the Temple in A.D. 70 and the prohibition of Hadrian in A.D. 135. If the Temple had been the only religious institution and sacrifice the only religious practice, the destruction of the Temple and the cessation of the cult might almost certainly have been the death of the entire religion. The only thing that could have saved Judaism was something like the synagogue. Such an institution may have developed after A.D. 70 as a substitute for the Temple, but fortunately it was already an accepted, well-organized, and healthy institution before then, and it provided for the survival, in a modified form, of Judaism up to modern times. In addition, the existence of synagogues outside Palestine meant that separated Jewish communities could continue to function with or without the sacrificial cult. Nevertheless, the destruction of the Temple must be regarded as the end of an era for Judaism. The year 70 marks the point at which Judaism ceased to be a religion of ritual but continued as a religion of Torah.

MESSIANISM

The basis of Jewish Messianism is to be found in the fundamental approach to history which has been previously described. Messianic thought is simply a special variant of that way of thinking known as eschatological. Time is given by God and will be taken away by him; thus history can be looked on as having a terminus which God will bring about. The historical conditions during the early Roman period were such as to give life to this expectation, which was potentially significant at any moment. The Jew could reasonably feel that Roman occupation of Judaea was offensive to God and that soon God would act to bring it to an end. This act would involve a reversal of present historical circumstances, for God would see to it that the righteous Jews would come out on top.

Messianism becomes a part of eschatological expectation when one speculates about the agent God will use in accomplishing his purposes. The word *Messiah* is a derivative of the Hebrew verb which means to anoint. It specifically referred to the act of pouring oil on the head of a king or high priest when he was installed in office. Anointing is equivalent to coronation and ordination, and it signifies God's choice of king and priest. We may recall the mission of Samuel to anoint David as king of Israel in I Samuel 16:1–13. The king or priest who had been so anointed could be called Messiah, and this title is frequently applied to Saul, David, and other kings of Israel and Judah. It may even be applied to a foreign king who is thought of as chosen by Yahweh for a special function, such as the Persian Cyrus in Isaiah 45:1.[30]

---

[30] The word *Christ* is the English equivalent of the Greek *Christos*, which was used to translate the Hebrew word *Mashiach* or *Messiah*. Thus, Christ and Messiah can be used interchangeably.

At a later time the word *Messiah* came to be used as a title for the agent who was expected to initiate the end time. Such a designation is not found in the Old Testament, where the word is always associated with a specific historical personality.[31] Neither do the Apocryphal books speak of an individual Messiah, although they contain many ideas associated with eschatological expectation, such as the destruction of Israel's oppressors, the glorification of Jerusalem and the Temple, the coming of Elijah, and the resurrection of the righteous dead. In several Apocryphal books, the eternity of the house of David and of the Aaronic priesthood is also affirmed. It is in the books of the pseudepigrapha that widespread speculation about the Messiah is found, but in this literature we are faced with bewildering variety. There is as yet no rigid, orthodox timetable for the coming of the Messiah. Joseph Klausner, in his definitive study of Messianic expectation among the Jews, delineates certain elements which seem to be basic in the documents.[32] There are three ages: (1) the birth pangs of Messiah; (2) the days of Messiah; and (3) the Age to Come. Klausner also compiles a list of what he calls the complete Messianic chain, composed of the following links: "The signs of the Messiah, the coming of Elijah, the trumpet of Messiah, the ingathering of the exiles, the reception of proselytes, the war with Gog and Magog, the Day of Judgment, the resurrection of the dead, the World to Come."[33] But this complete picture is not found in any one document; it is rather a composite formed by an analysis of the varied elements in the sources.

The documents of the pseudepigrapha present us with a most unconsolidated picture. In some the Messianic age comes suddenly, in others gradually, while in still others there is no Messianic age at all. In the Similitudes of Enoch, dated by Klausner about 68 B.C., the Messiah is said to have existed before the creation of the world. This document describes the Messianic age as a time when righteousness will prevail and unrighteousness will disappear. The Son of man will put down kings and the mighty, and the things of civilization will evaporate. Leviathan and Behemoth, the great beasts of primeval times, will serve as food for the righteous. Finally, the Messianic age passes over into the Age to Come. In the Assumption of Moses, written in the early decades of the first century A.D., there are descriptions of something like a Messianic age, but there is no Messiah. In II Baruch, probably written toward the end of the first century, there is a

---

[31] The one possible exception is in Daniel 9:25, on which see p. 111.

[32] Klausner, *The Messianic Idea in Israel*, trans. W. F. Stinespring (New York: The Macmillan Company, 1955).

[33] Ibid., p. 385.

timetable of events. The end will come when the number of men to be born has been fulfilled. But before Messiah comes, there are to be twelve periods of commotions, wars, death, famine, oppression, and wickedness. Next there is to be a general judgment day on which each individual's book is opened, and then comes the Messianic age, not an endless period, but one of transition, during which the Messiah conquers Israel's enemies and establishes peace. In the Messianic age nature produces in a remarkable way. At the end of it the Messiah is taken to heaven, and the birth pangs of the Age to Come begin. This last is an eternal age in a renewed creation. IV Ezra has a pattern similar to that of II Baruch up to the end of the Messianic age.[34] This age lasts four hundred years, and at the end Messiah and all survivors die. Then there is a primeval silence for seven days (or seven years), a resurrection, a day of judgment which lasts seven years, and finally the Age to Come.

Amid all of this diversity, the place and function of the Messiah is fairly consistent. Where a Messiah is mentioned, his function is to close the present age, to initiate the age that bears his name, and to preside over it until the final judgment. Usually he has no further part to play in bringing in the Age to Come.

When we come to efforts to define the person of Messiah, we meet still further diversity. In some passages God is his own Messiah. In others, although Messiah has a function, there is no description of his person and little interest in him as an individual. In those documents which display interest, there are five forms which can be delineated.

1. In some cases, Messiah is a human being who is raised up by God to perform this special function. He is assumed to be a Jew, but he has no special ancestry. The historical parallel for such thought would be found in the period of the Judges, who were chosen by Yahweh to lead various tribes into battle against their enemies.

2. In some cases, although Messiah is human, he has a special ancestry. A crucial passage in the Dead Sea Scrolls speaks of two such Messiahs. In the so-called Manual of Discipline, we have a reference to the Messiahs of Aaron and Israel.[35] Throughout this document, it is clear that the former is a descendant of Aaron and therefore a priest and that he has precedence over the other Messiah, who is the secular-political ruler.[36] The origin of this

---

[34] Klausner dates IV Ezra c. A.D. 90–100.

[35] Column ix, lines 10–11.

[36] See Karl Georg Kuhn, "The Two Messiahs of Aaron and Israel," in Krister Stendahl, *The Scrolls and the New Testament* (New York: Harper, 1957), pp. 54–64. Kuhn finds the same idea in the pseudepigraphical Testaments of the Twelve Patriarchs and

conception is not known, but it is possible that the combination of priestly and royal functions in the Hasmonean rulers fed the idea. Certainly, the importance of the priesthood in the Qumran community is compatible with the greater weight given to the priestly Messiah.

3. Another human Messiah with special ancestry is the Son of David. The veneration of Jews for David and his descendants is reflected in this belief, which has roots in the Old Testament.[37] Jeremiah and Ezekiel both looked forward to a restoration of the Davidic line. Haggai and Zechariah, writing about 520 B.C., actually proclaimed a Davidic descendant named Zerubbabel to be Messiah. The idea of a restored Davidic dynasty seems strong during the postexilic period, and the function of a Son of David-Messiah would be to bring back to Judaea the glory once associated with the house of David. In Jesus' day this would include ridding Judaea of Roman occupation and establishing the nation as an independent monarchy once again. Evidence in Josephus indicates that this was the most popular of all forms of Messianic expectation and that there were several persons claiming this kind of Messiahship before and after Jesus.

4. In other cases Messiah is thought of as a resurrected figure of the past —for example, the new Moses. Mosaic speculation is based upon Deuteronomy 18:15ff., which projects the coming of a prophet like Moses. This figure would frequently be called simply "the prophet." Although we might expect the prophet-Messiah to be a person other than Moses, most speculation felt that he could not be like Moses without being Moses. Similar expectation revolved around the person of Elijah and was based upon passages in Malachi. The situation here is not quite the same as with Moses, for the Biblical narrative states that Elijah did not die but was taken up to be with God. Furthermore, most documents which mention Elijah place him as a herald of Messiah.

5. Finally, we come to the phrase "Son of man." The phrase is common enough in Aramaic, where it is used in place of the first person singular pronoun or to stand for a human being. Even in Hebrew the latter usage is found in Ezekiel. The use of the phrase in connection with the events of the end begins with the Book of Daniel, which was written about 165 B.C. In the seventh chapter, the author narrates an apocalyptic vision of the events of past, present, and future. He does this in terms of beasts which rise up out

---

in the so-called Zadokite Fragment, which was originally discovered in 1910 but which is now generally regarded as an Essene document.

[37] See II Samuel 7:16, 29, 23:5; Psalm 89:3-4, 29-37.

of the sea—a lion, a bear, a leopard, and a beast with ten horns. The usual interpretation is that these beasts stand for the great empires of the ancient Near East, the fourth being the Seleucid. Then the author describes, in 7:13, "one like a son of man" who comes on the clouds of heaven and establishes an everlasting dominion. The phrase probably signifies a fifth beast, one with a human appearance. In the interpretation of the vision, which follows in Daniel 7:15–27, the place of the one like a son of man is taken by "the people of the saints of the Most High" (verse 27)—that is, the Jewish nation. Daniel expects this nation to be the fifth empire, one which will last forever. At this point the conception is a corporate one, and there is no attempt to make it Messianic. In a later vision in Daniel 9:25 f. a Messiah is mentioned whose function is to rebuild Jerusalem. But this rebuilding is that which followed the decree of Cyrus of 540 B.C., and the Messiah would be either the Davidic Zerubbabel or the priestly Joshua, who attempted this work. In the following verse the author says that this prince will be cut off; thus, this is not the everlasting kingdom established by the one like a son of man.

The figure in Daniel proved to be an attractive one and reappeared in the Similitudes of Enoch.[38] Here the phrase becomes *the Son of man* and is clearly identified with the Messiah. He existed before the creation of the world and at the end will put down the kings of the earth; he will be a staff to the righteous and a light to the Gentiles. He will annihilate all those who mislead men and will be worshiped by all men.[39] It is this Enochic figure that forms a fifth Messianic conception. The Son of man is understood as supernatural and pre-existent, and he is expected to come on the clouds.

Unfortunately, it is not possible to make clear identifications between these conceptions and known Jewish groups. The double Messiah idea with precedence going to the priestly one may be tentatively identified with the Qumran community. All the rest seem to be rather widespread conceptions and might be found in any community. It is probably the case that the Davidic Messiah was the most popular in the time of Jesus, but the other conceptions were not absent, as the early Christian writings bear evidence. The hope itself was a general one, at least in Palestine, and many would-be leaders took full advantage of it.

---

[38] The Similitudes form chapters 37–71 of the Ethyopic Enoch, which Klausner dates in 68 B.C.

[39] In Enoch 71:14–17, Enoch himself is identified with the Son of man.

SECTARIANISM

There was a time when first-century Judaism was thought of as a monolithic religion, which insisted on a rigid orthodoxy and allowed for no variations in belief or practice. Both early Christian writings and post-Christian Jewish literature contributed to this view. Largely because of the Dead Sea Scrolls, we have begun to take a fresh look at this phenomenon and, in so doing, have discovered a great deal of variety. The kind of unformed diversity exhibited in Messianic expectation is one aspect of this. Another is the existence of a number of sects among the Jews, each of which held its own distinctive ideas and practices. It will be valuable to be acquainted with four of these groups.

Our information on Sadducees comes mainly from Josephus, although a few verses in the Synoptic Gospels and in Acts relate to them. In explaining Jewish sectarianism, Josephus says that Sadducees do not believe in fate. This probably means that they believe man has freedom of will and the ability to do what God requires. He also says that Sadducees accept only the written Torah. This does not mean that they reject the prophets and writings as uncanonical but that they accept only the Pentateuch as Torah. As we have seen, this was one of the chief distinctions between Pharisees and Sadducees. According to Lauterbach, Sadducees rejected oral tradition on the grounds that their ancestors had vowed to keep the words Ezra read to them, namely the Pentateuch.[40] Thus, the Sadducees made a distinction between the divine words of the Pentateuch and the human traditions of the Pharisees. Josephus also says that the Sadducees rejected the belief in life after death, a fact borne out in Acts 23:8.[41] The passage in Acts adds that they rejected belief in angels and spirits. So far as we can tell, their Messianic speculation was nil, and their political position was one designed to preserve the status quo. Josephus identifies them with the rich and indicates that their views were not popular. He says that they sometimes posed as Pharisees in order to hold public office.[42]

· The meaning of the name, *Sadducee* is debatable, but most scholars trace it to Zadok, the high priest during the reign of Solomon. According to Ezekiel, only the sons of Zadok were to minister in the Temple, and it is possible that the Sadducees originated as a party committed to that principle. Their origin dates to the early Hasmonean period, when they supported

[40] Lauterbach, op. cit.
[41] See Matthew 22:23; Mark 12:18; Luke 20:27.
[42] Josephus, *Antiquities* XVIII, 1:4.

these priest kings. Their basic association is with the Temple and its priest-hood, and it is possible that their initial opposition to an oral Torah sprang from their recognition that the legitimate function of teaching was being taken from the priests by the scribes.

Josephus attempts to show that Pharisees represent the best in Judaism, and he maintains that this was the most popular group. On the latter point he must certainly have been correct. This was the one party that survived the great catastrophe of A.D. 70, and what we know of it indicates that it was the only group that could have survived. The first notice Josephus gives to them is in the time of John Hyrcanus (135–105 B.C.). But they clearly con-stituted a strong and well-established body by that time. They probably are rooted in the scribes, that group of nonpriestly interpreters of Torah which goes back to early postexilic times. There may be a relationship between them and the Hasidim, who originally supported the Hasmoneans.[43] The name is probably derived from a Hebrew verb meaning to separate, and it signifies their insistence on separating from all impurity.

The central focus of Pharisaic thought is the Torah and the oral tradition, as we have seen. Although they separated from the Sadducees on this point, one must not think that they were uninterested in ritual matters. In fact they made no distinction between ritual and moral matters, and a great deal of their emphasis was on ritual observances, some relating to the Temple, some not. In all these matters they were highly meticulous. Their tendency to avoid distinction between more and less weighty regulations earned for them the condemnation of their Christian contemporaries.

The basic institution with which Pharisees were associated was the syna-gogue. Although they did not neglect the Temple, priests and Sadducees controlled it. The synagogue was a perfectly appropriate institution for Pharisees, for it had developed as a teaching place, and it had brought to-gether the scribes, most of whom must have been Pharisees. This association gave to Pharisees the opportunity to come into contact with the great masses of Jews, and this would account for the popularity Josephus says they had. Because there were synagogues in every town and village, Pharisees would be found all over Judaea and Galilee in the first century. It has recently been maintained that the Pharisaic party was, from an economic point of view, the party of the shopkeepers and businessmen, whereas the

[43] The Hasidim are first mentioned as a party or sect in I Maccabees 2 : 42, 7 : 13. They originally supported the Hasmoneans, but some later questioned the legitimacy of their claim to the high priesthood. The group split into rival wings, and this may be the origin of both Pharisees and Essenes.

Sadducees were associated with the landed aristocracy.[44] This is just what we would expect from the Pharisees' association with the synagogue.

Although Josephus is silent about their Messianic expectation, Pharisees clearly condoned it. In the Psalms of Solomon, a Pharisaic document produced about 63 B.C., we find an expectation of the Davidic Messiah. While some may have held to other types of Messianism, the Davidic must have been fundamental for them. In general they seem to be willing to wait for God to send his Messiah, but when Bar Cochba was proclaimed Messiah in A.D. 132, he was supported by Rabbi Akiba, the leading Pharisee of the day.

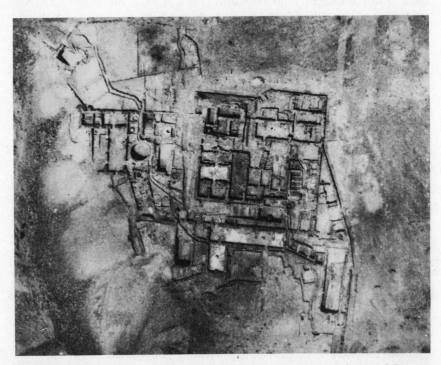

The remains of the Qumran community. (Photo by courtesy of the Israel Department of Antiquities and Museums.)

On doctrines where our information is less full, we can only say that they believed in resurrection, although this probably took the form of a belief in a general resurrection in the Age to Come. Josephus says that they believed in angels and in some cooperative arrangement between free will and fate.

[44] See Louis Finkelstein, *The Pharisees: the Sociological Background of Their Faith* (Philadelphia, Pa.: Jewish Publication Society of America, 1962).

Although there was probably very little speculation on such matters, Rabbi Akiba's saying may be typical: "All is foreseen, but freedom of choice is given."[45] Nothing is solved by such a statement, but the probable Pharisaic balance is illustrated.

The fundamental beliefs and practices of the Essenes are better known since the discovery of the Dead Sea Scrolls. Both Philo and Josephus had dealt with them, and they tell us that there were Essene colonies throughout Judaea. The Roman writer Pliny pinpointed one of the settlements near the Dead Sea. This is certainly the site we now know as Qumran, where archaeologists have unearthed a series of buildings, including a domitory and a refectory. This must have been the head house of the Essene order. The scrolls that the community produced were discovered hidden away in nearby caves. In addition to Biblical texts, the community produced a number of scrolls that record their beliefs and practices.

The distinctive feature of the Essene community was its monastic life. Members held no private property but pooled their resources and labor. They probably did not marry, although there is a lack of clarity on this point. Josephus says that they adopted young boys and prepared them for initiation into the movement. The community was ritually self-contained. It rejected the Jerusalem priests and had its own, who made sacrifices within the community. Although they sent contributions to the Jerusalem Temple, they did not appear there out of fear of being contaminated. Baptism was a daily practice as well as a rite of initiation and seems to take the form of a self-immersion in special tubs. They also had a common meal which featured the use of bread and wine, but we are not certain what these elements signified.

The Qumran scrolls speak with reverence about a *teacher of righteousness,* an apparently historical figure whose identity cannot be determined. He had been persecuted and put to death by a *wicked priest.* Their belief in a Messiah of Aaron and a Messiah of Israel has already been noted. On points relating to Torah, we cannot say whether or not they subscribed to Pharisaic interpretations, but they were regarded as being even more meticulous than Pharisees in their observances.

The origin of the community goes back to Hasmonean times, and many scholars see a relation between them and the Hasidic supporters of Mattathias. In the rebellion against Rome in A.D. 66, at least some came over to the Zealot position, and one was a leader of Jewish forces. Archeological evidence indicates that the Romans attacked the Qumran community during the war. As a result, the community was disbanded and the scrolls

---

[45] Mishnah, Pirqe Aboth 3:16.

Genesis Apocryphon Scroll, one of the Dead Sea Scrolls, before it was unrolled. Fragment at upper right was removed from the back of the roll in April, 1948. Lower fragment was received loose but probably came from break on lower part. (Photo by John C. Trever.)

Piecing together fragments of a Dead Sea commentary on Isaiah. (Photo by John M. Allegro.)

were hidden in caves. It is reasonable to expect that further light will be thrown on the Essenes by materials yet to be discovered, but even now we are able to understand them as varying in significant ways from the dominant traditions of Pharisees and Sadducees.

Josephus speaks of the Zealots as the fourth major group of Palestinian Jews, and he feels that it was the group chiefly responsible for the outbreak of war in A.D. 66. While Josephus probably overstates the case, the Zealots must be regarded as a strongly militant group. Their origin may be sought in Hasmonean times, when a militant nationalism pervaded the country, but their chief notoriety is to be found in the first Christian century. Their zeal was for the Torah, and in this they may have been similar to the Pharisees. But they equated Torah with Jewish independence and oriented themselves toward a war against the oppressors. Even their Messianic expectation, which was imprecise, was subservient to their revolutionary teaching. They felt that God's displeasure with the present situation of Roman occupation demanded that his people drive them out and so pave the way for his kingdom. With the motto, "We have no king but God," they preached a holy war against Romans and even against more patient Jews.

In addition to these four, some early Christian writers were aware of several others—Galileans, Baptists, Genistae, Meristae, Hellenists, and Nasaraioi.[46] We know next to nothing about these groups, but their existence reinforces the impression of diversity in first-century Judaism. It is, therefore, impossible to speak of orthodox Judaism prior to A.D. 70.

After the rebellion against Rome, Pharisaism came to be known as Rabbinic Judaism. This signalizes the fact that the Pharisaic was the only major movement to survive the war. Just before the city of Jerusalem fell in 70, Johanan ben Zakkai obtained permission from Titus to go to Jamnia and there set up a Rabbinical school. Many renowned scholars joined Johanan, and Jamnia became the new Jerusalem. Under his leadership the school set up a common calendar for religious observances and dealt with questions relating to the cessation of worship in the Temple. In time, some Temple practices were incorporated into the synagogue services. Under the leadership of Johanan's successor, Gamaliel II, Jamnia became the recognized authority in religion. In the eighties, a prayer against heretics (probably Christians) was permitted for use in the synagogues, and about A.D. 90 the canon of sacred Scripture, which included the thirty-nine books, was adopted. Gamaliel's successor, Rabbi Akiba, who supported Bar Cochba in the rebellion against Hadrian, began a written codification of the oral law. The process was continued by Akiba's pupil, Rabbi Meir, and concluded by Judah ha-Nasi, about A.D. 200. Judah's product is called the Mishnah, and it achieved a status tantamount to canonical authority among Jews in Palestine and Babylonia.

It was not only because Johanan ben Zakkai went to Jamnia that Pharisaism survived; there were elements in the movement itself that assured its continuation. Sadducees were too closely identified with the Temple and the sacrificial cult to survive their loss. The Essene community was largely destroyed, and the group disbanded. The Zealots had thrown all their force

[46] See Marcel Simon, *Jewish Sects at the Time of Jesus,* trans. James H. Farley (Philadelphia, Pa.: Fortress Press, 1967).

behind a losing war. Since Pharisees had identified with synagogues rather than exclusively with the Temple, the fall of the Temple, though a grievous calamity, was not the end of their movement. The Pharisaic development of oral tradition demonstrates their adaptability to changing situations. They do not bend to every wind, but they can understand the word of God to be relevant, come what may. Since Sadducees had committed themselves to the written word alone, they were not prepared to see its relevance to contemporary situations. The Pharisees also retained a hope in their Messianic expectation which did not focus on a particular war. They were willing to wait for God to bring in his own kingdom. This expectation, together with the assurance that God would destroy Judaea's enemies and raise the dead, gave to Pharisees a hope even in the darkest of times. After the war, the name Pharisee does not appear in Jewish literature because it does not need to. It is no longer a distinctive party; it is Judaism. The synagogue is the gathering center for all Jews; the oral tradition becomes a written word in the Mishnah and the Talmud; and the Messianic hope continues for Jews even to modern times.

Diaspora Judaism[47]

Judaism was found not only in Palestine but in Babylonia and in most major centers of the Roman world. In the first century, Jews in Egypt numbered a million and constituted about 15 per cent of the population there. Many diaspora Jews were slaves, and few were Roman citizens. There is evidence that they were allowed to form courts to decide cases involving purely religious matters. They were frequently granted local citizenship and could sometimes participate in local politics. But we read of very few Jewish diplomats or ambassadors on the international scene. During the Palestinian rebellions, sympathetic uprisings occurred in the Diaspora, and we know of an insurrection among the Jews in Egypt against Trajan in A.D. 116–117. In spite of these evidences of disloyalty, Jews were not exempt from military service.

Diaspora Jews struggled with the problem of maintaining community identity and yet living in predominantly Gentile communities. Their efforts were aided by an imperial ban against circumcisions after A.D. 135. The ban was enacted by Hadrian after the Palestinian rebellion, and it functioned to

[47] The word *Diaspora* designates the dispersion of Jews to lands outside Palestine. The beginning of Jewish emigration is to be identified with the Babylonian conquest of Judaea in 587 B.C.

eliminate proselytism almost totally and to minimize assimilation of Gentiles into Judaism. In addition, the scattered communities attempted to maintain close contact with Jews in Palestine. While the Temple stood, contributions to its support flowed in from the Diaspora. Counterparts to the school at Jamnia were established in Babylonia and in Rome. Many Babylonian scholars were trained in Jamnia or later in one of the Galilean schools. The school of Torah in Rome was established before the war under Hadrian, and both Johanan ben Zakkai and Gamaliel II visited there. Both these diaspora schools accepted in general the interpretive principles of Jamnia. Moreover, the synagogue served as a unifying institution within each diaspora community. Jews who frequented their local synagogues would hear the Scriptures read and interpreted and would come to know their ancient tradition as a living force.

But diaspora Jews could not completely isolate themselves from the wider community. In spite of the ban against circumcision, some Gentiles were attracted to the synagogue service. Some were positively influenced by Jewish practices and, in turn, influenced the Jewish community. The Jews in Alexandria seem to be the most thoroughly Hellenized of all those in the Diaspora. Philo, an Alexandrian Jew, who wrote during the first half of the first century, is a direct source of information about this community. He was, in fact, an esteemed leader among the Jews there.

It is significant that Philo could assimilate so much from Hellenism and still consider himself a Jew. His Judaism is maintained in his defense of Torah, and in this he is above reproach. But he thinks of the Mosaic books as a written embodiment of the universally revealed law. He uses allegory to bring together the Jewish Scriptures and his own universalism and attempts to establish a reasonable basis for each of the Jewish laws.[48] Even the food laws are so interpreted: God allows men to eat the flesh of gentle animals but forbids that of birds of prey and carnivorous mammals in order to elevate the virtue of peace. The allegorical method is, for Philo, an aid in discovering the distinction between the soul and the body of law, a distinction which he also accepts in the nature of man.

In his understanding of God, Philo is more Platonic than Biblical. He accepts the revelation to Moses but speaks of God in philosophical terms as Absolute Being. In this understanding he develops a whole system of intermediaries between God and the world, headed up by one called the *Logos*.[49]

---

[48] Allegory was commonly used by Hellenistic philosophers in the attempt to interpret the Greek myths in such a way as to be more intellectually satisfying.

[49] Cf. the Stoic use of *logos*.

This *Logos* is the sum of all created beings, and yet he is not different from God himself. Philo's thought at this point is an attempt to combine general Hellenistic thought with Jewish monotheism and may be compared with the understanding of Wisdom in other Jewish writings. It is the kind of amended monotheism that allowed early Christians to think of their Messiah as uniquely related to God. Whether typical or not, Philo represents an attempt to solve a problem which must have vexed most diaspora Jews, that of retaining their Judaism and not neglecting important aspects of the thought of their neighbors. We shall see that this is a problem which their Christian counterparts also shared.

Such is the multifaceted heritage of early Christianity. At different times and different places, particular aspects of this heritage will be more important than others, as we shall presently see. No part may be neglected in a study of early Christianity.

Part Two

The Literature of Early Christianity

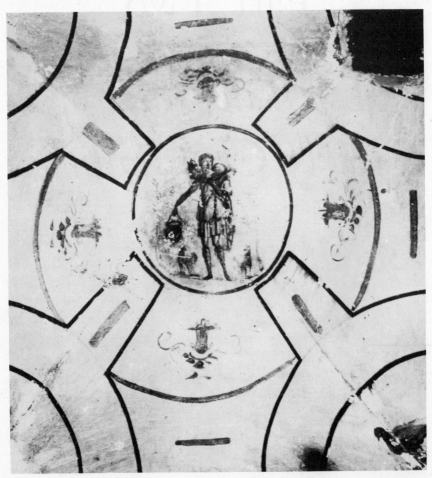

The Good Shepherd, fresco, early third century, Catacomb of St. Callixtus, Rome. Jesus as the good shepherd was a favorite theme in catacomb paintings. (*Courtesy* Pontifical Commission for Sacred Archives, Rome.)

Before we can investigate the nature and character of early Christianity, it is necessary to analyze the literary material which it left behind. In this section, we shall catalogue the most important examples of this material and indicate the background out of which the various documents came, their purposes, and character. The documents are arranged according to literary type.

(Approximate Dates)

Letters	Gospels	Histories	Sermons	Apocalypses	Apologies	Anti-heretical Literature
Paul, 40–60	Mark, 66–70 Matthew, 70–80 Luke, 80–85 John, 80–130	Acts, 80–85	Hebrews, 81–95			
Pseudo-Pauline, 90 James, 90–95 I Clement, 95 I, II, III John, 100 Jude, 100–125 I Peter, 115 Ignatius, 115 Polycarp, 115 & 135 Barnabas, 130	Book of James, 100–150		Hermas, 100–150	John, 95/96		
II Peter, 150	Infancy Thomas, 150 Peter, 150 Ebionites, 150 Thomas, 150		Didache, 150	Peter, 150		
Letter from Smyrna, 155			Melito, 167/168 II Clement, 150–175		Justin, 155	
Letter from Gaul, 177					Athenagoras, 176/177	Irenaeus, 180

FIGURE 14 A Time Chart of Early Christian Literature

Chapter Four

Letters

The letter is probably the most widely used form of writing. It is a direct communication between people. In the world of the first and second century, we find two types of such communication: one consists of those documents that grew out of specific, usually local, situations and addressed themselves to those situations; the other uses the letter form as a work of literary art. In the latter case, the background circumstances are more general, less local, and less personal. These we may call epistles. The difference is rather easy to spot, for the letter is intended for a specific person or group, while the epistle is meant for quite general consumption. Most of the materials that will be considered here are letters, although a few epistles will be found in the group.[1]

Although there are certain disadvantages in the use of letters as historical sources, the advantages far outweigh them. The major disadvantage lies in the fact that a letter is written against a background which is shared by author and recipient but which is no longer available to a modern scholar. Kirsopp Lake long ago noted that "the writer of a letter assumes the knowledge of a whole series of facts, which are, as he is quite aware, equally familiar to his correspondent and to himself. But as time goes on this knowledge is gradually forgotten and what was originally quite plain becomes difficult and obscure."[2] On the positive side, the letter is innately more honest than any other form of literature. Because a genuine letter is, by its very nature, private, the author may make little effort to hide facts that he would be reticent to reveal to a wider public. The modern historian is frequently privy to a good deal of information which might never appear except in letter form.

---

[1] Some documents which are frequently treated as letters or epistles will not be included in this section. The so-called letter to the Hebrews and the *Epistles of the Apostles* have none of the formal characteristics of the letter and are best omitted in a catalogue of letters.

[2] Kirsopp Lake, *The Earlier Epistles of St. Paul* (London: Rivingtons, 1919), p. vii.

THE LETTERS OF PAUL

The earliest Christian letters extant today are those of Paul, and these form the oldest bit of Christian writing there is. A number of Paul's letters contain autobiographical traces, which enable us to ascertain some of the basic facts of his life.[3] Paul was a Jew, whose birth date would not be far from that of Jesus. He was a Pharisee, and he exhibited an unusual degree of zeal for the Torah. His dedication to Judaism led him to become a persecutor of the emerging Christian movement. It is probable that he was in the act of persecuting the Church at Damascus when he felt himself to have a revelation from the Christ. To him this revelation meant that he was to preach Christ among the Gentiles. He went into Arabia, then returned to Damascus and to Jerusalem.[4] In Jerusalem, he was known only by reputation, as a former enemy of the church who was preaching the faith he once tried to destroy. On this visit to Jerusalem, Paul became acquainted with Cephas (that is, Peter), a disciple of Jesus, and with James, whom he called the brother of the Lord, but he met none of the other Christians. Still, he felt himself obliged to preach to Gentiles, and out of response to his revelatory experience he spent the next eleven to fourteen years preaching and establishing churches in Asia Minor, Macedonia, and Greece. About A.D. 51 he made a second trip to Jerusalem and conferred with James, Peter, and John (another disciple) on the question of the treatment of Gentiles in the church. The chief question was whether such persons should be required to be circumcised, and on this issue Paul stoutly affirmed the negative. His position prevailed, and Paul was given the task of collecting money for the Jerusalem Church. The next few years were spent in taking these offerings and preaching in Asia Minor and Greece. When he completed this work, he returned to Jerusalem for the third time in A.D. 53 or 54. We have no autobiographical material on Paul's life after this point. He mentions a number

---

[3] The Book of Acts, a late first-century work, includes a detailed biography of Paul, which must be treated as a secondary source. The letters of Paul constitute the primary material for Pauline biography, and that which follows is drawn from that primary source. For a full survey of the relative value of Acts and the letters for Pauline biography, see John Knox, *Chapters in a Life of Paul* (New York: Abingdon Press, 1950).

[4] In Galatians 1:18, Paul says that he went to Jerusalem "after three years." The context does not make it clear whether he means that the trip to Jerusalem occurred three years after the conversion experience or three years after his return to Damascus. John Knox, op. cit., argues convincingly that the conversion occurred in A.D. 34 or 35 and the first trip to Jerusalem took place between A.D. 37 and A.D. 40. The chronology contained here follows largely that of Knox.

of imprisonments, and it is likely that Acts is correct in reporting that he was arrested in Jerusalem and then sent to Rome for an imperial trial. The letter of Clement says that he became a martyr.[5] Late second-century tradition affirms that he and Peter were both executed in Rome at the same time.[6]

The letters we have from Paul were written in the period between the first and third visits to Jerusalem—i.e., between A.D. 37 and A.D. 54. It is important that we understand the specific occasion and purpose of each of his letters.

Paul to the Thessalonians

The New Testament canon preserves two letters allegedly written by Paul to Christians at Thessalonica. Although certain questions have been raised about the authenticity of II Thessalonians, the first letter is accepted by almost all scholars as a letter written by Paul, with the concurrence of Silvanus and Timothy. In addition, almost all scholars agree that I Thessalonians is the earliest of Paul's letters and, thus, the oldest piece of Christian literature available to us. The Book of Acts produces a date of A.D. 50 or 51 for the composition of this letter, but there is sufficient reason to think that it was composed as early as A.D. 40.[7] Although the precise date may be uncertain, we are clearly closer to primitive Christianity in this letter than in any other written material.

Behind the writing of I Thessalonians lies a visit that Paul, and probably Silvanus and Timothy, had paid to this Macedonian city, where they established a church. They had come from Philippi, also in Macedonia, where they had been "shamefully treated." In Thessalonica they preached "in the face of great opposition," and their word was received "in much affliction." It is not possible to document the nature of the trouble these missionaries met

---

[5] On the letter of Clement, see p. 152 ff.

[6] See Irenaeus, *Against Heresies* III, 1:1; Eusebius, *Church History* II, 25:8.

[7] The Book of Acts traces the geographical movements of Paul in general conformity with the pattern we get in the letters, i.e., from Philippi down to Athens and Corinth. In addition, Acts dates Paul's stay at Corinth to overlap with the appearance there of Gallio, who came as Roman governor of Achaea in or about A.D. 51. On this basis it is legitimate to date I Thessalonians somewhere in the neighborhood of A.D. 50. John Knox has shown, however, that nothing in the letter itself would force us to accept a date as late as this. He is convinced that Paul's second visit to Jerusalem occurred about A.D. 51 and that the Thessalonian correspondence preceded that visit by a significant span of time. I Thessalonians, says Knox, was clearly written soon after Paul's visit to Thessalonica, and that visit was early in Paul's career, perhaps about A.D. 40. See Knox, op. cit., pp. 85 ff.

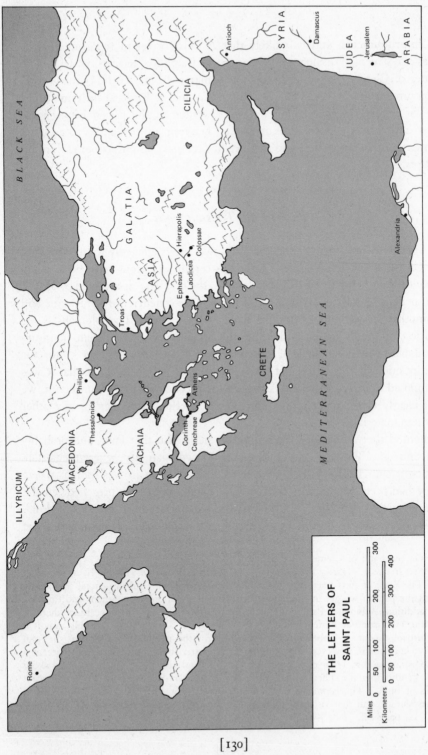

FIGURE 15   The Letters of Paul. (Copyright 1949 Thomas Nelson Inc.)

THE LETTERS OF
SAINT PAUL

Miles 0   50   100   200   300
Kilometers 0 50 100   200   300   400

in Thessalonica, but it is probable that they were greeted with some hostility. The Book of Acts says that Paul and Silas (probably Silvanus) spent three weeks in Thessalonica and preached there in a Jewish synagogue. While some Jews embraced their preaching, most opposed them and caused an uproar, which brought the missionaries to the attention of the city fathers. Acts concludes the narrative by saying that Paul and Silas were spirited away before they could be arrested. I Thessalonians may be understood as saying that opposition came from Jews, but nowhere is this explicitly stated. Moreover, the letter does not indicate that the primary contacts were with Jews. On the contrary, it says that the converts were those who "turned from idols to be servants of the living and true God"[8]—namely, Gentiles. Perhaps Jews had no significant part to play in the mission to Thessalonica. It also appears that Paul and his companions spent more than three weeks there. Although no specific period of time is mentioned in the letter, the impression of duration is stronger than that of speed. Paul says that they worked night and day so as not to burden their hosts. He speaks of treating the believers as children, exhorting and encouraging them and treating them with gentleness. In all probability the mission to Thessalonica was one of months rather than weeks and was marked by hostility from some Gentiles and acceptance by others.

After Paul and his companions left Thessalonica and came to Athens, Paul desired to see his converts again. He apparently made plans, at least on two occasions, to return, but he was prevented from doing so. When he "could bear it no longer," he sent Timothy to see if they had remained faithful to the newly embraced religion. The lapse of time between the departure from Thessalonica and Timothy's departure from Athens is spoken of as a short time.[9] The letter, I Thessalonians, was written when Timothy rejoined Paul, bringing news that the converts had indeed remained steadfast even in the face of persecution.

The letter, jointly written by Paul, Silvanus, and Timothy, was primarily intended to express their joy over the news from Thessalonica. But it is apparent that Timothy's visit also uncovered some problems which had to be faced. There was a need for a sexual ethic, probably brought to light by cases of adultery or promiscuity among Christians.[10] In addition, probably because some among them had died, the Thessalonians needed an understanding of life after death.[11] Finally, they needed a clarification of the

---

[8] I Thessalonians 1 : 9.
[9] I Thessalonians 2 : 17.
[10] See I Thessalonians 4 : 1–12.
[11] See I Thessalonians 4 : 13–18.

Christian future expectation.[12] It looks as if Paul had preached to them that the end of history was imminent and that some of the converts had begun to believe that that end was already upon them.[13] The letters, therefore, had a twofold purpose: to congratulate the Thessalonian Christians on their steadfastness and to answer their questions related to sex, death, and the future. It closes with the request that it be read to all the Christians in Thessalonica.

From time to time the authenticity of II Thessalonians has been seriously questioned. Scholars who doubt that Paul wrote this letter cite two reasons for suspicion. In the first place, the bulk of the letter seems too much like the first, so much so that some call it a slavish imitation of the first.[14] The same themes are found in both letters, but the second lacks the warmth of the first. It is difficult to imagine Paul copying himself, and it is possible that a later writer used I Thessalonians as a model for his own letter. The second ground for suspicion lies in the apparently different eschatological expectations presented in the two letters. The first had said that the day of the Lord would come without warning, "like a thief in the night,"[15] but the second insists that "the man of lawlessness" must precede the coming of the Lord and that something is now restraining him.[16] This passage says directly that signs will accompany the appearance of the lawless one and that one of the signs will occur in the Temple (presumably in Jerusalem).

These objections to authenticity can be answered. The similarities between the two letters would not appear to be unusual if both were written within a brief period of time. The formality and lack of warmth may be due to the gravity of the problem Paul faced in the second letter and to the continued persecution of the church. As for the different eschatological expectations, we may observe this same kind of inconsistency in Jewish apocalyptic writings, where we read that the end comes suddenly and that it is preceded by signs. Some of these writings make the period of lawlessness the initial stage of the end rather than a sign of the end, and this idea may be what Paul is alluding to. To him, the end has not come because the first stage, the birth pangs of the Messiah, has not occurred. The appearance of the man of lawlessness is not a warning that the end *will* come, but a

---

[12] See I Thessalonians 5:1–11.

[13] Some may have quit work in the exuberance of their faith, so that Paul calls upon the church to "admonish the idle" in 5:14. By the time of II Thessalonians, this had become an even more serious problem. See p. 133.

[14] See, e.g., Morton S. Enslin, *The Literature of the Christian Movement* (New York: Harper & Row, 1938), p. 242.

[15] I Thessalonians 5:2.

[16] II Thessalonians 2:1–12.

signal that it *is* here. This is not inconsistent with the idea that the day of the Lord comes without warning.

In addition, there are positive reasons for regarding II Thessalonians as a genuine letter of Paul. In the first place, it includes a reference to his visit to Thessalonica. In speaking of the man of lawlessness, the author says, "You cannot but remember that I told you this while I was still with you."[17] It would be difficult for an imposter to make such a statement to people who might be in a position to refute it. Secondly, there is a probable reference to a fraudulent letter in 2:2. A person writing a fraudulent letter would not be likely to call attention to fraud. But the remark is natural for a man who has been embarrassed by a letter written over his signature by an imposter. Finally, the letter is signed with the conscious intention to validate it as genuine.[18] This would be a bold stroke indeed, if the letter is not by Paul, but a natural one for a man who has had trouble before. Although there are difficulties, it seems probable that Paul did write II Thessalonians not long after he wrote the first letter.

The occasion for the letter, if genuine, is sufficiently clear. The first letter had been dispatched (2:15) by a messenger, who returned to Paul with more information about the church. In this way Paul learned of continued persecution in the church and of the existence of extreme eschatological expectations.[19] The latter troubled him. He may have felt partially responsible, since he had preached the return of the Lord and had gone into it again in the first letter.[20] It is also probable that a letter purporting to be by Paul had circulated in Thessalonica and had proclaimed that the end had arrived. Whatever be the cause, some Christians in Thessalonica were saying that the day of the Lord had already come. Some of these people had quit work as a result of their zealous belief, and they were drawing on the contributions of working Christians. Paul wrote II Thessalonians to correct these errors and to assure the church that the day of the Lord had not yet come. He ordered that those who had quit work must not be fed. The gravity of these problems for Paul is displayed toward the end of the letter, where he advises that shunning should be invoked against those who do not go back to work.

[17] II Thessalonians 2:5.
[18] II Thessalonians 3:17.
[19] This is a problem that Paul faced in I Thessalonians, but there it seems to be less serious than it does here.
[20] I Thessalonians 4:13–5:11.

Paul to the Galatians

The location of the letter to the Galatians within the general chronology of Paul's other letters is far from certain. We know only that it was written after his second visit to Jerusalem, a report of which forms a significant part of the letter. John Knox's date of A.D. 51 for the second Jerusalem visit may be taken as the earliest possible date for the letter, but it could have been written a few years later.[21] Its authenticity has never been questioned.

The churches to which the letter is directed are in Asia Minor,[22] and it seems to be occasioned by a controversy there over the necessity of circumcision. The trouble probably dates back to the earliest days of the Galatian churches. This part of Asia Minor must have been invaded by a rather large number of Christian preachers, some of whom retained the Jewish practice of circumcision. But others, such as Paul, did not make this a requirement for entry into the Christian fellowship. As the converts of the various missionaries mixed, circumcision became a hotly debated issue. Some of those who advocated it felt that the pillars of the Jerusalem Church were on their side and that Paul also agreed with them. Paul, in the letter, takes great pains to refute these assumptions, affirming that the Jerusalem pillars do not require circumcision for Gentiles and stating his own case against this requirement.[23]

Because this letter includes certain details of Paul's life, it is a valuable source for his biographers. Because it deals extensively with a rite associated with Jewish exclusivism, it has frequently been used to support a proclamation of freedom from Judaism and of opposition to any exclusivistic limitations in Christianity.

---

[21] See Knox, op. cit. p. 85.

[22] Doubt persists on the specific localities to which the letter was addressed. The Roman province of Galatia is in north-central Asia Minor and includes the towns of Ancyra, Pessinus, and Tavium. Before imperial days, Galatia included cities in south-central Asia Minor, namely Iconium, Lystra, and Derbe. The Book of Acts reports visits of Paul only to this latter group of cities. The letter gives no indication of the specific locality other than the address to the Galatians. Certainty on this issue is not possible, but there is a strong probability that the southern cities were the recipients. The geographical proximity of the southern cities to one another would allow them jointly to receive a single letter, but distances between the cities in the north would seem to require either a separate letter to each or a request that the single letter be passed around.

[23] See Joseph B. Tyson, "Paul's Opponents in Galatia," *Novum Testamentum* **10**: 241–254 (1968).

Paul to the Corinthians

In writing to the Galatians, Paul had said that the Jerusalem leaders required an offering from the Gentile churches.[24] In his correspondence with the Corinthians and Romans, he is in the process of collecting this money. The Corinthian correspondence may be dated between A.D. 51 and 53.

Although the New Testament contains two letters from Paul to Corinth, this is not all that he wrote, and II Corinthians almost certainly includes two letters. I Corinthians 5:9 refers to a previous letter, a portion of which may now be found in II Corinthians 6:14–7:1, which does not fit its present context and contains the substance of what we should expect. A full catalogue of Paul's correspondence with the Corinthians would be as follows:

A. II Corinthians 6:14–7:1 (a fragment).
B. I Corinthians.
C. II Corinthians 10–13.
D. II Corinthians 1–9 (minus letter A).

Paul's founding visit to Corinth was followed by letter A, in which he warned his converts not to associate with immoral persons and probably made a number of other ethical pronouncements. After sending the letter, he received additional information about Corinth from two sources: a letter from some Corinthian Christians[25] and an oral report from the people of Chloe.[26] The reports bring to Paul's attention a number of problems in the church, such as dissensions, problems of sexual morality and food regulations, perplexity about worship practices, spiritual gifts, and the resurrection of Christians.

The source of these difficulties is not easy to find. It is possible that the problem of sexual morality was caused by the general background out of which Paul's converts came and by the environment of Corinth. Sexual promiscuity in Corinth was legendary, but promiscuity was not the only problem which came to Paul's attention. There were some Christians in Corinth who visited prostitutes, but there were others who advocated complete celibacy within and outside of marriage.

If the general society did not foster all problems, it may be possible to find the source of difficulty in the diverse preaching of Christian missionaries.

[24] Galatians 2:10.
[25] See I Corinthians 7:1.
[26] The people of Chloe are otherwise unidentified, but the phrase suggests that they were her associates or agents, not members of her family; see I Corinthians 1:11.

Paul's letter indicates that quarrels arose over allegiances to different personalities—Paul, Cephas, Apollos.[27] It is possible that the preaching of these three missionaries was not identical. This supposition is attractive, because some of the information we have on Peter (Cephas) connects him with a problem of food regulations.[28] Of Apollos we know next to nothing.[29]

Several modern scholars have suggested that the problems arose because of the presence of Gnostic influence in Corinth.[30] W. Marxsen finds several characteristically Gnostic features in the Corinthian Church, such as the esteem for knowledge, possession of the spirit, moral freedom, and a denial of future resurrection.[31] If this is the case, as seems likely, we have here a record of the first confrontation between Gnostic and Pauline Christianity.

In a painstaking analysis of I Corinthians, John Hurd has attempted to reconstruct the main lines of Paul's initial preaching in Corinth, the letter A, and the letter from the Corinthian Christians to Paul.[32] He suggests that Paul's preaching allowed for a good deal of ethical freedom, but that, after he left Corinth, he found it necessary to reach an agreement with the Jerusalem apostles which involved more restriction than he would have liked. In letter A, he attempted to communicate these restrictions, presenting them as his own. The Corinthians replied, expressing perplexity over this new information and accusing Paul of inconsistency. Paul then wrote letter B, or I Corinthians, in which he attempted to justify the restrictions and maintain his consistency.

However we may account for the problems, it is clear that I Corinthians is occasioned by disagreement and perplexity on a number of moral and doctrinal issues. Paul addresses himself to each of the problems, always with an eye to the unity of the church within itself and with other churches. At the end he mentions his plans: he is now in Ephesus, whence he has sent Timothy to Corinth. Upon Timothy's return he expects to go to Macedonia and then down to Corinth, where he plans to spend some time.

The unity of II Corinthians has been seriously questioned by almost every

[27] See I Corinthians 1:12. In addition to those who ally themselves with Paul, Apollos, or Cephas, there are others who say, "I belong to Christ." The fourth group is probably composed of those who wish to have nothing to do with the partisanship inherent in the other three groups.

[28] See Galatians 2:11 ff.; Acts 10:1–23.

[29] But see Acts 18:24–28.

[30] On Gnostic Christianity, see pp. 316 ff.

[31] Willi Marxsen, *Introduction to the New Testament*, trans. G. Buswell (Oxford: Blackwell, 1968), pp. 74 ff. See also Walter Schmithals, *Gnosticism in Corinth*, trans. John E. Steely (Nashville, Tenn.: Abingdon, 1971).

[32] John C. Hurd, *The Origin of I Corinthians* (New York: Seabury, 1965).

writer on the subject. Willi Marxsen finds six letters, one of them probably not by Paul.[33] Most scholars find three letters—A, C, and D, to use the notations above. After we remove 6:14–7:1 and designate it as a fragment of letter A, two serious problems remain. The first is a lack of clarity in Paul's travel plans. At the end of I Corinthians he had said that he would not come to Corinth until after Pentecost. In II Corinthians 1:16 and 2:1, it is apparent that a projected trip has been canceled because Paul is sure that it would have increased animosity. In 9:3–5, he speaks of coming to Corinth to receive the offering for Jerusalem. In 12:14 and 13:1, he speaks of a third visit to Corinth, in which he intends to deal severely with his opponents. The comment on the visit in chapter 9 carries no note of hostility, while the animosity in chapters 12 and 13 is plain. The more serious problem is the tonal change within II Corinthians. Chapters 1–9 are conciliatory and were written after some serious controversy involving the personal relations between Paul and his readers had been resolved. But chapters 10–13 seem to be written during the midst of such a controversy. For this reason, we may turn the letter around and designate II Corinthians 10–13 as letter C and 1–9 as letter D. This solution is confirmed by references in the latter to the former. In II Corinthians 2:3 f., 2:9, and 7:8, Paul refers to a letter written with tears, a letter which caused the recipients grief. This cannot be I Corinthians, but II Corinthians 10–13 is exactly that kind of letter.

The problem around which letters C and D revolve is probably basically personal. Paul's defense in II Corinthians 10–13 is almost altogether personal, and indicates that he has been charged with being humble when present and bold when absent, with boasting, and with showing favoritism. He has been compared unfavorably with other apostles and apparently has been accused of not speaking in Christ. In writing letter C, probably from Ephesus, he threatens to come to Corinth for the third time and act severely against his opponents. We may also conjecture that some kind of trial awaits Paul in Corinth. He speaks of "passing the test" and seems to prepare for a trial by reminding the readers that "all facts must be established by the evidence of two or three witnesses."[34]

Letter D seems to say that Paul has not yet made that third visit. He has apparently been accused of vacillation, because he had planned to visit Corinth on his way to and from Macedonia.[35] In fact, however, he now confesses that he had decided against any further visits because he felt they

[33] Marxsen, op. cit., pp. 77 ff.
[34] II Corinthians 13:1.
[35] II Corinthians 1:16.

only caused pain. Instead, he sent Titus with letter C and agreed to meet him in Troas. He missed him there and went on to Macedonia, where Titus appeared with news that the majority at Corinth were still zealous for Paul and wished to see him. It then came to light that a single person had been causing the difficulty and that the majority had censured him. Paul even finds it necessary to ask them to forgive this former enemy. Letter D is, therefore, written out of joy at reconciliation with friends. It looks as if Paul sent Titus back to Corinth once more, with letter D and with orders to receive the collection for Jerusalem in preparation for the long-projected visit of Paul.

Paul to the Romans

The last Pauline letter to be related to the Jerusalem offering is that to the Romans.[36] It was probably written in A.D. 53 or 54. The occasion for the letter is stated in some detail at 15:22-29. These verses indicate that Paul has, for some time, planned a trip to Rome and that now he expects to stop by there on the way to Spain. He must, however, first go to Jerusalem to deliver the offering, the collection of which is now complete. Thereafter he will come to Rome.[37] The general background of the letter is sufficiently clear: Paul had been through serious controversies with the Corinthians, but these have been settled amicably. He has fulfilled his obligation to Jerusalem, although he has some apprehension about his reception there.[38]

---

[36] One ninth-century manuscript of this letter lacks the word *Rome* in 1:7 and 1:15, but this must be regarded as an error of omission, for all other manuscripts have Rome as the letter's destination. Two other facts raise a question about the integrity of the letter. A doxology, which sounds like the conclusion, appears in different places in the various manuscripts. Most modern editions of Romans place the doxology at 16:25-27. Although some scholars feel that the variable position of the doxology means that the letter has been expanded by later copyists, it is equally possible that Paul wrote all sixteen chapters and that later copyists abbreviated it. A second problem revolves around the nature of chapter 16, which contains greetings to twenty-five persons and two families. This appears incredible in a letter addressed to a place where Paul is a stranger, and some scholars suggest that chapter 16 was originally addressed elsewhere (e.g., Ephesus) and was attached to Romans by mistake. Nevertheless, it is not impossible that Paul knew so many people in Rome. He certainly would wish to cite all his acquaintances there if he intended to establish good relations with the Church.

[37] References in the Corinthian and Roman correspondence give a fairly complete account of the process of raising the collection. The Corinthian correspondence (I Corinthians 16:3; II Corinthians 8:6; 9:1-5) indicates that Paul wished to culminate the collection in Corinth and carry it from there to Jerusalem. II Corinthians 9:1-5 implies that Paul is just about ready to come to Corinth for that purpose. Romans 15 reveals that the task of collecting has been completed.

[38] See Romans 15:30 ff.

He has fulfilled his mission in the east, preaching "from Jerusalem as far round as Illyricum."[39] He has looked forward to visiting Rome for many years and is now planning for wider areas of work, even in Spain.[40] It is in this relatively peaceful but expectant mood that Paul writes this letter to a church he had not previously visited.

At first glance, the purpose of the letter seems to be threefold: to establish relations with Christians in Rome, to acquaint them with his travel plans, and to ask for their help on the projected trip to Spain. But the letter does more than meet these needs, for in it Paul gives the most complete and systematic statement of his theology we have. This was certainly not necessary, and a much briefer note would have been sufficient, unless he had another purpose in mind. It has been suggested that Paul was in such urgent need for money that he felt it necessary to explain his thinking as fully as possible.[41] Other scholars feel that he wished to allay the kind of misunderstanding he encountered in Galatia and Corinth.[42] Still others suggest that he had heard of controversies within the Roman Church and that he wrote in order to aid their resolution.[43] It is most likely that the reason for the letter lies within Paul himself. He seems to be conscious of a kind of turning point in his life. He has completed a number of things and now intends to begin work in a totally new region. He has preached his gospel in the east; now he expects to preach it in the west. This is indicated by the fact that in Romans he deals with a number of topics that he has already covered in other letters. He must intend this letter to be a summary and restatement of his basic thinking and also an introduction to Pauline Christianity for the Christians at Rome.[44]

The bulk of the letter deals with the problem of sin and what God has done about it. But Paul also deals carefully with the relationship of Jews to Christianity and to some ethical problems, such as the use of spiritual gifts, eating of food offered to idols, and allegiance to the ruling powers. Although it covers again some old territory, Romans may be evaluated, as it usually is, as the most important of Paul's letters, for in it he deals with topics more systematically and with cooler deliberation than he does elsewhere. It probably represents Pauline Christianity at its best.

[39] Romans 15 : 19, 23.

[40] Romans 15 : 23, 24, 28.

[41] See E. F. Scott, *Paul's Epistle to the Romans* (London: S.C.M. Press, 1947), pp. 21 ff.

[42] See John Knox, in *The Interpreter's Bible* (New York: Abingdon, 1951–1957), Vol. 9, pp. 358 ff.

[43] Kirsopp Lake, op. cit., pp. 379–418.

[44] See Günther Bornkamm, "The Letter to the Romans as Paul's Last Will and Testament," *Australian Biblical Review* 11: 2–14 (1963).

Paul: Letters from Prison

In addition to the Thessalonian correspondence and the letters concerned with the collection, we have three letters that Paul wrote from prison. Our knowledge of his life is not full enough to allow us to specify the number, duration, dates, or locations of Paul's imprisonments. He speaks of them in the plural without giving the locations.[45] The material in Acts describes imprisonments in Jerusalem, Caesarea, and Rome, all at the end of Paul's career.[46] But many scholars feel that Paul refers to an earlier imprisonment in Ephesus.[47] Since the material does not present a clear and precise picture of the imprisonments, we must be content to say only that the letters were written from prison but that the locations and dates are unknown.

Two of the letters, Philemon and Colossians, must have been written at the same time. That there is a relationship between the two letters has been noted from earliest times. Although some scholars feel that this relationship can be explained by assuming Colossians to be an inauthentic letter, most accept it as Pauline in spite of its stylistic differences. Colossians is addressed to a church founded by one Epaphras. Paul had not been to Colossae and was personally unknown there. The letter was written, in part, to provide ammunition for attack against a form of thought similar to Gnostic Christianity, although it was probably not a full-blown system of thought so early.

In Colossians, Paul calls upon the recipients to read another letter "from Laodicea," a possible reference to the letter we call Philemon.[48] This letter is actually addressed to three persons—Philemon, Apphia, and Archippus—and to a church that meets in the house of one of them. It is mainly concerned with the fate of a slave named Onesimus, who has been with Paul during his imprisonment. Although he seems inclined to keep the slave with him and hints that he would like to have him returned, Paul sends him to his master (either Philemon or Archippus) and promises to repay anything Onesimus might owe. It is probable that the slave had left without permission, for Paul appeals to the master that he be taken back and treated with kindness. The question of his freedom is not raised.

The other prison letter is known as Philippians but was probably com-

---

[45] See II Corinthians 6:5; 11:23.
[46] See Acts 21:27–28:31.
[47] See I Corinthians 15:32.
[48] See John Knox, *Philemon Among the Letters of Paul* (New York: Abingdon, 1959).

posed as three letters.[49] The complete story of the three letters to Philippi goes something like this: After Paul's imprisonment he received a gift from the Christians in Philippi, delivered by one Epaphroditus. Paul sent a note of thanks for it, namely Philippians 4:10–23. Later on, Epaphroditus, who remained with Paul, fell ill, and when this word reached Philippi there was grave concern. Paul then received word about their concern and also about some adversaries at Philippi, and he wrote Philippians 1:1–2:30. He then sent Timothy, who wrote him of further difficulties, and Paul wrote Philippians 3:1–4:9 to try to deal with these problems. In the second and third letters, Paul attacked certain adversaries, who are difficult to identify. It is probable that they are associated with a group of Jewish Christians who have certain Gnostic traces. They require circumcision, but they also believe that the resurrection has already occurred. In the letters Paul rejects both of these points.

THE PSEUDO-PAULINE LETTERS

Four letters in the New Testament which bear the name of Paul are generally regarded as pseudonymous: Ephesians, I, II Timothy, and Titus. Although Ephesians was known by Christian writers in the early second century and was accepted as Pauline, the majority of scholars today doubt that Paul wrote it. There are five main reasons for doubt. (1) No indication of a specific background, occasion, or purpose is included in Ephesians. The genuine letters of Paul were written in response to specific occasions and for certain purposes. They included definite notices of Paul's relationship to the recipients. Ephesians has none of this. (2) A number of early manuscripts of the document do not mention Ephesus or Ephesians. Several attempts have been made to account for this omission, including the attractive suggestion that Ephesians was intended as a circular letter.[50] A blank was included so that the person who delivered copies of the letter could fill it in as appropriate. E. J. Goodspeed and others have suggested that the author of Ephesians also collected the other Pauline letters and intended his to be a covering letter or introduction for the entire corpus.[51] However we account for those manuscripts that omit the address, we can be certain that the

---

[49] The three letters in order are: Philippians 4:10–20 or 23; Philippians 1:1–2:30; and Philippians 3:1–4:9.

[50] This hypothesis was first set forth by James Ussher in 1654.

[51] See Edgar J. Goodspeed, *The Meaning of Ephesians* (Chicago: Univ. of Chicago Press, 1933).

author of Ephesians did not have a specific locale in mind when he wrote. (3) The Ephesian letter is an expansion of Colossians. It is true that it also contains allusions to passages in other Pauline letters, but the similarities in content and style between Ephesians and Colossians are far greater than between any two of the genuine letters of Paul. (4) In Ephesians, several characteristic Pauline words are used without their Pauline meanings. For example, the word *mystery* is used with three different meanings, all strange to Paul.[52] A similar treatment of the word *plan* or *arrangement* is found in Ephesians.[53] (5) Some key ideas in Ephesians are at variance with the genuine letters. In I Corinthians 3:11, Paul emphatically stated that Jesus Christ is the only foundation of the church, but Ephesians 2:20 makes the apostles and prophets the foundation and Christ the cornerstone. In I Corinthians 7 Paul displayed no appreciation for matrimony, but in Ephesians 5 marriage is treated as a symbol of the union of Christ and church. The eschatological expectation characteristic of Paul is explicitly denied in Ephesians 3:21. W. G. Kümmel is certainly correct in saying that "the theology of Ephesians makes the Pauline composition of the Epistle completely impossible."[54]

Although we may not finally account for the writing of this document, we must assume that its author counted himself a disciple of Paul. The phenomenon of pseudonymity is neither unusual nor dishonorable in the ancient world, and it is possible that the author intended no deception in writing under Paul's name. D. E. Nineham offers an interesting parallel: "The Neo-Platonist Iamblichus praises the Pythagoreans for ascribing their work to their master; in this way, he thinks, they renounced all praise for themselves and turned everything to the honour and glory of their masters."[55] Plato's use of Socrates is also a form of pseudonymity. Dishonesty is not involved if we take seriously Goodspeed's suggestion that Ephesians was written to introduce the entire collection of Paul's letters. The work of collecting these letters was no mean task, for it would not be immediately obvious to the recipients of a Pauline letter that Paul wrote other letters. Nor would they know where to look. A clue could have been provided by a reference in Colossians to the letter from Laodicea (Philemon?). He who initially became intrigued by this reference may have begun the long search for other Pauline letters in the places associated with the apostle. After

[52] Ephesians 3:3 ff.; 1:9; 5:32.
[53] Ephesians 1:10; 3:9.
[54] W. G. Kümmel, *Introduction to the New Testament*, trans. A. J. Mattill (Nashville: Abingdon, 1966), p. 254.
[55] D. E. Nineham, in *Studies in Ephesians*, ed. F. C. Cross (London: A. R. Mowbray, 1956), p. 22, note 1.

bringing the letters together, he wrote a covering letter, modeled on the letter he knew best, namely Colossians. In doing so, he could not avoid interjecting his own point of view, which was not consistent with that of Paul at every point.[56] Goodspeed believes that the collection of letters was made about A.D. 90.

The author of Ephesians mainly devotes himself to a celebration of the unity of Jews and Gentiles in the Christian church, but he also includes a detailed table of suggestions on the application of Christian love to everyday relationships. Although the letter is pseudonymous, it may be regarded as an example of Pauline Christianity in the broad sense. It stands within that tradition which found its origin in Paul but demonstrates a more developed stage of the tradition.

The other three pseudonymous letters, two to Timothy and one to Titus, are usually grouped together and called Pastoral letters. This designation recognizes that a significant aspect of their content is devoted to prescriptions for pastors and officers in the churches. Qualifications for deacons, presbyters, and bishops are given in some detail, but the latter two terms seem interchangeable, and the functions appear to be the same. The probable situation is that the bishop is one of the presbyters, probably a first among equals. The attention paid to these officers constitutes a significant aspect of the non-Pauline character of the Pastorals. In the unquestioned letters of Paul, little attention was paid to church officers. Paul had referred to bishops and deacons in the letter to the Philippians, but he included no description of their qualifications or functions.[57] We may there translate these words in the nontechnical sense of "overseers" and "servants." By contrast, the Pastoral letters treat these as special offices within the church. In addition, the author understands Timothy to be in charge of the Church at Ephesus and Titus of that in Crete. Both are subject to Paul, who grants to them authority to appoint presbyters or bishops. In short, the situation required for these letters is not that of Paul's lifetime. They must have been written at a later time when the various churches were beginning to stabilize themselves and create a suitable and lasting organization. No longer does the vivid eschatological perspective dominate Christian thought and life. The Pastorals come from a time when Christians are beginning to adjust to an indeterminate extension of time.

Another aspect of the Pastoral letters is their attack on unacceptable interpretations of Christianity. It has long been recognized that the kind of

[56] See also Knox, *Philemon*.
[57] Philippians 1 : 1.

thought under attack is similar to Gnostic Christianity. There is a warning about myths and genealogies, which may be those of the Gnostics. The heretics also forbid marriage and the eating of certain foods. There may be a direct reference to Gnosticism and to a book by the second-century Marcion in I Timothy 6:20–21, where Timothy is warned to beware of the *Antitheses* of what is falsely called *Gnosis* (knowledge). Resistance to these objectionable ideas is so important for this author that he transforms the Pauline understanding of faith as a matter of relationship to the concept of faith as a body of doctrine which stands opposed to heresy.

In the case of Ephesians one may say that the pseudonymity is not intended to mislead those who read or hear the letter. The same cannot be said of the Pastorals. Not only is Paul's name used in the addresses, but the pose of Pauline authorship is carried through all three letters. Personal details are given, and names of Paul's erstwhile companions are sprinkled throughout. Although modern readers generally reject Pauline authorship because of the divergent conceptions and practices alluded to, it is evident that the author intended people to believe that Paul wrote the letters. He imagines that Paul has gone through his trial at Rome, has survived to travel further in the eastern Mediterranean, and that he is now facing a new trial. The probable reason for his procedure is that he wishes to invoke the authority of Paul in strengthening the hands of leaders in the churches of Ephesus and Crete.[58] We may assume that the letters were made available to those leaders, who felt themselves to be the successors of Timothy and Titus. They would be able to say that Paul granted authority to Timothy and Titus and thence to their successors.

It is difficult, if not impossible, to arrive at a satisfactory date for the Pastorals. They could not have been written before the collection of Paul's letters was made around A.D. 90, for they show familiarity with several letters in the collection. Moreover, they must have been written at such a time when the authority of Paul was widely acknowledged in the eastern Mediterranean. Many scholars tend to date them toward the middle of the second century because of the reference to Gnosticism. But such a verdict is based on the assumption that Gnosticism is strictly a second-century phenomenon. More recent scholars have shown the error of this assumption and have demonstrated that, although the system of Gnostic Christianity is a second-century phenomenon, there may well have been certain Gnostic ideas much earlier. If we could be assured that the reference to the *Antitheses* in

---

[58] Some scholars feel that a few genuine fragments of Paul's correspondence may be found in the Pastorals. See, e.g., P. N. Harrison, *The Problem of the Pastoral Epistles* (London: Oxford University Press, 1921).

I Timothy is to a book by Marcion, we could confidently date the letters in the mid-second century. Unfortunately, other interpretations are possible, for the author may simply be thinking of the contradiction between true and false Christianity or of the self-contradictory teaching of his opponents. It may be possible to date the letters on the basis of the kind of church organization represented in them. We shall see that the letters of Ignatius, written during the reign of Trajan, assume the existence of a monarchical episcopate—i.e., a system in which a single bishop holds supreme authority in the churches of a city and the surrounding region.[59] The Pastorals seem to represent a somewhat less formal structure, with a bishop presiding over a board of presbyters. Caution must be exercised, however, for we cannot assume that church organization developed uniformly in every place. It is more likely that some cities had a monarchical episcopate while others had a board of presbyters. In view of this complexity, the best we can do is to date the Pastorals some time after A.D. 90.

OTHER PSEUDONYMOUS LETTERS

Four writings in the Christian canon may be considered in this group: James, Jude, I, II Peter. In each case the document claims to have been written by an apostle. In each case the claim is probably not justified. Although there is no common theme which dominates all four documents, there is in each one an awareness of the larger community outside the church and an attempt to come to terms with it. In addition, we ought to call them epistles rather than letters. It is true that they contain addresses and other characteristics of letters, but the basic form of each indicates that they were not originally intended as letters in the usual sense.

James

The only letter forms in this document are the address, in which the author is identified as James and the recipients are called the "twelve tribes in the dispersion," and the one-word salutation, "Greeting."[60] In the body, there is no reference to a specific occasion to which a letter might respond and no personal detail. The form is probably that of the sermon, but a sermon intended for widespread publication among Christians in the

[59] On the letters of Ignatius, see pp. 154 ff.
[60] James I : I.

Hellenistic world. Christian writers must have adopted the practice of writing general epistles from Hellenistic philosophers. J. H. Ropes cites examples from Isocrates, Aristotle, and Epicurus, who wrote treatises intended for an indefinite number of audiences.[61]

The author is intended to be taken for the James who was regarded as the brother of Jesus. No one else by this name would have carried the weight that naturally belongs to the relative of Jesus, who held a chief position in the Jerusalem Church. For most of his life he was respected by both Jews and Christians, until his execution in the early sixties, probably by the Jewish high priest.[62] That this James is the intended author is beyond dispute. That he is the actual author is improbable. The use of the Greek language is a strong counter-indication. So is the use of a Greek style of writing. Ropes has pointed to the use of a number of elements associated with the diatribe, such as a dialogue with an imaginary interlocutor, a series of brief questions and answers, and the use of paradox, irony, imperatives, comparisons, figures of speech, and examples from famous individuals.[63] The author of James is also aware of a misinterpretation of the Pauline contrast between faith and works, which maintained that the Christian life required no good works.[64] He counters this with the assertion that faith without works is dead and that faith is brought to life and demonstrated only in certain moral activities. It is not impossible that the interpretation which James opposed arose during Paul's lifetime, but it is not likely that it would have achieved such significance until some time later. The clearest evidence against authorship of this document by James is its use of the Synoptic Gospels, in particular Matthew. G. Kittel counted twenty-six borrowings from the Synoptics.[65] Finally, the letter was not included in the earliest canonical lists, and even as late as the fourth century, the church historian Eusebius did not accept it as genuine.[66] These evidences would, taken collectively, rule out the possibility that this document was written by James. It must have been written by a later Christian in the name of the revered brother. It must be dated around A.D. 90, after the Synoptic Gospels, which it uses, and before I Clement, which uses it.[67]

[61] J. H. Ropes, *A Critical and Exegetical Commentary on the Epistle of St. James*, International Critical Commentary (New York: Scribner's, 1916), p. 7.

[62] See Josephus, *Antiquities* XX, 9:197–203.

[63] Ropes, op. cit., pp. 12 ff.

[64] See James 2:14–26.

[65] G. Kittel, "Der geschichtliche Ort des Jakobusbriefes," *Zeitschrift für die neutestamentliche Wissenschaft* 41:71 ff. (1942).

[66] Eusebius, *Church History* II, 23:24 ff.

[67] On the date of Clement, see pp. 152 ff., and on the Synoptic Gospels, pp. 190–212.

James has usually been characterized as a Jewish Christian writing because of its use of the Old Testament and Jewish Wisdom literature. Many scholars, however, observe that there is no indication of loyalty to the Jewish people and nothing on Sabbath observance or dietary regulations. Many have also noticed the absence of specifically Christian ideas; for example, the phrase *Jesus Christ* appears only twice. But there is no reason to classify it as a non-Christian document. The ethic is not inconsistent with what we know from other sources. It includes love of the neighbor as the summary rule of the Christian life, patience, humility, and service to the oppressed. It includes an eschatological expectation as does traditional Christianity. It speaks with considerable force on the necessity of moral activity, on control of one's desire and control of the tongue, and against discrimination in favor of the rich. As for the Jewish Christian character of James, it is true that it lacks many of the elements we should expect and represents no systematic partisan approach.[68] But there is in it one theme which makes it lean toward Jewish Christianity, namely the understanding of law as constituting the basic character of Christianity. In 1:25, Christianity is looked upon as the perfect law, which makes us free. In 2:8, the rule of neighbor love is called the royal law. In 2:10 ff., the author accepts the principle that breaking one part of the law makes a man guilty of breaking all of it, and it is clear that he means the Torah, for illustrative quotations from the Ten Commandments follow. In 4:11 f., he says that the one who speaks evil against a brother really does so against the law. The author contrasts keeping the law with judging it and condemns the latter. To be sure, there is no polemic against other forms of Christianity nor any partisanship. Nevertheless, James is best seen as coming out of that side of Christianity which continued to revere the Jewish Torah and to use it, together with the teaching of Jesus, as the basic ethic of Christianity. Such writings are best classified as Jewish Christian, although we shall later see that this group of Christians developed a more distinctive theology as time passed.[69]

Jude

This little letter claims to be the composition of a brother of James. This must be the same James who was intended in the previous document. Jude

---

[68] B. S. Easton classifies James "in the broad and nonpartisan 'center' of non-imaginative but earnest and common Greek-speaking Christians." In *The Interpreter's Bible*, Vol. 12, p. 9.

[69] See pp. 312 ff.

or Judas is named as one of four brothers of Jesus in Mark 6:3 and Matthew 13:55. We know nothing further of him except that Hegessipus reports an interview between Domitian and two of his grandsons.[70] The emperor decided that these two unlearned farmers were harmless, and they lived on into the reign of Trajan. That this document could not have been written by a contemporary of Jesus is demonstrated by the fact that the author looks upon the apostles as men of the past. These men, says the author, warned us about our own later time.[71]

The purpose of Jude is to warn the faithful about certain people within the church whose ideas and actions are perverting Christianity. Jude's attack on these people is strictly *ad hominem*: they are licentious and immoral; they do not respect authority or the men of the past; they revile what they do not understand; and they cause divisions in the church. The recipients of the letter are advised to hold onto their faith, to convince and save some of the heretics, and to have a fearful mercy on others. Although the information provided in the letter is not sufficient to permit a precise identification of the movement under attack, Albert Barnett is probably right in pointing out similarities with that group attacked in the Johannine epistles and in the letters of Ignatius.[72] On this basis, Barnett says that the letter may have been directed to the churches of Asia Minor, which also received the letters of John and Ignatius. He dates Jude about A.D. 125, but there is no good reason for excluding an earlier date of A.D. 100.

I Peter

The author of this letter writes in the name of the apostle Peter. Petrine authorship is generally denied because the letter lacks any firsthand knowledge of Jesus, uses impeccable Greek, and reflects Pauline theology. In the acceptance of the atoning significance of Jesus' death as well as in the use of distinctive Pauline phrases, the author is to be seen as a representative of Pauline theology. Peter could hardly be so characterized, for Paul himself describes him as uncertain on significant issues.[73] Some scholars believe I Peter was written by Silvanus, who once served as co-author of certain Pauline letters. He is mentioned in 5:12 as the secretary who worked at

---

[70] In Eusebius, *Church History* III, 20:1 ff.
[71] Jude 17–18.
[72] Albert E. Barnett, in *The Interpreter's Bible*, Vol. 12, p. 318.
[73] See Galatians 2:11–21.

Peter's dictation.[74] If Silvanus composed the letter, we could understand the quality of the language and the use of Pauline theology, for Silvanus must have known Greek and he certainly knew Paul. A. M. Hunter, for example, suggests that Peter dictated the main lines of the letter and Silvanus shared in its composition.[75]

One may be able to approach the question of authorship by reference to the historical situation presupposed in the letter. Here, however, we come upon a further problem: the situation reflected in the first part does not appear to be the same as that of the latter part. Up through 4:11, the author warns that Christians may face suffering. But he has in mind a kind of animosity which would naturally arise as Christians attempt a new kind of life in their old environment.[76] There is no hint that a persecution is underway. After 4:12, however, it is apparent that a fiery ordeal is in progress. This phenomenon has led some scholars to conclude that an earlier letter (1:1–4:11) has been expanded to meet the conditions of a more violent time. Others—for example, C. F. D. Moule—suggest that the author wrote two versions of a letter and sent one to the persecuted churches and the other to the more fortunate ones.[77] It is possible, however, to exaggerate the difference between the two parts of the letter. John Knox is probably correct in saying that the entire letter reflects the time of Trajan, when obstinate confession of Christianity was taken to be a crime subject to capital punishment.[78] The author of I Peter, says Knox, wishes to make sure that Christians are not persecuted as murderers or thieves but as Christians and that they defend themselves with gentleness and reverence, always remembering that they are subject to the emperor and his governors. If Knox is right, there is a unity in the letter, and it reflects the time of Trajan. In that case it was composed about A.D. 115 and was not written by Peter or Silvanus.

II Peter

There are several signs of a late date for the composition of II Peter. It must come after Jude and I Peter, for almost all of chapter two seems dependent

---

[74] See, e.g., Bo Reicke, *The Epistles of James, Peter, and Jude*, The Anchor Bible (Garden City, N.Y.: Doubleday, 1964), pp. 69–75; Archibald M. Hunter, in *The Interpreter's Bible*, Vol. 12, pp. 77 ff.

[75] Ibid.

[76] See Marxsen, op. cit., p. 234.

[77] See C. F. D. Moule, "The Nature and Purpose of I Peter," *New Testament Studies* 3: 1–11 (1956–1957).

[78] John Knox, "Pliny and I Peter," *Journal of Biblical Literature* 72: 187 ff. (1953).

on the former, and the latter is specifically referred to in 3:1. The author is also aware of several of the letters of Paul and of misinterpretations of them. There is reference to a group which looks upon the apostles as living deep in the past and as doubting the second coming of Christ because the first coming was so long ago. All of these matters show that in II Peter we are dealing with materials of a relatively late date, certainly in the second century. This conclusion based on internal evidence is confirmed by external evidence. The remarkable fact is that this document is unknown to every second-century writer we know. The first writer to mention it was Origen, in the middle of the third century, and he doubts the genuineness of it.[79] Eusebius, in the fourth century, reflects the continuing doubt about its authenticity.[80]

Like I Peter, this letter attacks a form of Christianity considered by the author to be heretical. Much of the argument is familiar: the heretics are licentious and immoral. In addition, there is allusion to "cleverly devised myths,"[81] which may be those of the Gnostics. The most distinctive aspect of their thought is an agnosticism in regard to the Parousia, or coming of Christ: "Where now is the promise of his coming? Our fathers have been laid to their rest, but still everything continues exactly as it has always been since the world began."[82] Doubt about the Parousia is characteristic of certain second-century Gnostic systems. The author answers their rhetorical question by asserting that our time is not God's time and by assuring his readers that the heavens and the earth will be dissolved by fire. The letter represents a reaction against a Gnostic Christian group and should be dated about the middle of the second century. In character it represents the developing proto-catholic Christianity of the second century.

THE LETTERS OF JOHN

Three letters in the New Testament are traditionally attributed to John. In fact, however, the letters do not make any such claim. The one which bears the title I John was probably not a letter, although it has traces of being written with certain readers in mind. The other two are genuine pieces of correspondence, the sender of which is called the presbyter. The three documents are called Johannine because the ancient church assumed that

[79] Origen, *Commentary on John* V, 3.
[80] Eusebius, *Church History* II, 23:25; III, 3:1, 4.
[81] II Peter 1:16. *The New English Bible* has: "tales artfully spun."
[82] II Peter 3:4.

one person wrote all three letters as well as the Fourth Gospel and that this man was John bar Zebedee, an apostle of Jesus.

The question of authorship has been variously answered by recent scholars. Many agree that one person wrote the Gospel and the three letters. There is a great deal of similarity between the linguistic style of the Gospel and I John, and a few stylisms reappear in II or III John. There are also some similar themes and theological conceptions. But there are certain ideological differences which preclude the possibility of a common author for the letters and the Gospel. They may all have been produced by the same school of writers, but not by the same writer. The identification of the author of the letters as the son of Zebedee is certainly incorrect. The writer identifies himself in II and III John as the presbyter. This may mean simply the old man, or it may be a title for an officer in the church. Eusebius has a confused account drawn from Papias about a presbyter at Ephesus named John, in which account presbyters seem to serve as links between Papias and the disciples of Jesus.[83] The presbyter John would be dated in the late first century. The evidence for connecting John of Ephesus with the letters is slim indeed, but Papias' remark may have led certain early Christians to confuse the presbyter with the apostle and so identify John bar Zebedee as the author of the letters. The use of material from I John by subsequent writers tends to date that document at the end of the first century, a date satisfactory for all three Johannine epistles.

The author of I John has in mind a certain interpretation of Christianity which he believes is dangerously false and which has already caused division in some churches. Some people have already left the church, possibly forming new Christian groups on the basis of their theology. The most significant feature of their theology is a Docetic Christology—that is, a denial of the humanity of the Christ. This idea frequently formed a part of Gnostic Christianity in the second century. It is based on the assumption that human flesh is essentially evil and could not have been present in the earthly appearance of the Christ. It assumes that the Christ did truly appear on earth and appeared to be human.[84] But to Docetism the human appearance was deceptive. The disciples saw something they thought was human, but their eyes deceived them. The Christ was a thoroughly divine, spiritual being. Against this form of thought, the author of I John sets forth his own version of

---

[83] Eusebius, *Church History* III, 39. Papias was bishop of Hierapolis in Asia Minor until c. A.D. 130. See also Irenaeus, *Against Heresies* II, 17:5, 8.

[84] The word *Docetism* is derived from the Greek word *dokeo,* which means to think, suppose, believe. It emphasizes the disciples' erroneous supposition that they saw a fleshly being when they saw Jesus.

Christianity, with belief in the humanity of Jesus and identification of the man Jesus with the Christ as necessary ingredients. In addition, the author affirms that love of the brethren is essential. His aim is to unify the church in belief and brotherly love.

The purpose of II John is much the same. It is a genuine letter written to a church ("the elect lady and her children") by the presbyter. The author warns the Church that some are preaching a Docetic Christology and that such persons are not to be received in the Church.

III John was written to a man named Gaius, who supported some missionaries sent by the presbyter. Gaius has, however, had opposition from Diotrephes, who refused to welcome the missionaries and excommunicated their supporters. The presbyter threatens to intervene personally in the case and challenge the authority of Diotrephes. It is tempting to speculate on the issues at stake in this incident. Some have suggested that there is a conflict between two different kinds of church organization, perhaps between that of the monarchical episcopate and that of the board of presbyters. But the short note is not adequate to bear the weight of such a theory. W. G. Kümmel has said about all that can be said: "We can think of a conflict between a fixed ecclesiastical organization and an earlier, freer charismatic situation. ... Yet it is not clear that 'the elder' represents the freer charismatic situation."[85]

A Letter of Clement[86]

Near the end of the first century, the Church at Rome addressed a letter to the Church at Corinth. It was occasioned by a controversy in Corinth over that Church's leadership. Certain younger members of the Church had apparently challenged the presbyters and had taken over the organization of the Church. Although this was certainly more than a simple power struggle, we have no way to determine the issues that may have been involved, nor do we know how word got to Rome about the incident.

Although the letter is known as I Clement, it was actually written in the name of the Roman Church. The identification of the author as Clement is not given in the best manuscripts of the document. Dionysius of Corinth (c. A.D. 170) is the first to ascribe it to Clement, whom Irenaeus identifies

[85] Kümmel, op. cit., p. 314.
[86] For an English translation, see *Early Christian Fathers*, ed. Cyril C. Richardson, Library of Christian Classics (Philadelphia, Pa.: Westminster Press, 1953), Vol. I, pp. 43–73. Translations below are from this edition.

as bishop of Rome from A.D. 88–97.[87] According to Irenaeus, Peter appointed Linus as the first bishop of Rome, and Linus was succeeded by Anencletus and then Clement. Irenaeus may be incorrect in using the title bishop for so early a figure as Clement, but he is probably right in identifying him as a leading figure in the Roman Church. He may have been a member of the board of presbyters, in an organization similar to that which the letter describes for Corinth. A second-century work, the Shepherd of Hermas, mentions Clement as a kind of foreign secretary for the Roman Church.[88]

The external witnesses tend to a date of c. A.D. 95 for the letter. With this the internal evidence agrees. Clement looks back upon the time of the apostles and recognizes that some of the presbyters appointed by them are dead. He says that some of the members of the Roman Church have been in it from youth to old age. Corinth is called an ancient church. The persecution of Nero, in which Peter and Paul died, is well in the past. But the author is living in the generation after the apostles, for he says that some of their appointees are still alive. It is probable that he speaks of a persecution under Domitian as his own historical context.[89] He apologizes to the Corinthians for not writing sooner, saying that "sudden and successive misfortunes and accidents"[90] have been encountered by the Church. In several places he speaks of current imprisonments of Christians and of potential dangers. The prayer at the end of the letter includes the petition, "Deliver us, too, from all who hate us without good reason."[91] In spite of all of this, the author upholds the virtue of obedience to the governors. A date of A.D. 95 for I Clement would satisfy all known conditions.

The chief purpose of the letter is to resolve the problem of rebellion in the Corinthian Church. It seems to be addressed to those who now hold power in Corinth, and Clement appeals to them to return the Church to its former situation. He does not regard the ringleaders of the rebellion as non-Christians or as heretics, and he seems to be unaware of any ideological issues. His appeal is from Christian to Christian, and he expects the Corinthian rebels to understand order as a Christian virtue. To Clement, the gravity of rebellion lies in the fact that the presbyters who were overthrown were appointed by the apostles or stood in succession from them and governed with the consent of the whole church.

---

[87] See Eusebius, *Church History* IV, 23:11; III, 6; Irenaeus, *Against Heresies* III, 3. On the date of Clement, see Eusebius III, 15:34.

[88] Shepherd of Hermas II, 4.3. See pp. 246 ff.

[89] For evidence of a persecution under Domitian, see Eusebius, *Church History* III, 17, and pp. 256 ff.

[90] I Clement 1:1.

[91] I Clement 60:4.

A significant implication of Clement's letter revolves around the assumed relations between the Churches of Rome and Corinth. It appears that, even at this early date, the Church at Rome feels responsible for maintaining order in other places. Not only does Clement write to Corinth in the name of the Church, he also sends ambassadors to mediate and restore peace. He writes without apology for interfering, as if such were his acknowledged right. There is no other evidence that Corinth naturally looked to Rome for leadership or that Rome had yet maintained a position of supremacy over others. It is more likely that the letters arose out of a genuine concern and that Clement saw his authority as based on moral right rather than ecclesiastical position. The tone of the letter is that of one who sees his brother acting in error and speaks with the conviction of being in the right. Witness the concluding statement: "You will make us exceedingly happy if you prove obedient to what we, prompted by the Holy Spirit, have written, and if, following the plea of our letter for peace and harmony, you rid yourselves of your wicked and passionate rivalry."[92]

As for the character of the letter, it is distinguished by a dependence on the Old Testament; but it is also influenced by the Pauline literature and Stoic thought. The last seems to be a dominating influence, for Clement establishes the need for order on the basis of natural law. He uses natural law to prove the validity of belief in resurrection, and he concludes the argument by reference to the incredible legend of the phoenix, known widely in the Roman world. The letter is strongly moral in tone, emphasizing the virtues of patience, sobriety, and self-discipline. The attitude toward the state is positive, and the Roman army is understood as a good example of the kind of order which should prevail in Christianity. In general, the letter is an example of a developing catholic Christianity, now significantly influenced by Stoicism.

THE LETTERS OF IGNATIUS[93]

During the reign of Trajan (A.D. 98–117), Ignatius, the bishop of Antioch, in Syria, was arrested and taken to Rome to be thrown to the wild beasts in the Colosseum. On the trip he was escorted by ten Roman soldiers, who did little to make his trip comfortable. They traveled mainly by land, coming through Asia Minor and stopping at Philadelphia, Smyrna, and Troas.

[92] I Clement 63:2.
[93] For an English translation, see Richardson, op. cit., pp. 87–120. Translations below are from this edition.

FIGURE 16 The Journey of Ignatius. (From *The Early Christian Church* by Philip Carrington. [Cambridge: Cambridge University Press, 1957.] Used with permission of Cambridge University Press.)

From Troas they crossed to Neapolis and thence to Philippi and finally Rome. Despite his condition, Ignatius was allowed to have contact with Christians in the layover towns. In Smyrna he was met by a delegation headed by four bishops representing their constituency: Polycarp of Smyrna, Onesimus of Ephesus, Damas of Magnesia, and Polybius of Tralles. Before he left Smyrna, Ignatius wrote letters to the congregations in Ephesus, Magnesia, and Tralles, thanking each for their encouragement and address-ing himself to certain ecclesiastical problems which the bishops must have brought to his attention. From Smyrna he also wrote to the Christians at Rome, asking them not to interfere with his impending martyrdom. From Troas he wrote three more letters: one to Philadelphia, where he had stopped on the way to Smyrna, one to Smyrna, and one to bishop Polycarp. Thanks to Polycarp, all seven letters were preserved. They all must have been written within a relatively brief period of time, but we can date them no more precisely than in the time of Trajan.[94]

Ignatius' desire for martydom is probably the most interesting theme in the letters. He feels that the martyr is the only true disciple of Jesus. His thought is largely bound up with a mystical conception of the unity of the

---

[94] On the date of Ignatius, see Eusebius, *Church History* III, 22.

believer with Christ. To Ignatius, the believer must imitate Christ not only by adhering to the moral teachings of Jesus but also by living and dying as he did. Genuine discipleship to Christ is demonstrated by sharing his passion. For this reason Ignatius writes to the Romans to dissuade them from making any attempt to defend or rescue him, for that would frustrate his efforts to be a true disciple. He can foresee himself pleading with the beasts and provoking them if they avoid him out of fear. As they eat him, he will become God's wheat, "being ground by the teeth of wild beasts to make a pure loaf for Christ."[95]

A secondary theme in the letters is Ignatius' insistence on good order and unity in the church. The key to both is the bishop. In every letter except that to Rome, he speaks of the respect and obedience which is owed to the bishop. This is to be granted even if the bishop is a young man, such as Damas of Magnesia. The bishop presides in God's place, and nothing may be done without his approval. "Where the bishop is present, there let the congregation gather, just as where Jesus Christ is, there is the Catholic Church."[96] "But he who acts without the bishop's knowledge is in the devil's service."[97] These letters quite clearly present the picture of a single chief officer in a community, the so-called monarchical episcopate. It is equally clear that the bishop is associated with a board of presbyters and assisted by deacons. Ignatius compares the relative position of the three orders as follows: "Let the bishop preside in God's place, and the presbyters take the place of the apostolic council, and let the deacons (my special favorites) be entrusted with the ministry of Jesus Christ."[98] Although he carefully deals with the authority of church leaders, Ignatius has no explicit doctrine of apostolic succession and does not enlighten us on the method of selecting leaders.

Ignatius is also concerned with divergent forms of Christianity. He warns the Magnesians and Philadelphians to beware of Judaism, by which he must mean a form of Jewish Christianity which emphasized observance of the Sabbath and dependence on the Old Testament. A more serious danger is posed by Docetism, and Ignatius gives an explicit description of it. He takes the denial of Jesus' humanity as a perversion of truth and calls on Christians to believe in the death of Jesus in spite of Docetic denials. The denial of the reality of Jesus' passion seems to Ignatius the most serious error made by Docetists. In his letters, belief in Jesus' death does not appear to mean belief in its redemptive quality but simply belief that it really occurred.

[95] Ignatius, Romans 4:1.
[96] Ignatius, Smyrneans 8:2.
[97] Ignatius, Smyrneans 9:1.
[98] Ignatius, Magnesians 6:1; see Trallians 3:1.

Unfortunately, we know nothing of the circumstances which led to Ignatius' arrest. There are some indications in the letters that other Syrians had already become martyrs in Rome and that still others were in the same circumstances with Ignatius.[99] By the time he reached Troas, he received word that the Church in Syria was at peace, and he asked the Philadelphians and Smyrneans to send delegates to Antioch to give them aid and encouragement. We lose sight of Ignatius after he left Troas, and we can only assume that he met the fate he so fervently desired.

A remarkable sense of solidarity is implied in the correspondence of Ignatius. Christians in Asia Minor have met with a transient prisoner from a distant country and are called upon to send delegates back to Syria. Ignatius can write to Rome on the assumption that Christians there will want to come to his aid. He calls upon Polycarp to write to the other churches in towns where he expects to be. A significant network of communication within the church seems to present itself at this point, a fact we might not have expected at such an early date and at a time when travel was not without difficulty and danger. A deep sense of solidarity among individual Christian communities is indeed developing in the early second century.

POLYCARP TO THE PHILIPPIANS[100]

Polycarp, bishop of Smyrna, was Ignatius' host and a recipient of one of his letters. Ignatius had requested Polycarp to appoint a delegate to go to Antioch to help that Church celebrate its return to peace. Polycarp had also received a request from the Church at Philippi to forward a letter of theirs to Syria and to send them copies of Ignatius' letters. In his letter to Philippi, Polycarp agrees to the first request and sends along copies of the Ignatian correspondence. He specifically remarks that this includes the letters he has received (presumably the letter to Smyrna and the one to himself) and "others we had by us."[101]

Polycarp must, therefore, be the one who collected Ignatius' letters. He continued as bishop of Smyrna until his martyrdom at the age of 86 in A.D. 155 or 156. Many years later Irenaeus recalls meeting him, and Eusebius says he went to Rome shortly before his death to confer with Anicetus over

---

[99] See Ignatius, Romans 10:2.
[100] For an English translation, see Richardson, op. cit., pp. 131–137. Translations below are from this edition.
[101] Polycarp, 13:2.

the date of Easter.[102] Irenaeus further notes that Polycarp converted many heretics at Rome and met Marcion, whom he called the first-born of Satan.[103]

P. N. Harrison has claimed that Polycarp wrote two letters to Philippi and that they were assimilated into the one we know.[104] In the first letter (chapter thirteen), he states his willingness to accede to the request of his correspondents and forwards to them copies of the Ignatian letters. He also inquires about any information they may have of Ignatius and his fate. Ignatius had passed through Philippi after he left Asia Minor, and Polycarp assumes that the Philippians will be the first to receive news about him. This letter must have been written within weeks after Ignatius passed through. The second letter (chapters 1–12) was written some decades later (c. A.D. 135–137). In it, Polycarp looks upon Ignatius as having joined the ranks of the martyrs. Harrison has solved a peculiar difficulty by dividing the letter into two, for Polycarp could hardly speak of Ignatius as a martyr in the same letter in which he inquires about his fate. As Harrison says, "One does not include in a list of glorious dead the name of a man as to whose fate one is *in the same letter* asking for information, and who, for all that one knows, may be still alive."[105]

If Harrison is right, the purpose of the earlier letter would be to respond to the Philippians' request and to find out about his friend and colleague. It should be dated during Trajan's reign. The occasion for the later letter seems to be some crisis in the Philippian Church involving one of the presbyters, Valens, who was consumed by the love of money and was excommunicated. In it, Polycarp also alludes to the dangers of a heresy that denies the reality of Jesus' flesh, denies the testimony of the cross, perverts the sayings of the Lord, and denies resurrection and judgment. Harrison identifies the heretic in question as Marcion.[106] He feels it significant that Polycarp calls his heretic "the first-born of Satan" (7:1), the same phrase he used in meeting Marcion.[107] Although Harrison's thesis is attractive at this point, Polycarp's language seems more likely to point to a series of heretical points of view to which he is opposed rather than to a single individual who is guilty of all these errors. Some of the heretics are Docetists, similar to those Ignatius

---

[102] See Eusebius, *Church History* IV, 14; V, 24:16.

[103] See Irenaeus, *Against Heresies III*, 3:4.

[104] P. N. Harrison, *Polycarp's Two Epistles to the Philippians* (Cambridge: Cambridge University Press, 1936).

[105] Ibid., p. 152.

[106] Harrison believes that Polycarp met Marcion before the latter had arrived at his theory of two gods.

[107] See Irenaeus, *Against Heresies III*, 3:4.

attacked. Nevertheless, Harrison is probably close to the truth when he dates Polycarp's second letter in Hadrian's time, c. A.D. 135.

A LETTER FROM SMYRNA[108]

This letter about the martyrdom of Polycarp is a truly remarkable document. Although it includes certain miraculous details and perhaps some later additions, the core of it must be an eyewitness account of the death of Smyrna's bishop in A.D. 155 or 156. In form it is a letter from the Christians at Smyrna to those in Philomelium, also in Asia Minor, and sent at the latter's request. The author, identified as Marcion (certainly not Polycarp's first-born of Satan), requests that the letter be forwarded to Christians elsewhere. Although the specific reason for persecution at Smyrna is not mentioned in the letter, it is clear that Polycarp and others could have escaped by taking an oath and making a sacrifice to the Roman emperor. Quintus, a Phrygian Christian, had so escaped. The narrative also says that Christians were charged with atheism and that Jews fully cooperated with Roman authorities in persecuting the victims. Some of the martyrs were killed by wild beasts, but Polycarp was burned. A vivid, though partially miraculous, account of the burning is included in the letter. The author also tells of gathering the bones of the martyr and observing the day of martyrdom in the Church. This is the earliest reference we have about reverence for relics and memorials. The significance of Polycarp and his martyrdom is indicated by inclusion of the exact date and time of his death—2 P.M. on February 22.

THE EPISTLE OF BARNABAS[109]

Like the letters attributed to James, Jude, and Peter, the Epistle of Barnabas is no genuine piece of correspondence. It has certain formal characteristics of a letter—namely, a salutation, a benediction, and a few artificially personal words—but the body of the document is a teaching tract.

The purpose of Barnabas is to show that Christians have been given the divine covenant which Jews broke. The author attacks the more moderate

---

[108] For an English translation, see Richardson, op. cit., pp. 149–158.

[109] For an English translation, see *Apostolic Fathers*, trans. Kirsopp Lake, Loeb Classical Library (Cambridge, Mass.: Harvard University Press, 1949), Vol. I, pp. 337–409. Translations below are from this edition.

view which holds that the covenant belongs to both Christians and Jews. To him the sin of the Jews is complete, and they are no longer to be regarded as God's people. He explicitly condemns the Jewish sacrifices, as well as the observance of circumcision, Sabbath, and food laws. On the other hand, he holds to the authority of the Old Testament (which includes Apocrypha and pseudepigrapha). He maintains that Moses taught the things of God well, but that Moses' teachings must be subjected to an allegorical interpretation. Moses prohibited the eating of swine, but this means that Christians should not associate with men who are like swine. Circumcision is that of the hearing ear and the believing heart. The author seems most impressed with his interpretation of Moses' circumcising 318 men. This is not to be understood as a fleshly circumcision but as an anticipation of Jesus' death on the cross, because the 18 is the numerical equivalent of IE (or JE for Jesus) and the 300 means T (the shape of the cross). His basic attitude toward Scripture is stated in 10:12: "See how well Moses legislated. But how was it possible for them to understand or comprehend these things? But we having a righteous understanding of them announce the commandments as the Lord wished."

Near the end of the letter, the tone changes abruptly, and we move to an ethical section in which the way of light is contrasted with the way of darkness. The manuscript history of Barnabas allows for the possibility that this section was not a part of the original letter. It is quite similar to a section of the Didache,[110] and both are probably drawn from an older Jewish or Christian source.[111] This kind of ethical instruction seems to be associated with baptism, at which the initiate was taught the way which he was to follow and that which he must avoid. The material in Barnabas may have originally been part of the baptismal ritual.

External sources retain no information about the author of this document or of the circumstances under which it was written. The textual history indicates that it was first known in Alexandria, so it may have been written there. The author is aware of the destruction of the Jerusalem Temple in A.D. 70 and appears to allude to the construction in Jerusalem of a temple to Jupiter. Although this suggests a date of c. A.D. 130 for the composition of Barnabas, the allusion is not strong enough to enable us to date the letter confidently. It is also difficult to comment on the character of the author. He certainly is hostile to Judaism, but he has a deep respect for the old Scriptures. He is aware of the Jewish use of these writings, and he works

---

[110] See p. 245 f.

[111] This point of view has been presented in a manuscript by M. Jack Suggs, as yet unpublished.

hard to create an alternative method of interpretation. We shall later see that a group of Jewish Christians held some of the same ideas as Barnabas and were quite similar in their attitude toward the sacrificial cult. For this reason, several scholars classify the Epistle of Barnabas as a Jewish Christian writing, a classification we may provisionally accept, pending a further analysis of Jewish Christianity.

A Letter from Gaul[112]

The fourth-century church historian, Eusebius, quotes extensively from a letter sent by Christians in Gaul to those in Asia Minor and to the Roman bishop, Eleutherus. He dates the letter during the reign of Marcus Aurelius,

The flagellation of Aelia Afanasis, A.D. 270–280. Catacomb of Praetextatus, Rome. (*Courtesy* Pontifical Commission for Sacred Archives, Rome.)

and it narrates events of the year A.D. 177 or 178, events which occurred in the Rhone cities of Lyons and Vienne, the latter about nineteen miles south of the former. The letter is surely an eyewitness account of an atrocious persecution of Christians in those cities. Christians were suspected of eating children and of having Oedipal intercourse. Such rumors, once started, were substantiated by non-Christian slaves, who fearfully testified against their masters. The author of the letter categorically denies the charges and

---

[112] Found in Eusebius, *Church History* V, 1–4. For an English translation, see Eusebius, *The Ecclesiastical History*, trans. Kirsopp Lake, Loeb Classical Library (Cambridge, Mass.: Harvard University Press, 1949), 2 vols.

expresses outrage that anyone would do such things. Nevertheless, several people were killed on the charge of being Christians, for the emperor had decreed that Christians should be tortured to death but freed if they denied their religion. Those who were Roman citizens were beheaded; others were thrown to wild beasts or roasted in an iron chair.

Although the martyrs were put to death on the charge of being Christians, it appears that suspicion about their practices gave rise to the persecution. The citizens of Lyons and Vienne were not trying to get rid of Christianity because they were inimical to its basic theological tenets but because they suspected its adherents of vile practices. One need not wonder for long why Christians fell under suspicion, for such is the nature of many who fear that which is different.

These are the most significant extant letters written by Christians during the first two centuries. To be sure, many more must have been written, but they were not preserved. Nevertheless, the ones we have illustrate the extensive use of the letter by Christians. They wrote letters to aid in the solution of specific ethical or doctrinal problems in the churches, or to expound Christian teaching, to attack divergent groups or ideas, to express thanks, to seek information, or to convey it. If this small sampling of correspondence is representative, we may be astonished by one fact: although they generally affirmed the reality of Jesus' historical appearance and insisted on the fact of his death, Christians included in their letters very little information about the life and teaching of Jesus. This recognition raises a question which must next be faced: How did Christians preserve and transmit their information about the historical Jesus?

Chapter Five

Oral Traditions

Although the word *literature* properly designates that which is written, it is necessary at this point to turn to a study of unwritten materials. The necessity for so doing is posed by the fact that oral tradition underlay some important early Christian documents and served for several decades as a vehicle for the preservation and transmission of information about Jesus.

That there was a period in which sayings and stories of Jesus were circulated orally is not only to be expected but is also abundantly demonstrated. The major proof is to be found in the date of the earliest written material about Jesus. We shall see that, although Paul alluded to a few sayings of Jesus and narrated one incident, the first documents that dealt seriously with the career of Jesus were the Synoptic Gospels, the first of which is to be dated about A.D. 66–70. The author of the earliest gospel must have been dependent upon oral sources. Other writers, from Paul on down, cite words of Jesus, some of which are similar to those in the Synoptics and some of which have no Synoptic parallels. In each case, their citations must be from oral sources. The author of Luke seems keenly aware of the tradition on which he draws, for he prefaces his Gospel with a statement about those things which "have happened among us, following the traditions handed down to us by the original eyewitnesses and servants of the Gospel."[1] The tradition to which Luke referred may have been written, but it was probably oral, for he mentioned others who had attempted to compile a narrative from the tradition, that is, to write a book based on oral sources. Even in the second century, Christians remembered that an oral period had preceded the writing of the gospels. Eusebius quotes Papias (who in turn got his information from one he calls the presbyter) to this effect:

And the Presbyter used to say this, "Mark became Peter's interpreter and wrote accurately all that he remembered, not, indeed, in order, of the things said or done by the Lord. For he had not heard the Lord, nor had he followed him, but later on, as I said, followed Peter, who used to give teaching

[1] Luke 1:2.

as necessity demanded, but not making, as it were, an arrangement of the Lord's oracles, so that Mark did nothing wrong in thus writing down single points as he remembered them. For to one thing he gave attention, to leave out nothing of what he had heard and to make no false statements in them."[2]

Papias' remark is probably incorrect in understanding Peter to be Mark's only source of information, but he nevertheless was aware that the source was an oral one.

One's initial reaction to an oral tradition may be despair, for it is not immediately clear how it should be treated. Nevertheless, the study of oral traditions is generally one of the tasks of historical research, for oral materials almost always lie at the base of the historian's quest. An event is preserved in memory and discourse before it is reduced to writing. Historians, therefore, have found it possible to study these otherwise hidden times. In the first place, it is possible to learn a great deal about an oral period by studying the characteristics of oral traditions which lie close to our own time. There are living traditions of oral materials still available in some cultures, and in our own some materials have only recently been reduced to writing, such as fairy tales, nursery rhymes, folk songs, and folk tales. By studying these, one may become aware of rules which govern the transmission of oral materials. Secondly, in the case of the Christian oral tradition, we have in the gospels a deposit which it has left behind. We cannot regard the gospels as completely accurate or exhaustive recordings of oral traditions, but they represent a culminating stage of those traditions. It will be necessary to work back from the written to the unwritten. Thirdly, we must use historical imagination. This is not a device to fill the gaps between certainties; rather, it should function as a methodological tool for discriminating between the probable and the merely possible.

CONSEQUENCES OF ORAL TRANSMISSION

We may employ historical imagination to find the possible consequences of oral transmission. If we ask what happens to material preserved orally and in particular what happened to the material about Jesus, several things come immediately to mind.

A great deal of material about Jesus would not have been preserved. No person or aggregate of persons can remember everything, and most of what is remembered never comes to conscious expression. What may come to ex-

[2] Eusebius, *Church History* III, 39:15.

Bust of Christ, mid-fourth century, from the Catacomb of Commodilla, Rome. (*Courtesy* Pontifical Commission for Sacred Archives, Rome.)

pression is the significant moment or the meaningful pronouncement. The gospels verify this thesis, because they contain almost no details about the interesting externals of Jesus' life: What kind of education did he have? Was he associated with any partisan group? Where did he stay when he traveled away from home? What did he look like? Many of Jesus' acquaintances would have known the answers to these questions, but this information is not found in the gospels and probably never entered the oral tradition. Thus, some material disappeared because it was not remembered and some because it never came to expression. We may reasonably assume that the oral tradition retained only a minimal amount of the information about Jesus and that most of the facts about his life are forever lost.

Our earlier examination of the nature of human memory showed that persons tend to remember those things which have significance, that is, those incidents which serve as signals of a reality that is more than the incident itself. The signal of reality may be a glimpse into the character of another person, an insight into the meaning of one's own life, an understanding of the way things work, or a flash of awareness about the meaning of good and

[165]

evil. Quite incidental things may serve as vehicles for such insights. Long years after the event, a man may remember a certain Christmas morning as a particularly bright day, on which as a child he received some special gift from his parents. He may remember the gift, those who gave it, the wrapping, the Christmas tree, the house decorations, and any number of other details. And when he thinks of this incident he finds that his memory is surrounded by feelings of affection, joy, and pleasure. This is the reason that he remembers: the incident serves as a signal of the relations between himself and other members of his family, a signal of the meaning of human love. In general, human beings tend to remember significant events and to forget insignificant ones. But we must go a step further to say that such significance is not inherent in the event itself. It is a product of the interplay between the event and the persons involved, and this means that an event which is remembered is an event which has been interpreted. The disciples of Jesus must have been witness to any number of occurrences which carried no significance for them, but those matters that they remembered and brought to expression are those that they interpreted as having significance.

From time to time we are able to see the presence of an interpretive element by examining the deposit of the oral tradition. When the Christian gospels include two or more versions of the same incident, the interpretive element is not difficult to isolate. The saying about the sign of Jonah is a case in point. In Mark 8:11–12, Jesus, in response to a Pharisaic question, categorically refuses to cite a sign of his authority. In Matthew 16:4, he says simply that the sign of Jonah is the only sign to be given to that generation. In Luke 11:29–32, we have the same saying with an interpretation in which the sign of Jonah is his preaching of repentance. Men "repented at the preaching of Jonah; and what is here is greater than Jonah."[3] In Matthew 12, the statement reappears with the interpretation about repentance. But in between the saying and this interpretation, Matthew has sandwiched a further explanation which understands the sign as resurrection: "Jonah was in the sea-monster's belly for three days and three nights, and in the same way the son of man will be three days and three nights in the bowels of the earth."[4] This must mean that a saying has reached the Synoptic writers in several forms: (1) one in which there is no sign; (2) one in which there is a sign but no interpretation;[5] (3) one in which the sign is understood as repentance; (4) one in which the sign is understood as resurrection. The

[3] Luke 11:32.
[4] Matthew 12:40.
[5] In this case, an earlier interpretation must have dropped out.

various forms of the saying may stem from different disciples, to each of whom the saying was significant but in different ways. In this case it is possible to say that Jesus once cited the sign of Jonah but did so without an interpretation, so that various hearers preserved the saying in the light of the significance it had for them.

The saying about the sign of Jonah illustrates another consequence of oral transmission. Here an original statement of Jesus, subject to diverse understandings, has picked up different interpretations, which finally became part of the saying itself. Once the interpretation became attached to the saying, it would be difficult to distinguish between the two. Thus, the explanation came to be attributed to Jesus himself. This must have been the case when Matthew wrote. Aware of several forms of the saying, the evangelist felt that Jesus said all of them. So he recorded both primary and secondary elements with no attempt at discrimination.

We turn now to the context in which the oral tradition was carried on. It is a truism to say that the church itself was the context in which the oral tradition was preserved and transmitted, but it is a meaningful one. It implies that the tradition was largely a product of Christian reflection and activity and that the church provided certain vehicles for the transmission of oral material. One of those vehicles was preaching. Preaching is denoted by the Greek word *kerygma*, which literally means the act of proclamation. C. H. Dodd and others have been able to find an outline of the main features of this proclamation. In *The Apostolic Preaching and Its Development*,[6] Dodd investigated the letters of Paul and the speeches in Acts to determine the basic framework of the *kerygma*, which he defined as "the public proclamation of Christianity to the non-Christian world."[7] The most primitive form of the *kerygma* may be outlined as follows:

1. The age of fulfillment has dawned.
2. "This has taken place through the ministry, death and resurrection of Jesus, of which a brief account is given, with proof from the Scriptures that all took place through 'the determinate counsel and foreknowledge of God.' "[8]
3. Jesus has been exalted as Messiah.
4. "The Holy Spirit in the Church is the sign of Christ's present power and glory."[9]

[6] (New York: Harper-Row, 1939.)
[7] Ibid., p. 7.
[8] Ibid., p. 39.
[9] Ibid., p. 42.

[167]

5. "The Messianic Age will shortly reach its consummation in the return of Christ."[10]

6. An appeal is made for repentance and salvation is offered.

Although the purpose of apostolic preaching was not to convey information about Jesus, such information would be given indirectly. The *kerygma* would be punctuated throughout by illustrative material drawn from the Old Testament, from Jewish folklore, and from the memory of Jesus' life and teachings.

The sermon was not the only context in which oral traditions survived. In the early period, Christians were frequently engaged in debates with Jews, and in the course of them material from the life of Jesus would be cited. The church would also provide teaching for Christians who needed to know what their lives should be like. The church was also a worshiping community, which developed a cult with emphasis on baptism and a feast, and material from Jesus was cited in hymns and liturgy. Finally, the early church included people called prophets, who spoke in the name of the risen Lord. While such prophets may not have been eyewitnesses of Jesus' life, their words would come into the tradition as words of Jesus. All of these functions served as vehicles for the preservation and transmission of the stories and sayings of Jesus: sermons, debates, teaching, worship, and prophecy.

It is obvious that these methods of oral transmission would not produce a consecutive account of the life of Jesus. If the material about Jesus came into the tradition through these functions, then it came in in bits and pieces, not in sequential narratives. Papias was aware of this when he said that Mark did not write down the life of Jesus in order, because Peter used the teaching as necessity demanded. The various vehicles of transmission would bring to light a large number of sayings and stories of Jesus but would neither put them in order nor provide chronological or geographical notes, which might serve a biographer. We may be assured, therefore, that no connected account of the life of Jesus was preserved in oral tradition.

The fact that the materials about Jesus were used in the service of the church's functions means that only that which so served the church was retained and that the functional context determined the meaning. We are faced again with the disappearance of some remembered, but not useful, material. In addition, the interpretive force of the context must be considered. We are familiar with the possibility of using a quotation out of context. A public official who makes a statement in one context intends

[10] Ibid.

thereby to convey a certain meaning. But his friends or his enemies may use his statement in a different context in order to attribute a quite different meaning to it. That this happened to sayings of Jesus is illustrated in the Synoptic Gospels. Both Matthew and Luke have a saying of Jesus about going to court. Although the saying is substantially the same in both gospels, the context in Luke compels an eschatological understanding of it: Because of the imminent end of all things, make friends *now* with your accuser.[11] Matthew, however, places the saying within a group of prohibitions, where it is an expansion of a saying on hatred: Do not hate your brother and, above all, do not allow hatred to come to the level of legal proceedings, because you may lose your case, and this would be disastrous.[12] The Lukan version speaks of the urgency of settling disputes, while the Matthaean gives us a little bit of prudential advice. It is possible that the gospel writers provided the contexts for the saying, but it is more likely that the oral tradition did so. It is probable that the saying was used in preaching, where the eschatological context determined its meaning, and that it was also used in teaching, where prudence was emphasized.

A further observation may be made in this regard, namely, that sayings and stories which came to expression within the context of the church may have had sources other than Jesus. A statement made by a revered Christian in the act of preaching, or a story used in debates or teaching, or a prophetic pronouncement may have been accepted as a word of Jesus. In the course of the development of oral tradition, it becomes increasingly difficult to retain an awareness of the originator of a saying. Although the post-Gutenberg age is substantially different in this respect, there are still illustrations of this difficulty. We no longer know who originally said: "a stitch in time saves nine"; "a cat has nine lives"; "where there is smoke, there is fire"; "the grass is always greener in the other man's yard"; or "make love, not war." The Synoptic Gospels contain a number of sayings which are also found in Jewish literature, and it is possible that some of them came into the Christian oral tradition by that route. Hellenistic folklore may have provided another source for the oral tradition. Prophetic pronouncements would have caused great difficulty, because they were introduced as sayings of the Lord. Although this did not originally mean sayings of the historical Jesus, the distinction was not long maintained.

An important shift in the course of early Christianity points to a further consequence of oral transmission. Sometime during the four decades be-

[11] Luke 12:58–59.
[12] Matthew 5:25–26.

tween Jesus and the Synoptics, the church moved out from Palestine and began a successful Gentile movement. By the time the gospels were written, the church had become primarily a Hellenistic institution. The language of the oral tradition shifted from Aramaic to Greek, and Hellenistic thought forms and images began to dominate the picture. More and more, the tradition could draw on Hellenistic sources for use in preaching and teaching. Of course, the oral tradition did not lose its Aramaic background, but it did expand into Hellenism and used stories and sayings familiar in this world. A simple illustration of the adaptation to Hellenism may be seen in Matthew 5:18 (RSV): "Till heaven and earth pass away, not an iota, not a dot, will pass from the law until all is accomplished." The subject of the saying is the durability of the Jewish Torah, but its component parts are spoken of in terms meaningful to those who speak Greek. The iota is a Greek letter, and the dot is a breathing or accent mark used in written Greek. The saying as it stands would have no meaning in Aramaic, although a similar Aramaic saying may once have existed.

Although historians generally meet an oral source at the base of their quest, an *oral tradition* is not the same. A biographer may need to consult a number of individuals who can supplement the written information at his disposal. He will judge the quality of this material in terms of its evidential ability and its correspondence with his other information. It depends in the final analysis upon personal memory. The material about Jesus is, however, tradition, and this means that it has become the property of a group and that it has a history. Oral tradition is that unwritten material which has been delivered from one generation to another. The author of Luke is fully aware of this and claims to follow "the traditions handed down to us." In oral tradition, stories and sayings are not the conscious creation of individuals; they result from constant oral repetition and are unconsciously and spontaneously developed by a community. Thus, in oral tradition, whether folklore or religious material, certain patterns or forms develop. Kendrick Grobel correctly observed that "A given folk at a given time is likely to use a limited number of types of unit, into one or another of which by an instinctive mnemonic economy it pours the content of each particular tradition."[13] The key to understanding an oral tradition consists in an analysis of the forms with which that tradition operated.

We turn next to an analysis of the forms used by the Christian oral tradi-

---

[13] Kendrick Grobel, in *The Interpreter's Dictionary of the Bible* (New York: Abingdon, 1962), Vol. II, p. 320.

tion. Before doing that it is essential to have firmly in mind the consequences of using the material about Jesus in an oral tradition:

1. A great deal of factual information about Jesus did not enter the oral
   tradition.
2. The material which came into the oral tradition did so because it had
   been interpreted as significant.
3. The oral tradition contained diverse interpretations.
4. The oral tradition confused the original words of Jesus and the interpretations.

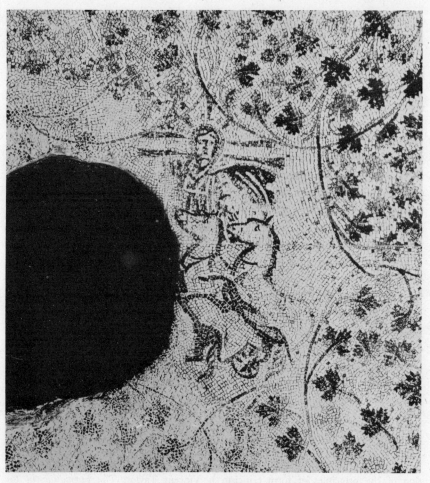

Christ as the Sun God, mosaic from third or fourth century, necropolis of
St. Peter's, Mausoleum Giulli, Rome. (*Courtesy* Fototeca Unione Roma.)

5. The oral tradition was carried on through preaching, teaching, debates, worship, and prophecy.
6. No connected account of the life of Jesus was preserved.
7. The context in which the material was used determined its meaning.
8. Sayings and stories used in the oral tradition may have had sources other than Jesus.
9. The Aramaic context of the oral tradition was modified and expanded by the Hellenistic.
10. The oral tradition made use of a limited number of forms.

Forms of the Oral Tradition

The study of forms, or form criticism, has been found to be very useful in dealing with oral traditions. Hermann Gunkel (c. 1900) was the first to apply the study of forms to Biblical, mainly Old Testament, materials. The most detailed early treatment of forms in primitive Christianity was that of Rudolf Bultmann and Martin Dibelius, after 1920. They began their study with the Synoptic Gospels and discovered that a number of primitive patterns underlie the written documents. These patterns can be analyzed in such a way that the secondary interpretive elements are separated from the primary saying or story. When the original form of the story is found, it is then possible to make a judgment about the context (or *Sitz im Leben*, life situation) in which the story first appeared. From there one can move on to discover the source for the story.

The forms delineated by Bultmann and Dibelius are not precisely the same, but the differences need not deter us. For purposes of simplicity we shall use those of Bultmann, but for detailed exposition the reader may consult the works of both scholars.[14] Bultmann divides the material about Jesus into two main categories: sayings and narratives. The sayings are subdivided into apophthegms, dominical sayings, and similitudes, the narratives into miracles and legends. It must be emphasized that the gospels do not preserve these forms in their original purity; the form is embedded in the gospel material.

[14] See Martin Dibelius, *From Tradition to Gospel*, trans. B. L. Woolf (New York: Scribners, 1935); *The Message of Jesus Christ*, trans. F. C. Grant (New York: Scribners, 1939); Rudolf Bultmann, *The History of the Synoptic Tradition*, trans. John Marsh (New York: Harper-Row, 1963 [first German edition, 1921]). A good English adaptation of the principles of form criticism is Vincent Taylor, *The Formation of the Gospel Tradition* (London: Macmillan, 1935). The most recent work is Klaus Koch, *The Growth of the Biblical Tradition*, trans. S. M. Cupitt (New York: Scribner's, 1969).

Apophthegms[15]

An apophthegm may be defined as a saying with a narrative introduction. It is generally marked by an absence of detail. There are almost no references to time or place. Most of the participants are representatives of a group (a scribe, a Pharisee, a disciple), and personal characteristics are either not given or given indirectly by reference to something done or said. The action is generally initiated by something that happens to Jesus. The chief interest of each is in the saying of Jesus, which is the culmination of the apophthegm. The saying is probably the most nearly original part. In the course of preaching, teaching, and debates, the saying picked up the explanatory narrative. Further details, such as more elaborate descriptions of the situation or the participants, were added at an even later time. Bultmann finds three types of apophthegms: controversy dialogues, scholastic dialogues, and biographical apophthegms.

The general pattern for a controversy dialogue may be illustrated by Mark 3:1–5, in which Jesus heals a man on the Sabbath. He entered a synagogue, in which opponents waited to see if he would disobey the Torah. Jesus said: "Is it permitted to do good or to do evil on the Sabbath, to save life or to kill?" The opponents remained silent, and Jesus healed the man. The initiation of the action is provided by a confrontation between Jesus and his silent accusers. The saying is central to the narrative and is intended to answer their question. Here the attack on Jesus is a silent one, but in other cases the opponents do something or say something to which Jesus makes reply. The reply may be a counter question, a metaphor, a scriptural quotation, or a symbolic action. The secondary nature of the narrative portion of a controversy dialogue can be seen rather clearly in Mark 2:15–17, where Jesus hosts a meal for his disciples, tax collectors, and sinners. The scribes of the Pharisees question the disciples about this, and Jesus replies, "It is not the healthy that need a doctor, but the sick; I did not come to invite virtuous people, but sinners." In this case the story does not fit with the saying, nor is the story consistent. The saying relates to the work of a physician, while the narrative pictures Jesus as host. The scribes question the

---

[15] Dibelius and Taylor both recognize the materials in this section as having a distinctive form, which Dibelius calls paradigms and Taylor pronouncement stories. Robert M. Montgomery and W. R. Stegner have recently prepared some programed instructional material on the pronouncement story. Studies of other forms should come out shortly. Use of this material should help the student recognize the meaning of form critical study and should facilitate his ability to distinguish between primary and secondary elements in the pronouncement stories. Cf. *Auxiliary Studies in the Bible: Forms in the Gospels: I. The Pronouncement Story* (New York: Abingdon, 1970).

disciples, but Jesus answers. We are not told how the scribes found out about the meal. In context with the narrative, the saying equates Pharisees with the righteous, a fact which Jesus challenges elsewhere. We can assume that the narrative came into the tradition to clothe the saying with an interpretation, and not a very good one at that. Bultmann feels that, although the central saying in a controversy dialogue may go back to Jesus, the narrative section originated "in the discussions the Church had with its opponents, and as certainly, within itself, on questions of law."[16] The dialogues are imaginary constructions of debates between Jesus and opponents. In the earlier stages of the tradition, the opponents were not named, but there was an active tendency in the later stages to use scribes and Pharisees in these roles. In reference to the historical authenticity of these apophthegms, Bultmann says: "The individual controversy dialogues may not be historical reports of particular incidents in the life of Jesus, but the general character of his life is rightly portrayed in them, on the basis of historical recollection."[17]

The scholastic dialogue is another kind of apophthegm, which starts with a question rather than an action or situation. The question may be posed by a disciple of Jesus or by an opponent. The form suggests the rise of this type within the teaching function of the church, for it is markedly similar to the question-and-answer pattern of a catechism. Mark 12:28–34 is such a form. A scribe asks Jesus which is the greatest commandment, and Jesus answers with citations from Deuteronomy and Leviticus.

The biographical apophthegms are more varied in form and include such stories as the calling of the disciples, the blessing of the children, and Jesus' rejection in Nazareth. Bultmann regards them as intended to present an ideal: "They embody a truth in some metaphorical sort of situation which, by reason of its wider reference, gives the apophthegms their symbolic character."[18] The context for these is best seen in preaching, because "they help to present the Master as a living contemporary, and to comfort and admonish the Church in her hope."[19]

Dominical Sayings

Dominical sayings are those attributed by the tradition to Jesus (from the Latin *dominus,* Lord), but they are sayings which could have had a free-float-

16 Bultmann, op. cit., p. 41.
17 Ibid., p. 50.
18 Ibid., p. 56.
19 Ibid., p. 61.

ing existence. They were not embodied in an apophthegmatic form. Bultmann discusses four basic types of dominical sayings: logia, which present Jesus as a teacher of wisdom; prophetic and apocalyptic sayings; legal sayings and church rules; and I-sayings.

The logia are mostly proverbs, such as the following: "For the words that the mouth utters come from the overflowing of the heart";[20] "Each day has troubles enough of its own";[21] "The worker earns his pay";[22] "What God has joined together, man must not separate";[23] "Leave the dead to bury their dead."[24] By the time the logia reached the Synoptic authors, some were expanded or combined with similar sayings, illustrations, or explanations. The main content of the logia consists of "observations on life, rules of prudence and popular morality, sometimes a product of humor or scepticism, full now of sober, popular morality, and now of naif egoism."[25] Some logia breathe the atmosphere of popular piety and are concerned with such things as the sovereignty of God, retributive righteousness in world affairs, trust in God's providence, and the efficacy of prayer. Most of these motifs and many similar sayings are found in Jewish literature, and most of them probably came out of the Jewish oral tradition. The Palestinian church quite unconsciously introduced these sayings into Christianity out of its lore of folk wisdom, and the words were soon attributed to Jesus.

The prophetic and apocalyptic sayings are those concerned with the imminence of the kingdom of God and with the effects of its coming. They include a "little apocalypse" in Mark 13, the beatitudes in Luke 6 and Matthew 5, woes on the rich, woes on the scribes and Pharisees, and other admonitions. Many of the sayings have been taken over from Jewish traditions. The "little apocalypse" is a Christianized form of a Jewish apocalypse. This group also includes a number of prophetic sayings which originated with revered Christians. Bultmann observes, "The Church drew no distinction between such utterances by Christian prophets and the sayings of Jesus in the tradition, for the reason that even the dominical sayings in the tradition were not the pronouncements of a past authority, but sayings of the risen Lord, who is always a contemporary for the Church."[26]

The legal sayings and church rules include certain comments on the Torah

[20] Matthew 12:34.
[21] Matthew 6:34.
[22] Luke 10:7.
[23] Mark 10:9.
[24] Matthew 8:22; Luke 9:60.
[25] Bultmann, op. cit., p. 104.
[26] Ibid., pp. 127 f.

(such as those in Matthew 5:27–48) and certain rules on prayer and church discipline. These materials are not so old as the similar sayings among the controversy dialogues, and most have come out of Jewish tradition or Christion preaching.

A fourth category of dominical sayings is called the I-sayings, that is, those in which Jesus makes some pronouncement about himself. In them Jesus appears as eschatological prophet, Messiah, and judge of the world. According to Bultmann they appeared relatively late in the oral period and were mainly products of Christian prophets in the Hellenistic church.

Jesus Teaching Among the Apostles, fresco, early fourth century, Catacomb of Domitilla, Rome. (*Courtesy* Pontifical Commission for Sacred Archives, Rome.)

Similitudes

Similitudes include metaphors and parables. A metaphor is a concrete statement based on an implied comparison. The Synoptic Gospels include a number of metaphors, such as "no one puts new wine into old wineskins";[27]

---

[27] Mark 2:22.

"if a kingdom is divided against itself, that kingdom cannot stand";[28] and "can one blind man be guide to another?"[29]

The parable is a metaphor told as a story. It "gives as its picture not a typical condition or a typical recurrent event, but some interesting particular situation."[30] The parable is a specific form in the oral tradition, but there are variations in the pattern. Many begin with an introductory question (what is the kingdom of God like?) or with a formula of comparison (the kingdom of God is like this). A story is then told with marked brevity. There are few characters, never more than three. They are usually not described except by what they do or say. A single course of action is described with economy of language. At the conclusion of the story, the hearer's judgment is called for on the point of the story. No attention is devoted to the moral quality of the characters or their motivation. Some have an application introduced by the words, "Truly I say to you . . ." or simply "Thus . . ." Others end with no explicit application.

No one parable can demonstrate all of these characteristics, but we may examine two for illustrative purposes. The brief parable in Matthew 18 : 12–14 begins with a question: "What do you think?" Then follows a narrative about a man who has one hundred sheep, loses one, and rejoices when it is found. The character of the shepherd, his location, and his family are all ignored in the narrative. No other characters enter. There is no description of the search. At the conclusion the point is made, "In the same way, it is not your heavenly Father's will that one of these little ones should be lost." The story is told to establish this one point. No other application is called for, although readers may be interested in subsidiary questions. The parable of laborers in a vineyard in Matthew 20 : 1–15[31] has an introductory formula: "The kingdom of Heaven is like this. There was once a landowner who went out early one morning to hire labourers for his vineyard." Then follows the story in which the landowner employs people for various lengths of time and then pays all of them the same wages. The ones who had worked all day grumbled, but the landowner explained that he had cheated no one. He paid those who worked all day the contracted wages, and he was generous to the rest. He claims that he can do what he will with what he has. No application is drawn. The brevity of style is notable. Although many people are involved in the story, the workers are treated as groups. The only

[28] Mark 3 : 24.
[29] Luke 6 : 39.
[30] Bultmann, op. cit., p. 174.
[31] Verse 16 must not have belonged to the parable originally, for the point of it is quite different from that of the parable itself.

dialogue is between the landowner and a representative of the first group. Above all, the parable illustrates the fact that only one point is involved, namely, that the kingdom of God is somehow similar to this situation. Some people come in early and some late, but all receive the same reward. One certainly may make a moral judgment about an employer who would treat his workers without due consideration for the quantity of their work, but this is not the point of the parable. The context is probably to be found in the Hellenistic church, which attempted to justify its existence vis-à-vis the older Jewish Christian church.

Many of the parables contained in the Synoptic Gospels must have come from Jewish tradition, for similar parables are found in Jewish literature. Some may have originated with Jesus, but it is extremely difficult to be certain on this point, because the form of the parables was altered during the history of the oral period. They were frequently provided with introductions and conclusions. Sometimes two or more were grouped together. Explanations were added, and in some cases the explanation turned the parable into an allegory. When the gospel writers found the parables, they already contained these secondary features, which were then included in the written compilations. The parable of the marriage feast in Matthew 22:1–10 was given an allegorical expansion in 22:11–14. The parable of the sower in Mark 4:3–9 had a detailed interpretation in 4:13–20. By the time of the Synoptics, the changes in the parable form were so extensive that Bultmann concludes: "*The original meaning of many similitudes has become irrecoverable* in the course of the tradition."[32] He feels that the only ones which might go back to Jesus are those that express a distinctive eschatological temper and that lack any features characteristic of Jewish piety or Christian thought.

We now turn to the narrative material about Jesus, in which Bultmann includes miracles and legends.

Miracles

A large number of Synoptic narratives are told in the form of miracle stories. These can easily be spotted on the basis of content, but they also have a particular form. There are two types found in the gospels: healing miracles and nature miracles. The former include the curing of disease, exorcism of demons, and resuscitations of the dead. Nature miracles are those performed on inanimate objects.

[32] Bultmann, op. cit., p. 199.

In the usual healing miracle, the story begins with a description of the illness and sometimes includes a statement on its duration, the dreadful and dangerous character of it, and the ineffective treatment of former physicians. In the performance of the miracle, all attention is focused on Jesus, and the person being cured is of no significance. The miracles frequently work in an automatic fashion and without the agency of Jesus' will. The woman with a hemorrhage, for example, is cured by touching Jesus' garment without his prior knowledge.[33] The healing generally takes place by means of a gesture, a touch, a word (frequently incomprehensible or foreign), a name, or by a threat to the sickness or demon. Then follow certain features which demonstrate the successful performance of the miracle: a lame man walks, a blind man describes what he sees, or an exorcised demon creates a disturbance. The story concludes with the dismissal of the healed person and a report of the crowd's response.

There are very few nature miracles in the Synoptics. Bultmann finds only six, and they do not present a consistent pattern. In general, Jesus encounters some problem which he solves by controlling the elements. In Mark 4:36–41, Jesus and his disciples are in a boat when a storm begins, threatening to capsize it. Jesus is awakened from his sleep, he commands the storm to cease, and the disciples are filled with awe. Most of the nature miracles probably came out of the general lore of folk stories in the Hellenistic world. Bultmann cites a number of parallels to the walking on water in several traditions, including one in which a disciple walks across water to Buddha. Some of the stories may have arisen within the Christian tradition, where they were first told as Easter stories. The conception of the risen Lord presiding at a Messianic banquet may have become a story of miraculous feeding.[34] Other nature miracles may have been fashioned out of dominical sayings or parables. The parable of the fig tree in Luke 13:6 ff. probably became the story of the cursing of the fig tree in Mark 11:12 ff., where it is told as a nature miracle. No one can, of course, be certain that historical incidents do not underlie the nature miracles, but that is another study which will engage us later.

The form of both healing and nature miracles was altered to some extent by the oral tradition in two particulars: there was a tendency to increase the miraculous element, and there was a tendency to develop a novelistic (or romantic) interest in the secondary participants. When the narratives reach a literary stage, it is possible to trace the tendency to heighten the miraculous

[33] See Mark 5:25–34; Luke 8:43–48.
[34] See Mark 6:34–44; 8:1–9; and parallels.

element. The miracles in the later gospels are more stupendous than those in the earlier. We must assume that this tendency was at work in the oral stage as well. The same is true of the novelistic interests. Characters who are barely mentioned in the earliest gospels are given names and detailed treatment in the later. In Mark 14, at the arrest of Jesus, an unnamed person cut off an ear of the high priest's slave. In Luke 22, it is the right ear which is cut off, and Jesus heals the ear. In John 18, it is Peter who cut off the right ear of the slave, whose name is given as Malchus. At each stage the story has become more specific, as details and names are added.

Legends[35]

Legends are those stories about the events in Jesus' life which function as religious or edifying narratives. It is possible that the stories embody some authentic historical recollections, but their chief value lies in their suitability for Christian preaching and teaching, which must have been the context for most of the legends. The passion narrative, including the trial and execution of Jesus, the resurrection narratives, and the birth and infancy accounts are the longer legends, but the shorter ones dealing with the baptism, temptation, and transfiguration of Jesus are to be included. Although the passion narrative is composed of a number of independent narratives, it was probably combined into a coherent sequence of events during the oral period. A number of motifs are found in the passion and resurrection narratives: apologetic motifs, in which the Jews are blamed for the death of Jesus and the Romans are nearly exonerated; paradigmatic motifs, in which the execution of Jesus is presented as an example to protomartyrs; cultic motifs, in which Jesus' last supper serves as an institution of the Christian eucharist; and missionary motifs, in which the risen Lord commands his disciples to preach to Gentiles. The earliest form of these narratives is the primitive Christian *kerygma*, in which the death and resurrection of Jesus was proclaimed. This proclamation gave rise to the more developed narratives, and we need not look outside the Christian movement for their origin. The form of the individual narrative in the tradition is marked by a conciseness of style and an economy of characterization. Bultmann feels that the legendary narratives consistently present Jesus in terms of Messianic ideas and that this is a sign that they arose among Christians of a Jewish background. The treatment of Jesus as Messiah accounts for the lack of legends such as those

---

[35] Bultmann uses two terms to designate this group of narratives—legends and historical stories—but he does not distinguish between the two.

later Christian stories of saints. The legends do not treat Jesus' life as a pattern of devotion, and there is little interest in his life in the historical sense, because he is believed to be the Messiah. The legends tell of evidences of his Messiahship and acts of the Messiah, not the acts of a saintly man.

There is no escape from the fact that oral materials are more difficult to work with than written ones, because they are not directly available to us. Nevertheless, it has been possible to say some definite things about this body of material. The early church received some sayings and narratives from the recollections of the eyewitnesses of Jesus' life, from Jewish oral tradition, and from Hellenistic stories. These began to circulate in the form of apophthegms, dominical sayings, similitudes, miracles, and legends. They were used in the context of sermons, debates, instruction, worship, and prophecy. In time, the simpler forms were altered by way of expansion and change of context. They were finally grouped together into gospels, a type of literature we shall next investigate.

Chapter Six

The Synoptic Gospels

In Greek, the word *euangelion,* which we translate gospel, literally means good news. It was often used as the object of "to preach," and thus it defined the content of the Christian *kerygma.* Only later did it come to signify a book, and Mark seems to be the first writer to use the term in this capacity. He opens his book with: "Here begins the Gospel of Jesus Christ," and this was intended as a title. The superscription, "According to Mark," was added later. The other evangelists—writers of gospels—did not use the term. Matthew's title is: "The book of the generations of Jesus Christ, son of David, son of Abraham." The titles of Luke and John, if there were any, are not preserved. Nevertheless, the designation *gospel* has become a convenient way to describe a particular literary genre. It may be defined as *a formulation of the Christian message in terms of sayings and actions of Jesus.* The purpose of a gospel writer is not materially different from that of those who preserved and transmitted the oral tradition. Both are kerygmatic, and the evangelists intended to preach and teach just as their predecessors did. Although they preach by presenting a good deal of material about Jesus, their purpose is not to write biographies. After all, they include very little of the personal information that should be included in a biography. Their writing is motivated by their faith, and all of their work is infused with a belief in Jesus as uniquely related to God. Thus, Jesus is not presented in a way that a human being might be presented; he is exhibited as the object of faith.

The remark of Papias that connects Mark with Peter illustrates the relationship the evangelists had with the oral tradition.[1] The first gospel, whether one of these or some lost document, was compiled largely from the oral tradition. It was an attempt to bring together the various apophthegms, dominical sayings, similitudes, miracle stories, and legends, and to put them into some order. Since the materials came to the evangelists in random order, it was necessary for them to impose a structure on them. It was up to

[1] See p. 163 f.

[183]

them to develop a chronological sequence and to put the materials into some geographical setting. In the process they would group materials in such a way that one saying would inevitably affect the meaning of an adjacent one. The evangelists also provided connecting links for their materials and felt free to introduce their own interpretive comments. In other words, the gospels represent the final stage in the history of the oral tradition.

The practice of writing gospels was popular well into the third century. It began with the Synoptic Gospels: Matthew, Mark, and Luke. They are called Synoptic because they present an approach to Jesus which is similar in many basic respects and because they share a great deal of material. The similarities in these three gospels have attracted the attention of scholars from the earliest days. Scholars have rightly felt that the similarities deserved some explanation and that they could not be accounted for by a common dependence on the oral tradition. The similarities frequently extend to a duplication of entire sentences, with word-for-word agreement. Moreover, for extended periods the gospels are in agreement on the sequence of events. The oral tradition would not have provided a basis for such agreement in language or order. We can only conclude that copying has occurred in the writing of the Synoptics, that there is, in fact, a literary relationship among these gospels. Papias offered an explanation for this in saying that Matthew drew up the logia (words of Jesus) in Hebrew and that each one translated them as he was able.[2] Augustine believed that Mark was a kind of abridgment of Matthew.[3]

We can gain some perspective on the relationships if we first catalogue the various kinds of material in accordance with its appearance in one, or two, or all three Synoptics:

Class I. Material in all three gospels. About 480 verses appear in all three gospels.[4] In this material the verbal agreements are very high in frequency, but occasionally one gospel may differ from the other two, or all three may have different words. It is rare that Mark disagrees in wording where the

---

[2] In Eusebius, *Church History* III, 39 : 16. If Papias meant that Mark was one of those who copied Matthew, he seems to contradict himself in saying elsewhere (in *Church History* III, 39 : 15) that Mark depended on Peter.

[3] *De Consensa Evangelistarum* I, 2–3.

[4] The computations used here are based upon those of Allan Barr in *A Diagram of Synoptic Relationships* (Edinburgh: Clark, 1938). Although the proportionate relationships are usually judged in the same way, computations by scholars differ because of various ways of counting verses and judging agreements. For other computations, see B. H. Streeter, *The Four Gospels* (London: Macmillan, 1953); and Frederick Gast, in *The Jerome Biblical Commentary* (Englewood Cliffs, N.J.: Prentice-Hall, 1968), Vol. II, pp. 1–6.

other two agree. In reference to the order of events, there is basic agreement, although one may occasionally depart from the other two. This is rarely the case with Mark. In respect to style, Mark appears to be somewhat less smooth than the other two.

Class II. Material in Matthew and Mark. This consists of some 120 verses, but since Matthew and Mark also share the 480 verses in Class I, these two gospels have a total of about 600 verses in common. This amounts to about 90 per cent of Mark and about half of the longer Matthew. The material in these two classes seems to include most of the framework for both gospels.

Class III. Material in Mark and Luke. Less than two dozen verses are found in this class, but Mark and Luke actually share a good deal more than this, namely, material that makes up over half of Mark and one third of Luke. This material alternates in Luke with large blocks of material from other classes.

Class IV. Material in Matthew and Luke. About 170 verses belong in this class. They are found throughout the two gospels, but not always in the same sequence or context. It consists mainly of the teaching of John the Baptist and Jesus. The verbal similarities are, on the whole, not so high as those in Classes I–III, but in some sections they reach as high as 97 per cent.

Class V. Material in Mark alone. Only about 50 verses are included in this group, constituting about 10 per cent of Mark. It includes some details in several stories and two complete narratives—the healing of a dumb man in 7:32 ff. and of a blind man in 8:22 ff.

Class VI. Material in Matthew alone. About 280 verses are found only in Matthew, including the stories of the birth of Jesus, the resurrection appearances, and many teachings which have a Palestinian character, some of which show a special Jewish Christian interest.

Class VII. Material in Luke alone. About 500 verses are found only in Luke. These materials are found primarily in the Lukan infancy narratives and the resurrection appearances, but they are also found in many of Luke's parables.

Nineteenth-century scholarship produced a theory of Synoptic literary relationships which is still held by most Biblical scholars. Fundamental to the theory is the acceptance of Mark as the earliest of the three gospels. Some early nineteenth-century scholars had imagined a lost source from which all three writers had copied. It was frequently assumed that Mark had copied this document most faithfully, so it was called Ur-Markus, a primitive Mark. By the end of the nineteenth century, many scholars began to feel that the similarity between Ur-Markus and Mark was so great that it was not necessary to speak of a hypothetical source, and they began to identify the two. Thus, it seemed best to say simply that Matthew and Luke each had a copy of Mark, which they independently used as a source for their longer gospels. In 1924, B. H. Streeter[5] was able to cite five basic reasons for accepting the priority of Mark. (1) Matthew reproduced 90 per cent of Mark, and Luke more than half of it, both in language nearly identical with that of Mark. (2) The majority of Mark's words are found also in Matthew or Luke, or both. (3) The relative order of Mark's material is preserved by one or both of the others. Although one or the other may rearrange some of the narratives, they almost never agree in their rearrangement. (4) Mark's language appears more primitive than either of the other two. (5) The distribution of material in Matthew and Luke indicates that each had Mark before him and was faced with the problem of combining this with material from other sources.

The priority of Mark and its use by Matthew and Luke would explain the material in Classes I, II, and III. Material in Class V is simply that small amount which neither of the others cared to use. Material in Classes VI and VII must be regarded as having its source in private documents used respectively by Matthew and Luke or in oral tradition known by the authors. A serious problem remained, however, for material in Class IV could not be explained simply by the thesis of Markan priority. Here we have a significant amount of material in Matthew and Luke which could not have been obtained from Mark. Since the later evangelists worked independently, an additional source must be assumed for these 170 verses. To explain this phenomenon, scholars called upon a hypothetical source called Q, from the German word *Quelle,* meaning source. This document must be at least as old as Mark but was unknown to Mark. It consisted mainly of teaching material and lacked the stories of Jesus' birth, death, and resurrection.

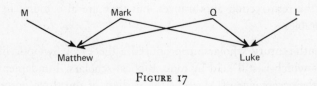

FIGURE 17

Figure 17 explains these relationships (M stands for material in Class VI, and L stands for material in Class VII).

Although most scholars today adopt this solution to the Synoptic problem,

[5] Op. cit.

it is not without its difficulties. For one thing, the dependence of the theory on a hypothetical Q document is something of an embarrassment. A theory without hypothetical sources would certainly be stronger. Evidence for Q as a document is not particularly strong, since Matthew and Luke vary considerably in the order and wording of this material. In addition, the arguments presented by Streeter and others are subject to question. In general, Streeter's arguments are phrased in such a way that they presuppose Markan priority. It is not correct to say that Matthew reproduces 90 per cent of Mark unless you already know that Mark came first. The fact that the three gospels have similar material does not dictate any one solution. It may suggest that Mark is dependent on one or both of the others or that they are dependent on him. Streeter's second argument says that Matthew and Luke both follow Mark's wording very closely. In fact, however, there are places where the two agree with each other but disagree with Mark, and this in sections where they are allegedly using Mark. These phenomena are minor but occur frequently enough to be significant. Some may be accidental and some may be due to changes in the text by later copyists, but a number of others raise serious objections against the theory of Markan priority. It is to be expected that two authors who use the same source would alter a word or two here and there, but it is surprising when they both make precisely the same change. Streeter's third argument on order can, of course, cut both ways. If the basic sequence is the same in two or more documents, we can assume that one has been copied. But order does not dictate which one.

Streeter's fourth argument suggests that Mark's language and grammatical usage is more primitive than that of the other two. This, however, can be questioned. William R. Farmer[6] feels that Mark committed no more grammatical errors than did the other two. He uses some Latinisms in writing Greek, but this may be due to his background, and he has some Aramaic terms, but he almost always translates them.[7] Streeter had also observed that, although his Gospel is shorter, Mark is actually more verbose than the others in the narratives he includes. His stories are expanded by the inclusion of relatively insignificant details which are not found in the others. Streeter is quite sure that Mark could not have copied Matthew, because "Only a lunatic would leave out Matthew's account of the Infancy, The Sermon on the Mount, and practically all the parables, in order to get room for purely verbal expansion of what was retained."[8] Farmer has, however, shown that many of the Markan narratives are, on form critical grounds, less primitive

---

[6] *The Synoptic Problem* (New York: The Macmillan Company, 1964).
[7] The lone exception is in 10:51, where Jesus is addressed as rabbi.
[8] Streeter, op. cit., p. 158.

than the comparable ones in Matthew and Luke. The study of oral tradition has shown that miracle stories tend to pick up details of a romantic interest, precisely those details that Streeter said only a lunatic would prefer. Lunatic or not, Mark seems to stand closer to the gospels of the second century than do Matthew and Luke, and for this reason may actually be later.

These difficulties have led a few recent scholars to reopen the question of Synoptic relationships. Most notable among these is William R. Farmer,[9] who has proposed consideration of a theory first formulated by the eighteenth-century scholar Johann Griesbach. This hypothesis maintains that Matthew was the earliest Gospel, that Luke used Matthew as a source, and that Mark used both (see Figure 18).

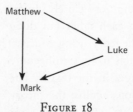

FIGURE 18

The material in Classes I, III, IV, and VI would be accounted for in this theory, and that in Class V is minimal enough to cause no problem. Class III and Class VII material must be from a version of the oral tradition that Luke preferred to Matthew or to something like an L source. The theory has a number of advantages. It eliminates the hypothetical Q source, which is essential for the theory of Markan priority. Matthew and Luke share this material, because Luke copied it from Matthew. The large amount of agreement among the three occurs because Mark used both of the others. The agreements of Matthew and Luke against Mark are not problematical, for under this theory Mark is not bound to copy every word exactly. Mark's similarity with second-century gospels is also explained.

Nevertheless, there are serious problems with the Griesbach hypothesis. Although it eliminates the necessity of a Q source, it requires another hypothetical source to account for non-Matthaean material in Luke. Moreover, Luke does not simply use this material to amplify Matthew; in many cases, he uses it instead of Matthew, and this creates a major difficulty for the Griesbach hypothesis. If Luke had seen Matthew's birth story, why did he use a totally different one that had the same religious function? If he had seen Matthew's genealogy, why did he use a different one? If he had seen

[9] Op. cit.

the narrative of resurrection appearances in Matthew, why did he substitute his own? And why did he make all of these substitutions but retain the great bulk of Matthaean material elsewhere? A related problem has to do with the purpose of Mark. Did he produce a gospel only to duplicate what he found in his sources? After all, he has almost nothing new. And if this is his purpose, why does he omit the birth narratives and so much of the teaching? Even if his purpose was to include only that material on which his sources agreed, he omitted 170 of such verses (Class IV material).

It must be admitted that, for all its work, scholarship has produced no unassailable theory of Synoptic relationships. If one is impressed by scholarly consensus, he will adopt the theory of Markan priority, and almost all contemporary literature is based on this premise. Otherwise, it comes down to a matter of informed judgment: Which proposal has fewer and less weighty problems? At first glance, the Griesbach hypothesis might appear more attractive. But for all its merits it is difficult to see how Luke and Mark could have written as they did under the circumstances this theory assumes. Moreover, the strength of Streeter's fifth argument has not been diminished. This argument states that the distribution of material in Matthew and Luke indicates that they combined Mark with other sources. The arrangement of Synoptic material is striking. Mark begins with the baptism of Jesus and ends with the discovery of the empty tomb. Matthew and Luke both have material which they place before the baptism, and they both narrate material which they place after the story of the empty tomb. But this material is unique to each gospel. It looks as if these writers used Mark as a basis for their gospels, for they begin to agree with each other at the point where Mark begins and cease their agreement where Mark leaves off. Both must have felt that Mark was incomplete at both ends, and they added comparable but different material to what they found in Mark. In Figures 19 and 20, parallel lines indicate agreement, and tangential lines indicate nonagreement.

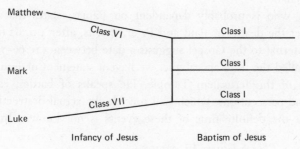

FIGURE 19 The Beginning of the Gospels

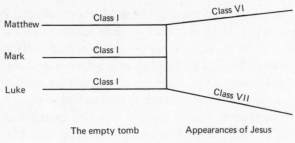

FIGURE 20   The End of the Gospels

We shall follow the scholarly consensus but must point out problems as they occur. Although we use the theory of Markan priority as an operative principle, we must not be blind to its problems and must keep an open mind on the subject.

THE GOSPEL OF MARK

Since gospels depend on traditional material and are written as the documents of a movement, their authors do not make themselves visible. Although the superscription, "The Gospel According to Mark," did not appear in the oldest manuscripts of this book, by the middle of the second century it was known as the work of a man bearing that name. Papias speaks of Mark as the interpreter of Peter,[10] but he gives us no hard information about him, and none of the earliest witnesses are able to remove the anonymous character of the work. There is some slim evidence that it was written in Rome, and the use of Latinisms in the Greek text tends to confirm this evidence. A number of scholars maintain a Palestinian provenance for the Gospel, and their argument is difficult to refute. Nevertheless, the basic tendencies seem to be those of a Gentile Christian, and Rome is a more likely provenance.

Irenaeus, who is probably dependent on Papias, states that Mark was written after the deaths of Paul and Peter, that is, after A.D. 62 or 64.[11] The evidence internal to the Gospel suggests a date between A.D. 66–70. In Mark 13, often called the little apocalypse, we have a statement of Jesus about the destruction of the Jerusalem Temple. He speaks of battles, earthquakes, famines, and persecutions, which will precede the actual destruction, and he admits that the definite time of these events is not known. In 13:14, he

[10] In Eusebius, *Church History* III, 39:15.
[11] *Against Heresies* III, 1:1.

The opening of the Gospel of Mark from the Lindisfarne Gospels, seventh century. (*Courtesy* the Trustees of the British Museum, London.)

speaks of an "abomination of desolation" being placed where it does not belong and says that the disciplines are to flee to the hills when they see it. Mark adds the significant rubric, "let the reader understand," clearly indicating that the words are intended for those living in his own time. It is obvious that 13:14 is the key to the entire passage, for most of the rest is standard apocalyptic language, probably drawn from a Jewish apocalypse. The verse is taken from Daniel, where it probably referred to the altar to Zeus set up by Antiochus IV in 167 B.C. The threatened Roman conquest of the Temple would be seen as an analogue to the situation described in the Book of Daniel and as a signal that the end has drawn near. When these events take place, the Christian is to leave Jerusalem and run to the hills, as the Maccabean rebels did in 167 B.C.

In this connection, Eusebius refers to an oracle given to the Jerusalem Christians before the destruction of the Temple, warning them to flee from the city:

> The people of the church in Jerusalem were commanded by an oracle given by revelation before the war to those in the city who were worthy of it to depart and dwell in one of the cities of Peraea which they called Pella. To it those who believed on Christ migrated from Jerusalem, that when holy men had altogether deserted the royal capital of the Jews and the whole land of Judaea, the judgement of God might at last overtake them for all their crimes against the Christ and his Apostles, and all that generation of the wicked be utterly blotted out from among men.[12]

It is just possible that Mark 13:14 is a record of that oracle. Although Mark does not mention Pella specifically, he does speak of the hill country, which would have included it. Eusebius says that the Christians received the oracle before the war broke out, but Mark must not have recorded it until afterward, for he has Jesus affirm that the battles are preparatory to the end and are not to be mistaken for it. The end is the destruction of the Temple, and that event has not yet occurred. If this is correct, we may be safe in dating Mark between A.D. 66 and 70.

Mark's story begins with the appearance of John the Baptizer, who calls for repentance in view of the imminence of the kingdom of God. After his baptism and temptation, Jesus goes into Galilee, preaching the same message. He gathers a group of disciples and moves about in Galilee, exorcising demons, healing the sick, lepers, and paralytics, and performing a resuscitation. He teaches about the kingdom and allows his disciples a certain freedom in reference to Pharisaic observances. He restores the sight of a blind man, feeds a multitude on a small amount of food, and walks on the sea. In chapter 8, Peter expresses his belief that Jesus is the Christ, and Jesus speaks (on three occasions) of his pending suffering, death, and resurrection. In chapter 9, three of the disciples see him transfigured, in company with Elijah and Moses. When Jesus arrives in Jerusalem, he cleanses the

[12] Eusebius, *Church History* III, 5:3.

Temple and is arrested a few days later. Between the cleansing and the arrest, Mark includes a number of Jesus' teachings, his condemnation of Pharisees, and the apocalyptic discourse of chapter 13. Jesus is arrested after a meal with the disciples, one of whom, Judas, reveals his identity to the authorities. He is tried before the Jewish Sanhedrin and found guilty of blasphemy. The following morning he is taken before Pilate and charged with political treason, found guilty, and crucified. On the following Sunday, three women come to Jesus' tomb and find it empty, except for a young man dressed in white, who tells them that Jesus has risen from the dead and will meet them in Galilee. Mark ends abruptly: "Then they went out and ran away from the tomb, beside themselves with terror. They said nothing to anybody, for they were afraid."[13]

In writing his Gospel, Mark has drawn on the tradition of Jesus' deeds and sayings, most of which must have come to him in oral form. If he used any written sources, they are no longer available to us. Nevertheless, many scholars believe that some of the material had previously been written down. The story of the passion, the collection of parables in chapter 4, and the group of conflict situations in 2:1–3:6 may have circulated in written form before Mark. Although he acts in the capacity of an editor in bringing these various materials together, he should not simply be regarded as a compiler of old traditions. He is dependent on the material he knows, but he gives it a structure, and he comments upon it from his own point of view. There are certain themes which run through the Gospel and give to it its unique character. We shall look at four of them: the Messianic secret, the misunderstanding of the disciples, martyrdom, and the significance of Galilee.

William Wrede, in 1901, was the first to call attention to the motif of the Messianic secret and to the significant part it played in Mark's interpretation of the history of Jesus.[14] Mark seems to have believed that Jesus' Messiahship was not openly proclaimed until after the resurrection. An exorcised demon who proclaims Jesus to be the Christ is commanded to be silent.[15] Jesus explains that the purpose of his teaching in parables is to hide the truth from nonbelievers.[16] The disciples are commanded to be silent about Jesus' Messiahship until after the resurrection.[17] Wrede accounted for this

[13] Some English translations include additional material, but the earliest and best texts of Mark end at 16:8. It is possible that Mark wrote more and that the last portion was lost, but it is more likely that the author intended his Gospel to end precisely at this point.

[14] *Das Messiasgeheimnis in den Evangelien* (Göttingen: Vandenhoeck and Ruprecht, 1901).

[15] See Mark 1:23–25, 34; 3:11–12; 5:6, 7; 9:20.

[16] See especially Mark 4:12.

[17] Mark 9:9; see also 7:26; 8:30.

phenomenon by suggesting that Mark was aware that Jesus was not proclaimed to be Messiah during his lifetime. Mark, however, felt that Messiahship was recognized but suppressed at Jesus' command. Mark does not suggest why Jesus should want to hide his identity; he simply assumes that whatever happened must have been intended.

A closely related theme in Mark is that of the misunderstanding of the disciples. A central place is given to the confession of Peter, who, in chapter 8, comes to recognize Jesus as Messiah. It is significant that the association of disciples with Jesus begins before their recognition of his identity and that even when their recognition is expressed, it is treated as partial and possibly inadequate. Elsewhere, Mark implies that the disciples have a wrong conception about the nature of Jesus. They do not understand a number of things Jesus does and says: the stilling of the sea (4:41), the feeding of the five thousand (6:52), Jesus' attitude toward children (10:13 ff.), the saying about the rich entering the kingdom (10:23). They are characteristically unable to understand parables (4:1–20, 33 f.). Above all, they do not understand the necessity of Jesus' suffering. Mark has Jesus speak of his coming passion on three occasions. In the first (8:31–33), although Peter has just confessed Jesus to be Messiah, he cannot accept the fact of suffering and death. At the end of the section, Jesus impatiently condemns Peter's point of view: "Away with you, Satan, you think as men think, not as God thinks." In the second, Mark says that the disciples did not understand what Jesus said and were afraid to ask him about it.[18] After the third, two of the disciples ask for special privileges in Jesus' kingdom.[19] It is difficult to know why Mark felt it necessary to emphasize the disciples' lack of understanding, unless he was trying to mitigate their authority or to object to a point of view that did not sufficiently emphasize the significance of Jesus' death. Some Christian preachers accepted the death of Jesus as simply an unfortunate historical fact and emphasized the resurrection as the moment of divine significance. In Acts 2, Peter preaches in precisely this way. The author of Luke, as we shall see, understood that the death of Jesus was in accordance with divine plan, but he saw no redemptive significance in it. Mark, however, not only emphasizes the inevitability of the death; he once refers to it as a ransom.[20] His emphasis on the significance of Jesus' death is a creative theme, which reappears as Mark treats of martyrdom.

[18] Mark 9:32.
[19] Mark 10:35–40.
[20] Mark 10:45.

Not only does Mark use the motifs of secrecy and misunderstanding in narrating specific incidents, but he also uses them in the basic organization of his material. The centrality of Peter's confession in chapter 8 has already been noted. T. A. Burkill[21] and others regard the confession and transfiguration narratives as the climax of Mark's Gospel. Before the confession, Mark portrays Jesus as teaching the crowds, healing the sick, and exorcising the demons. In these stories, only the demons recognize the truth about Jesus, and they are commanded to be silent. Not until we get to 8:29 do we have a Messianic recognition by a human being, as Peter proclaims, "You are the Messiah." Even here Jesus commands strict secrecy and then begins to teach the disciples about the necessity of his coming suffering and the certainty of his resurrection. As we have seen, Peter does not understand this teaching. Six days later, Peter, James, and John experience the transfiguration of Jesus on a high mountain.[22] Although several scholars believe that this is a misplaced story of a post-resurrection appearance of Jesus, Burkill feels that Mark intentionally placed it here to show that the disciples finally began to understand the true nature of Jesus. The transfiguration demonstrates the glory that belongs to Jesus as Messiah and confirms Peter's recognition in 8:29. Burkill writes: "For a few fleeting moments the veil of the flesh is withdrawn and the three disciples are privileged to behold their Master as he really is and as he will be made manifest to the world when he comes in clouds with great power and glory."[23] These narratives form a turning point in the Gospel, for before them Mark is mainly interested in portraying the "esoteric manifestation of the secret fact of the Messiahship [and afterward in showing] how the fact of the Messiahship mysteriously meant that Jesus had to endure the shame of crucifixion in the fulfillment of his redemptive mission in the world."[24] The remainder of Mark concentrates on Jesus' teaching about his death and resurrection and culminates in the passion story. At his trial before the Sanhedrin, Jesus openly proclaims his Messianic status.[25] The Gospel concludes with the discovery of the empty tomb by women who "said nothing to anybody, for they were afraid" (16:8). The conclusion, nevertheless, points forward to an appearance of the risen Christ in Galilee (16:7), which is not described. Although Mark believes that Jesus was

[21] *Mysterious Revelation* (Ithaca, N.Y.: Cornell University Press, 1963).
[22] Mark 9:2–8.
[23] Op. cit., p. 164.
[24] Ibid., p. 5.
[25] Mark 14:62. Neither Matthew nor Luke follows Mark at this point, and this raises a doubt as to the presence of the verse in the original text of Mark.

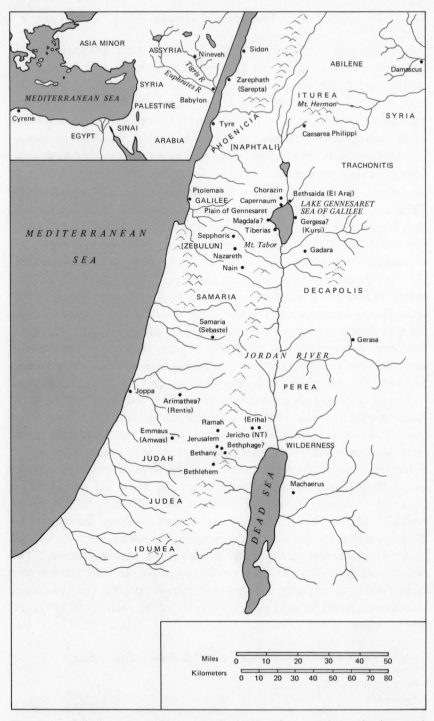

FIGURE 21 Palestine, the Synoptic Gospels. (Copyright 1949 Thomas Nelson Inc.)

[196]

designated Messiah at the time of his baptism, he looks forward to an appearance, or Parousia, of Jesus in Galilee, in which the fact of the Messiahship will be made known universally. Until that time it is to be proclaimed and maintained within the church. Mark never specifies the exact time of the Parousia, but he expects it within his own generation and probably feels that it is to be signalized by the abomination of desolation.[26]

There are several indications in the Gospel that Mark intends to speak to a situation in his own time which called for moral and physical strength on the part of Christians. Jesus is portrayed as an example to later martyrs, and the disproportionate space which is given to the passion narrative testifies to Mark's intention to speak about martyrdom. From the narrative of Peter's confession on to the crucifixion, well over half the book, the death of Jesus is discussed. It is Jesus' death and resurrection that is fundamental for this Gospel, which has frequently been called a passion narrative with a long introduction. The emphasis on the divine necessity of Jesus' death carries with it the corollary that the disciples must be prepared to meet the same fate, and Jesus' teaching makes this explicit. In 8:34, Jesus defines a disciple as one who, like him, is crucified, and he condemns those who are ashamed of him. In 10:35 ff., James and John are vying for the chief places in the kingdom, and Jesus says that it is necessary for them to "drink the cup" that he drinks—namely, the cup of martyrdom. Specific statements are included in the apocalyptic thirteenth chapter—betrayals, arrests, trials, and persecutions for the disciples. Peter's greatest failing is his denial under stress.[27] The emphasis on martyrdom would admirably fit the situation of Christians in Rome in the sixties. Nero had persecuted the church there in the early part of the decade, and it was then that Peter and Paul were probably executed. No Christian in Rome could feel secure during Nero's reign. The situation in Jerusalem was somewhat different, for Christians there were not being singled out for persecution, but the times were fraught with danger for all residents, as Mark 13 makes clear.

In discussing the nature of oral traditions, it was observed that the separate sayings and narratives would normally be preserved without geographical notes. Those who transmitted the stories in oral form had no interest in preserving information on where Jesus was when he said or did certain things. Geographical notes are, however, relevant in a continuous narrative like Mark. Since they were probably not available in his sources, he was

[26] See Mark 9:1.
[27] Mark 14:66 ff. See D. W. Riddle, "The Martyr Motif in the Gospel According to Mark," *Journal of Religion* 4: 397–410 (1924). Riddle points out that *denial* is a hated word in martyrologies.

obliged to supply them. Thus, his selection of locations is significant for an understanding of his Gospel. The striking fact is that Mark organizes his material about two locations: Galilee and Jerusalem. The ministry of Jesus takes place in Galilee; his death occurs in Jerusalem. Although Mark tells of only one trip to Jerusalem, he could have done it differently. There are indications that Jesus was familiar with the city and that he had acquaintances in nearby Bethany. In 14:49, Jesus claims that he has preached daily in the Temple. These minor traces demonstrate that the oral tradition permitted Mark to present several trips to Jerusalem, as John does. But for some reason Mark describes no other trips and places the bulk of Jesus' activity and teaching in Galilee. What is his reason for doing this? He seems to have thought of Galilee as the place where Jesus' work was secretly revealed and Jerusalem as the place of doom.[28] The initial proclamation of the kingdom by Jesus is in Galilee. It is only in Galilee that exorcism takes place, and Mark understands an exorcism as the clearest demonstration of Jesus' eschatological work, for it manifests his victory over Satan.[29] The eschatological significance of Galilee is further enhanced by the fact that, although the death of Jesus takes place in Jerusalem, the Parousia is expected in Galilee. The Gospel ends by pointing forward to the definite appearance of the risen Lord in Galilee. Mark succeeds in raising Galilee to a position of pre-eminence within the Christian tradition, and he does it at the expense of Jerusalem. This seems to be a conscious revolution of roles, for, in Jewish thought, Jerusalem is the holy city, and Galilee is despised and frequently called "Galilee of the Gentiles." According to the Book of Acts, Jerusalem had also been significant in the earliest Christian period and had served as the seat of an apostolic group that had tremendous prestige. In his evaluation of the two locations, Mark may have been deeply influenced by the oracle cited in 13:14, which called upon Christians to abandon Jerusalem, and he must have been keenly aware of the fate the city was to meet from the Romans. For whatever reason, he felt that God had rejected Jerusalem and chosen Galilee as the place of present and future revelation. W. Marxsen believes that Mark may actually be calling the church to assemble in Galilee to await the Parousia, in the conviction that Jesus is hidden there now and is soon to be revealed.[30]

[28] In spite of the redemptive significance of Jesus' death, Mark cannot portray it without tragedy.

[29] See Mark 3:23 ff.

[30] *Mark the Evangelist*, trans. James Boyce et al. (Nashville, Tenn.: Abingdon, 1969). See also Ernst Lohmeyer, *Galiläa und Jerusalem* (Göttingen: Vandenhoeck and Ruprecht, 1936).

In his own way, Mark has created a literary genre by using materials from the life and teaching of Jesus and organizing them in order to make them relevant for Christians in his own generation. The success of Mark is demonstrated by the fact that he had many imitators, some of whom not only adopted his format but also used his material.

Jesus, Mary, and Joseph in Egypt, fourth-century mosaic in Santa Maria Maggiore, Rome. (*Courtesy* Alinari-Art Reference Bureau.)

THE GOSPEL OF MATTHEW

The same Papias who wrote about the origin of Mark also spoke of Matthew. He said that Matthew collected the oracles in Hebrew and that others interpreted or translated them as they were able.[31] In speaking of oracles, Papias may have been thinking of a collection of Old Testament texts or a collection of Jesus' sayings, or he may have meant the Gospel. His second-century interpreters assumed that he was speaking of the Gospel, and so the name Matthew was given to the unknown author of the book.

[31] In Eusebius, *Church History* III, 39 : 16.

This meant that Papias was affirming Matthew to be the earliest Gospel and the others to be dependent on it. In addition, second-century writers felt that the Matthew of whom Papias spoke was that apostle mentioned in Matthew 9:9 and 10:3.[32] It is apparent that the second-century statements about the authorship of this Gospel rest upon Papias and that those writers select one of several possible interpretations of the original statement. Even if Papias thought that Matthew wrote the Gospel, he tells us nothing further about him, and he does not clearly identify him as an apostle. Although he speaks of a writing in Hebrew, all extant manuscripts of the Gospel are in Greek.[33] Many passages are virtually identical with Mark, and his language bears little trace of being a translation. In the final analysis, this Gospel must be regarded as anonymous.

If Matthew is dependent on Mark, as most scholars believe, we have a *terminus a quo* for its composition. Furthermore, one passage seems to look upon the destruction of the Jerusalem Temple as an event in the past. This is the parable of the wedding feast in 22:1–10, a story substantially the same as one in Luke 14 and possibly drawn from Q. In the Lukan version, a host invited some people to a banquet, and the guests declined. The host then issued a general invitation to the poor, maimed, and blind, and indeed compelled them to attend. In Matthew, the host is a king, who gave a wedding feast for his son. Some of the invited guests not only declined the invitation but murdered the king's servants. The king then sent troops to kill the murderers and burn their city, and he issued a general invitation, which was accepted by good and bad alike. One man who came was found to be unprepared and was dismissed. The background for both forms of the story is probably the Jewish rejection of Jesus and the consequent preaching to Gentiles. Luke's form, however, is that of the parable, and Matthew's is an allegory. The king is God, who gives a feast for his son, Jesus. The Jews refuse to come, and they murder God's messengers, the prophets and apostles. God then sends Roman troops, who defeat the Jews and burn Jerusalem. The Gentiles heed God's invitation, but not all are worthy, and some are cast out of the church.[34] If this interpretation is correct, the reference to the burning of the city is to the destruction of Jerusalem. Since the allegory

[32] Matthew is also mentioned in Mark 3:18 and Luke 6:15.

[33] There are versions of Matthew in other languages, but these are dependent upon the Greek.

[34] The man without a wedding garment represents a general Matthaean point of view. Matthew believes that the church is now composed of both good and bad and that the separation of the two groups will not occur until the end comes. See, for example, Matthew 13:47–50.

speaks of this event in the past tense, Matthew must be looking back upon it and must have written after A.D. 70.[35]

As a *terminus ad quem* we have the use of Matthew by Ignatius in A.D. 115. It is difficult to narrow these limits and determine a more precise date, but we may surmise that Matthew would not have used Mark until it had achieved some degree of authority in the church. Nor would Ignatius have used Matthew until it had a similar authority. It is probably safe to say that the Gospel of Matthew was written some time between A.D. 80 and 100. Because of its use by Ignatius and because of certain relationships with Jewish Christianity, Matthew's provenance is usually understood to be Antioch or, more broadly, Syria.[36]

Matthew followed the Markan framework for his Gospel but rearranged it at several points and mixed in a good deal of non-Markan material. He preferred a topical arrangement of the teaching material, collecting the teaching about the law in chapters 5–7, about missions in chapter 10, about the kingdom of God in chapter 13, and the eschaton (or end) in chapters 24–25. Some of the non-Markan material has parallels in Luke, but a good deal of it is unique to Matthew. Either the author took these sayings and narratives from some lost document or documents, or he knew them from the oral tradition, or he composed them himself. His most extensive unique material comes at the beginning and end of the book. The first two chapters tell the story of Jesus' birth and include a genealogy, which contains David and the Davidic kings of Judah among Jesus' ancestors. They tell of the visit of astrologers from the east at Jesus' birth, the escape of the family to Egypt, the massacre of the infants by Herod the Great, and the return of the family to Galilee after the king's death. In the last chapter, Matthew tells of the discovery of Jesus' empty tomb, an appearance of the risen Christ near the tomb, and one on a mountain in Galilee. Many scholars have found a religious significance in Matthew's literary structure. There are five great discourses,[37] most of which conclude with a formulalike statement, and Matthew may have intended the reader to be reminded of the five books of the Torah. On the other hand, this arrangement is not sufficiently clear to have been obvious to the average reader, and we cannot be certain that the parallelism was intended.

There is, however, sufficient indication in the Gospel that the author in-

---

[35] In his version of Mark's apocalyptic chapter, Matthew makes more explicit reference to the destruction of the Temple. See Matthew 24:15.

[36] See G. D. Kilpatrick, *The Origins of the Gospel According to St. Matthew* (Oxford: Oxford University Press, 1946).

[37] Namely, 5:1–7:29; 9:35–11:1; 13:1–58; 18:1–19:1; 24:1–26:2.

tended to present Jesus in the light of the Old Testament generally and the stories of Moses specifically. The birth of Jesus has affinities with the story of Moses: Herod's massacre of the children is reminiscent of the angelic killing of first-born Egyptian males; the flight to Egypt and the return is a repetition of the sojourn of Israelites in Egypt and the Exodus. Several times Jesus teaches from a mountain, as Moses delivered the Torah from Mount Sinai, and, in the Sermon on the Mount, Jesus' teaching is a commentary on the Mosaic commandments. Matthew's presentation of the transfiguration seems explicitly intended to present Jesus as the new Moses.[38] It is Moses' function as lawgiver which is most important in this regard, and this theme is expressly developed in the Sermon on the Mount (Matthew 5-7). In these chapters, Jesus speaks of various Mosaic commandments. Recall that the Pharisaic oral tradition developed as various scribes commented on the Torah. But the words that Matthew records are quite unlike those associated with the oral tradition, in which one searched for the proper application of Moses' words. Jesus emphatically contrasts his own commands with those of Moses: You have heard that it was said by the ancients, do not murder; but I say, do not be angry. You have heard, do not commit adultery; I say, do not lust. You have heard, do not commit perjury; I say, do not be insincere. In each case there is a reference to one of the Ten Commandments, and in each case Jesus makes his word antithetical to that of Moses. Matthew does not present Jesus as a follower of Moses, as one who develops and renews the commandments. He is the *new Moses* giving the *new Torah*. The life demanded by the new Torah is usually designated as the higher righteousness, a degree of obedience that exceeds that of the Pharisees. It is both deeper and more intensive than that which can be found in the best of Judaism. Matthew brings his book to a conclusion with a final presentation of Jesus as the new lawgiver. At the end, the risen Christ appears to his disciples on a mountain in Galilee and says to them: Go and baptize Gentiles, teaching them to obey my commandments.[39]

Although he emphasizes the newness of Jesus, Matthew sees him in the light of the old. He is new, but his character is best illuminated by the Moses of ancient times. More than the other Synoptic writers, Matthew relates Jesus to the Old Testament. He looks upon the Old Testament as a set of predictions of Jesus, so he sometimes interprets his life by an Old Testament passage and sometimes molds his story so that it conforms to the predictions. He regards the Old Testament as the word of God, the word

[38] See W. D. Davies, *The Sermon on the Mount* (Cambridge: Cambridge University Press, 1966), pp. 15 ff.

[39] Matthew 28 : 19-20.

that has its fulfillment only in Jesus. He, therefore, works with two seemingly paradoxical emphases in his presentation of Jesus: Jesus as continuous with the past and as discontinuous. The paradox is stated in Jesus' description of the ideal teacher of the law who becomes a disciple in the kingdom of heaven: " He is like a householder who can produce from his store both the new and the old."[40]

The old-new pattern relates to another complexity in Matthew's Gospel, namely the relationship of Gentiles and Jews. On the one side, Jesus appears as a devout Jew whose mission is not to abolish the Torah but to fulfill it.[41] On the other, he denounces the Pharisees in vehement terms.[42] About his own mission he says, "I was sent to the lost sheep of the house of Israel, and to them alone,"[43] and, in missionary instructions to the disciples, he forbids them to go to any but Israelites.[44] But in the concluding charge he commands the disciples to go to all nations (or Gentiles).[45] Even in chapter 15, where Jesus claims a mission only to Israel, he accedes to the request of a Canaanite woman and heals her daughter.[46] The paradox is a bold one: Jesus confines himself to Jews but is open to Gentiles.

Matthew's use of the Old Testament, his presentation of Jesus in the light of Moses, his teaching on law and on the relationship of Jews and Gentiles, all demonstrate his proximity to Judaism. This is also notable in a number of linguistic details. He refers to Jewish usages without explaining them. He has Jesus' questioners use Rabbinic formulations. He uses characteristically Hebraic phrases, such as *kingdom of heaven* rather than *kingdom of God*, and thus avoids the use of the divine name. In spite of these pro-Jewish tendencies, his strong anti-Jewish feeling is evident in the polemic against Pharisees and his condemnation at the crucifixion, in which he has the Jewish accusers say, "His blood be on us and on our children."[47] Most scholars take this two-sided emphasis to be characteristic of one who was raised a Jew and converted to Christianity. The Jewish background accounts for the author's deep interest in problems of the Torah, the Old Testament, Moses, and the meaning of Israel. His hostility to Judaism is accounted for by his belief that Jews had rejected the very one whom their Scriptures predicted. This animosity is typical of one who has consciously turned away

[40] Matthew 13 :52.
[41] See, e.g., Matthew 5 :17 ff.
[42] See Matthew 23.
[43] Matthew 15 :24.
[44] Matthew 10 :6.
[45] Matthew 28 :19. The Greek can be translated by either word.
[46] Matthew 15 :21–28.
[47] Matthew 27 :25.

from the religion of his fellows and embraced something new. He cannot understand why his fellow Jews could refuse the new things that he sees so clearly indicated in the Scriptures, that he and they both acknowledge as authoritative.

What is true of the author must also be true of the congregation for which he wrote. His interests in writing must have been dictated by the problems encountered in his own church—problems of applying the Torah in the light of the higher righteousness that Jesus demanded. Matthew and his congregation must be regarded as Jewish Christians. The continuing regard which later generations of Jewish Christians held for Matthew confirms this thesis. Nevertheless, Matthew's context was not a form of Jewish Christianity which denied the validity of the Gentile church, as Jesus' last words indicate. W. G. Kümmel correctly states:

> The author not only lives in a Jewish-Christian tradition but also wishes to offer to his readers the message about the omnipotence of the risen Jesus, and salvation through baptism, and keeping of his commandments (28:17 ff.) in a form which will reveal to them as Jewish Christians Jesus Christ as "the son of David, the son of Abraham" (1:1), whose "gospel of the kingdom will be preached throughout the whole world, as a testimony to all nations; and then the end will come" (24:14).[48]

In summary, the Gospel of Matthew was written by a Jewish Christian, probably living in Syria, sometime between A.D. 80–100.

THE GOSPEL OF LUKE

The third member of the Synoptic trio is also the first of a two-volume set. The Gospel of Luke and the Book of Acts are from the same author. Both are addressed to Theophilus,[49] and the prologue to Acts refers to the earlier work. An analysis of linguistic style makes common authorship of the two books a certainty, a fact which the earliest Christian commentators recognized. Any evaluation of the Gospel of Luke must recognize the unity of the two books and consider the material in Acts as having a direct bearing on the meaning of the Gospel.

[48] W. G. Kümmel, *Introduction to the New Testament*, trans. A. J. Mattill (Nashville: Abingdon, 1966), p. 82.

[49] Theophilus is not identified. He may have been a high-ranking government official, since Luke addresses him as "most excellent" or "your excellency." The name means "lover of God," and the author may have intended to designate his potential readers by the phrase.

A miniature of St. Luke from a manuscript written in gold, c. A.D. 800, under the influence of Charlemagne. (*Courtesy* the Trustees of the British Museum, London.)

Like the other Synoptic writers, the author did not identify himself in the text. Irenaeus was the first to write about its authorship, and he said it was written by Luke, a companion of Paul.[50] The Muratorian Canon (c. A.D. 200) refers to the author as Luke, a physician and companion of Paul, and states that he was not an eyewitness of the things he described in the Gospel. In both references, the Luke in question is the one mentioned in Colossians 4:14, Philemon 24, and II Timothy 4:11. Colossions and Philemon state that Luke was present with Paul when the letters were written. We have seen that both were written at about the same time. The reference in II Timothy, a pseudo-Pauline letter, probably has no historical significance. From the time of Irenaeus on, the church attributed the authorship of both Luke and Acts to the companion of Paul, but many modern scholars doubt the validity of the traditon. They point out that Acts, which contains a life of Paul, is not fully consistent with what we know from his letters and shows little awareness of his major theological viewpoints. It is thought that a companion of Paul would have known him better and described him differently. Many other scholars accept the tradition of Lukan authorship, because they find it hard to understand the motivation for a false attribution in this case. There was a strong tendency in the early centuries to attribute apostolic authorship to the treasured books of the church. If one was not really sure who wrote the Gospel, he probably would have assumed it to be the work of an apostle or at least of someone better-known than Luke, who is, after all, fairly obscure. Furthermore, authorship by one such as Luke is consistent with the prologue to the Gospel, which implies that the author was not an eyewitness of Jesus' life. There are also some interesting sections in Acts where the author seems to identify himself with the major partici-pants in the story. These are called "we" sections, because in them the author uses the first person pronoun instead of the more usual third person. The author may have used a diary written by a participant. But if he did, he was careful to rewrite it in his own style and leave the "we" standing. It seems easier to conclude that the author is quoting from his own diary at these points and that he actually was associated with Paul on several trips. To the argument that Acts does not adequately represent Paul's life or thought, we may say that Luke was not constantly with Paul and was writing at a time when the issues that engaged Paul were no longer paramount points of dis-cussion in the church. Although the arguments for Lukan authorship seem sufficient, it makes very little difference in our understanding or evaluation of his work. In the prologue to the Gospel, he has identified himself as a

[50] *Against Heresies* III, 1:1.

Christian of the second generation, as one who consulted and studied other documents, and as one who intended to tell the story of his religion in an orderly fashion. His tendency to favor Gentile Christianity probably means that he was not a Jew. To know this much is to know a good deal, and the supplying of a name and a limited contact with Paul adds very little. We may call the author Luke, but we should not categorically identify him as the medical companion of Paul.

In the prologue to the Gospel, Luke states that he has consulted other documents about Jesus. Our theory of Synoptic relationships says that he not only consulted but actually used both Mark and Q. His use of Mark means that he wrote after A.D. 70. In his version of the apocalyptic chapter he makes explicit reference to the Roman conquest of Jerusalem:

> But when you see Jerusalem encircled by armies, then you may be sure that her destruction [desolation] is near . . . for there will be great distress in the land and a terrible judgement upon this people. They will fall at the sword's point; they will be carried captive into all countries; and Jerusalem will be trampled down by foreigners until their day has run its course.[51]

The word translated *destruction* is the same as that in Mark's "abomination of desolation." Luke is interpreting Mark's passage so that the desolation is clearly understood to be the fall of Jerusalem. His reference to the encircling armies and the prisoners of war must be based upon his knowledge of the actual events of A.D. 70. Nevertheless, he does not make the fall of Jerusalem the end of all things, for he has Jesus warn his listeners to be wary of people who claim that "the day is upon us."[52] It is nearly impossible to set a firm *terminus ad quem* for the Lukan writings, for no writer used them before A.D. 140. Marcion is said to have had an abbreviated version of Luke, and Justin certainly used it. Its use by both shows that it was highly regarded by the middle of the second century. The most significant evidence relating to a *terminus ad quem* is the author's ignorance of the Pauline letters. He has no quotation from them, never mentions the fact that Paul wrote letters, and composes a number of Pauline speeches that allude to none of the chief ideas in the letters. In addition, he narrates a council meeting in Jerusalem, which Paul also wrote about in Galatians.[53] But Luke had obviously not read Galatians, for his description is at odds with it at a number of significant points. We have previously ascertained that Paul's letters were collected and published about A.D. 90, and thus we may assume that Luke wrote both

[51] Luke 21 : 20, 23–24.
[52] Luke 21 : 8.
[53] See Acts 15 : 1–29 and Galatians 2 : 1–10.

volumes of his work prior to that date. We would not err very far if we set the date for Luke and Acts at A.D. 80–85.

The location of the author is almost impossible to determine. Eusebius[54] puts him in Antioch, and he does display a keen interest in affairs there. But if Matthew is from Syria, Luke could not be, and Ignatius makes no reference to Luke. Other suggestions have been made, including Caesarea, Alexandria, and Rome, but no certainty is possible.

Although Luke uses some of the same sources as Matthew, he edits them in quite a different way. He regularly follows Mark's sequence, but he uses far less of his material than Matthew did, and he arranges it in three large blocks (3:1–6:19; 8:4–9:50; 18:15–24:11). In between, he inserts material from Q and from his own special tradition. He has a narrative about the birth of Jesus, affirming the Davidic ancestry and the virgin birth. But these narratives are not those of Matthew and could not have come from the same source. The genealogy is totally different—even Jesus' grandfather is not the same. At the end of the Gospel, Luke includes a series of resurrection appearances in Jerusalem and its environs; he seems to know nothing of appearances in Galilee. In the passion narrative, Luke weaves material from Mark with some from his own special source and conveys quite a different impression of Jesus' trial.

The character of Luke's writing may be seen in his adoption and modification of sources and his editorial comments. Of major importance, however, is the fact that Luke wrote two books. Although each book has its own integrity, the two most have formed a unity in the author's conception. When he writes that he proposes to provide Theophilus with authentic knowledge about the things of which he had been informed (1:4), he means to tell not only about what Jesus did and said (Acts 1:1), but also about the early history of the church. The unity of the two books is displayed in their overlapping. The Gospel ends with a disappearance of the risen Christ,[55] which is referred to as an ascension in Acts 1:2. The first narrative in Acts is a description of the ascension, probably a repetition of that in the Gospel.[56]

Luke's work has frequently been described as a history of salvation. His interest in history is visible not only from his production of two books but also from his statement of purpose: to write an orderly account (Luke 1:3)—that is, to write "in a logically unbroken sequence."[57] Although it is not a

---

[54] *Church History* III, 4:6.

[55] Luke 24:51.

[56] Acts 1:9.

[57] M. S. Enslin, *The Literature of the Christian Movement* (New York: Harper-Row, 1956), p. 409.

Giotto, *The Kiss of Judas*, Scrovegni Chapel, Padua. (*Courtesy* Alinari-Art Reference Bureau.)

strictly chronological account, it is one that takes history seriously. The author's eschatological outlook appears to be the major reason for his interest in history. With Luke we have none of the eschatological fervor of the early Paul or even of Mark. To be sure, Mark, in his apocalyptic chapter, meant to put a damper on enthusiastic proclamation of an imminent end, but Luke does it even more forcefully. Both Mark and Luke advise their readers to beware of those who claim to be the Christ, but Luke adds a caution about those who proclaim that the end time has arrived.[58] According to Luke, Jesus told the parable of the pounds,[59] because some people wrongly felt that he was about to bring in the kingdom. When Pharisees ask Jesus when the kingdom will come, he answers that there will be no visible signs, and he says to the disciples: "The time will come when you will long to see one of the days of the Son of Man, but you will not see it. They will say to you,

[58] Luke 21 :8.
[59] Luke 19 : 11–27.

'Look! There!' and 'Look! Here!' Do not go running off in pursuit."[60] Luke is unique in his emphasis on patience, a prime virtue for people waiting for a consummation which is not imminent. The expectation of a delayed fulfillment is characteristic of Luke. But, as Henry Cadbury observed, early Christian writers generally did not take an extreme position on eschatological matters, neither proclaiming an immediate end nor a continuing history. The difference among them lies in "their skillful adjustment between these extremes as regards imminence rather than in their acceptance or rejection of apocalyptic as a whole."[61] Nevertheless, Luke moves in the direction of a delayed consummation, and this tendency forces him to take history seriously. He must treat the history of the church as part of God's entire plan of salvation, not as some inexplicable but brief interim.

Hans Conzelmann has recently produced an analysis of Luke and Acts as a history of salvation.[62] He believes that Luke understood history as made up of three periods: the time of Israel, the time of Jesus, and the time of the church. The time of Israel is one of the law and the prophets, and it extends to John the Baptist. Luke makes this explicit: "Until John, it was the Law and the prophets; since then, there is the good news of the kingdom of God, and everyone forces his way in."[63] As the last man of the time of Israel, John is geographically separated from Jesus, and he does not preach the coming of the kingdom. He cannot, because only Jesus possesses knowledge about the kingdom. The second period is that of Jesus, which Conzelmann calls "the center of history." It is a special time of salvation, characterized by the departure of the devil at Luke 4:13 and concluded by his return at 22:3. During this period, Luke portrays the ministry of Jesus, drawing on the sources at his disposal and filling in his outline with the same kinds of material that Mark and Matthew used. The time of Jesus includes three subdivisions. In the first, Jesus is active in Galilee, assembling the witnesses who are to convey the traditions to the later writers. During this period, Jesus also proclaims the kingdom to Israel and demands a decision about it. The second part consists of Jesus' trip to Jerusalem, which consumes the entire middle section of the Gospel, 9:51–19:28. The death of Jesus is constantly in view here, and the entire section is intended to express the divine necessity of Jesus' suffering. The third section tells of Jesus' arrest, trial, crucifixion, resurrection, and ascension. Strictly speaking, this is a transition section, for the devil is active once again, entering into Judas to bring about his be-

[60] Luke 17:22–23.
[61] *The Making of Luke-Acts* (London: S.P.C.K., 1958), p. 290.
[62] *The Theology of St. Luke*, trans. G. Buswell (New York: Harper-Row, 1960).
[63] Luke 16:16.

trayal of Jesus. Jesus' death is described as a judicial murder by the Jews. It has no redemptive significance but is part of God's plan and serves as the means of Jesus' resurrection and glorification. The final period of history is that of the church, a period marked by the presence of the spirit, which comes upon Jesus' disciples at Pentecost.[64] During this time the Lord is in heaven, and his church is on earth, preaching those things communicated to it by the eyewitnesses. The church takes over its heritage from Israel and, indeed, becomes the new Israel by virtue of its adherence to the Torah and Temple in its earliest days. The church lives amid persecution and must learn to endure it. Endurance is made possible by the expectation that the time of salvation, once known in the time of Jesus, will return. This is the message which the church preaches: Once again there will come a time when the devil will be inactive.

Although Luke is vitally interested in history, we should not expect him to write as a modern historian might. He is interested in the past, but he is no antiquarian. He looks upon the past and the present as the unfolding of the divine plan of salvation. In the final analysis, his major interest is in the church of his own time and the problems it faces in maintaining a continuity with the past and living in the expectation of a delayed consummation. His solution to these problems is to affirm that the conditions of the past will once again manifest themselves in the future, though that future is not imminent.

A few additional emphases in Luke's writing must now be observed. He understands Christianity as a universal religion. It is true that he limits the activity of Jesus to Israel and that of the disciples to Jerusalem, but this is for a particular historical time. After the first days of the church, it has become clear that the Jews have rejected Christianity and have no more share in salvation history. The people of God are now the Gentiles. Luke's sympathies are with Paul, whose universalistic tendencies are made emphatic in Acts. Before a crowd of Jews in Pisidian Antioch, Paul and Barnabas boldy state: "It was necessary that the word of God should be declared to you first. But since you reject it and thus condemn yourselves as unworthy of eternal life, we now turn to the Gentiles."[65]

Luke also has a lively interest in classes of people who are usually objects of discrimination, namely the poor and women. His interest in the poor, however, is not so much a pity for them as it is a condemnation of the self-assurance of the rich. He includes in the teaching of Jesus as much material about the duty of the rich toward the poor as he does words of assurance

[64] See Acts 2 : 1.
[65] Acts 13 : 46. The same statement is made on two other occasions. See Acts 18 : 6; 28 : 28.

to the poor. He seems to adopt an equation found in contemporary Judaism and probably widely adopted by Christians in which poverty is understood to be the inevitable result of piety.

There is also a strong note of optimism pervading Luke's writing. The expectation of judgment is not absent, but the hopeful future is a distinctive emphasis in Luke. Jesus is pictured as basically kind and a doer of good deeds. God is giving and forgiving. The kingdom of God is a gift to be sought, not feared. The birth of Jesus is greeted with great joy by angels,[66] and at the end of the Gospel the disciples are filled with joy and spend their time praising God in the Temple.[67]

Luke is not easily categorized. He displays no particularistic tendencies except those that we might identify broadly as Gentile Christian. He is interested in the function of the church but not in its organization, ministry, or authority. He does not explicitly condemn a variant Christianity except that which expected an imminent kingdom. Although he displays no deep understanding of Paul, he nevertheless sides with him in his basic universalistic thrust. We probably should count Luke as standing within the broad tradition of Pauline Christianity.

---

[66] Luke 2 : 10.
[67] Luke 24 : 52–53.

Chapter Seven

—————◆◆◆—————

Other Gospels

The Gospel of John

A fourth attempt to publish the major aspects of Christian faith in terms of the ministry and teaching of Jesus is the Gospel of John. In certain respects this Fourth Gospel is similar to the first three. It contains some of the same material about the deeds of Jesus and concludes with a narrative of the trial, death, and resurrection. Like Mark, it tells of John the Baptist, of a feeding of the multitude, and of a walking on the water. The story of Jesus' cleansing the Temple is included but placed earlier in John. There are a few places where the verbal similarity between Mark and John is fairly close, and a number of Synoptic sayings are placed within John's larger discourses. In spite of the similarities, the reader is overwhelmingly impressed with the contrast between John and the Synoptics. The differences are intentionally designated by our terminology, in which the word *Synoptic* specifically excludes John, and by a popular habit of calling the Fourth Gospel the spiritual Gospel.[1] The contrast is evident from the very beginning of the Gospel. Whereas Mark begins with the ministry of John the Baptist and Matthew and Luke with Jesus' birth, the Fourth Gospel starts with a hymn to the *Logos* and follows that with the Baptist's testimony to Jesus. John has no story of Jesus' birth, no narrative of the baptism, no temptation story, and no exorcisms. Several Johannine narratives have no Synoptic counterparts: for example, the story of Jesus' turning water into wine and his resuscitation of Lazarus. At the last supper, which is not a Passover meal in John, Jesus does not serve bread and wine; rather, he washes the disciples' feet. Even in narratives dealing with Synoptic incidents, John presents a different picture. Jesus is arrested by the Jewish police and a cohort of Roman soldiers. He is tried by two high priests and by Pilate. There are

---

[1] Clement of Alexandria, in the third century, seems to be the first to use this expression. He says: "But that John, last of all, conscious that the outward facts had been set forth in the Gospels, was urged by his disciples, and divinely moved by the Spirit, composed a spiritual Gospel." In Eusebius, *Church History* VI, 14:7.

The opening of the Gospel of John, eighth century. (*Courtesy* the Master and Fellows of Corpus Christi College, Cambridge.)

differences in the location and, perhaps, the duration of Jesus' ministry. Instead of the Synoptic pattern of a ministry in Galilee followed by death in Jerusalem, John places most of Jesus' ministry in Jerusalem and has him make several round trips between the two. The Synoptics had mentioned only one Passover, the one at Jesus' death. John has three, and he implies that Jesus' ministry covered more than two years. The difference in the style of Jesus' teaching is easily observed. Instead of the Synoptic parables, apophthegms, and brief dominical sayings, we meet several long and involved discourses. These have a characteristic pattern, which begins with a question posed by Jesus. Jesus replies to the question but is misunderstood. He then corrects his interlocutor and launches into a long speech, which is frequently inappropriate to the original subject. Throughout the discourses he employs words that have both an obvious meaning and a deeper significance. Often, the miracle stories are used as points of departure for long discourses of questionable relevance. The subjects of the discourses are also different. In the Synoptics, Jesus speaks of the kingdom, repentance, and the law; but in John, he speaks of eternal life, the contrast of true and false, light and dark, good and evil, believing and not believing. He frequently speaks of his unique relationship with God. In brief, the Fourth Gospel employs a vocabulary familiar to Gnostic Christianity and to general Hellenistic thought.[2]

The resemblances and contrasts between John and the Synoptics raise the question of their relationship. On this question scholars are deeply divided. The use of Matthew is not seriously entertained, but many scholars feel that John probably used Mark and may have used Luke. C. K. Barrett, for example, feels that John's use of Mark is shown by the fact that the two gospels share a sequence of ten events.[3] Barrett's evidence, however, is not so strong as one might like. The ten events cited are not found in a continuous section of either gospel but are interrupted by material that is not shared. Of the ten, two are geographical notes, which have no bearing, because the overall geographical scheme is not the same in Mark and John. Four are incidents within the passion narrative, several versions of which must have been the common possession of Christians from an early date. The material about the work of John the Baptist should not be regarded as the same story, since the character and function of the Baptist are not the same in John and Mark.[4] The confession of Peter in John bears no resemblance to that in

---

[2] The best analysis of the ideological background of this Gospel is C. H. Dodd, *The Interpretation of the Fourth Gospel* (Cambridge: Cambridge University Press, 1953).

[3] *The Gospel According to St. John* (London: S.P.C.K., 1960), pp. 34-45.

[4] In John, the Baptist is portrayed as the first Christian confessor. There seems to be,

Mark. This leaves two incidents: the feeding of the multitude and the walking on the water. These occur in both gospels in the same order, and there are a few common expressions in the narratives.[5] But it is very precarious to assume literary dependence on the basis of a scant nineteen verses where

The Sea of Galilee. (*Courtesy* Israel Government Tourist Office, Atlanta, Georgia.)

verbal correspondence is slight. It is possible to explain the similarities between John and the Synoptics by assuming a dependence on a continuing oral tradition. The Christian community did not cease to transmit narratives

---

in the Fourth Gospel, a serious attempt to limit the sphere of the Baptist. This is probably due to conflicts between Christians and the followers of the Baptist. There is sufficient evidence that a Baptist group existed in the early centuries. Acts 18:25 and 19:1–7 speaks of such a group. The *Clementine Recognitions* preserve a notice about the existence of a group in the third century which claimed that John was the Messiah. A small sect of Mandaeans exists today, and it preserves some literature which speaks of John as the Christ and Jesus as the false prophet. It is precisely the belief in the Messiahship of John which the Fourth Gospel attacks.

[5] It may be significant that the two stories in Mark form the first of a pair of doublets; Mark 6:34–7:37 is parallel to Mark 8:1–26.

and sayings in oral form the moment written gospels appeared, and even in the second century Papias said he preferred oral to written accounts.[6] Furthermore, the alterations in the Fourth Gospel narratives are precisely the kind we would expect in a highly developed oral tradition. Although it is not possible to be certain, it seems more likely that John did not use the Synoptics as sources for his Gospel.

But John was not entirely or even directly dependent upon the oral tradition. There are a number of rough spots in the Gospel which indicate that the author was joining together some written material. These rough spots create certain geographical and chronological difficulties in the text. In chapter 5 Jesus is in Jerusalem and in chapter 6 in Galilee, but no trip has taken place. In chapter 10 there is a controversy over a remark Jesus had made six months earlier. In 14:31, Jesus invites his disciples to depart, but the departure does not occur until 18:1. There is also an inconsistency in the enumeration of Jesus' deeds. In 7:21 he claims that he has performed only one Sabbath miracle, but John had recorded others. John 2:21 calls the miracle at Cana the first sign, but 2:23 speaks of signs in the plural. In 4:45 there is a reference to all that Jesus had done, but 4:54 says he had only accomplished two signs. To know that John used written sources is not to know what sources, for none of them is now extant. Bultmann has suggested three major sources.[7] One is the passion narrative, which is not that of the Synoptics. A second is a collective of signs, which partially overlapped the Synoptic miracle stories and included the calling of the disciples, the miracle at Cana, the story of the Samaritan woman, the healing of the ruler's son, the feeding of the multitude, the walking on water, the healing of the impotent man and of the man born blind, and the raising of Lazarus. The third source was a collection of revelation discourses, which included the prologue, a discourse with Nicodemus, and discourses on water, testimony, bread, and the good shepherd. It concluded with the long speech in John 14–16 and Jesus' prayer in 17. This means that almost all of the long discourses of Jesus are from a single source. It goes without saying that the evangelist has rearranged and assimilated his sources and has sprinkled them with his own comments. It must also be noted that this analysis does not put the evangelist in immediate contact with oral tradition, although it is still possible to assume that the authors of his sources drew on it.

---

[6] In Eusebius, *Church History* III, 39:4.

[7] *The Gospel of John*, trans. G. R. Beasley-Murray et. al. (Philadelphia, Pa.: Westminster, 1971). An excellent analysis of Bultmann's work can be found in D. M. Smith, *The Composition and Order of the Fourth Gospel* (New Haven, Conn.: Yale University Press, 1965).

A recognition of sources utilized by the fourth evangelist may be of significant help in solving some problems relating to the character of the Gospel. Allusion has been made to the use of certain Gnostic ideas in the Gospel. In particular, there is a tendency to portray Jesus in something approaching Docetic terms. Ernst Käsemann has forthrightly called attention to this element in the Fourth Gospel, making clear, however, that the brand of Docetism there "is present in a still naïve, unreflected form and it has not yet been recognized by the Evangelist or his community."[8] It is difficult to read this Gospel without asking whether Jesus is human or not. It is true that he performs fewer miracles than in the Synoptics, but they are more stupendous and are motivated only by Jesus' intention to authenticate himself. He weeps at the distress of Lazarus' sister, but he purposefully waits until Lazarus has died and been dead four days before visiting the family, and then he raises him from the dead. The delay is said to be good for faith. Jesus' discourses frequently center on himself, and he demands that his hearers believe that he is the Son of God. He claims to be one with the Father and a visible manifestation of the Father. He is the light, the true bread, the water of life, the resurrection and the life, the shepherd, the door of the sheep, and the way to eternal life. He has supernatural insight and is completely self-motivated. He never consorts with sinners. The discourse source and the signs source are consistent in this respect, for they both present Jesus in something like Docetic terms.

The prologue to the Gospel (1:1–18) illustrates the point of view of the discourse source. The evangelist used it but added some notes on John the Baptist (1:6–8, 15). Bultmann believes that the original source was a Gnostic hymn to John the Baptist as the *Logos* and that the fourth evangelist felt it necessary to explain to the reader that the Baptist was only a witness to Jesus, the real *Logos*. Although *Logos* is customarily translated as "word," its essential meaning is by no means clear. *Logos* was used by Stoics to designate a divine element present in all men. Philo used it as a mediator between God and man and as a translation of the Hebrew Wisdom, a personal agent of God in the creation of the world.[9] It is probably this last which is intended by John 1, for the prologue is a creation story. The evangelist uses this pre-Christian hymn to picture Jesus as the divine being whose existence antedates the world itself. He was present with God, dwelt with God, and was God. All things were created through him. Light was present with *Logos* and overcame the darkness of precreation chaos. The *Logos* entered

---

[8] *The Testament of Jesus* (Philadelphia, Pa.: Fortress Press, 1968), p. 26.
[9] See Proverbs 8:22–31.

the world he created but was not recognized. Indeed, the *Logos* became flesh. This ringing affirmation of the fleshly nature of Jesus has usually been understood as a denial of Docetic thought. But what is really meant by flesh? The following phrase says: we beheld his glory. We can only determine the meaning of this by asking what it was that Jesus revealed, and we have seen that the remainder of the discourse source presents a far-from-human-Jesus. If we ask which is fundamental for the discourse source, the glory of the heavenly Christ seen as Jesus, or the true humanity of Jesus, the answer is clearly the former. This source falls heavily on the side of a glorified Christ, a pre-existent divine being who enters the world with no diminution of his divine nature. The flesh is real, but it is only the means by which humans are able to behold the true glory of God's Son. To be sure, this is not a full-blown Docetism, for the reality of the flesh is not denied, but it surely moves in that direction.

In certain respects the passion source differed from the other two. At two points it seems consciously to reject Docetic implications. Just before he died on the cross, Jesus said, "I thirst" (19:28). And in 19:17 a point is made of the fact that Jesus carried his own cross. In the Synoptics, Simon of Cyrene carried the cross partway, and this led some Docetists to claim that it was he who was crucified and not Jesus.[10] The passion source leaves no doubt that Jesus really died.

The presence of Docetic tendencies in the discourse source and of certain anti-Docetic notes in the passion source creates a bewildering problem in the Fourth Gospel. Where does the evangelist himself stand? Probably somewhere between. He does not really doubt that Jesus has come in the flesh, and he believes the flesh is real and that Jesus was a historical person. It is significant to him that Jesus has really come, but the significance is that in him humans beheld the glory which properly belonged to God's Son. Käsemann is probably right in referring to the author's position as a naïve and unreflective Docetism, but the emphasis should be placed on his naïveté at this point. He probably has not faced the real implications that a strong Docetic movement can make clear.

Another serious problem in the Fourth Gospel is its attitude toward Judaism. In all of the sources there are signs of a Jewish background, and some material of the evangelist's composition indicates an acquaintance with Jewish ideas and procedures. C. H. Dodd is impressed with this quality, and he states: "The Fourth Evangelist, even more definitely than the Synoptics, is developing his doctrine of the person and work of Jesus with conscious

[10] See Irenaeus, *Against Heresies* I, 24:4.

The Resurrection of Lazarus, fresco, fourth century, Catacomb of the Via Latina, Rome. (*Courtesy* Pontifical Commission for Sacred Archives, Rome.)

reference to Jewish messianic belief."[11] Over against this, however, there is a good deal of hostility toward Jews in the Gospel. Jesus' opponents are styled as Jews, rarely as Pharisees, Sadducees, or simply individuals. J. Louis Martyn accounts for this paradoxical attitude by suggesting that there was a proximity between the evangelist and the Jewish synagogue.[12] Martyn further thinks that in John's locality certain Jews were being excluded from the synagogue because they believed Jesus to be the Messiah. Other Jews, represented by Nicodemus, secretly held the belief and remained within the synagogue. These all held to an understanding of Jesus as the Mosaic-type Messiah, but John was intent on proclaiming Jesus as the Son of man.[13] By this he understood Jesus as the Messiah of Jewish expectation but more than that, as the heavenly man, as the glorified divine being who has come to earth and returned to heaven. The influence of the local synagogue may have given to John (or his sources) an acquaintance with Jewish ways, but

---

[11] Op. cit., p. 92.

[12] *History and Theology in the Fourth Gospel* (New York: Harper & Row, 1968).

[13] Martyn says that the author of the signs source also believed that Jesus was the Mosaic-type Messiah. Ibid., p. 108.

the practice of excluding Christians created a polarity in the community and increased hostility between the two groups.

It is not likely that we can identify the author of any of the sources or the evangelist himself. Since the last quarter of the second century, it has been believed that the entire Gospel was the composition of John bar Zebedee, but it is difficult to accept this testimony for several reasons.[14] The son of Zebedee was an eyewitness, but an eyewitness would not have found it necessary to depend on written sources. Neither John, nor his brother James, nor Zebedee are even mentioned in the Fourth Gospel, except in chapter 21, a late addition. All the Synoptic narratives which have John as a participant are missing. Although John is, according to the Synoptics, from the north, the Fourth Gospel has no interest in Galilee. The world of thought in which the Gospel moves is not the world of a Galilean fisherman. Furthermore, until late in the second century there was some reluctance to accept the Gospel. Many people thought that it was written by a Gnostic, and Irenaeus even knew some Christians who still rejected it.[15] It is difficult to account for such widespread doubt about the validity of the Fourth Gospel if it had been generally regarded as the work of an apostle. If it had not been so regarded earlier, where did the later writers get their information?[16]

The earliest attempt to identify the author is in John 21, a late addition to the Gospel. The unknown author of chapter 21 claims that the first twenty chapters were written by the "beloved disciple." The "beloved disciple" is the nameless man who figures into three Johannine narratives: he was present at the last supper; he received Jesus' mother at the crucifixion; he, with Peter, discovered the empty tomb.[17] In the body of the Fourth Gospel he is never named and is not designated as the author. Nor does chapter 21 give him a name. He must be either one of the unnamed disciples in 21:2 or else one of the sons of Zebedee. It is not clear that the author of John 21 thought the evangelist was John bar Zebedee, but if he did not we are in no position to name the "beloved disciple."

We cannot agree that the author of the Fourth Gospel was the son of Zebedee, and the reference to the "beloved disciple" is not helpful. Nevertheless, we should be able to account for the traditional attribution to John.

[14] The tradition was first recorded by Irenaeus, *Against Heresies III,* 1:2.
[15] Ibid., III, 11:12.
[16] It is possible, but by no means certain, that Mark 10:39 embodies an authentic tradition to the effect that John and James had been martyred during the sixties.
[17] John 13:23; 19:26; 20:2. According to Bultmann's source analysis, all three of these are from the hand of the evangelist.

It may be possible to assert that second-century writers, such as Irenaeus, had confused John the apostle with the author of the Johannine epistles.[18] This view is attractive, because of the linguistic similarities between the Fourth Gospel and I John. But it breaks apart when we recognize the ideological differences between the two writings. The first letter of John was written in reaction against a group of Docetists, but the evangelist in the Fourth Gospel took no hard line against such people. In the final analysis, although modern scholarship has produced a number of elaborate and fascinating theories about the authorship of this gospel, we must admit our complete ignorance on this score.

In 1935, a small fragment of the Gospel of John turned up in Egypt. Although minute, its significance is great. The fragment is almost certainly not the original, but it must be a very early copy. It was produced in the middle of the second century and, thus, sets for us a *terminus ad quem* for the Gospel at about A.D. 130. The determination of the *terminus a quo* is not so easy. If we could be sure that the evangelist or his sources used the Synoptics, the task would not be so difficult. Still, whatever contact the sources had with the Christian oral tradition must have come at a fairly late stage. Generally speaking, the Synoptics are related to a more primitive form of the tradition than is John.[19] If the Jewish practice of excluding Christians from the synagogues plays a part in the background of the Gospel, then A.D. 80 becomes a *terminus a quo*.[20] Influences from Docetic thought would tend to put the Gospel toward the end of the first century at the earliest. Thus, any date from A.D. 80–130 would be appropriate. The place of writing is not recoverable, but Ephesus and Alexandria are the most frequently chosen alternatives.

In the third and subsequent centuries, the Gospel of John had a tremendous impact on the church. People felt that it contrasted with the other gospels in that it went directly to the heart of the matter to present the reality of the Christ. The evangelist must have had something like this in mind as he wrote. He was not so interested in matters of historical fact as he was in affirming that in Jesus Christ we have a direct revelation of God. He presents a unique form of Christianity. He has not neglected the Jewish background and preserves an awareness of it. But he has moved away from it to a significant degree and has embodied ideas from non-Jewish sources.

[18] See p. 150 f.

[19] Although ancient testimony accepts authorship by John, it looks upon this Gospel as the last of the four. See Clement of Alexandria in Eusebius, *Church History* VI, 14:7 and the Muratorian Canon.

[20] See Martyn, op. cit.

He is aware of Gnostic ideology and moves toward it far enough to present a naïvely Docetic picture of the Christ. Because this Gospel occupies a unique position in the spectrum of early Christianity, we must place it in its own category as a representative of Johannine Christianity.[21]

Giotto, *The Presentation of the Virgin in the Temple*, Scrovegni Chapel, Padua. The painting was inspired by the Book of James. (*Courtesy* Alinari-Art Reference Bureau.)

THE BOOK OF JAMES[22]

The church never canonized but, nevertheless, deeply revered the so-called Book of James. We know it now from one third-century manuscript and

---

[21] We shall join with it the Johannine Epistles, recognizing that the same author did not write both but also recognizing that the two shared a certain body of ideas.

[22] For an English translation, see Edgar Hennecke, *New Testament Apocrypha*, ed. W. Schneemelcher, trans. R. McL. Wilson (Philadelphia, Pa.: Westminster, 1963), Vol. 1, pp. 374–388.

from several later fragments. It has influenced popular Christian piety almost as much as the canonical gospels have.

The Book of James is properly called a protogospel, for it deals with events prior to the beginning of the other gospels and ends with the birth of Jesus. In it Joachim and Anna are introduced as a childless couple. For this reason, Joachim was not allowed to make a sacrifice in the Jerusalem Temple. He went into the wilderness to fast for forty days and forty nights, and his wife Anna went into her garden to pray. An angel appeared to her and promised that she would conceive, and Anna vowed to dedicate the child to God. The child was called Mary, and at three she was taken to the Temple to be brought up by the priests. When she was twelve, the widower Joseph, an old man with sons, was chosen to be her husband. He considered Mary to be sacred and preserved her virginal state. When she became pregnant, however, Joseph was afraid that his neglect had allowed an adulterer to seduce her. But the priests gave both of them a trial by bitter water, and they survived. In response to the census decree of Augustus, Joseph went to Bethlehem, and Jesus was born there in a cave.

The author draws heavily on the infancy narratives of Matthew and Luke, quoting large segments of them. The book may have been known by Justin in the second century, and if so it should be dated between A.D. 100 and 150. In any case, it was known in the third century, so could not be written later than A.D. 200.

The title, which comes at the end, refers to the author as James, a half brother of Jesus. But this James would not have been alive during the second century. In addition, the book includes erroneous references to certain Jewish features. For example, nothing is known of the exclusion of a childless man from the Temple or of the rearing of a virgin in the Temple. James would not have committed such errors. Furthermore, in the body of the book, the author never indicates that he has a firsthand acquaintance with the persons in the narrative. Yet, according to his own claim, he would have been one of the sons of Joseph by a former marriage. We can only conclude that this James was not the author and that the author was an anonymous Gentile Christian of the second century.

The book appears to be a unified composition rather than a collection of oral or written traditions.[23] It is a single story told meaningfully and in chronological order. It is probably the product of pious speculation on the birth of Jesus. Three basic features in the narrative may indicate the purpose.

In the first place, the major emphasis is on Mary herself. Her miraculous

---

[23] A few sections, however, appear to have been added to the original work. See Hennecke, op. cit., I, 372 f.

birth and upbringing in the Temple are reminiscent of the story of Samuel in the Old Testament. Her virginity is especially cared for by the priests and by Joseph. The author emphasizes the distance between Mary and Joseph. When Joseph sets out for Bethlehem, he debates with himself whether to register her in the census as his wife or his daughter, for she is in fact neither. The perpetual virginity of Mary is strongly implied in the document. Here we have an elaboration of the Synoptic infancy narratives in the direction of the elevation of celibacy. Thus the focus of attention subtly shifts from Jesus to Mary, and the reader is called upon to agree that the life most pleasing to God is the celibate life.

A second feature is the claim that Mary is of Davidic ancestry.[24] Matthew and Luke had created a certain problem at this point, for they asserted both that Jesus was virgin-born and a son of David, and they traced his relationship to David through Joseph. Both assume that Joseph is of David's lineage, but neither says this of Mary. The author of the Book of James must have been aware of this problem, and he deftly solved it by making Mary carry the Davidic genes.

A third feature is similar. Matthew and Luke had affirmed the virginity of Mary, but they referred also to brothers and sisters of Jesus. Jesus is called the first-born but never the only child of Mary. In the early Jerusalem community, James was commonly known as the brother of the Lord. The author of the Book of James is not so much interested in the birth of Jesus as he is in the virginity of Mary, so he accounts for the other brothers as sons of the widowed Joseph.[25]

The purpose of the author must have been threefold: (1) to glorify Mary; (2) to emphasize the value of celibacy; and (3) to solve some problems in Matthew and Luke. His book was never canonized, but his point of view has been widely accepted in the church. The perpetual virginity of Mary was taught by the church fathers from the fifth century on. The Immaculate Conception of Mary, another teaching that is rooted in the Book of James, was proclaimed as a dogma for Roman Catholics in 1854.

The Infancy Gospel of Thomas[26]

The canonical gospels are almost silent on the childhood of Jesus. Luke contains one narrative about a conversation between the learned men of the

---

[24] Book of James 10:1.
[25] Note that Joseph has no daughters in the Book of James.
[26] For an English translation, see Hennecke, op. cit., 1, 392–401.

Temple and the twelve-year-old Jesus, but that is the extent of it.[27] The Infancy Gospel of Thomas attempts to fill this gap by narrating a number of incidents involving Jesus between the ages of five and twelve. He makes clay sparrows on the Sabbath, and they fly away when he claps his hands. A child who hit Jesus on the shoulder dies immediately. On one occasion, several children were playing together in the upper story of a house. One of them fell to the ground and died, and Jesus was blamed. So Jesus revived the child, who confessed that his death was an accident. When Joseph cut a board too short, Jesus stretched it to its proper length. When he was sent to school to learn the alphabet, he refused to hear about the second letter until his teacher should fully explain the first. Then Jesus explained *alpha* to his exasperated and dumbfounded teacher. The Gospel concludes with the Lukan story of Jesus in the Temple.

The Infancy Gospel of Thomas fits into the same time period as the Book of James. Its dependence on Luke places it in the second century. Irenaeus[28] alludes to it in A.D. 180, so a date around A.D. 150 would seem appropriate. It seems to have no relationship to the Gospel of Thomas, to be discussed later.[29] The attribution to Thomas is certainly erroneous but probably arose in Gnostic circles, where Thomas was one of three highly revered disciples (the other two being Matthew and Philip). The actual author is unknown.

In character, the Infancy Gospel appears to be a collection of popular legends, many of which may have circulated orally. If so, they must have originated in a Gentile environment, because they contain no knowledge of Judaism except that which could be learned from the canonical gospels. The childhood of Jesus is looked upon as an anticipation of his later miracles and teaching. In the teaching material, which is minimal, there is a definite leaning toward Gnosticism. Jesus' allegorical interpretation of the letter *alpha*, for example, is similar to many Gnostic speculations. The church did not canonize this Gospel, but its translation into several languages and its appearance in a number of collections attest to its continued popularity.

THE GOSPEL OF PETER[30]

At about the end of the second century, Serapion, bishop of Antioch, referred to a gospel in use at the Church of Rhossus.[31] It was called the

---

[27] See Luke 2.41–52.
[28] *Against Heresies* I, 7:1.
[29] See pp. 230 ff.
[30] For an English translation, see Hennecke, op. cit., 1, 183–187. Translations below are from this edition.
[31] In Eusebius, *Church History* VI, 12:2–6.

A silver plaque showing the apostle Peter carrying a cross on a staff. Found near Antioch, Syria, and dating from the sixth century. (*Courtesy* the Metropolitan Museum of Art, Fletcher Fund, 1950.)

Gospel According to Peter. At first the bishop saw no harm in its use, although he was sure that Peter had not written it. But on closer examination he concluded that it must not be used because of its Docetic viewpoint. In 1886, a fragment of the Gospel was discovered in Upper Egypt. It begins with the Matthaean story of Pilate's washing his hands at the trial of Jesus and continues with the crucifixion, burial, and resurrection. The most notable feature in the fragment is the description of the resurrection itself. On the Saturday night after the crucifixion, the soldiers guarding Jesus' tomb saw the heavens open and two men descend to enter the sepulcher. A few moments later they saw three men come out—two whose heads reached heaven and one even taller. They were followed by a cross. A voice from heaven proclaimed that Jesus had preached to the dead, and the cross answered, "Yes." Then another man descended from heaven and entered the tomb. The scene is now set for the discovery of the empty tomb by the women on Sunday morning, and that episode is described in Markan terms.

Serapion was certainly correct in suspecting the authorship of this document. The author made use of all four canonical gospels and so could not have lived during the apostolic period. In addition, although the Gospel claims to be by Peter, the central event took place before soldiers, who agreed to tell no one what they saw. While the resurrection was taking place, Peter was off fishing, according to the Gospel. Once again we have an unknown author. The document should be assigned to the middle of the second century, since the Rhossus Church was using it a few decades later.

Although Serapion judged the Gospel to be Docetic, it is hard to find any clear traces in the fragment we have. During the crucifixion Jesus held his peace "as if he felt no pain."[32] It does not say that he died but that "he was taken up."[33] It is doubtful if we would have spotted these traces as Docetic if Serapion's condemnation had not warned us to look out for them. There is a third possibly Docetic reference in the cry of Jesus from the cross: "My Power, O Power, thou hast forsaken me."[34] As a Docetic statement, this would imply that the Power, which is the real Christ, has left the pseudo-body, which is then seen to expire. The cry is, however, subject to other interpretations that do not question the real humanity of Jesus and was so understood in some non-Docetic Jewish Christian groups. Serapion had said that most of the Gospel was acceptable, and it is probable that only the more acceptable portions of it were preserved to appear in our fragment, which is not the original but a fourth-century copy.

[32] Gospel of Peter 4:10.
[33] Gospel of Peter 5:19.
[34] Gospel of Peter 5:19, see Mark 15:34; Matthew 27:46.

The Baptism of Jesus, third-century fresco from the Catacomb of Sts. Peter and Marcellinus, Rome. (*Courtesy* Pontifical Commission for Sacred Archives, Rome.)

THE GOSPEL OF THE EBIONITES[35]

The fathers of the church frequently referred to gospels used by Jewish Christians, variously titled. There is a good deal of confusion in the references and citations, but it now appears that there were at least three distinct Jewish Christian gospels—the Gospel of the Ebionites, the Gospel of the Hebrews, and the Gospel of the Nazaraeans. Unfortunately, no manuscript of any of the three has turned up. It is possible, however, to judge something about the contents and character of these writings from citations in the fathers. Our sole authority for the Gospel of the Ebionites is Epiphanius, the fourth-century bishop of Salamis, who says that it was used by a sect called Ebionites (that is, the poor) and was a falsification and abridgment of Matthew.[36] It was probably written in the middle of the second century. It

[35] For an English translation of the citations by Epiphanius, see Hennecke, op. cit., I, 156–158.
[36] Epiphanius, *Refutation of All Heresies* XXX, 13:2 f.

claims Matthew as the author and may have been combined with the canonical Matthew and designated by that name by the Ebionites.

In the fragments that Epiphanius cites we have the call of the disciples, the baptism of Jesus, and a few of his words. In the description of the baptism, it is stated that the Holy Spirit entered into Jesus at the moment when the dove descended from heaven. It was in that moment that the heavenly voice said: "This is my beloved son. I have this day begotten thee." Here the baptism is not a symbolic act of the human Jesus. It is the actual birth of the Messiah. Thus, the Gospel denies that Jesus was the son of Mary and Joseph, for he was born at the baptism. Equally strong emphasis is placed upon the vegetarianism of John the Baptist and Jesus and upon Jesus' mission to abolish sacrifices. We shall see that these principles were fundamental for some Jewish Christian groups.

THE GOSPEL OF THOMAS[37]

In 1945 and 1946, near the town of Nag Hammadi in Egypt, a remarkable discovery was made. Several Coptic manuscripts of original Gnostic Christian works were found. The manuscripts undoubtedly form the remains of an extensive Gnostic library. Among the texts, there were three so-called gospels. The Gospel of Truth is actually a meditation probably composed by the Gnostic Valentinus about A.D. 140. The Gospel of Philip may be a later composition by a pupil of Valentinus. The Gospel of Thomas may turn out to be the most significant discovery of the group. We had previously known of the existence of a Gospel by this name, and from Hippolytus we knew one of the sayings it contained.[38] Now we can see just what the document looked like.

The Gospel consists of some 114 sayings of Jesus. There is no narrative framework except the general introduction, which states: "These are the secret words which the living Jesus spoke, and Didymus Judas Thomas wrote them down." All the sayings are addressed to disciples, individually or collectively, some in response to their questions. Although a pattern may be discerned within a short series of sayings, no overall structure is ap-

[37] For an English translation, see Hennecke, op. cit., 1, 511–522. Translations below are from this edition.

[38] Hippolytus, *Refutation of All Heresies* V, 7:20. At least three sayings in Thomas are also found among the Oxyrynchus papyri. Thousands of these papyri were discovered in 1897, and until the Nag Hammadi find we were ignorant about the source of these sayings.

parent. The sayings take the form of parables, proverbs, and short exhortations. In both form and content, many sayings are similar to those in the Synoptics and may be drawn directly from them. Others appear to be taken from the Gospel of the Hebrews or the Gospel of the Egyptians. But still others have no parallels elsewhere. In a form critical comparison of parables in Thomas and in the Synoptics, Hugh Montefiore has concluded that, while many parables in Thomas depend on the Synoptics, others have come from an independent source, namely an oral tradition of a Jewish Christian character.[39] Montefiore writes: "Occasionally this source seems to be superior [to that on which the Synoptics drew], especially inasmuch as it seems to be free from apocalyptic imagery, allegorical interpretation, and generalizing conclusions."[40] The implication of this discovery may be startling: namely that, if we are looking for historically authentic words of Jesus, we cannot afford to overlook the Gospel of Thomas.

The sayings in the Gospel are said to be the secret sayings of Jesus recorded by Thomas. Even so, Thomas does not reveal all that Jesus said even to the other disciples.[41] The disciples here are understood as an elite group, and the message of Jesus is intended for a limited number. Many sayings relate to the kingdom of God, but the eschatological note is absent. The kingdom is not something to come; it is to be found. This means that some effort is called for from the disciples, but the effort is largely a matter of self-knowledge. The kingdom is a present spiritual phenomenon to be found within the disciples. "The Kingdom is within you, and it is outside you. When you know yourselves, then shall you be known, and you shall know that you are the sons of the Living Father."[42] The resurrection of the dead is no eschatological occurrence of the future but an event of the past: "His disciples said to him: on what day will the rest of the dead come into being? And on what day will the new world come? He said to them: That which ye await has come, but ye know it not."[43] In some sayings the kingdom is equated with Jesus, and there is a kind of incorporation of the disciple with Jesus. There is also a degree of pantheism in one saying: "Jesus said: I am the light that is over them all. I am the All; the All has come forth from me, and the All has attained unto me. Cleave a (piece

---

[39] Hugh Montefiore and H. E. W. Turner, *Thomas and the Evangelists* (Naperville, Ill.: Allenson, 1962).

[40] Ibid., p. 78.

[41] See Saying 13.

[42] Saying 3.

[43] Saying 51.

of) wood: I am there. Raise up a stone, and ye shall find me there."[44] Jesus is the Light and the All; he is one with the Father. But not everyone can see him for what he is. Some may mistake him for a human being: "Salome said: Who art thou, O man? And whose son? Thou hast mounted my bed, and eaten from my table. Jesus said to her: I am he who is from that which is equal; to me was given of the things of my Father."[45] In this Docetic passage, Salome has mistaken Jesus for a human being, and Jesus has corrected her.

The method by which one attains to the kingdom is *Gnosis,* which means knowing oneself and knowing God. There are few moral duties, and the ways of the Old Testament and Judaism are specifically rejected. Above all, one must despise all things material and abhor sex. The ideal is a unisex, which means the abolition of the female. In the last saying, Peter calls for the exclusion of Mary from the group, but Jesus says: "Behold, I shall lead her, that I may make her male, in order that she may become a living spirit like you males. For every woman who makes herself male shall enter into the kingdom of heaven."[46] This ideal state of life is signalized by nudity: "When you unclothe yourselves and are not ashamed, and take your garments and lay them beneath your feet like little children, and tread upon them, then [shall you see] the Son of the living One, and ye shall not fear."[47]

The Gospel of Thomas is a strange mixture of secret sayings about self-knowledge and inwardness. It brings together mysticism, pantheism, Docetism, antimaterialism, anti-Semitism, and antifeminism. And yet, as R. M. Grant notes, this Gospel should have a strong attraction for men of the twentieth century. He writes: "Thomas is silent about sin and forgiveness. He records no miracles or, indeed, deeds of Jesus. There are no embarrassing stories about demons and the exorcism of demons. The kingdom of God is almost entirely inward, unrelated to time or history. One need not love his enemies. . . . Self-knowledge is all-important."[48]

The date of the Gospel of Thomas must be sometime between the Synoptic Gospels and Hippolytus—that is, some date in the second century, probably about A.D. 150. The attribution to Thomas is, of course, erroneous

[44] Saying 77.

[45] Saying 61.

[46] Saying 114.

[47] Saying 37. Although the plain meaning of this saying is that one should become nude, the garments may refer to the human body. The meaning would be that one should strip off the body and become a pure spirit.

[48] R. M. Grant and D. N. Freedman, *The Secret Sayings of Jesus* (Garden City, N.Y.: Doubleday, 1960), p. 112 f.

but interesting. He is here referred to as Didymus (meaning the twin) Jude Thomas. In the Gospel of John, Thomas was called Didymus, but the author does not say whose twin he was. The Synoptics, Acts, and the letter of Jude call attention to a brother of Jesus by the name of Jude or Judas. In another Nag Hammadi document and in the third-century Acts of Thomas, Thomas is called the twin brother of Jesus. These traditions evidently rest upon the assumption that Jude and Thomas were the same person. Furthermore, in the Gnostic *Pistis Sophia*, Thomas is one of the three authorized recorders of the teaching of Jesus. He is, thus, highly regarded in the Gospel of Thomas. The only competitor is James, who is proclaimed to be the leader of the community after the departure of Jesus. In a saying probably coming out of Jewish Christian circles we have: "In the place to which you come, you shall go to James the Just, for whose sake heaven and earth came into being."[49]

Christians in the second century produced other gospels, most of which have disappeared without a trace. Nor did the practice of publishing gospels cease with the second century. Nevertheless, the nine we have examined here have set the main lines of development and presented the major ideas on which later writers will comment and elaborate. In concluding this section, we should notice a problematic feature in the history of gospel writing. Although the gospel form is the most suitable one for the transmission of material about Jesus, not one of the gospels was written with the express and sole purpose of narrating his life. In the final analysis, a gospel is not a life of Jesus but the preaching of the church. The writers of gospels had neither the tools nor the inclination for biographical work. This does not mean that the gospels contain no historically accurate information, for they are valuable records of the history and beliefs of the church. If we are after a life of Jesus, we may also find some accurate information in the gospels. But we shall need to devise certain principles for the use of this material and must understand that the gospels contain historical evidence, not historical testimony.

[49] Saying 12.

Chapter Eight

Other Writings

In addition to letters, oral traditions, and gospels, early Christianity produced a variety of other writings. In this chapter, some examples of the other types will be considered.

A HISTORY OF THE CHURCH

Among the Christian writings of the first two centuries, only the Acts of the Apostles can qualify as a history, and that only in a restricted sense. All early Christian writing is religious, and Acts is no exception. But Luke is interested in history and sees in human events the working out of God's plan. Conzelmann's term, history of salvation, aptly describes both Luke and Acts. Since we have discussed the date, authorship, and character of Luke and Acts together, it remains now to say something about the contents and character of Acts itself.[1]

The Book of Acts is Luke's description of the third period in the history of salvation, the period of the church. It begins where the Gospel leaves off. The time of Jesus is concluded with the ascension, and the last period is initiated by the descent of the spirit at Pentecost. Luke offers a vivid description of the latter event, in which the disciples' ability to speak in foreign languages is pictured as the outward manifestation of the spirit. Just before the ascension Jesus gives certain orders to the disciples, and these words determine the outline for the remainder of the book. He tells them to remain in Jerusalem until they receive the spirit and then to become his witnesses first in Jerusalem, then in Judaea and Samaria, and finally to the ends of the earth.[2] J. C. O'Neill has shown that the book follows this scheme and has suggested a fivefold division of the work.[3] It will be good to use this outline to examine the contents of Acts.

[1] See pp. 204–212.
[2] Acts 1:4, 8.
[3] *The Theology of Acts* (London: S.P.C.K., 1961).

In the first section (1:9–8:3), the apostles are witnessing in Jerusalem. The congregation of Christians meets in a portion of the Temple and observes Jewish customs, but it has opposition from the priests. The Church also practices a sharing of resources, and internal friction develops between a group of Hellenistic Christians and one of Hebrew Christians. Stephen, a representative of the former group, is executed by the Jews, and a period of persecution ensues, which causes a scattering of Christians throughout Judaea and Samaria.

In the second section (8:4–11:18), the church spreads out into Judaea, Samaria, and Syria. Philip works in Samaria, where he converts Simon Magus, and in Gaza, where he converts an Ethiopian government official.[4] The conversion of Paul occurs on the road to Damascus. Peter goes out into Judaea and then to Samaria, where he converts the first Gentile, Cornelius. Before he goes, he receives a vision that convinces him that there is no distinction between kosher and nonkosher food and that it is appropriate for him to eat and talk with Cornelius. Nevertheless, he has to defend this conversion before the other apostles, who agree that "this means that God has granted life-giving repentance to Gentiles also."[5]

In the third section (11:19–15:35), the interest shifts to Asia Minor, where Paul and Barnabas preach. They speak first in Jewish synagogues, but after opposition from Jews they decide to go to the Gentiles. Both success and violence meet them in every town. When they return to Antioch, they find that a group of Judaean Christians is insisting that Gentile converts be circumcised. The Antioch Church decides to raise this question with the Jerusalem apostles and sends Paul and Barnabas to a council there. At the session it is decided that Gentile Christians must avoid adultery and must obey three of the food laws. Circumcision is not included among the requirements. The way has now been prepared for the admission of Gentiles on an equal footing with Jews.

In the fourth section (15:36–19:20), Paul launches out still farther to Macedonia (Philippi and Thessalonica), Greece (Athens and Corinth) and Asia (Ephesus). Near the end of the section, Luke notes that "the whole population of the province of Asia, both Jews and Gentiles, heard the word of the Lord."[6]

In the final section (19:21–28:31), the gospel has reached to the ends of

---

[4] It is probable that the official was a Jew, since he was reading from the Old Testament. But he could not be counted as a full member of the congregation of Israel, because he was a eunuch.

[5] Acts 11:18.

[6] Acts 19:10.

the earth when Paul arrives at Rome. There is a strong motif of divine necessity in this section, and the description is reminiscent of Luke's portrayal of Jesus' journey to his death. Paul undergoes a number of hearings in Jerusalem and Caesarea, before the Sanhedrin, before the procurators Felix and Festus, and before King Herod Agrippa II. All of these are inconclusive, but Paul appeals to Caesar and is transported to Rome for the trial. In the last two chapters of Acts we have a detailed description of the voyage to Rome. Upon his arrival Paul is assigned to a private lodging with military escort, and he preaches there for two full years, openly and without hindrance.

Since Luke used written sources for his Gospel, we would expect him to do the same for Acts. But no such material has survived. It is probable that he put together the traditions of various localities, notably Jerusalem and Antioch, and added to them a number of speeches of his own composition. The "we" sections may rest upon personal recollection, perhaps his own.[7] They generally deal with sea voyages, and the information in the last two chapters betrays such extensive knowledge about and interest in sailing, that we may say that the author of these sections was a seaman.

It is apparent that Luke has built the Book of Acts on a geographical framework. As the map (Figure 22) shows, Luke is interested in the progressive spread of Christianity from Jerusalem in section one, to Judaea, Samaria, and Syria in section two, to Asia Minor in three, to Macedonia and Greece in four, and to Rome in five. Jerusalem and Rome form two foci for his attention. Jerusalem is the pivot for the entire work, for Jesus brought the gospel to it, the apostles received the spirit there, and from there the gospel spread to the rest of the world. Rome is the goal, for that is where the gospel is headed, and there the book ends. When Paul has reached Rome, Christianity has spread to all the world. Luke is not simply interested in the spread of the gospel but in its progressive independence from Judaism. Paul is important to him not simply as a missionary but as the one who established an independent religion. Although he is the hero of the last part of Acts and his arrival in Rome is the culmination, he is not the first to bring Christianity to the capital. Italian Christians meet Paul's boat at the port of Puteoli. The gospel has actually outrun the hero. Paul's importance for Luke is indicated in his last recorded words, which repeat an affirmation made twice before: "Therefore take notice that this salvation of God has been sent to the Gentiles; the Gentiles will listen."[8] Luke's geo-

---

[7] See p. 206.
[8] Acts 28:28; see 13:46; 18:6.

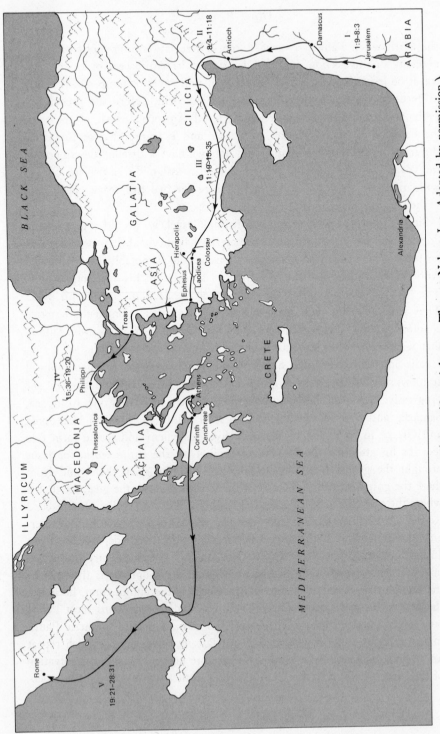

FIGURE 22   The Geographical Structure of Acts. (Copyright 1949 Thomas Nelson Inc. Adapted by permission.)

graphical structure, thus, indicates his interest in the spread of Christianity and an even deeper interest in its independence from Judaism.

Luke's attitude toward Judaism comes through clearly. He believes that Jews have heard the gospel but have not heeded it. As a result, God has rejected them. He also shows that Jews are the troublemakers; it is they who execute Stephen and pursue Paul. At the same time, Luke presents Christians as completely without offense. Paul, Peter, and James never disobey a Mosaic law. The earliest Christians meet in the Temple and remain faithful to Judaism. This means to Luke that Christians have taken the place of the Jews as God's people. God has rejected the Jews because of their disobedience, and Christians have become the people of God through obedience.

A related theme is Luke's attitude toward Jewish Christians. He is aware that the earliest Christians had been Jewish converts and that they practiced Judaism with devotion. He seems proud to report that the Jerusalem Church was attractive to Pharisees and some priests, and that the apostles were held in high regard by their fellow Jews. But his sympathies are obviously with Peter and Paul, who accept Gentiles. For Luke, not only must Gentiles be admitted but they must not be required to be circumcised. He believes that the demand for circumcision was made by a group of Jewish Christians who had no standing in the church and that the apostles settled the issue by requiring only a minimal burden for Gentile converts. In short, Luke has respect for Jewish Christians, and he accepts their continued practice of circumcision, but he strongly denies their right to impose this practice on Gentile Christians.

For Luke, the apostles form a distinct group. Although they have come out of Judaism, it is not they who demand the circumcision of Gentiles, and they cooperate in the Gentile mission. In a sense they are lifted above all partisanship. They support Paul, but they do their best not to inflame the Jews. They are twelve in number, and this number must remain constant. At the death of Judas, Matthias is chosen to bring the apostolate to its full strength. The title is restricted to these twelve, except in one reference, where Paul and Barnabas are called apostles.[9] Although he gives us no explicit information on the organization of any church, he understands that the apostles occupy a dominant position for the entire church. It is they who must decide the issue of circumcision; they recognize the validity of converting Gentiles; they set requirements for Gentile Christians; they authorize Paul. Among the twelve, Peter appears to be the leader until his

[9] Acts 14:14.

[239]

arrest by Herod Agrippa I. After that he does not disappear, but leadership is exercised by James.[10] At the apostolic council in chapter 15, James makes the decision, and, when Paul returns to Jerusalem for the last time James suggests a ritual of purification. Thus, Luke has assigned a special position to the apostles and, in particular, to James. They are qualified for leadership in the church, not because they are Jewish Christians, but because they were eyewitnesses of the ministry of Jesus.

It is now generally agreed that Acts is not an adequate source for the life of Paul and that our fundamental understanding of his life must come from the letters. It is also clear that Luke had not seen the collection of Paul's letters. But when we have in mind the information that the letters contain, it is remarkable that a number of points are also reflected in Acts. Luke has much of his material in the wrong order and context, but he has some accurate information. He knows that Paul was a missionary to the Gentiles, that he was opposed to the circumcision of Gentile Christians, and that some Jewish Christians opposed him. He knows that Paul had been a Pharisee and a persecutor of the church. He knows that he brought a collection to the Christians in Jerusalem. He is correct on some of the localities that Paul visited—Thessalonica, Philippi, Corinth, Ephesus. He knows that he attended an apostolic council in Jerusalem, which dealt with the circumcision issue. He knows that Paul intended to go to Rome. Certain details on Paul's travels are consistent with what we have in the letters. There are, to be sure, some major disagreements on historical details and on Paul's theology. If we do not press the Book of Acts into service as an exhaustive account of Paul's life and thought, it may yield a correct impression of him.

A particular problem adheres to the ending of Acts. Readers are frequently puzzled by the fact that Luke does not state what finally happened to Paul. This appears to be a problem, because at least half of the book has Paul as the hero and his journey to Rome is described in minute detail. But at the end he is awaiting trial and preaching. It has been suggested that the original ending was lost, or that Luke intended to write a third book, or that he wrote before the final outcome was decided. Three considerations show, however, that these suggestions are unnecessary. (1) The book could not have been written prior to the final outcome, because that would date it in the early sixties. (2) Even if Luke's source omitted the outcome, it is inconceivable that Luke was ignorant on this score. He has made it perfectly clear that Paul *must* die in Rome in obedience to the divine impera-

---

[10] James, nevertheless, is not counted as one of the twelve.

tive. It is equally inconceivable that Luke's readers were ignorant on this point. If both author and readers knew full well what happened to Paul, the ending takes on a highly dramatic tone. In writings of all ages, we meet a similar phenomenon. A few years after the assassination of President John F. Kennedy, John Connally, then governor of Texas, wrote as follows:

> This was the final success and the last of my worry evaporated. The people on the street were his. The business community whose help he needed had been impressed and would be more so at the luncheon that day and at Austin that night. The President looked strong and confident, obviously delighted with his reception. Nellie [Mrs. Connally] leaned back between the jump seats and said proudly over the crowd's roar, "You can't say now that Dallas doesn't love you, Mr. President," and he smiled and nodded. The big car turned off Main Street and slowly negotiated the turn under the looming School Book Depository building and started down the hill in the bright sunshine.[11]

Governor Connally knew that his readers were well aware of the outcome, and he omitted it precisely because it was well known. (3) When we fully appreciate the dominant motif in Luke-Acts, we find that a narrative about Paul's death would be an anticlimax. Luke is not writing a life of Paul; he is telling the story of the church. The importance of Paul is that he carried the gospel to the capital of the world and made it independent of Judaism. His fate is secondary to the fact that he preached the gospel in Rome, "openly and without hindrance."[12]

The Book of Acts has sometimes been called an apology, that is, a defense of Christianity directed to Roman authorities. Under this interpretation, Theophilus (in 1:1) is understood as a Roman official, who is investigating the movement. The book is also notable for its high regard for Roman justice. At every opportunity Luke calls attention to the favorable attitude of Romans and the opposition of Jews. Witness the treatment of Paul, whom Luke designates as a Roman citizen. He is mobbed by Jews in Jerusalem and rescued by the Roman commandant. The Jews plot to ambush him, but the Romans issue him a safe conduct. The Jewish high priest appears before Felix to accuse Paul, but the procurator adjourns the court. The same Felix would have freed Paul except for his desire not to offend the Jews. This is just the kind of defense one might give to a Roman official. The purpose is not to curry favor but to show that Rome has nothing to

[11] John Connally, "Why Kennedy Went to Texas," *Life* 63: 104 (November 24, 1967).
[12] Acts 28:31.

fear from Christians. We would not seriously err by classifying Acts as an apology, but we should refrain from doing so, because it appears to be so much more as well. In order to give full weight to the two volumes of Luke, the Book of Acts appears in a unique category. There were other writings, such as the Acts of Peter, the Acts of Paul, and the Acts of John, which tell the deeds of these apostles. But they lie outside the range of our study and, in spite of their titles, belong to a different literary genre. It is best, therefore, not to classify the Acts of the Apostles either as an apology or with the other Acts, but as the continuation of Luke's history of salvation.

SERMONS AND TEACHING TRACTS

The sermon and the lesson were two of the earliest vehicles for the transmission of oral traditions. Although we have been able to determine the main outlines of the earliest Christian *kerygma*, we have no copies of the earliest sermons.[13] Since the sermon was an oral proclamation, this unfortunate fact should cause no surprise. Preachers generally did not write out their sermons in advance or record them after delivery. But as time passed, some sermons were written down and, perhaps, circulated. The Epistle to the Hebrews, the second letter of Clement, and the sermon of Melito represent this genre. Teaching material is contained in letters and gospels, but the Shepherd of Hermas appears to be a teaching tract, and the Didache preserves material which may have been part of the initiatory instruction given to Christians at baptism.

The Epistle to the Hebrews

There is no address or salutation in this document, but there is an epistolary-type conclusion. Chapter 13 has several moral injunctions, a doxology, a farewell, a reference to Timothy and to the author's travel plans. In 13:22, the document is explicitly called a letter. It is possible that the introductory material was lost, although the document reads well enough as it is. It is equally possible that chapter 13 was added at a later time either by the author of chapters 1–12 or by some strange hand. In either case, the basic document is not a letter but a sermon. It contains references appropriate to oral communication and exhortations to a listening rather than a reading

---

[13] For an outline of the early *kerygma*, see p. 167 f. The apostolic sermons in Acts are largely the composition of Luke.

audience.[14] It is possible that we have in Hebrews a sermon, which was initially preached and later circulated to a distant congregation.

The author is deeply disturbed by a kind of apathy among Christians. His Church has faced opposition before and may need to again. In citing the courage of Christians in the first blush of enthusiasm, he raises a question about the preparedness of his contemporaries. He fears that they may not remain faithful and may fall away from the true religion, and he challenges them by cataloguing the faithful men of the past in chapter 11. That he anticipates bloody persecution is indicated in a threatening word: "You have not yet resisted to the point of shedding your blood."[15] The implication is that martyrdom may be necessary in the future. The author, therefore, must be associated with a Church that passed through a persecution in the previous generation and is facing another. Such a situation did in fact exist in Rome in the late first century. That Church was attacked by Nero in the sixties and by Domitian in the nineties. Clement of Rome first cited Hebrews in A.D. 95,[16] and it could have been written any time during the reign of Domitian, which began in A.D. 81. Clement's knowledge of it also argues for a Roman provenance, as does the greeting "from our Italian friends" in the epistolary addition.[17]

The title is fairly early but no part of the original document. There is no internal evidence that the author was addressing Hebrews or Hebrew Christians. The title must have been the result of speculation by people who were impressed with the weighty Old Testament material contained in the document and by the contrasts between Christianity and Judaism. Actually, the sermon is addressed to Gentile Christians who are in danger of falling away from the living God.

The author is anonymous, but Christian writers began speculating about him very early. In the east, Hebrews was accepted as Pauline, but western writers were not so sure. Clement of Alexandria thought that Paul wrote it in Hebrew and that Luke translated it,[18] while others attributed it to Paul's companion, Barnabas. Not until the fourth century did the western churches accept it as Pauline. Almost all modern scholars deny Pauline authorship to it on the grounds that it does not claim it, its ideas are different, and its date is too late. Speculations continue, however, and author-

[14] References to the act of speaking may be found in 2:5; 5:11; 6:9; 8:1; 9:5. A listening audience seems to be addressed in 5:11 ff.; 6:9 f.; 10:25, 32 ff.; 12:4 f. In 11:32, the speaker refers to a lack of time to cover the subject.

[15] Hebrews 12:5.

[16] I Clement 17:1; 36:2–5.

[17] Hebrews 13:24.

[18] In Eusebius, *Church History* VI, 14:2 f.

ship by Barnabas, Apollos, Priscilla, or Acquila is frequently proposed. Interesting as these suggestions are, they do not remove the anonymous character of the work. Although we do not know his name, we are able to describe the author with a high degree of exactitude. He is a Christian of the second generation. He is acquainted with the Old Testament, and his principles of interpretation are, on the whole, those of Philo. His basic philosophy is Platonic, which he may also have understood by reading Philo. His literary style is the best Greek in the New Testament. He knows about Judaism from the Old Testament, but not from firsthand experience. The casual way he dismisses the food laws suggests that he did not come from a Jewish background. He is an intelligent and skillful writer, deeply influenced by the Old Testament, Plato, and Philo.

The framework of Platonic thought is fundamental to our author's understanding of Christianity. He accepts Plato's distinction between the world of ideas and that of shadowy phenomena. The latter contains visible objects, which are imperfect copies of those real entities found only in the world of ideas. He believes, further, that Jesus has brought about a direct revelation of reality. To make his ideas clear, he contrasts Christianity with Judaism, a respected religion, but an imperfect copy of reality. If Plato is one source of authority for the author, the Old Testament is another. From it he gains the idea that sacrifice is necessary for the forgiveness of sins. With the Platonic framework in one hand and the Old Testament demand for sacrifice in the other, the author goes to work. Judaism is correct, he says, in its recognition of the necessity for sacrifice, but its application of the principle is inadequate. Jews sacrifice animals in a temporary sanctuary. They have a succession of priests who sin and must sacrifice for themselves and who die and must be replaced. Christians, however, have a direct and real application of sacrifice. Instead of the repeated sacrifice of animals, they have the one sacrifice of the Son of God. Instead of a temporary tabernacle, Jesus has entered the heavenly sanctuary, which is permanent and real. Instead of sacrifice by priests, Christians have Jesus as the one high priest. In his function as high priest, Jesus is the one mediator between man and God, for he is both human and divine. As a human being, he committed no sin, but he knew both humanity and temptation. As divine, he is able to effect absolute forgiveness. His dual nature means that he is the mediator, but it is necessary for the author to qualify Jesus as priest in another way. He knows that Jesus was not a Levite, so he cannot associate him with the Levitical priesthood. He affirms, however, that he is a priest of the Melchizedek order. Melchizedek is described in Genesis as a priest to whom Abraham paid a tithe. He appeared without ancestry or progeny, but his temporal priority to Levi proves to our author that his priesthood was superior. Jesus is the only other member of that priesthood, and he is the true high priest; the Levites are imperfect copies. Thus, Jesus, as both priest and victim, has performed the ultimate and perfect sacrifice, and there is no need for repetitions.

In his own context, the author must have intended his sermon to combat lethargy in his Church. He elevates his congregation by claiming that their religion is the one reality in a world of imitations, and he threatens them by affirming that sin after baptism is not forgiven. Although his motive is practical, he does not speak as a church official but as a great thinker. A. C. Purdy describes him "as perhaps the first Christian known to us who attempted to present the gospel in the form of a philosophy of religion, authenticating it over against another religion, Judaism, as fulfilling the valid ideas imperfectly realized in that religion."[19] His thought was unique at so early a date, but the book came to exercise a significant influence on developing catholic Christianity.

The Didache[20]

The Greek word *didache* means teaching, and the full title of this little document is, "The Lord's Teaching to the Heathen by the Twelve Apostles." It, and a companion known as the Latin Doctrina, were discovered in the nineteenth century. They both probably came from an original source in Greek, for the first half of the Didache is about the same as the Doctrina. The Latin Doctrina is probably a translation of the Greek original, and the Greek Didache is a copy. The Epistle of Barnabas has this same material, and it appears in a fourth-century document, *The Apostolic Church Order*.

The shared material is instruction about "two ways," which sets forth a comprehensive body of early Christian ethical teaching. The way of life includes loving God and the neighbor and following the Ten Commandments. The Christian is told not to get angry, because that leads to murder, and not to lie, because that leads to theft. He is also commanded to share freely with the brethren. The way of death is the neglect of the Ten Commandments. To this teaching about the two ways, the Didache adds a set

[19] In *The Interpreter's Bible* (New York: Abingdon, 1951–57), Vol. XI, p. 586.
[20] For an English translation, see Cyril C. Richardson, *Early Christian Fathers*, Library of Christian Classics (Philadelphia, Pa.: Westminster Press, 1953), Vol. I, 171–179.

of instructions for churches about food regulations, baptism, fasting, prayers, the Eucharist, itinerant teachers, prophets, and apostles, and about the election of bishops and deacons. It closes with a warning about eschatological judgment. The character of this teaching is quite different from the preaching of Hebrews. There is nothing approaching speculation about the nature of Christ, no metaphysical language, and no sign of philosophical influence. It is all very practical and quite valuable as a source of Christian ethical teaching and church practices. The two ways section sets forth a perfectionist ideal, but the church regulations seem much more moderate. In regard to food, the Christian is advised to do what he is able, so long as he eats no idol meat. Baptism should be in running cold water, but may be in still warm water. If a body of water is not accessible, pouring is permitted.

The anonymity of the Didache is no disadvantage, for it is certainly a community document. The two ways section was probably read at baptisms, and the regulations formed a kind of church manual. It probably came out of Syria and may be dated in the mid-second century. It shows acquaintance with the Synoptic Gospels and quotes extensively from Matthew. The Epistle of Barnabas and the Shepherd of Hermas also lie behind it. It was quoted in some early third-century documents. The Greek two ways source, which it used, probably dates from the early second century. The Didache came close to being canonized and was highly revered in the early church. It represents a moderate Christianity which was moving toward catholicism. But there is a residue of Jewish Christianity in it, as may be seen in the weight given to the Ten Commandments and the regulations about eating. Although it recognizes a danger from false prophets, it seems unaware of divisions in the church, and there is no partisan character to it.

The Shepherd of Hermas[21]

Hermas' book is usually classified among the apocalypses, because it is written in the form of a series of visions and contains a number of revelations. The author, who calls himself Hermas, speaks in the first person and describes himself as one who had been sold into slavery to a lady named Rhoda in Rome. He tells how he fell in love with her and subsequently

---

[21] For an English translation, see *Apostolic Fathers*, trans. Kirsopp Lake, Loeb Classical Library (Cambridge, Mass.: Harvard University Press, 1950), Vol. II, pp. 1–305. Translations below are from this edition.

had a vision of her in heaven. In the vision she accuses Hermas of his sins, claiming that his evil desire was sinful in spite of the fact that he had committed no sinful act. Hermas later finds that the woman is actually the church, and she appears to him on several occasions. He also meets a shepherd, or pastor, who interprets the visions to him, gives him a set of commandments, and presents him with some parables. Throughout the book there is a running allegory, in which the church is presented as a woman and in some cases as a tower. Although there are visions and allegories, there are good reasons against classifying the Shepherd of Hermas as an apocalypse. The fact is that the essential apocalyptic element is missing. Beyond a few stereotyped warnings about the approaching end, there is no eschatological perspective in the narrative. Hermas has a stronger relationship to the teaching literature of early Christianity than to the apocalyptic.

In content if not in form, the Shepherd of Hermas is a teaching tract dealing with Christian ethics. It probably represents the normative ethic of the Church at Rome in the second century. It is composed of four visions, twelve commandments, and ten parables, in that order. The twelve commandments are quite different from the ten in the Old Testament. They are more lengthy and contain the command, interpretations of the command, and exhortations. Some are vague, but in them we are able to see some of the values which second-century Roman Christians preached. The first commandment is to believe in the one creator-God. In those that follow, the believer is told to give to the needy, to love and speak only the truth, to be patient, to speak no evil, and to avoid adultery, anger, doubt, grief, lust, and luxury. In the eighth commandment, evil is defined as adultery, fornication, drunkenness, luxury, overeating, extravagant wealth, boastfulness, haughtiness, pride, lying, slander, hypocrisy, malice, and blasphemy. The righteous life is one of faith, fear of God, love, harmony, truth, and patience. The servant of God is expected to "minister to widows, to look after orphans and the destitute, to redeem from distress the servants of God, to be hospitable . . . to resist none, to be gentle, to be poorer than all men, to reverence the aged, to practice justice, to preserve brotherhood, to submit to insult, to be brave, to bear no malice, to comfort those who are oppressed in spirit."[22]

Hermas encourages the Christian to live a gentle life, but he is not so gentle in his urgings. The demands on the Christian seem to be more rigorous than on the non-Christian. The non-Christian, for example, is

[22] Hermas, Mandate VIII, 10.

permitted to repent even on the last day, but the Christian has an earlier limit, namely the publication date of Hermas' book.[23] After that day, no sin committed by a Christian will be forgiven. Even before the deadline, only one such sin may be forgiven. Hermas makes a distinction between the remission of sins in baptism and repentance for subsequent sins, and he specifically warns that "the servants of God have but one repentance."[24]

The ethical principles that Hermas upholds are not significantly different from those in similar writings, such as the Didache and II Clement. There are a few nods in the direction of Paul, for example: "The man who has the Lord in his heart is able to master all things and all these commandments."[25] But the general tone of the document shows that this thinking is secondary, peripheral, and unassimilated to the whole and that the Pauline understanding of good works as products of the spirit is lacking. The quality of the Christian life is judged on the basis of performance, and Christians who sin do themselves irreparable harm. They may repent of one sin, but even in that case they suffer a great deal of punishment and are demoted to a less honorable place in the church.[26]

The Muratorian Canon, probably adopted in Rome about A.D. 200, does not accept the Shepherd of Hermas among the sacred writings. It claims that it should not be read in church, although it is worthy of private reading. The reason given is that it was "written very recently in our time by Hermas, in the city of Rome, when his brother, Bishop Pius, was sitting in the Chair of the Church of Rome."[27] The episcopacy of Pius is dated c. A.D. 140–155. But there are signs that some parts of the Shepherd were written at an earlier date. Its influence on the Didache argues for a date early in the second century. In the second vision, Hermas is told to make two copies of his book and send one to Clement, who will forward it to the cities abroad.[28] If this is a reference to the famous Clement of Rome, author of I Clement, it must have been written around the turn of the century. Some scholars have suggested that the document was the product of several authors; others argue that a single author compiled it over a period of several decades. The only certainty is that it came from Rome in the first

[23] See Hermas, Vision II, 2:3 f.
[24] Hermas, Mandate IV, 1:8; see Hebrews 6:4, which seems to allow no repentance for postbaptismal sins.
[25] Hermas, Mandate XII, 4:3.
[26] Hermas, Vision III, 7:5–6.
[27] Henry Bettenson, ed., *Documents of the Christian Church*, 2nd ed. (London: Oxford University Press, 1963), p. 41.
[28] Hermas, Vision II, 4:3.

half of the second century. In its ethical prescriptions and its attitude toward postbaptismal sin, it contributes to a growing consensus that we designate protocatholic Christianity.

A Sermon of Melito of Sardis[29]

According to Eusebius, Melito, bishop of Sardis, was one of the most prolific writers of the ancient church. He lists some twenty of his works, including a sermon dated in A.D. 167–168.[30] Only fragments of his works survive, but in 1940 an almost complete manuscript of the sermon came to light. In 1958, an even earlier copy appeared, dating from the third century and entitled, "On the Passover."

Melito was involved in a second-century controversy that deeply disturbed relations between Asian and western churches. The former observed the crucifixion of Jesus on the first day of Passover as calculated by the Jewish calendar—namely, on the fourteenth of the month Nisan. Christians in Asia Minor were referred to as Quartodecimans, or fourteenthers. In the west it was customary to observe the crucifixion on the Friday following the first day of Passover—that is, on Good Friday.[31] Melito, of course, followed the Asian practice, and his sermon is a contribution to the discussion. Although he does not discuss the date of the crucifixion directly, he treats the subject of Jesus' suffering in such a way as to identify it with the observance of Passover.

The sermon begins with a review of the Scripture for the day, namely the Passover narrative from the Book of Exodus. Melito vividly describes the escape of Hebrews and the slaughter of the Egyptians. Then follows his interpretation of the passage. The Passover holds a dual significance for him. It is both a Jewish institution commemorating a historical event and a "type" of the sacrifice of Christ. Melito's interpretive method is called typological, because it attempts to find in the Old Testament evidences for the work of Christ. Such evidences serve as examples or types of Christ.[32] Melito accepted Christ as pre-existent and active in the history of Israel.

---

[29] For an English translation, see Campbell Bonner, *The Homily on the Passion by Melito Bishop of Sardis* (Philadelphia: Univ. of Pennsylvania Press, 1940). Translations below are from this edition.

[30] See Eusebius, *Church History* IV, 26:2.

[31] Polycarp of Smyrna was also involved in this controversy. See p. 157 f.

[32] The Greek word *typos* means pattern, model, or example. The author of Hebrews used a similar method.

Working on this assumption, he finds it possible to discern pre-Jesus examples of Christ's work, examples which are consistent with the deeds of Jesus. He states his own principle: "So the people became the pattern of the Church, and the Law the writing of a parable, and the Church the reservoir of the truth."[33] Melito applies typological interpretation to the Passover narrative and explains that the slaying of the lamb means that Christ suffers for us. The Hebrew sons were spared from plague by the mark of lamb's blood on the doors. The Christian is spared from destruction by the death of Christ. But it is not only in the lamb that Christ's suffering is seen. "If you wish to see the mystery of the Lord, look at Abel who was slain like him, at Isaac who was bound like him, at Joseph who was sold like him, at Moses who was cast out like him, at David who was hunted like him, at the prophets who in like manner suffered for Christ's sake."[34] The Christ, therefore, appeared in all of these forms and came finally as a man born of a virgin.

In the latter half of the sermon, Melito turns his attention to the Jews, whom he makes responsible for the death of Jesus. He acknowledges that the suffering of the Christ was foreordained by God, but he believes that the Jews could have avoided guilt in the matter. They could have washed their hands of guilt as did Pilate; thy could have pleaded with God to let him die by the hands of the Gentiles; but they crucified him. As a result, the Passover of the Jews is a bitter feast, and they must eat bitter herbs.

Melito's interpretive method leads him into a virtual identification of God and Christ. "He who hung the earth in its place is hanged, he who fixed the heavens is fixed upon the cross, he who made all things fast is made fast upon the tree, the Master has been insulted, *God has been murdered*, the King of Israel has been slain by an Israelitish hand."[35] That Melito is not thinking of a spiritual death is demonstrated by his reference in the next verse to Jesus' naked body. In the fourth century, the kind of theology for which Melito stood was condemned on the ground that it did not make sufficient distinction between the person of God and the person of Christ. It is probably for this reason that Melito's work was so long neglected. The fortunate recovery of the sermon provides a demonstration of the character of second-century preaching in Asia. Melito's typological interpretation was not condemned. On the contrary, it became an exceedingly useful tool for protocatholic and later Christianity.

[33] Melito, 40.
[34] Melito, 59.
[35] Melito, 96 (author's italics).

The Second Letter of Clement[36]

That this document was originally a sermon is hardly subject to doubt. Two sentences say this clearly: "Not only at this moment, while the presbyters are preaching to us, should we appear believing and attentive."[37] "I am reading you an exhortation to heed what was written."[38] That it was written by Clement of Rome is hardly credible. The text makes no such claim, and the document reflects a somewhat later situation. How it came to be attributed to Clement is a mystery. Some scholars feel that the sermon was sent as a letter from Rome to Corinth, as had Clement's genuine letter. If so, it may have been deposited with it and later mistakenly confused with it. The document is known by writers of the later second or early third century; it appears in two New Testament manuscripts and in one fourth-century canonical list. The probable date of composition is in the third quarter of the second century.

This sermon is chiefly a call to repentance directed to Christians. The author has no patience with professed believers who do not obey God; but, in contrast to the author of Hebrews, he allows the possibility of repentance after baptism, and unlike Hermas, he sets no limit. The obedience which God requires consists of acts of charity, fasting, prayer, and love, and the virtues are ranked in that order. The author also stresses the reality of Christ over against Docetism and the resurrection of the flesh over against Gnosticism. His doctrine of the church is a combination of Gnostic and Pauline thought. The church is the flesh of Christ, and Christ is the spirit of the church. In this sense, the church is a continuation of the incarnation. Moreover, the Christian who harms his own flesh harms the church. The sermon also includes an eschatological emphasis along with a recognition that the consummation has been delayed. The preacher's congregation is apparently losing its zeal for the end, for some are saying, "We have heard these things long ago, even in our fathers' time, and day after day we have waited and seen none of them."[39] The preacher also counsels that Christians do not receive their rewards immediately, for in that case they would be working solely for the reward.

We have in II Clement another example of a moderate thinker moving

---

[36] For an English translation, see Richardson, op. cit., pp. 193–202. Translations below are from this edition.

[37] II Clement 17:3.

[38] II Clement 19:1.

[39] II Clement 11:2; see II Peter 3:4.

toward catholic Christianity. We should not fail to note, however, a tinge of Gnosticism in his contrast of flesh and spirit. Even so, he emphasizes the importance of the flesh and consciously reacts against Gnosticism.

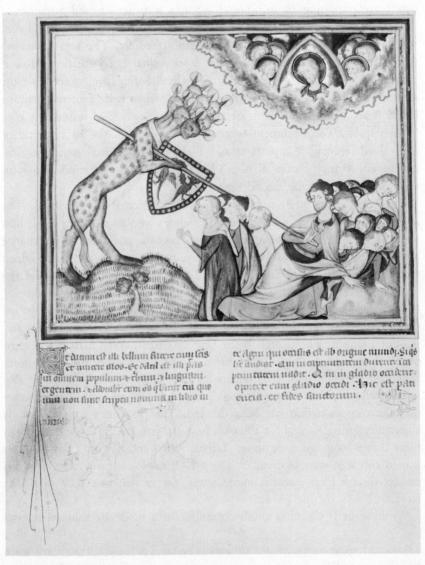

A parchment painting illustrating the Book of Revelation, from a fourteenth-century German manuscript ("The Apocalypse"; folio 23, verso). (*Courtesy* the Metropolitan Museum of Art, The Cloisters Collection, 1968.)

Apocalypses

In the two centuries preceding the rise of Christianity, Jewish authors had produced a distinctive writing known as the apocalypse, or revelation. A portion of the Old Testament Book of Daniel is an apocalypse, and several are contained in the pseudepigrapha. Christians soon began to use the form. Paul included a few apocalyptic verses in II Thessalonians, and Mark had an apocalyptic chapter that the other Synoptists used.

The basis of apocalyptic thought is the typically Jewish eschatological view of history. Apocalyptic writers add a good deal to this base. The Old Testament prophets, who adopted an eschatological point of view, attempted to understand events of their own time as the activity of God. They frequently felt that God was bringing an end to history but that history was nevertheles meaningful. The apocalyptic writer also feels that the end is near, but he has deep doubts about the meaningfulness of history. Instead of seeing the activity of God in history, he looks upon history as the effect of events which occur elsewhere. He modifies the Platonic distinction between ideas and phenomena and builds his thought on the basis of a two-level universe. The visible level is history; the invisible is reality. On the historical level one may see events taking place, but the events are only effects of actions that take place on the level of reality. All earthly history is, thus, controlled in heaven, and earth is very much like a puppet show. Although a person may see certain things take place on the stage, he does not understand what is really going on unless he looks behind the scenes to see the puppeteer. We may experience an epidemic, but we do not understand it unless we see an angel pouring out a pestilence on the earth. But no one can see into the realm of reality, or heaven, unless it is revealed to him. The apocalyptist feels that a special privilege has been given him, which enables him to see into the other world, and he describes the process as an opening of the veil which separates reality and history. So he looks into heaven and receives an apocalypse, or revelation. The distinction between the simpler eschatological view and the apocalyptic may appear subtle but may be expressed in this way: The eschatologist looks at historical events and *in them* sees the actions of God. The apocalyptist receives a direct revelation of God's activity and uses it to interpret historical events. The eschatologist looks at earth to see heaven; the apocalyptist looks at heaven to understand earth. The eschatologist sees reality in history itself; the apocalyptist sees reality in heaven only.

When he looks into heaven, the apocalyptist usually sees a mighty contest. Heaven is a well-populated place, not yet fully under God's control.

In addition to God and his angels, there is also the devil with his angels, and these forces fight for control. An apocalyptist generally believes that the devil has control of earth but that God is beginning to gain his proper ascendancy and will soon defeat him.

The apocalyptic writer also thinks in terms of a definite schedule of events. If history is a puppet show, it should have a program, a succession of predetermined events. Sometimes the apocalyptist looks back in time to describe the schedule, but he characteristically looks forward to see a plan, which he describes. With the schedule there is an assigned duration for each historical period. Thus, heaven is a contest between God and devil, and earth is the battlefield; but the contest has a predetermined battle plan and outcome.

The history of apocalypticism produced a more or less definite form and style for the apocalypse. The author feels himself to be especially endowed with the ability to see reality, but he usually has assistance from an angel, who interprets what he sees. His communication with heaven takes place through dreams and visions, and he is easily and quickly transported from place to place. His literary product records the dreams and visions, and he includes with them a good deal of animal symbolism and allegorical inter- pretation. In many cases the author uses pseudonymity, and he frequently antedates his book by setting himself back in time. He speculates in num- bers and sets the time for events in semiveiled language. The style makes the apocalypse a particularly difficult book for the modern reader or for anyone who does not share the apocalyptic world view. We must assume, however, that apocalypses were meaningful for their own times, and we can be assured that they contain a good deal of information about the re- ligion of their times.

The apocalypse usually made its appearance at a time of religiopolitical difficulty. The Christian apocalypses represent the religious response to political oppression, and they served to proclaim the reality of God to a world which could see no signs of it. We must not underestimate the effect of such a proclamation. When Christians were beginning to doubt the meaning of their own lives and the reality of God, an apocalyptist was able to say with conviction: The Lord God Omnipotent reigns!

The Revelation of John

The only full apocalypse in the New Testament is that called the Revela- tion, or Apocalypse, of John. The Muratorian Canon accepted it as sacred,

FIGURE 23 The Seven Churches of Asia. (From *The Early Christian Church* by Philip Carrington [Cambridge: Cambridge University Press]. Used with permission of Cambridge University Press.)

but questions were raised about it from several quarters, and Eusebius said that one could take it or leave it.[40] It was included in the decisive canonical list of Athanasius in A.D. 367.[41] It begins with seven letters to churches in western Asia Minor, contains a series of visions, and concludes with a description of the new Jerusalem.

Unlike most apocalypses, this one is neither pseudonymous nor antedated. It claims to be written by a prophet named John, who has been exiled to the island of Patmos during a persecution of Christians. Justin claimed that it was written by an apostle of Jesus,[42] but the author calls himself a prophet, not an apostle, and speaks of the twelve as a group in the past. The letters to the churches suggest that the author was a Christian of some influence in western Asia Minor, and his acquaintance with the apocalyptic tradition indicates that he may have come from a Jewish background. Differences in diction, vocabulary, style, and phraseology demon-

[40] *Church History* III, 25:2.
[41] For the text of Athanasius' letter, see Edgar Hennecke, *New Testament Apocrypha*, ed. W. Schneemelcher, trans. R. McL. Wilson (Philadelphia, Pa.: Westminster, 1963), Vol. 1, p. 59 f.
[42] *Dialogue with Trypho* 81:4.

A coin of Nero. (*Courtesy* The American Numismatic Society.)

strate that he is not the author of the Fourth Gospel or the Johannine letters.

Irenaeus said that the Revelation of John was written "toward the end of Domitian's reign."[43] The internal evidence suggests the same period. It is evident that the historical situation that prompted the book was a persecution of Christians, brought about by their failure to obey an order to conform to imperial religion. At least one well-known man, Antipas of Pergamum, has been killed, and John has been exiled to Patmos. The book refers to divine claims made by the ruler and to marks which were required of his subjects. The Roman state cult, rooted in the worship of Roma, began with the posthumous worship of Julius Caesar.[44] It arose quite naturally among religious polytheists, who found in the emperor the chief example of divine power. To most it was simply an expression of patriotism and gratitude for the peace and security the Empire afforded. Augustus attempted to discourage it, and the Senate restricted it to a select group of deceased emperors. But it was difficult to control an emperor who wished to receive the benefits of worship in his lifetime. There is evidence that Domitian was one of these and that he practiced religious persecution.[45] In

[43] *Against Heresies* V, 30:3.

[44] See p. 77.

[45] Eusebius, *Church History* III, 17; Dio Cassius, *Roman History* 67:14. For an analysis of the relevant literature on Domitian's enforcement of the imperial cult, see Donald McFayden, "The Occasion of the Domitianic Persecution," *American Journal of Theology* 24: 46–66 (1920).

addition, there are certain allusions in Revelation that point to Domitian. The author speaks of a series of rulers and identifies his own time as the reign of the sixth. Domitian was not the sixth Roman emperor, but he was the sixth ruler to be declared divine.[46] In the enumeration of rulers,

Head of Domitian, Museo Communale, Rome. (*Courtesy* Alinari-Art Reference Bureau.)

John says there will be one more, and then one of the previous six will return. This may reflect the *Nero redivivus* legend, which arose near the end of the first century. Nero had died in A.D. 68, but it was believed that he would return. Finally, in Revelation 6:6, there is a possible allusion to

[46] The first five were Julius Caesar, Augustus, Claudius, Vespasian, and Titus. See Martin Rist in *The Interpreter's Bible* (New York: Abingdon, 1951–57), Vol. XII, p. 495.

Domitian's edict on Asian vineyards. In A.D. 92, he ordered that half the vineyards in Asia be plowed under in order to protect the price of Italian wine. The various internal evidences indicate that Irenaeus was right and that Revelation was written toward the end of Domitian's reign, that is, about A.D. 95–96.

Most of the apocalyptic trappings are present in Revelation. The author describes his vision as a revelation of what is shortly to happen. After the seven letters, he narrates a series of visions, the first of which features a scroll containing a schedule of events. Only the Christ, described as a lamb, is able to open the scroll. The events to come include famines, rebellions, wars, pestilences, and conflagrations. The devil is described as a dragon, who has an earthly counterpart, a beast, which is an obvious representation of the Roman Empire. The central section of the book is largely descriptive of the time of the author. In 19:11, however, begins a chronological sequence that projects into the future. Christ appears as head of an army, conquers the beast, and throws him into a lake of fire. The dragon is bound and thrown into a bottomless pit for a millennium (one thousand years). During this period the Christian martyrs come back to life and reign with Christ. At the end of the millennium, the dragon is released, and he, with the help of the nations, makes war on Christ and the saints. But the dragon and its allies are finally defeated and thrown into the lake of fire. Then earth and sky disappear, and all the dead are raised for judgment, the canon of which is the book of life. All those whose names are not recorded therein are thrown into the fiery lake. In the final scenes we have the creation of a new heaven, a new earth, and a new Jerusalem. God is eternally and immediately present in the new creation, and there is no pain, sorrow, or mourning. The new Jerusalem is characterized by order, beauty, riches, and righteousness.

The Revelation of John has been the object of a wide diversity of interpretation. Many understand it as intended for a modern audience and attempt to interpret its symbols as twentieth-century figures and events. It is inevitable that latter-day Christians will see their own time reflected and anticipated in a book which is regarded as sacred, and Revelation's obscurity lends itself to this tendency. Modern readers should, however, keep in mind the fact that the book was written for people living at the end of the first century. These Christians were facing persecution and needed encouragement to endure. They would not have found it if John of Patmos had been speaking over their heads to us. Nor is it likely that they would have preserved a book that was totally meaningless to them. Any interpretation must be controlled by this fact.

The Apocalypse of Peter[47]

The concept of eternal rewards and punishments formed a part of Christian thought from early times. Matthew had contained a picture of the last judgment, in which Jesus separates the sheep from the goats, and the Revelation of John left no doubt about the fate of the wicked. But it is with the Apocalypse of Peter that we first have a detailed description of the localities of punishment and reward—hell and heaven.

Most of the apocalyptic features are missing in this document, and there is concentration on the existence of the unrighteous and righteous dead after the Parousia of Jesus. The author sets the scene on the Mount of Olives, where Peter asks Jesus to relate the signs of his Parousia. After he gives the fig tree as the sign, he shows Peter the fate of all men. The righteous are in Jesus' right hand and the others in his left. The reader's attention is almost entirely focused upon the fate of the wicked. Some two-dozen types of sinners are listed, including apostates, idolaters, fornicators, murderers, unwed mothers, abortionists, persecutors, slanderers, false witnesses, moneylenders, disobedient slaves, and sorcerers. Each sin has its own punishment, and the punishment is sadistically described. Persecutors are cast into a dark place, where "a worm that never sleeps consumes their entrails."[48] Some punishments are intended to be appropriate to the crime. Women who procure abortions are swallowed up to their necks in excrement, and their children stand facing them from a distance. "And lightnings go forth from those children which pierce the eyes of those who, by fornication, have brought about their destruction."[49] By contrast, this author has little interest in the rewards of righteousness.

The Muratorian Canon seems to have accepted the Apocalypse of Peter as sacred and lists it as the last New Testament book but says that some refuse to have it read in church. Clement of Alexandria, in the third century, thought that Peter had written it.[50] Since it shows acquaintance with the Synoptic Gospels and is listed in the Muratorian Canon of A.D. 200, it must be dated about the middle of the second century. Its description of heaven and hell as localities had a long-lasting influence on the Christian church.

---

[47] For an English translation, see Hennecke, op. cit., Vol. II, pp. 668–683. Translations below are from this edition.

[48] Apocalypse of Peter 9.

[49] Apocalypse of Peter 8.

[50] In Eusebius, *Church History* VI, 14:1.

APOLOGIES

The political difficulties of the Christian movement gave rise to apocalypses, directed to the persecuted, and apologies, directed to the persecutors. The apocalypses were intended to convince Christians that they were on the side of right and ultimate victory. The apologies were written to defend Christianity against misunderstanding and false charges. The apologists were not regretfully acknowledging an error and asking for forgiveness; they were acting as advocates for the faith. They tried to present Christianity in the best possible light and to show that the state had nothing to fear from it. Christianity was widely misunderstood by Roman officials and by the general populace. It was like Judaism but seemed new. It challenged all other religions. It upset economic patterns and social relationships. It admitted women and slaves, but its meetings were open only to members. It spoke of a kingdom to come. It revered a criminal. The Christian apologists attempted to explain these difficulties to Roman authorities and to show that the teachings of their religion were compatible with the best thought of the culture.

The literary form of the apology had a time-honored history, dating back to the Apology of Socrates. The customary approach was to take the charges, explore their meaning, and demonstrate their erroneous nature. Their style was characterized by clarity of exposition and interesting detail. Many were replete with quotations from poets and philosophers. They generally concentrated on one major point and gave slight attention to one or two minor matters. A concluding appeal summed up the argument. It takes a learned man to be an apologist. He must write in a clear, forceful, and appealing style, and he must be familiar with a wide range of literary allusions. He must be aware of the basic ideas and motivating forces of his opponents and must know what in his defendant will appeal to them. It is notable that second-century Christianity could produce so many apologies, including one by Aristides, an Oration to the Greeks by Tatian, three books addressed to Autolycus by Theophilus, and the anonymous Epistle to Diognetus. The chief principles, methods, and viewpoints of the apologists may be illustrated by reference to two—Justin and Athenagoras.

The Apology of Justin[51]

Justin, called the Martyr, was born in Samaria of Gentile parents. He had a passing acquaintance with Stoics, Peripatetics, and Pythagoreans, but was

---

[51] For an English translation, see Richardson, op. cit., pp. 242–298. Translations below are from this edition.

deeply attracted to Platonic philosophy. About A.D. 150 he met a Christian who exposed him to the writings of the Old Testament prophets. Impressed with the correspondence between these writings and the life of Jesus, he became a Christian convert. Eusebius lists a number of his writings, most of which have been lost.[52] His *Apology* and his *Dialogue with Trypho* have, however, come down to us in late manuscripts. The former is his defense of Christianity addressed to Roman authorities; the latter is addressed to Jews. Both are characterized by an irenic spirit and seek to convince by persuasion without depreciating the opponent. The *Apology* was written in Rome about A.D. 155 and the *Dialogue* a few years later. Sometime between A.D. 163 and 167, Justin was executed for refusing to make the imperial sacrifice.

The *Apology* is addressed to Antoninus Pius, Roman emperor from A.D. 138 to 161. It begins by calling on him to investigate the charges brought against Christians and not to persecute them simply for the name. As early as A.D. 117, the emperor Trajan had virtually declared Christianity illegal. Although he took a moderate attitude on searching out Christians and on receiving complaints, his decision meant that they could be persecuted for bearing the name. Justin's *Apology* reflects the fact that Trajan's decision became official policy. Justin admits that some Christians have been convicted of criminal activities, but this should not mean that all Christians are criminals.[53] If all philosophers do not say the same thing, then all Christians are not alike. In fact, says Justin, Christianity opposes those activities that harm the state. It teaches its adherents to pay taxes and pray for the emperor. Christians have such a high sexual standard that some in their sixties and seventies are still virgins. Because they are taught that God judges all men on the basis of their virtue or vice, Christians are the emperor's best helpers in securing order.

But Christians were arrested not only for bearing the name; they were accused also of atheism. Justin admits that Christians neglect the worship of the demons and the sons of Zeus. Nor do Christians make sacrifices to any God, because they believe that God has no need of offerings. Christians are not atheists, however. They refuse to worship the demons and Zeus because of their immorality, but they worship the one true God.

Justin also objects to the charge that Christianity is novel and strange. Throughout his *Apology* he makes comparisons between Christianity and

---

[52] *Church History* IV, 18.

[53] Contrast Athenagoras, *Apology* 2, who said that no Christian had ever been convicted of a crime.

the other religions and philosophies. He asks: Why are we singled out for persecution, if we believe something like what is believed by others?

> When we say that all things have been ordered and made by God we appear to offer the teaching of Plato—in speaking of a coming destruction by fire that of the Stoics; in declaring that the souls of the unrighteous will be punished after death, still remaining in conscious existence; and those of the virtuous, delivered from punishments, will enjoy happiness, we seem to agree with [various] poets and philosophers; in declaring that men ought not to worship the works of their hands we are saying the same things as the comedian Menander and others who have said this, for they declared that the Fashioner is greater than what he has formed.[54]

Justin compares the virgin birth of Jesus with the births of the sons of Zeus, his healing with that of Asclepius, and his ascension with those of deceased emperors. In making these comparisons, Justin is in danger of overlooking the uniqueness of Christianity. In fact, however, he believes that the analogues are present because the other religions have imitated Christianity and the philosophies have been given a partial truth.

The key to the relationship of Christianity to the other religions and philosophies is Justin's understanding of *Logos*. He may have been familiar with the prologue to the Fourth Gospel, but Justin mainly expresses himself in Stoic fashion. He believes that *Logos* is in every man, but this presence does not impart a divinity to men. It acts, rather, as the means of the revelation of truth, given to the Old Testament prophets and to the Greek philosophers. Thus, Christianity is not to be regarded as some strange new thing. It was preached even by Moses, to whom the *Logos* was revealed, and by Plato, who learned from Moses. The relationship that Justin sees between Moses, Plato, and Christ appears fantastic to us, but his purpose is to point to the unity of truth. In a reference to Plato's *Timaeus*, Justin says that the Son of God was placed X-wise in the universe, that is, in the shape of a cross. Plato got this from Moses, who protected the people from snakes by a cross, and both Moses and Plato were speaking of the crucifixion of Jesus.[55] The *Logos,* then, is the source of truth for Moses, the prophets, the philosophers, and for Christianity. The latter has the fullness of truth, because the *Logos* has appeared in the man Christ Jesus. The evidence for the truth resident in the incarnation is the remarkable correspondence between the Old Testament prophets and the life of Jesus. Some of these spoke five

---

[54] Justin, *Apology* 20.
[55] Justin, *Apology* 60.

thousand years beforehand. The *Logos* revealed these things then so that they would be believed when they occurred.

In the concluding chapters, Justin gives a description of Christian worship in order to show its inoffensive nature, and he ends with a letter of Hadrian, which he takes to be helpful to the Christian cause.

The two notable features of Justin's thought are his understanding of *Logos* and his accommodation to Greek philosophy. The *Logos* is the son of God and that of which "every race of man partakes."[56] But the *Logos* was also born, taught, was crucified, died, and ascended. Although other religions have imitated Christianity, they have nothing like the crucifixion. In fact, however, Justin underplays the uniqueness of Christianity. For not just the crucifixion, but the incarnation itself, is lacking a parallel in contemporary religion and philosophy. Justin's accommodation to philosophy may be deceptive. Although he finds much of value in Platonism and Stoicism, he makes it abundantly clear that whatever truth they have is revealed by the *Logos*. The essential difference between the philosophies and Christianity is that the former have a knowledge that is the result of human conjecture and an incomplete divine revelation, whereas the latter is altogether the product of divine revelation.

The Apology of Athenagoras[57]

Athenagoras may have borrowed certain ideas from Justin, but the style of his *Apology* is far superior. He quotes several of Jesus' teachings, but he has nothing on the life, and he has no emphasis on Old Testament prophecy. Nothing is known of the author's life. His *Apology* is directed to the emperors Marcus Aurelius and Commodus, so it must date from A.D. 176 or 177.

Athenagoras sets out to answer three charges: that Christians are atheists, that they practice incest, and that they are cannibals. Some seven eighths of the work is devoted to the first charge. Having answered that Christians are not atheists, he finds no difficulty in demolishing the others. He does not suggest the source of the moral charges, but we may guess that they arose out of a misunderstanding of the Christian emphasis on love and of the closed communion service, where the body of the Lord was eaten.

Athenagoras clearly regards the charge of atheism to be the most serious.

[56] Justin, *Apology* 46.
[57] For an English translation, see Richardson, op. cit., pp. 300–340. Translations below are from this edition.

He defends Christians by affirming their monotheism, and he shows that Plato, Aristotle, and the Stoics were also monotheists. He claims, "All philosophers, then, even if unwillingly, reach complete agreement about the unity of God when they come to inquire into the first principles of the universe."[58] He then turns to a proof of monotheism based upon rational argument and Scripture, and he expounds upon the Trinity in the clearest statement of any second-century writer. He bolsters his monotheistic affirmation by an attack upon the other religions and the immorality of their gods. He claims that demons draw men to idolatry and to the worship of gods who were originally men.

One cannot fail to be impressed with the learning and wit of Athenagoras. Nor should we overlook his courage, for he was challenging the basic religious ideas of his day. But we fail to find in him the central themes we have learned to associate with Christian tradition. There are a few quotations from Jesus' ethical teachings but nothing about his life or death. There is no emphasis on Hebrew prophecy, no redemption theology, no eschatology. To be sure, the *Apology* may not be the full expression of Athenagoras' religion, but it is evidence that one could be a Christian and write a fairly lengthy document without these items. Furthermore, the central monotheistic affirmation is not defended by appeal to revelation but to reason and to revered men of the past.

The Apologies are signals of an emerging alliance between Christian religion and Platonic-Stoic philosophy. The alliance originates as a useful device for communicating with the Roman world but will come to play a leading role in the history of Christian thought. We do not know if the Apologists achieved their desired result. Certainly, Justin's writing did not save him from martyrdom in the time of the Stoic philosopher-emperor Marcus Aurelius. But their writing produced a significant, if unintended, effect by opening up lines of communication that proved to be of immense value in the centuries to come.

ANTIHERETICAL LITERATURE

The word *heresy* is derived from a Greek word which means choice. It was used to designate the particular teachings of philosophical schools, and it denoted the opinions that each one had chosen. Christian writers began to

[58] Athenagoras, *Apology* 7.

use the term and soon gave it a pejorative significance. To them a man or school does not have the right to choose an opinion, hold it, and teach it. Opinion is a humanly derived idea, the result of conjecture and speculation. Truth, however, is given to man by revelation. Heresy, therefore, involves not only choosing an opinion but rejecting revelation. Thus, it has an evil significance, and the heretic is evil.

The antiheretical literature arose to deal with those who were teaching divergent opinions. As we shall see in the next section, early Christianity was full of all sorts of movements, sects, and teachers, all claiming the name Christian. Justin was embarrassed by the fact that the name covered such a wide diversity of beliefs and practices. We may ask if each group would not have claimed that the teachings of other Christian groups were false. Surely they would, and it is something of a historical accident that the literature we have represents only one side of an argument. Precious little Gnostic literature was preserved, and none of this explicitly attacks other forms of Christianity or responds to attacks. Some such writing may have been suppressed by the victorious group. We may, nevertheless, assume that there were internal arguments, charges, and countercharges within the Christian movement for several decades. A Gnostic would claim that other forms of Christianity were deficient in knowledge. A Jewish Christian would feel that the church had largely diverged from its heritage. The antiheretical writings we have make the claim that problems in Christian faith are caused by the act of choice in matters of belief. Man simply does not have the right to choose an opinion in theological matters. Although one may say that this claim is itself a chosen position, writers such as Irenaeus felt that the distinguishing characteristic of Christian faith was the acceptance of a revealed tradition. Although a number of earlier writers had addressed themselves to the problem of Christian diversity, the earliest systematic attack on heresy preserved for us in that of Irenaeus of Lyons.

Irenaeus[59]

Irenaeus says that when he was a boy he knew Polycarp of Smyrna, so he must have been born and raised there. He later became a presbyter in Lyons and carried correspondence from there to Rome. He may have taken the letter about persecution at Lyons and Vienne to the Roman bishop,

[59] For an English translation of the most important sections of Irenaeus' *Against Heresies*, see Richardson, op. cit., pp. 358–397. Translations below are from this edition.

Eleutherus.[60] Returning to Gaul in A.D. 177, he found that his bishop had been executed and that he had been selected as his successor. About A.D. 180 he wrote *A Refutation and Overthrow of Pseudo-Gnosis*, usually referred to as *Against Heresies.* In the five books that make up this work, he gives detailed descriptions of numerous heresies, which he claims to have studied extensively, and he destroys them. His attention is mainly focused upon the thought of Valentinus and Marcion. His descriptions are fundamental sources for our understanding of these sects, but we must remember that Irenaeus was not an objective reporter.

Irenaeus has a strongly pastoral intent in writing, and he is disturbed at the damage done to the simple Christian by the heresies. To him the heresies are wrong chiefly because they deny monotheism. They set up a pantheon of deities, attribute the work of creation to a lesser god, and separate redemption from creation. This is the fundamental error, because, for Irenaeus, there is but one God, who created the world and spoke his redemptive word in Jesus the Christ. How does he know that his opponents are wrong? For one thing, they use spurious Scriptures, such as the Infancy Gospel of Thomas and the Gospel of Truth. Some of them confine themselves to one Gospel, such as Marcion, who used a "mutilated" copy of Luke. When they comment upon the Scriptures, they misinterpret them and read fanciful speculations into them. In addition, their teaching is irrational, for polytheism cannot be defended by reason. They make Jesus superfluous, because they derive their systems from the Greek philosophers and mix them up in strange ways. They claim to have a secret tradition from Jesus, known only to themselves, but they are inconsistent with one another, and they all say different things.

By contrast, the monotheism taught by the church may be rationally defended. Both the Old and the New Testaments teach it consistently. It has been taught publicly by Jesus, the apostles, and all the churches. It is a more ancient teaching than that of Valentinus or Marcion.

If one should ask how a person in A.D. 180 should determine what true Christianity is, Irenaeus would answer that it is found in the church. But a number of complexities immediately arise, because there were churches which held to Marcionite teaching, and there were Christians who were Valentinians. We need, then, a definition of *church*, and Irenaeus provides one. The church is defined by three factors, which guarantee its possession of the truth. (1) The church is guided by the rule of faith, a creedal statement taught in all churches, whether in Spain, Gaul, Italy, or Asia Minor. This

---

[60] See pp. 161 ff.

creed, which Irenaeus quotes, expresses belief in "one God, the Father Almighty, who made the heaven, and the earth, and the seas, and all that is in them, and in one Christ Jesus, the Son of God, who was made flesh for our salvation, and in the Holy Spirit, who through the prophets proclaimed the dispensations of God."[61] Irenaeus believes that this rule was delivered by the apostles to the church. The church, therefore, is that which has received the revealed tradition expressed in the rule of faith. (2) The churches were established by the apostles, who also chose their successors. Irenaeus can point to an unbroken succession of bishops in the churches and, as an illustration, lists the bishops in the Church at Rome, from Peter to the current Eleutherus. He chooses Rome because of its age and pre-eminence. In this way he guarantees the authenticity of the rule of faith and guards against the notion of secret traditions. If Jesus had conveyed secret teachings to the apostles, they would have delivered them to their successors, and the church would now possess them, not the heretical groups. But the apostles did not deliver secrets; they delivered the rule of faith. (3) The church has the apostolic writings. The Old Testament contains the word by anticipation, but the apostles were eyewitnesses of the incarnation and vehicles for the transmission of Jesus' teachings. But since many books claim apostolic authorship, we need a definition of Scripture; and Irenaeus makes a significant contribution to the development of the canon. He maintains that there are four gospels, no more and no less. Matthew and John were written by apostles, Mark and Luke by disciples of apostles. Irenaeus also relies on the authority of Paul and quotes from every document now in the New Testament except Philemon, III John, and perhaps Jude. In citing the authority of the rule of faith, apostolic succession, and the apostolic writings, Irenaeus is certainly following the traditional practices of many, but by no means all, churches.

The demands of Irenaeus' historical situation and his response to them have made him a figure of crucial significance for early Christianity. He has seen the problem of diversity and the need for authority. The honest but simple Christian, who is anxious about his salvation, needs only to depend upon the church, its rule of faith, and its Scriptures. These have authority because the rule of faith is the content of apostolic teaching, because the church stands in an unbroken succession from the apostles, and because the Scriptures were written by the apostles. With these tools Irenaeus has laid the foundation for catholic Christianity and has brought to a close the ancient period of uncontrolled diversity.

[61] Irenaeus, *Against Heresies* I, 10 : 1.

The crypt of the Popes, Catacomb of St. Callixtus, Rome. (*Courtesy* Pontifical Commission for Sacred Archives, Rome.)

Our survey of early Christian literature is now complete. Not every writing has been covered, but enough has been examined to indicate the kinds of interests Christians had, the diverse points of view they held, the problems they faced, and the developments that were taking place. We shall next proceed to use this literature as source material for understanding the various Christian groups that were to be found in the early period.

Part Three

*Varieties of
Early Christianity*

The Breaking of Bread, third-century fresco from the Catacomb of Priscilla, Rome. (*Courtesy* Pontifical Commission for Sacred Archives, Rome.)

Our survey of the literature has shown that early Christianity was represented in a number of groups with diverse viewpoints and practices. Some of the differences are due to the creative impress of a personality, such as Paul or John. But most of the variation is the product of differences in traditions. Those documents that have an institutional character and include traditional material, such as the gospels, represent something akin to schools of thought, which may be distinguished on the basis of their theological orientation or their ethnic context. Within the period encompassed by our study, it is possible to distinguish some six varieties of early Christianity. In some cases there are differences within groups, and, in other cases, similarities between groups. Nevertheless, these six stand out with sufficient distinctiveness: primitive, Pauline, Johannine, Jewish, Gnostic, and protocatholic.

Although Christianity found its beginning with Jesus, he did not bequeath to it a set of clear and distinct ideas. As a result, early Christianity was marked not only by vital growth but also by lively diversity. The very earliest identifiable form of Christianity is given the name primitive. It designates the religion of the immediate followers of Jesus, some of whom had been with him in his lifetime. It was mainly a Jewish movement, located almost entirely in Palestine. But there was also a primitive Gentile Christianity, probably located in several cities of Asia Minor in the primitive period—that is, from A.D. 30 to A.D. 70. Pauline Christianity is, of course, the religion that Paul held, preached to churches in Asia Minor, Macedonia, and Greece, and communicated in his letters. But it is also to be associated with the pseudo-Pauline and other writings, which modified it in significant ways. Paul's period of activity was c. A.D. 40–60 and partially overlapped the primitive period, but Pauline Christianity continued into the second century. Johannine Christianity is found in Asia Minor after A.D. 90 or 100, although its influence is not well attested until the latter part of the second century. Jewish Christianity claimed to be the continuation of the most primitive form of the religion. It is best to treat it as a distinct group, however, because most of the literature about it comes from the mid-second century or later. It was located mostly in Syria and Palestine. Many second-century Christians regarded it as an antiquated phenomenon, although it seems to be fairly well known. The origin of Gnostic Christianity is obscure, although it is probable that a non-Christian Gnosticism preceded it. There are indications that it was known in the first century, even as early as Paul's time. By the mid-second century, it had become a significant expression of Christianity. The geographic center seems to be Asia Minor or Egypt, but it was to be found throughout the Mediterranean world. Protocatholic Christianity arose largely out of combat with Gnostics. We give this name to a form of the religion *that anticipated the development of a full-blown catholicism in the third and fourth centuries. It is best represented in the apologetic and antiheretical literature of the last half of the second century. The following chapters examine the groups in greater detail.*

Chapter Nine

The Earliest Varieties

Under this heading we shall consider primitive Christianity and Pauline Christianity.

PRIMITIVE CHRISTIANITY

The term *primitive Christianity* is used to designate the oldest form of the religion, which one would expect to find among those who had been Jesus' most intimate associates. Chronologically, it refers to Christian beliefs and practices of the first three or four decades after the crucifixion, and it partially overlaps Pauline Christianity. It is difficult to avoid assumptions about this period, and it seems easy to read back into it favorite concepts of later times. Because it should represent the original type of Christianity and includes Jesus' personal followers, it has its own special kind of authority for later Christians. A romantic aura frequently pervades our picture of these early times. One's impression is that of a handful of vigorously enthusiastic people who see themselves involved in a mystery and proclaim it in simple terms. The quality of freshness, mystery, and simplicity is difficult to avoid and, perhaps, should not be suppressed.

The difficulty in understanding the period is compounded by a lack of directly relevant material. Paul wrote his letters during the primitive period, but he represented a different variety in Christianity, and he was largely involved in issues relating to his own newly founded churches. The Book of Acts includes a history of the period, but, as we have seen, it was written later in the first century by an author who had a distinctive point of view. Nothing is directly relevant, but a cautious use of Paul and Acts may, nevertheless, serve our purposes. It is possible to distinguish between the creative, or Pauline, and the traditional, or primitive, elements in the letters of Paul. For example, he refers to a traditional catalogue of witnesses to Jesus' resurrection in I Corinthians 15 and to material about the last supper in I Corinthians 11. These are items of information he had received from primitive Christianity. In Galatians he describes some of the contacts he had with those who were Christians before him. Because Paul was in a position to know something about primitive Christianity and was careful

The city of Jerusalem, showing the Jaffa Gate in the foreground, the site of the Temple in the center, and the Mount of Olives in the background. (*Courtesy* Israel Government Tourist Office, Atlanta, Georgia.)

to distinguish between his own views and those of others, his letters are, when used properly, valuable sources for understanding primitive Christianity. Moreover, the Book of Acts may be useful, for Luke had sources which antedated him, and sometimes they can be spotted. In addition, we have been able to discover an outline of the primitive Christian *kerygma*.[1] Although it is lacking in details, the outline can serve as a guide to the beliefs of the earliest Christians. Finally, the study of oral forms has opened another set of sources. Since material about Jesus circulated orally in the primitive church, it should be possible to use the oldest forms deposited in the gospels for information on primitive Christianity. All of these materials must be used with great care, and we must constantly be aware of the distinction between elements in the tradition and those contributed by later writers. With these qualifications, the letters of Paul, the Book of Acts, the outline of the *kerygma,* and certain Synoptic forms make up a respectable body of source material.

The primitive *kerygma* is our fundamental guide to the basic spirit of the primitive church. This included a proclamation that the final age of history had begun in the ministry, death, and resurrection of Jesus, who has now been exalted as Messiah. History will soon reach its consummation at his return. The preachers further proclaimed that the spirit in the church was a signal of the Messiah's present power and glory and that there was still time for repentance before the end. The very earliest community must have been made up of those who had known Jesus and were convinced of his resurrection and his pending return.

The genesis of the religion was the belief in the resurrection of Jesus. Just what did the original Christians mean when they proclaimed the resurrection? The oldest statements we have suggest that some people had seen him alive after death. In I Corinthians 15, where Paul is clearly conveying traditional, primitive material, he catalogues a series of appearances to Cephas (Peter), the twelve disciples, five hundred brethren, James, and the apostles. To the traditional list, he adds a final appearance to himself. Unfortunately, the catalogue does not contain a description of the appearances, and we are not enlightened on their nature. Were they thought to be private, optical, or auditory experiences, or were they public and objective? When Paul says that there was an appearance to "over five hundred of our brothers at once,"[2] we may be led to think of a public appearance. But *brother* is Paul's technical term for Christian, so he cannot be thinking

---

[1] See p. 167 f.
[2] I Corinthians 15:6.

of a public appearance. The traditional material limits the resurrection appearances to believers. It never suggests that Jesus appeared to Pilate or Herod Antipas or the high priest. Although Paul claims an appearance to himself, he does not describe it, and all we know is that it caused a drastic reorientation of his life.[3] The material cited by Paul suggests that the church had early come to believe that the risen one had appeared to select people. But is the faith of the church based upon the claims of these people, or does the tradition of appearances result from a prior belief that Jesus had been raised?

We may get somewhat closer to the meaning of the resurrection faith in a speech of Peter in Acts 2. Although the speech is Luke's composition, it seems to contain a kernel of non-Lukan primitive material. The scene is Jerusalem at Pentecost. The disciples of Jesus are gathered together and suddenly begin to speak in tongues.[4] The phenomenon (called glossolalia) causes a great uproar, and Peter attempts to explain it to the crowd. He does so by quoting from the prophet Joel, who had predicted ecstatic phenomena on the last days. The fact of glossolalia, therefore, demonstrates that the end is upon us. Then Peter goes on to proclaim the resurrection of Jesus, and he quotes an Old Testament prediction of it. He concludes: "The Jesus we speak of has been raised by God, as we can all bear witness. Exalted thus with God's right hand, he received the Holy Spirit from the Father, as was promised, and all that you now see and hear flows from him. . . . God has made this Jesus, whom you crucified, both Lord and Messiah."[5] Peter is saying that the glossolalia is precisely what Joel predicted. It has been made possible by the risen Jesus. Although there are Lukan elements in the narrative, it is appealing as primitive, because it is not consistent with Luke's own presentation of the resurrection faith, which cites the empty tomb and visible appearances as evidence.[6]

The speech of Peter illustrates the eschatological climate in which the resurrection faith must have arisen. The disciples of Jesus came to the conviction that the last days were upon them and that they could expect to see visions and experience ecstatic phenomena. Since they were Jews, they understood the eschatological hope in terms of a Messianic age, one aspect

---

[3] The Book of Acts contains three detailed descriptions of Paul's conversion, 9:1–19; 22:4–16; 26:12–18. These are, of course, Luke's descriptions, not Paul's.

[4] The phenomenon of glossolalia is also dealt with in I Corinthians 14, where it appears to be ecstatic speech of an unknown tongue. Luke, however, understands it as the ability to speak an actual human language foreign to the speaker. Paul is certainly closer to the actual situation at this point.

[5] Acts 2:32 ff.

[6] See Luke 24.

of which was to be the resurrection of the righteous. They came to believe that this resurrection was represented by the resurrection of Jesus himself; it was the first act in the concluding period of history and an anticipatory confirmation of the life to come. The only way they could have come to their eschatological convictions is by their contact with Jesus. In some as yet undefinable way, they had focused on Jesus as their hope for the future and refused to believe that his defeat was God's final word. They knew that he had been killed by lawless men, but they were convinced that God had exalted him. Once this conviction was established, then ecstatic phenomena and reports of appearances would confirm their faith. It is not possible to describe fully the origin of their convictions, but it was surely in the certainty that the Messianic age was about to dawn that the disciples arrived at the belief in the resurrection.

To express their eschatological convictions, the disciples found in their Jewish heritage the concept of the Messiah, which was readily available for their use. Their feeling was that at the resurrection God had made Jesus the Messiah. Jesus was not Messiah in his lifetime, but he is now, and he will return to exercise his proper functions. The earliest Christians were not yet ready to raise any questions about the life of Jesus. To them, of course, it was a human life, for they were precisely those who had known him as human. So his humanity was part of the given situation, neither questioned nor explicitly affirmed, but not problematic. In no case do they think of Jesus as exercising the functions of Messiah during his lifetime, for the resurrection was the crucial point at which he became the Christ. Their Christology (speculation about the person and work of the Christ) is usually called adoptionistic. This means that God did not send Jesus from heaven as his Messiah but rather designated him as such at the resurrection. Even so, we are not to think of this as an idea which occurred to God only when Jesus died, for the early preachers were sure that the whole complex of events was in accordance with the definite plan and foreknowledge of God.[7] The point to be emphasized in the primitive Christology is that God did not send a divine being to earth as Messiah but selected a human.

Although the term *Messiah* was readily available for Christian use, it was not an unambiguous term. The primitive Christians certainly accepted Jesus as son of David, but soon they began to think of him as Son of man. Here was an Aramaic term, which was significant in the apocalyptic tradi-

[7] See Acts 2 : 23.

tion from Daniel on down.[8] The disciples of Jesus would have understood it as a divine figure who is expected to come on the clouds to bring about the end of the world. The use of the phrase demonstrates the community's orientation toward the future and its veneration of Jesus. In this respect, the most primitive Christian community maintained a sense of continuity with Judaism. Both Jews and Christians were looking forward to the coming of Messiah; neither believed that he had come. The Christians, however, affirmed that he is to come soon and that when he comes, he will be Jesus. The primitive Christian Christology runs as follows: Jesus, son of David, was born, lived, and died; God raised him up and made him Son of man-Messiah; he will soon return to bring in the Messianic age.

In their Christology, primitive Christians demonstrate their proximity to Judaism. Since the earliest disciples were Jews, this is precisely what we should expect. In other respects as well, this proximity is evident. These primitive Jewish Christians were monotheists and accepted the God of Moses as the one God. They accepted the Jewish Scriptures and felt that they stood in a continuum with Israelite history. They accepted Jewish institutions and presented themselves as the Israel of the latter days. They referred to themselves as the *ecclesia*, a term that we translate as church but that really means a gathered community. They felt that the initial stages of the eschatological collection of Israel had begun with them.

The leadership of the primitive community is far from clear. The city of Jerusalem seems to be a focal point for them, although communities quickly arose in Damascus and Antioch. Our sources sometimes speak of leadership by the twelve disciples. It is frequently stated today that the idea of the twelve is a legendary conception of later times.[9] The group is supposed to be representative of all Israel, which was originally made up of twelve tribes. That there never was such a formal group is shown by the fact that the Synoptic writers differ widely in their lists of those who were in it. The term *apostles* points to a genuine, but loosely organized, group of leaders. It is impossible to determine how many apostles there were, but Peter, John bar Zebedee, and Paul certainly belonged to it, and it probably included Barnabas, Andronicus, and Junias.[10] The word denotes persons who have been commissioned for a specific task, and most are described as traveling to make an initial proclamation of the gospel in foreign

[8] See p. 110 f.

[9] The conception is represented in Christianity prior to Paul; see I Corinthians 15:5.

[10] The last two names appear only in Romans 16:7. See Walter Schmithals, *The Office of Apostle in the Early Church*, trans. J. E. Steely (New York: Abingdon, 1969).

parts. According to Paul, apostles held a position of prime authority in the church, ranking ahead of prophets, teachers, miracle workers, and healers. In reference to the leadership of the Jerusalem Church, he speaks of three "pillar" apostles, namely Peter, John bar Zebedee, and James. The Synoptic writers also have a group of three intimates, but they have James bar Zebedee rather than the brother James. Paul is more dependable at this point, and his "pillar" apostles represent the top group of primitive Jewish Christians. If one is to point to a single leader, it would be either Peter or James. Luke says that Peter was the original head of the church and that James later took over. Paul says that on his first visit to Jerusalem, three years after his conversion, he saw Peter and James.[11] At his visit fourteen years later, the "pillars" are in charge, and they recognize Peter as apostle to Jews and Paul as apostle to Gentiles.[12] A certain time later, Paul meets Peter in Antioch and accuses him of acting hypocritically in response to criticism from Jews and other persons who came from James.[13] The picture is by no means clear, but there is a strong probability that James held the highest position in the church from the beginning. Although Paul made his first Jerusalem trip to see Peter, he could not leave without paying his respects to James. By the time of his second trip, James' position was firmly established. Leadership by James is perfectly consistent with the thinking of primitive Jewish Christians. They are anxiously awaiting the appearance of the Messiah, and it is appropriate that his nearest relative, also a son of David, should be his vicegerent until he comes.

The Jerusalem Church seems to exercise a kind of hegemony over other primitive Jewish churches, and Jews held it responsible for all Christian groups. James and the "pillars" therefore have something to say about the other Christian communities among Jews and Gentiles. We have just noted the influence that James exercised in Antioch. Paul also felt it necessary to present his gospel to the Jerusalem Church.[14] Although the "pillars" did not deem it necessary to require the circumcision of Gentile Christians, they requested Paul to take up a collection. The funds were probably necessary to enable the Jerusalem Church to exist in a precarious and volatile environment. Paul was eager to raise the money, because he was interested in the survival of the Jerusalem Church, and he made special efforts to take the collection and present it personally. Another indication of the

[11] See Galatians 1 : 18 ff.
[12] See Galatians 2 : 1–10.
[13] See Galatians 2 : 11–14.
[14] See Galatians 2 : 2.

dominance of the Jerusalem Church may be seen in its appointment of Peter and Paul as apostles to Jews and Gentiles respectively.

Baptism, a third-century fresco from the Catacomb of St. Callixtus, Rome. (*Courtesy* Pontifical Commission for Sacred Archives, Rome.)

The earliest Christians were Jewish Christians, and most of their beliefs and practices were either the same as those in Judaism or compatible with them. On the issue of the Torah, however, we find a degree of complexity. One point is fairly clear: the "pillar" apostles felt that such things as circumcision were optional. In their meeting with Paul, they agreed on this point. But Acts 6–7 suggests that one group of primitive Christians took a more liberal position and called for the total abolition of Torah for all

Christians. Luke's narrative in these chapters is intriguing, because he intends to portray the history of the church in terms of a harmonious unity, but chapters 6–7 betray the fact of division. He has, therefore, modified his source in order to play down the divisive factors and has produced a very difficult section. The Lukan story goes as follows. In the Jerusalem Church a dissension arose between Hebrews and Hellenists over the distribution of food to widows.[15] The Hellenists felt the effects of discrimination. In order to resolve the problem, the twelve disciples, representing the Hebrews, appointed seven men of good reputation and charged them with the serving of tables. Stephen, one of the seven, began to work miracles and signs. He met opposition from Jews, who accused him of making blasphemous statements against Moses and God. He was brought before the high priest, and he defended himself in a speech accusing Jews of disobedience to Moses and predicting the destruction of the Temple. When he claimed to see the Son of man at God's right hand, he was stoned to death, and a period of violent persecution gripped all of the Jerusalem Church except the apostles.

The narrative has numerous difficulties. Just who were the Hebrews and Hellenists? What were the issues between them? Why was Stephen executed? How widespread was the following persecution? Walter Schmithals[16] shows that the terms *Hebrew* and *Hellenist* were used by Jews in the first century to indicate cultural differences between groups of Jews. A Hebrew was a Jew who felt himself to have an intimate relationship with the religion of his fathers. A Hellenist was a Jew who was committed to the Greek way of life and was fairly lax on matters of the Torah. A similar distinction may have been utilized by Jewish Christians, but the words did not mean the same thing in this context. The issue of food distributed to widows may have been problematic, but it alone would hardly have caused the difficulty described in Acts 6. An inequity in allotments to two groups cannot be resolved by the appointment of a council composed solely of the representatives of one side.[17] The only possible interpretation is that there was a break-up between the two groups. The council of seven constituted the leadership for the more liberal group, and Stephen was their spokesman.

[15] The New English Bible gives an interpretation rather than a literal translation of these terms. Here, a Hellenist is one who speaks Greek, and a Hebrew is one who speaks "the language of the Jews" (Acts 6:1).

[16] *Paul and James* (Naperville, Ill.: Allenson, 1965), pp. 26 f. The present author is indebted to Schmithals for the analysis of Acts 6–7.

[17] That the council of seven was composed entirely of Hellenists is shown by the fact that they all bore Greek names, and one of them is explicitly called a proselyte.

His speech in Acts 7 must have been played down by Luke, for it was hardly enough to convict him. Nor does Stephen fit the definition of a Hellenist as one who is lax on Torah. Schmithals observes: "If a certain laxity in observing or esteeming the Law had brought Stephen to his death, it would have been consistent to depopulate half Palestine."[18] The only crime consistent with conditions in Jerusalem and the picture in Acts is that Stephen and his group advocated an abolition of the Torah for those Jews who became Christians. It is also probable that Paul understood that primitive Christians proclaimed the abolition of Torah. He persecuted them because of his zeal for Torah, and upon his conversion he gave it up.[19] He must have come in contact with a group similar to that of Stephen. It is probable that Stephen and the Hellenists were not simply lax about Torah, but that they actually preached against it and that Stephen was executed for his preaching. As for the persecution that followed the death of Stephen, Luke's picture is not credible. He suggests that it involved all of the church except the apostles. He uses the persecution within his geographical scheme as a device for scattering the church into Judaea and Samaria. It is more likely that the persecution was directed at the Hellenists, whom the Jews would correctly associate with Stephen. The more conservative wing of the Jerusalem Church, the wing of James, was unharmed. All details may not be completely clear, but an overall impression is hardly subject to doubt. There were at Jerusalem, in the primitive period, two groups of Jewish Christians—one, that of the Hebrews, which treated the Torah as a cultural phenomenon without religious significance; the other, that of the Hellenists, which called for its abolition. The latter group fared poorly in Jerusalem and probably centered its attentions on Antioch. In other respects—monotheism, eschatology, Christology—the two groups of Jewish Christians are not to be distinguished.

Sometime in the primitive period, Christianity came to Gentiles. Just when this happened nobody knows, although Luke shows that it was not an easy step for Jewish Christians to take. The conversion of Cornelius, the first Gentile, was preceded by a revelation to Peter and followed by confirmation by the Jerusalem apostles. A little later on, Paul conceived of himself as apostle to the Gentiles, but by his time Gentile Christianity had been established in principle and, in some places, in practice.

We should expect primitive Christianity to be the same, whether Jewish or Gentile, but things are rarely that simple. In this case, we have a com-

---

[18] Schmithals, op. cit., p. 22.
[19] See Philippians 3:6. See also pp. 290 ff.

munication problem of significant proportions. How can one preach a message which originated among Jews to non-Jewish people? How can you say to a Gentile that Jesus is Messiah? This term has familiar associations for Jews, but it is meaningless to Gentiles. Nevertheless, some term must

Sarcophagus showing a baptismal scene, third century. (*Courtesy* Soprintendenza alle Antichità, Rome.)

be found that expresses what Jewish Christians meant when they spoke of Messiah. What Gentile term is equivalent to Messiah, in terms of function and value? In terms of function, there is no equivalent, for Messiah was expected to act eschatologically, and there is no eschatological framework in Gentile thought. In terms of value, they could speak of Jesus as Son of God or Lord. The former term was familiar in the Roman world as a designation for the sons of Zeus. This does not mean that Gentile Christians thought of Jesus as one of the sons of Zeus, but it means that they found this term to be the closest equivalent in value to the term Messiah-Son of man. The case is nearly the same as one in which Americans attempt to express the significance of a British monarch. There is no equivalent, for the term *president* does not carry the same weight or express the same complex of meaning and feeling. But it is the closest term available. Similarly, for Gentile Christians, son of God is the nearest term available. The two terms, *Messiah* and *son of God,* may produce a similar reverential feeling but not the same meaning. In time the change of terms will produce a further change in meaning, for Gentile Christians will analyze the phrase son of God on its own merits. This will cause them to raise questions about the humanity and divinity of Jesus, the relationship of the two, the metaphysical nature of Jesus, and his relationship to God.

Another term that Gentiles began to use was *Lord.* The Greek word *kyrios,* which we translate Lord, was familiar in the Hellenistic world, where the Caesar was addressed as *kyrios* and, still earlier, the central deity in religious cults was so addressed. In primitive Gentile Christianity we find the practice of calling on the name of the Lord Jesus in prayer, exorcism in Jesus' name, and cultic veneration of the Lord in worship.[20] Here again we may point to a rough equivalency in terms of value. But Messiah is one whose future appearance is expected, and *kyrios* signifies a cult calling upon a deity present to the community. This shift not only effects a change in attention from future to present, it also looks to the past to assume a preexistence of Jesus. Paul will adopt the idea, which will be further elaborated in John and Hebrews, but he clearly did not originate it. Gentile Christology is profoundly affected by the lack of an eschatological back-

[20] It is possible that the primitive Jewish Christian communities also thought of Jesus as Lord. In I Corinthians 16:22, Paul refers to a liturgical phrase in Aramaic, *Maranatha,* that is, "Come, O Lord." W. Bousset, however, was convinced that the conception of Jesus as Lord was originally Gentile and that Aramaic-speaking Christians picked it up from them. See his *Kyrios Christos,* trans. John E. Steely (Nashville, Tenn.: Abingdon, 1970), pp. 119-152.

ground. Jesus is the son of God, who has come to earth and has died. God has raised him up and restored his divine status; he is now the Lord present to his community of worshipers.

If *Messiah* could be translated only with serious alterations in meaning, the term *Torah* could hardly be used at all. Only the term *nomos,* or law, came close in meaning, and it was generally assumed to mean such things as circumcision and food restrictions. Paul had some trouble with Galatian and Corinthian groups, which attempted to impose circumcision on Gentile Christians. To them the Torah was an eternally valid standard for the judgment of God, and Jesus did not abolish it. Unfortunately, we do not know whether these groups originated before Paul or arose in reaction to him. In spite of some controversy, we can be assured that the basic character of primitive Gentile Christianity did not include adherence to the Torah.

Several practices in the primitive communities deserve our attention. Luke has said that they practiced a sharing of possessions, and this must be historically correct. Those who were able donated money for the support of those who were not able to work. This practice must have been continued in the Gentile churches, for Paul alludes to it when he decrees that anyone who does not work shall not eat.[21] This is an unenforceable decree unless sharing was practiced. Baptism was used as a rite of initiation in the primitive period. It may have arisen in imitation of a practice in the sect originated by John the Baptizer, and it was associated with repentance. The Eucharist is probably a Gentile adaptation of a sacred meal observed among primitive Jewish Christians. The earlier practice was probably a continuation of fellowship begun in Jesus' lifetime. In the Gentile modification, the ideas of partaking of the body and blood of the Lord and remembering his death were uppermost. Paul indicates that the usual pattern consisted of a breaking of bread, followed by a full meal and then a partaking of wine.[22]

Primitive Christianity was, thus, not the same in all places. Those who came from a Jewish background were quite different from the Gentiles, and not all Jewish Christians were the same. From it spring other varieties of early Christianity. From primitive Jewish Christianity a more developed Jewish Christianity will emerge. Pauline Christianity combines elements from Jewish and Gentile Christianity of the primitive period.

[21] II Thessalonians 3:10.
[22] See I Corinthians 11:23–26.

Michaelangelo, *Conversion of Paul*, Capella Paolina, Rome. (*Courtesy* Anderson-Art Reference Bureau.)

PAULINE CHRISTIANITY

The obvious meaning of the phrase *Pauline Christianity* is the correct one. It stands for the specific contribution that Paul made to Christian faith. It is true that the authors of the pseudo-Pauline letters felt that they were writing within the Pauline tradition and that Luke and I Clement had a deep reverence for Paul. But the influence that Paul had over the other writers is very questionable, and their contribution is in any case ideologically minimal. Thus, Pauline Christianity is almost entirely represented by Paul.

Paul was one of the most crucial figures in the formative period of Christian history. As a Jewish convert who carried on work among Gentiles, he was in contact with the major Christian groups of his day. He knew many of the apostles personally and considered himself one of them. He traveled widely—in Palestine, Asia Minor, Macedonia, Greece, and Italy, and he was not fearful of controversy. The date of his conversion cannot be determined exactly, but it was surely some time in the thirties, so his association with the new religion coincides with its infancy. Indeed, his knowledge of Christianity may go back several years earlier, while he was persecuting the church out of zeal for the law. To belabor the obvious, Paul is the earliest Christian writer, knowledgeable about the religion almost from the first and in possession of traditional material which antedates him. The dates of Pauline Christianity, therefore, are from A.D. 35–60, and its geographical extent from Palestine to Rome.

Paul's interpretation of Christianity is basically a combination of his universalism and his understanding of grace. Neither word is adequately descriptive of his thought, but they form the foundation on which his more visible theology is built. Paul never questions the belief that his message is intended for all men. Since there is one God, there is one Christ and one gospel, and the gospel has universal applicability. With him the distinctive barriers between Jews and Gentiles, between slave and free, between men and women, are ignored. The other basis is his understanding of grace, which focuses attention on the part God plays in the salvation of man and virtually ignores man's part. Man is never pictured as deserving good treatment from God, for he is never in a position to deserve anything but condemnation. God's salvific action, therefore, is his gift, his graciousness, a totally undeserved way of treating man. With these basic ideas in mind, we shall now examine Paul's thought in several areas: eschatology, legal theory, ethics, Christology, and ecclesiology.

From his Jewish Christian colleagues Paul drew certain traditions about the teachings of Jesus, the last supper, and the resurrection. He also accepted the basic eschatological framework that the primitive church had taught. But in his thought the eschatological viewpoint receives quite different expression. In some of the letters it has a dominating force, while in others it is shoved to the background.

In the Thessalonian correspondence, his expression is vivid, and he expects to live until the end. In the first letter he attempts to answer a question about the death of Christians. The question is not literally preserved in Paul's letter, but it can be reconstructed as follows: "Although you have promised that we will be present when Jesus returns, some among us have died. What happens to those people?" The fact of the question indicates the dominating force of Paul's eschatological thought. When he preached in Thessalonica, he must have felt so strongly about the end that it never occurred to him that death might come to some of his converts. Nor would he have provided them with teaching that might have prepared them to accept death. Eschatological hope surely formed the basis of Paul's previous preaching in Thessalonica. But when some, or even one, among the converts died, a serious question arose, and Paul answered it in some detail.

He said that Christians will be raised from the dead, because Jesus was. We who are still alive when Jesus returns will join the resurrected Christians preparatory to meeting the Lord in the air. This resurrection will occur at the end and is limited to Christians. Paul gives no specific date for the resurrection and the return of the Lord. It comes, he says, like a thief in the night, and the Christian must always be prepared. There is no hint of a long delay; he confidently proclaims its imminence and assumes that it will occur in his lifetime. It is notable, however, that he had not previously expected even a brief delay.

In II Thessalonians, Paul finds it necessary to put the damper on some overly enthusiastic eschatologists. It appears that a forged Pauline letter had arrived and proclaimed the dawning of the day of the Lord. It was accepted at face value by some in the community. In his letter, Paul says that the day cannot have come because its initial signs have not yet occurred. Before the final day arrives, there must be a rebellion and a revelation of Christ's enemy. This cannot yet occur, because something is now restraining the enemy, although his secret power is already at work and is soon to be revealed. This line of thought appears to be inconsistent with that in I Thessalonians, where Paul said that the day of the Lord would come like a thief in the night. If Paul had had a chance to explain the apparent contradiction, he might have said that the initiation of the end—that is, the appearance of the enemy—would be like a thief in the night. At least, we have an apt figure in that case. At any rate, Paul assures his readers that he is telling them nothing new; the hope is still vivid, and Paul expects to be alive at the end.

A more detailed description of the events of the last day is included in I Corinthians 15. Here Paul describes the transformation which occurs for all Christians, living and dead. When the last trumpet sounds, the living will be changed within the twinkling of an eye. The mortal body will become an immortal, imperishable one. At the same time, the Christian dead are raised in spiritual bodies. This new resurrection body is unique—imperishable, glorified, powerful. To Paul, it was perfectly obvious that man should have a spiritual body at the resurrection, for he could point to all sorts of bodies, each one appropriate to some creature—beast, bird, fish, sun, moon, star. By *spiritual body* he does not mean an invisible, incorporeal soul, but a human form which is not subject to change, corruption, illness, or death. Paul was too Hebraic to think of man without a body, and he does not speak of immortality in the Greek sense. Neither could he think of the resurrection of the body that died. His thought is somewhere between. There is continuity between the dying one and the rising one, but not identity. There is resurrection in a body, but it is a spiritual body. Although this is a more detailed statement, it is consistent with that in I Thessalonians. There is no suggestion of postponement, and Paul still expects to be alive at the end.

In I Corinthians, Paul also makes certain suggestions about sex and marriage in the light of the impending end. He says that the status quo should be maintained, since the time is so short. The bachelor should remain celibate, and the married man should not seek divorce.[23]

In all of these letters—I, II Thessalonians, and I Corinthians—Paul's eschatological expectation plays a significant role, dominating his thought in the first two. In other places, however, it is not so prominent. In Philippians he expresses a doubt about staying alive until the end, and he says that he prefers to die and be with Christ.[24] The phrase seems peculiar when we compare it with what he had said in the other letters. Death does not seem to be overcome by a general resurrection at the time of the Lord's coming. It is rather a means by which one may instantly go to Christ. In other places, Paul implies a realized eschatology: a termination that has already occurred. In II Corinthians 3:18 he says that believers are already transfigured into the Lord's likeness. In II Corinthians 5:17 he says, "If any one is in Christ, he is a new creation; the old has passed away, behold, the new has come."[25] In Romans, although he still regards the resurrection as future, Paul feels that the Christian has begun to embark upon a new life in the spirit. He has been united with Christ in baptism and can expect to be raised as he was. Meanwhile, he lives in the spirit, dead to sin and law. In Colossians 3:1-4, Paul seems to take one more step. He there maintains that the Christian has been raised to life with Christ but that his life is now hidden. It will be made visible when Christ himself returns.

Although no precision is possible on the dates of Paul's letters, the distinction in eschatological thought conforms roughly to that between the earlier and the later letters. Thus, in his earlier letters he identified the resurrection of the dead and the transformation of the living with the future day of the Lord. He expected that event within his own lifetime. In the later letters he expressed doubt about his endurance, de-emphasized the future general resurrection, and spoke of a transformation at baptism. The day of the Lord seems to be a good deal farther off and less important than it did in the earlier letters. As time wore on, Paul probably played down eschatological hope precisely because he recognized that the day had

[23] See I Corinthians 7:26-29. See pp. 296 ff.
[24] See Philippians 1:21 ff.
[25] Revised Standard Version.

not come as soon as he had expected. The expanded time also forced him to become interested in matters affecting the contemporary church, among them problems of law.

It is in what he says about law that Paul makes his most distinctive contribution. He probably spent much time debating with opponents about the Torah and defending his activities before critics. He wrote the letter to the Galatians because some Christians had been demanding that his converts in Asia Minor become circumcised. It also looks as if some significant group had challenged Paul's position as an apostle. In the very salutation of the letter, he launches into a vigorous defense of his apostleship: "From Paul, an apostle, not by human appointment or human commission, but by commission from Jesus Christ and from God the Father who raised him from the dead."[26] He then accuses his converts of turning away from the gospel they had originally accepted and defends the divine origin of his own gospel. His language is so vehement in the opening of the letter that we suspect that he is reacting to some personal charges. It also appears that Paul had been accused of being dependent upon the Jerusalem apostles. He takes special pains to outline in detail his relations with this group—namely, with James, Peter, and John.[27] The central event in his relationship with them occurred in a meeting held in Jerusalem about A.D. 51. At the meeting, certain people (Paul calls them false brethren) insisted that all Christians must be circumcised. Paul and Barnabas opposed this group and introduced an uncircumcised Greek convert, Titus, as a test case. In his own account, Paul carried the day: the "pillars" authenticated his apostleship to the Gentiles and agreed "that we should go to the Gentiles while they went to the Jews."[28] Only one requirement was imposed, namely that Paul take up a collection for the Jerusalem "poor," a task to which he energetically dedicated himself.

The division of labor between Paul and the other apostles is significant. Although Paul is anxious to affirm his independence from any alleged authority except the divine, one cannot avoid asking if the division of labor involved something more than a mutual agreement. In the context of its time, such a division would probably be understood as a restriction on Paul. In order to maintain the existence of a Christian church in the heart of Jewry, the "pillars" must have felt that it was necessary to keep Paul from speaking to Jews.[29] They would control the mission to Jews, among whom

[26] Galatians 1:1.
[27] In Galatians 1:18–2:21.
[28] Galatians 2:9.
[29] See p. 279 f.

the alternative of uncircumcision was not a viable one. Paul, however, must confine himself to Gentiles but may present a gospel without the circumcision requirement. It is significant that the "pillars" accepted uncircumcised Gentile Christians, although they did not advocate the cessation of Torah. At this meeting with the "pillars," Paul appears to argue the position of Stephen and the Hellenists, who called for the total abandonment of Torah. But his position is not presented in its fullness in the letter to the Galatians, and we can only determine it by a thorough analysis of his complex legal theory.

The Greek word *nomos* is the closest equivalent to the Hebrew Torah. We translate it as law, but it basically means order and can be used for any kind of standard, principle, custom, or system. Paul rarely uses the word in its basic sense. He usually thinks of it as the Mosaic Torah or the Scriptures. He will speak of the law of Moses or the law of God, and there is no genuine distinction between them. God's law was revealed to Moses and is contained in the Scriptures. In most cases Paul speaks very positively about law: it is holy and just and good.[30] But in some cases he speaks of it in a highly pejorative way: "Those who rely on obedience to the law are under a curse."[31] The difference seems to depend upon the various ways in which he thinks of law, or the relationships in which law stands. There are four of these relationships of law: to God, to sin, to man, and to Christ.

Law and God. In this relationship, law is good. Paul is convinced that God gave the Mosaic Torah, embodied in Scripture, as his authentic demand and that he intended it to produce righteousness and to lead to life. The revelation of law is a gracious act on God's part, and it defines what God wills and what he opposes. Its authority is unquestioned. The point is simple enough: God gave the law, and he expected man to follow it. The intention of God is clearly expressed in Romans 2:13: "It is not by hearing the law, but by doing it, that men will be justified before God."

In this relationship Paul makes it perfectly clear that there are some things which God never intended. These are called "works of law." The phrase is subject to all sorts of interpretations but probably is meant to refer specifically to those acts that signify the conditions of Jewish existence. The "works of laws" are primarily circumcision and food laws, and Paul is able to separate them from God's law. To him they are opposed to God's will, because they are marks of exclusivism. They are ethnic practices which cause Jews to feel that they have a special relationship with God. But

[30] See Romans 7:12.
[31] Galatians 3:10.

such an assumption is intolerable for Paul, because it is inconsistent with his basic monotheism and universalism. God is God of both Jews and Gentiles, so marks of exclusivism cannot be in accord with his will. Those "works of law" are not to be generalized, as if Paul were condemning all so-called good works. He, in fact, speaks positively about good works, but negatively about those works which distinguish the Jew. He is quite clear on this point: "On the basis of works of law no flesh shall be justified."[32] "Whoever exists on the basis of works of law exists under a curse."[33] That such things as circumcision do not conform to the will of God is shown by the fact that Abraham was justified without it.

Law and Sin. To understand this relationship we must first comprehend Paul's use of the word *sin*. He seems to think of it on two levels. On one level it is an entity that stands outside the empirical world and dominates man. He does not personalize the concept, so it would be improper to think of a devil. Nevertheless, it is, in our terms, a mythological power, which we may designate as Sin with a capital letter. All men stand under the power of Sin.[34] Paul speaks of Sin reigning and having dominion; he thinks of man as being in slavery to Sin and of being freed from Sin. Sin works all kinds of desire in man; it dies and rises again; it deceives and kills and causes man to produce what he does not intend. It is allied with death, so that its slave inevitably dies. On the other level, Paul thinks of sin as disobedience or transgression, a human act made necessary by the domination of Sin. Sin controls man, so all men are sinners who have fallen short of God's intention.[35]

The law enters this picture in an unexpected way. It has been established that God gave the Torah as his authentic will. It, therefore, is a definition of those acts that God requires and forbids. It is the definition of disobedience or sin. Paul never questions its accuracy and dependability as a measure of sin. It comes from God, and it is absolutely correct. But because it defines sin it actually comes under the control of Sin. It comes to man not simply as definer of sin but as agent of Sin. As a result, man is able to say: I would not have known Sin if it had not been for the law.[36] This good law has been used by the demonic power to effect the reign of Sin in the world, and the evidence is that man disobeys the law when he hears it. This does

[32] Galatians 2:16 (author's translation).
[33] Galatians 3:10 (author's translation).
[34] See Romans 3:9.
[35] See Romans 3:23.
[36] See Romans 7:7.

not mean that man begins to commit forbidden acts only when he hears the law or that it would not have occurred to him to disobey if he had not heard the command. For example, the law says: Do not desire your neighbor's wife. A man can desire his neighbor's wife whether or not he has heard the commandment. But without the commandment he has no way to evaluate himself. He has a kind of ignorant innocence. With the law, however, he is able to evaluate himself, and he can only evaluate himself as sinner, as under the power of Sin, because he still desires his neighbor's wife and now knows it is wrong to do so. So law has brought about the knowledge of Sin. Although God intended law to produce righteousness and life, it does not do so, because this world is dominated by Sin. Even God's law is subject to its use.

Law and Man. Man attempts to exist in a situation in which he is dominated by Sin. Paul does not hesitate to cite the evidence for this situation. He finds it in man's disobedience of law and in the Jew's reliance on circumcision. The Gentile disobeys the common rules that all human beings acknowledge. The Jew is, if anything, more guilty, because he boasts in his status and produces a pseudorighteousness by misunderstanding the law. It is clear that in this situation the law is no real help to man. It is God's measure of a man, and when it measures it finds him to be controlled by Sin. In a profound passage in Romans, Paul explores the meaning of existence under law.[37] He finds that there is a deep rift between man's intention to live under law and the result of that intention. Although it is written in the first person, it is not an autobiographical passage but one that expresses the plight of any man who faces the law. Man discovers that he does not produce what he intends to produce.[38] He intends life, but death results, because he is dominated by Sin and his actions are not his own.[39] In this relationship, law designates an existential situation which is totally without hope. Law produces the wrath of God upon man.[40] It does so invariably and unavoidably, because it demands of the man under domination of Sin that he be righteous. Man, therefore, finds himself trapped. He cannot escape the trap by saying that the law is invalid or somehow inadequate or by denying his guilt. The trap is inescapable, and the law always produces condemnation.

---

[37] Romans 7:7-8:4. See R. Bultmann, "Romans 7 and the Anthropology of Paul," in *Existence and Faith,* trans. Shubert Ogden (New York: World Publishing, 1960), pp. 147–157.

[38] See Romans 7:15.

[39] See Romans 7:17.

[40] See Romans 4:15.

God really speaks in his Torah, but when he speaks he says to each man: "You are a sinner, and you must die." Man can only respond: "Who will deliver me?" [41]

Law and Christ. Existence in Christ is an alternative to existence in law. Life in Christ is marked by righteousness, guiltlessness, and freedom from Sin. Paul sometimes presents law and Christ in opposition to each other, but in most cases he affirms a profound harmony between them. In what is probably his fundamental statement on the whole issue, he presents Christ as the end of law. [42] Here *end* means fulfillment rather than conclusion. As *law* is God's first word, *Christ* is his second, but the second fulfills the first and was implicit in it. In Christ, God presents the ultimate meaning of law; Christ is what law is all about. It was possible, thus, to understand it before the appearance of Jesus, but it is in the death of Jesus that the meaning becomes explicit. Here we have arrived at the most difficult point in Pauline Christianity. How can the death of the Christ be the fulfillment of law? We cannot get at this without entering into the mythological world that Paul took for granted. Sin dominates man, controls God's law, and leads inexorably to death. Christ, who is not dominated by Sin, nevertheless, is condemned and dies. But at this point God intervenes and raises Christ from the dead. This breaks the power of Sin, for death is not the ultimate fate of Christ. Although he is condemned, his condemnation is ineffective. Sin now is powerless, for without the threat of death it is empty. Law now can have its intended result; it can produce life, not because man lives under law, but because he lives in Christ. In the death and resurrection of Christ, God has not condemned man, as he does under law; instead he has condemned Sin. Sin is dead, and man can live.

Paul uses a number of terms to express this new relationship, among them *justification, reconciliation,* and *redemption.* These point to the same thing but are intended to illuminate the situation by analogies. *Justification* is a legal term and refers to a verdict of not guilty. *Reconciliation* stands for the restoration of a broken friendship. *Redemption* means the recovery of lost property, animate or inanimate. In Christ, man's situation may be described by any of the three terms: a guilty man is pronounced not guilty; friends have become reconciled; the alienated have been recovered.

Of the four relationships, that between law and Christ is the most important for Paul, for it represents the solution to all things. The relationship to God only expresses God's intention, and that to sin and man is only

[41] Romans 7:25.
[42] Romans 10:4.

temporary. The relationship to Christ is the ultimate and permanent one, the final act of God in his defeat of Sin.

The ethical implications of this semimythological analysis are not easy to see. Paul's conviction centers in the belief that a situational change has taken place. Man now has an alternative to existence under law: he can live in Christ. If he does not recognize the alternative possibility, he is still doomed to exist under the domination of Sin and death. But if he does, he can live in faith. Faith can be interpreted mythologically, as belief that God has defeated Sin, or existentially, as one's understanding of himself as free of condemnation. There is no sense in which human effort carries any weight in this system, but man must make a choice between living under law and living in Christ. Man who lives in Christ lives in faith, and he also lives in the spirit. The spirit is the representative of the Lord to the Christian and functions as an ethical guide both for the community and for the individual Christian.[43] Under its leadership, the believer works out the meaning of freedom from Sin as he lives out his life.

Pauline Christianity is, therefore, characterized by the rarity of hard and fast ethical rules. The specifically required duties are those which express love of the brothers and helpfulness to the group. Nevertheless, Paul can be quite clear that leadership by the spirit produces a certain style of life. It is a life marked by "love, joy, peace, patience, kindness, goodness, fidelity, gentleness, and self-control."[44] Likewise, Paul does not hesitate to list the acts and qualities which do not belong to the Christian life: "fornication, impurity, and indecency; idolatry and sorcery; quarrels, a contentious temper, envy, fits of rage, selfish ambitions, dissensions, party intrigues, and jealousies; drinking bouts, orgies, and the like."[45] For the most part, the separate items are drawn from traditional lists of commonly acknowledged virtues and vices. Paul intends to provide a representation of required and restricted matters, not an exhaustive list of duties and prohibitions. The virtues are typical of the behavior which characterizes life in the spirit.[46]

On a few points Paul cannot escape from giving specific ethical advice. In fact, it appears that when he wrote I Corinthians several acute problems were developing. In the previous chapter we observed that a good deal of per-

[43] See Galatians 5 : 13–25.

[44] Galatians 5 : 22.

[45] Galatians 5 : 20 f. Similar lists are found in Romans 1 : 29 f.; I Corinthians 5 : 11; 6 : 9–10.

[46] See Victor P. Furnish, *Theology and Ethics in Paul* (Nashville, Tenn.: Abingdon, 1968), pp. 75 ff.

plexity formed the background for this letter. Paul's converts in Corinth were seriously confused on a number of points. Some were saying, "all things are lawful," but not all subscribed to this view. One problem came to the surface on the question of meat offered to idols.[47] The background of the problem lies in the widespread Hellenistic practice of placing previously sacrificed meat on the open market. It was presumed that such meat retained a degree of sanctity which would be a benefit to the secondhand purchaser. The Jewish Torah strictly forbade the eating of such meat on the principle that it brought one into contact with idolatry. It is possible that the Corinthians had recently received a decree forbidding their use of such meat, a decree such as that in Acts 15.[48] In this case, they would now be subject to a regulation that was not originally imposed on them. Whatever may be the cause, they were confused on the issue, and they presented the problem to Paul. Some argued that, because there is only one real God, the question of eating sacrificed meat is irrelevant. Others, either former Jews or former Gentiles, were not so sure. Those who had come out of a Jewish background would have retained their former fear of contamination. Former Gentiles would have been so accustomed to acknowledging the deity of the other gods that they would continue to look upon the meat as nearly sacred.

Paul approaches the problem of meat by agreeing with those who said that there is but one God. If this is the case, it follows that meat offered to a so-called god is in no way different from other meat. A false god can neither sanctify nor pollute anything. But he goes on to say that the Christian's actions must be governed by the recognition that some are unsure. Although Paul disagrees with those who are reluctant to eat sacrificed meat, he shows amazing respect for them. He calls them weak, but he requires the strong Christians to respect their weakness. His counsel is that strong Christians should forgo their right to eat meat if their eating causes the moral downfall of a weaker brother. Although this advice appears to move in the direction of regulation, upon closer examination it turns out to be an application of the basic Christian ethic, namely love of the brothers. Eating idolatrous meat is not strictly forbidden. Rather, the Christian is called upon to avoid contempt and to have consideration for one with whom he disagrees.

In Corinth there were also some problems of relations between the sexes.[49] Paul had heard reports of a man who slept with his stepmother and of

[47] See I Corinthians 8 : 1–13; also Romans 14 : 13 ff.
[48] See John C. Hurd, Jr., *The Origin of I Corinthians* (New York: Seabury, 1965), pp. 240–270.
[49] See I Corinthians 7 : 1–40.

several men who visited prostitutes. To him this kind of behavior was unthinkable. He retained from his Jewish background a deep respect for the body, and he argued that, since the body is the shrine of the spirit, it is not right to join it with the body of a prostitute. But the sexual problem had another side. There seem to be some men and women who practiced celibacy while living together. They apparently felt that God would be pleased with their denial of bodily desires and that their determination must be tested by exposure to temptation. The situation in Corinth was complicated by discussions on the relative value of bachelorhood and marriage.

In dealing with these questions, Paul initially agreed that "it is a good thing for a man to have nothing to do with women."[50] So, if a man has made a compact with a virgin and intends to preserve her in that state, he does well. But, says Paul, if this man finds that he cannot restrain himself, he does no wrong in getting married. Marriage is a permissible means of avoiding immorality, and in a strictly monogamous marriage sex has its proper place. In this relationship a man's body belongs to his wife and his wife's to him. Except for periods of abstinence mutually agreed upon for the purpose of praying, a husband and wife should not deny each other their sexual rights. On the relative value of bachelorhood and marriage, Paul clearly prefers the former. At one point he expresses a desire that everyone should follow his own example of bachelorhood. He knows, however, that this is impossible, and he is cautious to avoid downgrading the marital state. Some persons do not have the gift of celibacy, and they do not disobey God if they marry. He has only one substantively negative objection to marriage, and that is a practical one. The married man is forced by his position into a concern for worldly things, since he must devote himself to the wife. The unmarried man is able to devote himself completely to God, but the husband finds his loyalty divided. In spite of his preference for bachelorhood and his objection to marriage, Paul feels that the institution must be protected. Marriage is not dissoluble by divorce except in the case of a Christian's marriage to a non-Christian, and only then if the latter finds the situation intolerable. In one respect, Paul's treatment here is similar to that of the sacrificed meat. He is able to express and defend his point of view, but in the end he shows no disrespect for persons he regards as weak.

When he dealt with sacrificed meat, Paul based his argument partly on his monotheism. But what is the basis of his preference for bachelorhood? It is difficult to find anything in Judaism that would account for it, and his statements about divided loyalty sound too much like an attempted rational-

---

[50] I Corinthians 7:1.

ization. It is probable that we have here a matter of personal attitude rather than a profound theological or ethical consideration. It is consistent with his own bachelorhood and with his requirement that women veil themselves and remain silent in church. These matters of personal taste affected Pauline Christianity deeply, but they do not reflect a religious or ethical basis. At one point, however, Paul's theological views are clear. His eschatological considerations led him to say that the status quo should be maintained: the unmarried should remain unmarried, and the married should remain married. Since the time is so short, we should not make a big issue out of the matter of marriage and celibacy. The latter is preferable, but neither is wrong. More than likely, his eschatological expectation led Paul into a generally conservative attitude on social issues. In the letter to Philemon, he did not question the institution of slavery. In Romans, he expressed only a positive appreciation for Roman government.[51] Since he felt the time was short, he gave no serious attention to the structure of human society.

Paul also writes in I Corinthians an exalted analysis of the core of his ethics. In other places he said that the whole of one's ethical life is summed up in the maxim: "You must love your neighbor as yourself."[52] In I Corinthians 13 he writes on the meaning of this love. The chapter is frequently interpreted in isolation, but it can be properly understood only in context. In chapter 12, Paul introduces certain questions about spiritual gifts. He and his converts believe that the spirit let its presence be known in the community by granting certain abilities. So Paul discusses the gifts in the light of their benefit to the community. He seems to be aware of two problems. The first is that of distinguishing between the spirits, testing the spirits.[53] This must have been an acute problem in a community that tried to rely on spiritual guidance for its ethical life. How does one know if the gifts he has received are those of God's spirit or some other? Or what attitude can one take towards the spiritual claims of someone else? It would seem easy for anyone to claim the backing of the spirit for any position he wished to take. Paul lays down two principles for testing: one who lays a curse on Jesus is not led by the spirit; one who says that Jesus is Lord must be. Our sophisticated age may find these tests inadequate, for they appear not to admit the possibility of dishonesty. But Paul would take it for granted that a man's curse or confession is dictated by a spirit and that only the spirit of the one God can cause a man to confess Jesus as Lord.

The second problem about spiritual gifts was that they brought about

---

[51] Romans 13:1 ff.
[52] Romans 13:9; Galatians 5:14.
[53] The same problem is also dealt with in II John and in the Didache.

dissension within the Corinthian Church. Since the gifts came in a variety of forms, it was possible to compare them. Recipients of various kinds of gifts could claim positions of authority on the basis of them. In order to solve this problem, Paul does three things. First, he asserts that the community needs all of the spiritual gifts. Just as the human body needs hands, feet, and head and cannot function without a harmonious cooperation of all parts, just so the church needs all the spiritual gifts. Secondly, Paul lays down a list of gifts, ranked in order of importance, and he encourages the readers to seek the higher gifts. The order is:

1. Apostleship.
2. Prophecy.
3. Teaching.
4. Working miracles.
5. Healing.
6. Helping and guiding others.
7. Ecstatic utterance.

Thirdly, Paul offers "the best way of all." So, in chapter 13, he presents love as the best spiritual gift, and he contrasts it to them. Although a person engages in ecstatic utterance "of men and of angels,"[54] without love he produces only meaningless sounds. He may have the gift of prophecy or faith, but without love he is nothing. Even acts of self-sacrifice are meaningless without love. The trouble with the gift of prophecy is that it is partial and will evaporate with the appearance of ultimate truth. Prophecy can only be a matter of "puzzling reflections in a mirror,"[55] but in the future Christians may expect to see things as they really are. Paul compares spiritual gifts, such as prophecy and glossolalia, with the behavior and speech of a child. They are meaningful for a while, but they must be put aside as a man approaches maturity. In contrast to the temporary nature of the other gifts, love is permanent. A definition of the practices that love accomplishes is not a definition of love, but it is as close as Paul gets. In I Corinthians 13:4–7, we are at the center of the Pauline ethic:

Love is patient; love is kind and envies no one. Love is never boastful, nor conceited, nor rude; never selfish, not quick to take offense. Love keeps no score of wrongs; does not gloat over other men's sins, but delights in the truth. There is nothing love cannot face; there is no limit to its faith, its hope, and its endurance.

[54] I Corinthians 13:1.
[55] I Corinthians 13:12.

Even the catalogue of love's functions does not become a list of regulations for the Christian life. Paul does not mean that, if a person lives in love, he qualifies as a Christian. The case is rather the other way around. Since God has accomplished in Christ the justification of man, it is possible to live in Christ, to live under the guidance of the spirit, to live in love. Paul is not perfectly consistent on ethical matters. His personal tastes and his varying eschatological expectations sometimes enter the scene. But in the main his ethical pronouncements avoid concrete rules. In general, the life style of the Christian is to be governed by his love of others. The Christian should live in the faith that he has died to Sin and is able now to live righteously, in the joyful expectation that the end, the time of his salvation, is coming soon.

Paul's Christology is related to his legal theory. As the fulfillment of law, the death of Christ is also the defeat of Sin. The believer lives in Christ—that is, he experiences a mode of existence that means freedom, righteousness, and life. Paul uses a number of terms to express his understanding of Jesus. He uses *Messiah*, but for him it is more of a proper name than a title. He is more likely to say *Jesus Christ* or *Christ Jesus* than *Jesus the Christ*. The human existence of Jesus seems to have held little interest for him. In II Corinthians 5:16, he disavows knowing Jesus in a fleshly way. He concentrates his attention on the nonhistorical dimension of Christ. He speaks of Christ as the Wisdom of God, in reminder of the Wisdom of Proverbs.[56] He also presents Jesus as the second Adam, the originator of a new creation, a new race of men.[57] His most characteristic Christological expression is *Lord*, and by using it Paul allies himself with primitive Gentile Christianity.

Although he expresses little interest in the life of Jesus, he never displays any doubt about his humanity, and he even knows a few facts about his life. He believes also in the pre-existence and present existence, as did the Gentile church before him. The fullest expression of his Christological thought is found in a hymnlike expression that he was probably quoting.[58] Although it is not a passage of his own composition, it probably represents his thought adequately. It starts with the pre-existence of Jesus. He was in the form of God, but he did not "think to snatch at equality with God."[59] He divested himself of the divine nature and became human. In the human life he was humble and obedient to the point of death. But God raised him up and bestowed on him the title *Lord*, the highest status in heaven and earth (see Figure 24).

[56] See I Corinthians 1:24, 30.
[57] See Romans 5:12–19.
[58] Philippians 2:6–11.
[59] Philippians 2:6.

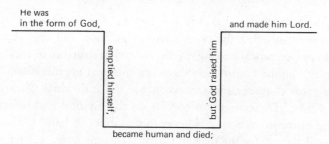

He was
in the form of God,

and made him Lord.

emptied himself,

but God raised him

became human and died;

FIGURE 24 Pauline Christology

Paul uses the quotation within a larger admonition to humility. He feels that it gives his readers the supreme example of humility, which is seen in Jesus' giving up of his divine nature. Two points in the quotation need further elaboration. (1) Nothing is said about the precise relationship between Jesus and God, but it is clear that Jesus is subordinate. In this light it is possible to say that when Jesus gave up his divine nature he did not expect to regain it. In fact, if he did so expect, the passage would lose its force as an example of humility. The giving up would be a form of condescension at best or a kind of pose at worst. But the giving up must be genuine if it is meaningful. No one receives an example of humility from a rich man who pretends to be poor for a time, but only from one who permanently gives away what he has. (2) The human life must be completely human. Paul is no Docetist. To him both the life and the death of Jesus are real. So when he became human, he became mortal, and only after death did God intervene and exalt him to the status of Lord. It is implied that God intervened because of the humble and obedient quality of Jesus' life. The intervention has given a cosmic dimension to the death, but the fact remains that God has not interfered with the purely human working out of Jesus' life. For Paul, the humanity is not only unquestioned, but it is devoid of any nonhuman quality. He never refers to a miraculous birth or to Jesus' performance of miracles.

It is perhaps significant that Paul does not have a full and independent treatment of Christology. When he deals with it, it is always within the context of some other topic. It is not presented as an isolable article of faith but as ancillary to themes of greater magnitude. Christology for Paul is not abstract metaphysical speculation, but it is functionally related to his eschatology, ethics, and legal theory.

Paul's ecclesiology, or understanding of the church, is also related to these other points. In terms of legal theory, the church is the community of those who see themselves as justified. In terms of eschatology, it is that group which expects the return of the Christ with salvation. Ethically, the church is composed of those who are led by the spirit. None of these relationships demands that the church have regulation and organization. But, as a matter of empirical necessity, groups develop structure or they evaporate. So, even in Pauline Christianity there is a minimal organization.

Paul's most characteristic expression for the individual Christian is the man in Christ. The conception borders on the mystical and reflects a belief in a kind of incorporation of believer in the object of faith. It also relates to Paul's legal theory, for the man in Christ is the one whose existence is determined by the word of God in Christ rather than the word in Torah. Existence in Christ is marked by righteousness, guiltlessness, and freedom from Sin, and it is possible because Christ is God's second word. When one thinks of the corporate life of those in Christ, he is thinking of the church. It is in this vein that Paul speaks of the church as the body of Christ. Because the community of those who find their existence in Christ manifests itself as Christ himself, the church is a kind of earthly counterpart to the heavenly Christ. At the same time, it is a community in waiting, not one of permanent duration but one whose existence is soon to expire.

Paul emphasizes the unity of Christ's body. He seems to proceed on the conviction that the one church manifests itself in the various localities. The church is primary, and the local groups are secondary. The importance of unity is signified by the agreement worked out in Jerusalem between Paul and the "pillar" apostles. In describing this meeting Paul says that he had received a revelation that told him to go to Jerusalem. But he also says that he needed to know if his missionary work was going to be in vain.[60] His meaning is not altogether clear, but the need for unity between the Pauline and Palestinian churches probably played a part in his concern. In a minor regulation, Paul chides the Corinthian Church for differing from the others.[61] The need for unity and mutual dependence within local churches has already been observed.[62]

The churches that Paul established probably met in private homes. The homeowner would be looked upon as convenor and in some cases may have become an authoritative leader of the church. But Paul himself continued to have a high degree of authority over these churches. The people felt it perfectly natural to ask him about ethical and doctrinal matters, and he did not hesitate to give answers. He insisted that he was an apostle, and in listing the gifts of the spirit he gave priority to apostleship. He assumed that the traveling apostle was the symbol of authority in the church. The local

[60] Galatians 2:2.
[61] I Corinthians 11:16.
[62] See p. 298 f.

churches, however, must soon have developed an independent stability. At first the leadership would have been charismatic, but as time passed it became more formal. Only once in Paul's letters is there a reference to these leaders by title. In Philippians 1:1, Paul addresses himself to the bishops and deacons. This may mean that by the time of this letter the situation was beginning to formalize itself or that the Philippian Church arrived at a point of organized development ahead of the others. On the other hand, there is no description of the functions of these officers, and the titles may be intended in an untechnical sense.[63] At any rate, it is clear that Pauline Christianity paid little attention to the matter of church organization.

There are certain corporate practices associated with Pauline Christianity. Ecstatic utterance seems to be a frequently practiced manifestation of the spirit. Baptism continued to be used as the rite of initiation. With Paul, however, it took on significance as a symbol of one's death to Sin and resurrection to life in Christ. It was also an anticipation of the resurrection to come:

> Have you forgotten that when we were baptized into union with Christ Jesus we were baptized into his death? By baptism we were buried with him, and lay dead, in order that, as Christ was raised from the dead in the splendour of the Father, so also we might set our feet upon the new path of life.[64]

Baptism is, thus, the passage from one form of existence to another and a guarantee of the life to come. The Pauline churches also celebrated the Eucharist, which Paul understood as the repeated proclamation of Jesus' death. It consisted of eating bread and drinking from the cup. For some in Corinth it had become an occasion for gluttony and drunkenness, a fact that Paul deplores. He requires that those at Corinth test themselves before they participate in the meal, for one must not desecrate the body and blood of the Lord. In the main the Eucharist is, for Pauline Christianity, a memorial of Jesus' death, not a means of union with him.

The other writers who consider themselves to stand within the Pauline tradition add little to Paul himself. The author of Ephesians takes a final eschatological step, maintains that the resurrection has already occurred, and implies a long period of time yet to come. Some writers begin the process of assimilating Paul to protocatholic Christianity. The author of the Pastoral epistles uses Paul's authority to establish that of bishops, presbyters, and deacons. I Clement recalls Paul's handling of problems in Corinth, as he

---

[63] See p. 143.
[64] Romans 6:3 f.

deals with the overthrow of presbyters there. Luke understood Paul's universalism but treated him as a link leading from the Jerusalem apostles to the Roman Church. These may be considered as representatives of Pauline Christianity at a later stage of development—in fact, at a time when its distinctiveness was being neglected and merged with protocatholic Christianity.

Chapter Ten

The Later Varieties

JOHANNINE CHRISTIANITY

Since Johannine Christianity is represented almost solely by the Gospel of John as a finished product, it was possible to analyze the basic character of this variety in a previous chapter. We should keep in mind the fact that the fourth evangelist used certain sources for his work, but at this point we are concerned with the thinking of the author who put the sources together. The Johannine epistles, though from a different hand, belong in the same general category.

We have seen that John was far more interested in the divine nature of Christ than in the history of Jesus. This interest is part of a general Johannine tendency to emphasize the spiritual at the expense of the physical, the eternal as opposed to the historical. John uses the gospel genre as his vehicle of communication, so he describes a number of things that appear to be events. But when we look closely we find that Jesus' teachings are not teachings about God but revelations of God. His deeds are not the visible events of ordinary life; neither are they done out of kindness or even power. They are rather symbols of truth for those who have the eyes to see it. The real nucleus of Johannine Christianity is a preference for a truth revealed to the intellect in nonhistorical terms. John cannot agree with Paul that the meaning of life is to be found in a single historical event, the death of Jesus. Nor can he believe that it matters whether Jesus was a Galilean, a Jew, or whatever. To John there is universal and eternal truth in this religion, and such truth cannot be identified with historical events, although they may be found within them. John surely finds a large number of sympathizers in the twentieth century among people who cannot believe that an event that occurred two thousand years ago can have any significance now. Such people are far more ready to accept an idea that seems to have eternal validity. It is possible to illustrate this dehistoricizing tendency by examining more thoroughly John's Christology, eschatology, and understanding of the Christian life.

The Fourth Gospel clearly affirms belief in the pre-existence of Jesus as *Logos*, his incarnation, and his return to the Father.[1] The incarnation is real and fleshly, but flesh appears to be a means of communication rather than a genuine participation in human nature. In Jesus' flesh, human beings are able to see the divine nature of the Christ. The basic elements of Pauline Christology are present in John's three stages: the eternally existent *Logos*; the incarnate *Logos*; the return of the *Logos* to its proper realm. But the dramatic force of Paul's Christology is missing. Instead of a Christological picture with sudden breaks and alterations of direction, the Johannine is one of continuous and rather gentle flow from one stage to another (Figure 25). Christ is an eternally divine being, present with God at the creation, appearing on earth as an incarnated but still divine being, and now eternally present with God and in the church.

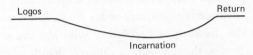

Logos   Return

Incarnation

FIGURE 25   Johannine Christology

The idea of the *Logos* may have been drawn from Philo's conception of the intermediary through whom the world was created.[2] The conception of pre-existence was already present in primitive Gentile Christianity. Jesus' return to the Father is related to earlier Christian speculation. In his description of the incarnate *Logos,* John uses some older conceptions but is not limited to them. He speaks of Jesus as the Christ, but he does not think of him in eschatological terms. One of his characters calls him the King of Israel, an acceptable but not very significant title for John.[3] He is also called Rabbi, but John probably understands this in a nontechnical sense.[4] Various characters in the Gospel address Jesus by the title Lord, and it has the customary meaning found in Gentile Christianity. John's favorite title is Son of God. By affirming the divine sonship of Jesus, the author means to say that in him we have a public revelation of reality, a thoroughly dependable communication from God himself. In him, and only in him, is real life possible. His words are trustworthy, and his promises are sure. It is essential to believe that Jesus is the Son of God, although not all people have the ability to do so. But he who has seen Jesus, really discerned him, has seen

[1] See p. 218 f.
[2] Ibid.
[3] John 1:49.
[4] See John 1:38, 49; 3:2, 26; 6:25.

the Father. John also uses the term *Son of man* in reference to the incarnate *Logos*. But the term has no eschatological significance for him. His understanding of the title is similar to that found in the Hermetic literature. This material is from the second and third centuries, but it is probable that some of it goes back much earlier and would have been available to John. It includes a series of revelations by Hermes Trismegistus, a supposed sage of ancient Egypt who was deified as Thoth, to a man named Poimandres. One of the revealed characters is the heavenly man, who had been sent to earth by Thoth, knew whence he had come and whither he was headed. He was divine and immortal.[5] John pictured Jesus as this kind of divine man, who had been sent by God to earth, knew his origin and destiny, and possessed unity with God. It seems clear that John had become acquainted with the Son of man title from earlier Christianity, but he was not equipped to understand it eschatologically. He was, however, familiar with a heavenly-man teaching in Hermeticism, and he naturally used it to interpret the title.

The titles do not tell the whole story. John must also have used a model for his life of Jesus, perhaps one drawn from Stoicism. Jesus, in the Fourth Gospel, does come off as a kind of ideal Stoic man of a-pathy. He does not struggle with his fate; he is completely self-possessed; he has no temptation; he is unaffected by popularity; he moves with divine necessity.

Thus we have a nearly ahistorical Christology. Even the picture of the earthly segment draws little from sources dealing with historical events but concentrates on mythological and theological conceptions. This Christology must be understood in context. It is a skillful blending of Gentile Christian, Stoic, Hermetic, and Philonic elements, and it constitutes an approach to the best popular thought of the day. John took the value of Jesus and put it in terms that were meaningful for his culture. Every Christian generation tends to see Jesus in terms of its own highest ideals, and to John this was the Stoic man, the Hermetic heavenly man, and the Philonic *Logos*. Since these represented the highest ideals of his place and time, John could not picture Jesus in a way that would make him less meaningful to men of morality and intellect. For the same reason he played down the historical. People of the Hellenistic world were not accustomed to attribute ultimate meaning to a historical event. To them, what is true must be eternally true, not historically conditioned. A form of Christianity that goes one step farther in the same direction is Gnostic Christianity. John is not usually classified among the Gnostics, because he does not totally disregard historical existence. He looks

---

[5] For a good analysis of Hermeticism and its possible influence on John, see C. H. Dodd, *The Interpretation of the Fourth Gospel* (Cambridge: Cambridge University Press, 1953), pp. 10–53.

upon history as a medium of revelation, even though he does not regard the revealing act as strictly historical. Johannine Christianity, nevertheless, opens the way for the further development of Gnostic theology and Docetic Christology.

Another indication of the dehistoricizing tendency of the Fourth Gospel is its lack of eschatological expectation. Its absence is a demonstration that it was very difficult for such thought to find a place in the Hellenistic world, which did not attribute religious meaning to history, even the end of history. To be sure, eschatological expectation in its most vivid form could not have lasted anyway, for groups cannot retain an intensity of feeling about a culmination that recedes farther and farther into the future. But there were Christian groups that retained a modified eschatological framework. Pauline Christianity, for example, came to de-emphasize the immediacy of the end but still expected it. Johannine Christianity seems only vaguely aware of such expectation. At one point there is an allusion to a future general resurrection and judgment,[6] but judgment is usually a present phenomenon, and the ideal of a general resurrection is partially corrected on the spot: "A time is coming, *indeed it is already here*, when the dead shall hear the voice of the Son of God, and all who hear shall come to life."[7] Aside from these questionable verses, there is no idea of a future resurrection, and there are no predictions of destruction. Some persons may not expect death, but not because the eschaton comes first. Such people by-pass death in their transition from life to life. There is no final judgment, for judgment is present now. In 14:3, Jesus speaks of his coming again in a way that could cause the reader to think of his coming as the apocalyptic Son of man. But this probably refers to the resurrection. The idea is clearer in 16:22, where Jesus speaks of a period of sadness to be followed by a time of joy. This is apparently a reference to the death and resurrection. Jesus also promises to send the Paraclete to the disciples.[8] The Paraclete is a substitute for Jesus after his return to the Father and is a near equivalent to the primitive and Pauline teaching on the spirit. It functions to aid a believer's understanding, to guarantee authenticity in the church, to intercede for the believer, and to be his advocate; it is the champion of the church. But this is no eschatological promise, for it was fulfilled on the day of the resurrection. On the evening

[6] John 5:28 f.

[7] John 5:25, author's italics. According to Bultmann, neither this verse nor 5:28 f. was in John's sources. See D. M. Smith, *The Composition and Order of the Fourth Gospel* (New Haven, Conn.: Yale University Press, 1965).

[8] *Paraclete* is translated as counselor in the Revised Standard Version and as advocate in the New English Bible.

of that day, Jesus was present with his disciples. "Then he breathed on them, saying, 'Receive the Holy Spirit.'"[9] In sum, all of Jesus' promises about the future have already been fulfilled, for he has returned, and he has granted the spirit. There is no unfulfilled promise or threat, no destruction, no resurrection, no judgment. John has not completely eliminated the historical, for he still describes the promises as having a fulfillment at a specific time. But the Christian is not encouraged to look toward a historical future that has religious significance.

The final area in which the dehistoricizing tendency of Johannine Christianity is apparent is in the teaching about the Christian life. The phrase *union with Christ* adequately describes this life. It is also called eternal life or, simply, life. The conception is similar to Paul's life in Christ, but it has more of the quality of mystic absorption. The believers are joined to Christ as branches are to the vine. This life is eternal in the sense that it is both unending and unchangeable. In this conception, death is meaningless, for one may enter into union with Christ now and continue unchanged in that relationship beyond death. Such a person does not die but passes from life to life.[10] To the extent to which the believer is united with Christ, to that extent he is separated from the world. John considers the world to be a place of evil, so the Christian must separate from it. This motif is present in chapter 17, where Jesus says: "I am not praying for the world but for those whom thou hast given me, because they belong to thee."[11] The disciples, who represent the Christian at this point, are spoken of as strangers in the world, and the world is alienated from God and Christ. It knows neither God, nor Christ, nor the Christian.

The individual Christian is not left alone to find his union with Christ, for there is a sense in which the church is such a united body. There is no explicit persecution language here, but there is a deep feeling for the estrangement between church and world. This feeling has produced in Johannine Christianity an ecclesiology of sectarianism.[12] Anyone familiar with small sects of fairly recent origin knows that a certain kind of psychology goes along with the movement. It is one that maintains the correctness of the small group and the error of the world as a whole. The sect may present its message to the world outside, but it always attempts to maintain

---

[9] John 20:22. In both Hebrew and Greek the words for *spirit* and *breath* are from the same root. The same is true in English; cf. *spirit* and *respiration*. In John, Jesus gives the spirit in the act of breathing.

[10] See John 8:51.

[11] John 17:9.

[12] See Ernst Käsemann, *The Testament of Jesus*, trans. Gerhard Krodel (Philadelphia, Pa.: Fortress Press, 1968), pp. 56–73.

its distance, feeling that its own integrity and purity depend on its separateness. It finds itself in union with the heavenly Christ, and this lifts the group and its members above the plane of ordinary existence. Johannine ecclesiology must have come out of this kind of sectarian psychology. As such, it is not appropriate for conditions that will meet the church in the centuries to come. When persecution and opposition ceased and the church began to equip itself to create a Christian world, Johannine ecclesiology would not do.

II and III John move in a different direction. In these letters we are exposed to a church official who has wide influence, and the issue is not one of the separation of church from world but of order within the church. The presbyter who wrote these letters was sufficiently well known so that he did not need to include his name. He addressed members of distant churches as his children. He probably sent out traveling missionaries, and he was in a position to receive reports on churches supposedly under his care. He set himself forth as the judge of truth and doctrine; he put his testimony on the side of truth; he was certain that his personal intervention in a dispute would turn the tide. Although he called himself a presbyter. Ignatius' description of the bishop fits him well. These letters represent a rather different kind of ecclesiology from that in the Fourth Gospel—one which emphasizes order within the church rather than the church's separation from the world.

The "sectarianism" of the Fourth Gospel opens still another door to Gnostic Christianity. We shall see that one of the fundamental assumptions of the Gnostics is the evil nature of the world. John is not entirely Gnostic at this point, because he affirms the creation of the world by God, but he is only a step away.

The church achieves its union with God and Christ through the sacraments. The Fourth Gospel has no record of a sacramental institution. The last supper, which served as an institution of the Eucharist in the Synoptics ("Do this in memory of me") is replaced by a foot-washing ceremony in John.[13] Despite this absence, there is a significant amount of material dealing with the sacramental meaning of water, bread, and wine. At Cana, Jesus turns water into wine. When Nicodemus complains that a man cannot re-enter his mother's womb to be born again, Jesus replies that he must be reborn from water and spirit. The water must be that of baptism and may have been suggested by the bag of waters in which the fetus develops. In conversation with the Samaritan woman, Jesus claims the ability to supply her with water sufficient for her entire life. At the last supper, the foot washing is a type of baptism. At the crucifixion, soldiers pierce Jesus' side,

[13] John 13:2–17.

and out pour water and blood. In the discourse in chapter 15, Jesus speaks of himself as the vine and of his disciples as the branches. It is no accident that the figure is that of the vineyard. Chapter 6 contains the most extensive treatment of the sacraments. It begins with a narrative about the feeding of the multitude. In the interpretive commentary which follows, Jesus affirms that it is necessary to partake of his body and blood in order to have eternal life. He claims to be the bread of life. He has come down from heaven as the manna descended during the time of Moses. Then he says that the bread he gives is his own flesh. His body is real bread, and his blood is real drink, and it is absolutely essential to partake of his body and blood.[14] The long discourse concludes with Jesus saying, "The spirit alone gives life; the flesh is of no avail."[15] Despite the importance of the material elements, it is the spirit that stands behind the sacraments and authenticates them. The language of the Fourth Gospel reminds one of the mystery religions, which emphasize the sacrament as a means of participation in deity. John is able to say that the unification of believer with Lord is made secure in the sacraments. At the same time, he intends to guard against highly materialistic interpretations of the sacraments by having the spirit as the guarantor of their efficacy.

The importance of the spirit in the Fourth Gospel led Clement of Alexandria to call it the Gospel of the spirit. This is an accurate generalization, because the author de-emphasizes historical, fleshly, and earthly phenomena. His Christology does not depend heavily on the life of Jesus of Nazareth. Futuristic eschatology is forgotten and replaced by a concept of eternal life. The believer does not find revelation in a series of historical events but in his own union with Christ. The church is not intended to create a Christian domain but is to understand itself as separated from the world. Although the teaching was used in connection with sacraments, it is appropriate to the whole of Johannine Christianity: "The spirit alone gives life; the flesh is of no avail."[16]

[14] In Bultmann's analysis of John's sources, the sacramental passages belong to the final redaction of the Gospel. See Smith, op. cit.

[15] John 6:63.

[16] John 6:63. The letters of John probably come from the same school of thought, for the language, especially in I John, is very similar to that in the Gospel. I John has, however, a good deal more anti-Docetic polemic and eschatological fervor. The two documents are close together in their understanding of eternal life and union with God and Christ. The similarities and differences are just the kind we should expect in a school of writers, who operate from a basically similar point of view but represent somewhat different times, situations, and predictions.

Reconstruction by Herbert S. Gute, Christian Chapel at Dura Europos, overall view. The chapel was built about A.D. 232 and is the oldest known Christian meeting house. (*Courtesy* Yale University Art Gallery, New Haven, Connecticut.)

JEWISH CHRISTIANITY

Although primitive Christianity included Jews, we give the name Jewish Christianity to a somewhat more developed form of that tradition that began with them. It is not to be regarded as a new variety, for those who represented it were extremely conscious of a continuity with primitive Christianity. Nevertheless, it is not to be equated with the earlier form, because it represents a more developed stage of religious thought and life. A precise definition of Jewish Christianity by first- and second-century authors is missing. Different writers use different names, such as Ebionites, Nazoreans, and Elkesaites. These may be distinctive names of different groups of Jewish Christians, or they may be locally variant designations for the same basic group. Justin, without using any names, speaks of two groups, one acceptable to him, the other not.[17] We know little about the

---

[17] *Dialogue with Trypho* 47.

subtle distinctions between groups, but it is possible to outline the main lines of Jewish Christian thought with a high degree of probability.

The literature on which we may draw is minimal, and not much of it comes directly from Jewish Christian writers. In previous chapters, we looked at four documents that bore some relationship to Jewish Christianity—the epistles of James and Barnabas, and the Gospels of Matthew and the Ebionites. The latter Gospel is known only through quotations in Epiphanius. There are at least two other gospels—the Gospel according to the Hebrews and the Gospel according to the Nazoreans, likewise known only by quotations from other writers. In addition, the third- and fourth-century pseudo-Clementine literature contains some Jewish Christian material of older date. Finally, the Old Testament translation by Symmachus, done late in the second century, is helpful, because the translator was a Jewish Christian.

The origin of Jewish Christianity is most appropriately found in the religion of the Jerusalem Church, led by the "pillar" apostles, James in particular. The death of James about A.D. 62 and the threat of war in Jerusalem brought about a flight of the community to Pella, described by Eusebius and reflected in the Synoptic Gospels.[18] Eusebius also tells of the successors of James. An uncle, Simon bar Clopas, led the community to Pella before the war and probably brought a small group back to Jerusalem afterward. Most stayed in the trans-Jordan area, and after the second Jewish revolt in A.D. 135, there was no significant Christianity in Jerusalem. Between the two wars (A.D. 70–132), there was a good deal of Jewish hostility toward Christians. They were specifically excluded from the synagogues, a fact probably alluded to in the Gospel of John.[19] Roman officials also saw them as potential rebels and executed Simon bar Clopas in A.D. 107, because he was a descendant of David.[20] Eusebius lists fourteen successors of James, each of whom headed the Jerusalem Church.[21] The last one ruled until A.D. 135. Some were relatives of Jesus, and one suspects an attempt to set up a dynasty of Jesus' family to rule the church. Our knowledge of the history of Jewish Christianity ceases at this point, but we may reasonably assume that it continued in the trans-Jordan area for three or four centuries.

A number of general characteristics may be derived from the literature at hand.[22] Jewish Christians were devout monotheists; they revered the Old

[18] See p. 192.

[19] See John 9:22; 12:42; 16:2.

[20] Eusebius, *Church History* III, 32:3-6.

[21] Ibid., V, 12:1–2; see III, 11:1.

[22] See H.-J. Schoeps, *Jewish Christianity*, trans. D. R. A. Hare (Philadelphia, Pa.: Fortress Press, 1969), for a lucid analysis of the subject.

Testament; they practiced circumcision; they saw a continuity between Moses and Jesus and between Jesus and themselves. They insisted that James was the first head of the church, and they expressed deep hostility toward Paul. In the pseudo-Clementine literature, Peter is called the true apostle, and Paul is the enemy of Christianity. Peter contests Paul's claim to be an apostle and insists that the prime qualification for apostleship is acquaintance with the historical Jesus. In other writings Paul is accused of the murder of James. This hostility does not seem to be anticipated by the primitive Jerusalem community of Christians. Although there were certain points of disagreement, there must have been a basic harmony between James and Paul. Paul vigorously affirms that he reached an amicable agreement with James and the other "pillars" in Jerusalem. Jewish Christian hostility to Paul must be a later development, occasioned by the increasing independence of Gentile Christians and their tendency to ignore Jewish Christians. As Jewish Christians looked back on the early history of the church, they came to feel that Paul was responsible for all their troubles. The hostility they felt toward the larger Gentile movement came to be focused on the one who, according to them, initiated it.

In many areas, Jewish Christians shared ideas with other groups of the time, but their Christology and their legal theory are distinctive. They looked upon Jesus as the prophet like Moses, who was predicted in Deuteronomy 18:15 ff. His life was purely human, and he was not born of a virgin. He committed no conscious sin but was not without unwitting sins. As the new Moses, he fulfilled and purified Mosaic institutions, including the Torah. To emphasize his continuity with Israelite history, they thought of him as one in a line of bearers of revelation. The glory of God passed from one bearer to the next in a line that started with Adam and went through Enoch, Noah, Abraham, Isaac, Jacob, and Moses, to Jesus, the final bearer of revelation. His Messianic designation came at his baptism, when the descent of the dove symbolized God's adoption of him. They believed also in his resurrection and his future return as Messiah. Because the earthly life was characterized by humility and suffering, he must return in conquest. Although his Messianic designation came at the baptism, he is not expected to function as Messiah until his return as Son of man. In most respects, the Christology of Jewish Christianity is similar to that of their primitive counterparts. Jesus was a human being upon whom the spirit of God descended; he will return as Messiah-Son of man. There is no pre-existence and no divinity in the earthly life.

To Jewish Christians the law was still of paramount importance, but they felt that Jesus had made some drastic modifications in it. The major

The Healing of the Paralytic from the Christian Chapel at Dura Europos. This
is the oldest known pictorial representation of Jesus. (*Courtesy* Yale University
Art Gallery, New Haven, Connecticut.)

change was the elimination of the sacrificial cult and the ritual of the Jerusalem Temple. The sacrificial slaughter of animals was abominable to them. In this light they held distinctive interpretations of the Old Testament. They objected to the idea of the Jewish monarchy, severely criticized Solomon and David, and did not look upon Jesus as son of David. They rejected all the prophets except the bearers of revelation mentioned above. They rejected certain Old Testament passages, namely those that spoke of God anthropomorphically and those that reported immoral acts by Old Testament worthies. Jewish Christians felt themselves relieved of the sacrificial laws, but they put correspondingly greater emphasis upon others. They refused to eat meat with blood and meat from an animal which had been sacrificed to an idol. They put a high value on poverty and personal ritual purity. Jewish Christianity did not direct itself toward a profound analysis of the meaning of law and did not question the status of Torah as the word of God. As men of a Jewish background, Jewish Christians retained and even intensified those legal matters relating to their personal lives. But, as Christians, they were convinced that Jesus had made significant changes in the content of the law. He had not abolished it but fulfilled it by relieving his followers of some parts and intensifying others. H.-J. Schoeps writes:

> The really creative contribution of the Ebionites to religion lay in their internalization of the Old Testament law. On the one hand they wanted to purge it of falsification, and so they abbreviated and lightened it; on the other hand, they wanted to augment it and make it more difficult by intensifying that which was essential.[23]

With some justification, Jewish Christians claimed to retain without change the earliest beliefs and forms of Christianity. It is not correct that they were unchanging, but we need to take seriously their claim of continuity with the original Christians. At the same time, their religion came more and more to be identified with a particular ethos and was less and less appealing to the church as a whole. Jewish Christianity was finally relegated to a position of interesting but irrelevant antiquity.

GNOSTIC CHRISTIANITY

A religion that intends to appeal to man must describe him in meaningful terms. It must tell him who he is, why he is here, what is expected of him,

[23] Ibid., p. 76.

and where he is headed. To put it another way, religion is not so much an abstract speculation about God as an interesting but irrelevant subject as it is an expression of man's deepest feelings about the nature and context of his own existence. A meaningful religion is one to which men can make positive responses. It is meaningful if a man can listen to its assertions and say: Yes, that adequately describes me. Generally optimistic people may not respond to a religion that tells them they are in a hopelessly depraved situation, and slaves may reject a religion that tells them that all is right with the world. Gnostic Christianity appealed to large numbers of people in the world of Roman Hellenism, because it seemed to address them where they were with a message of hopeful change.

We know Gnosticism only as a variety of Christianity, which reached full bloom in the second century. Modern scholars are convinced, however, that it arose prior to and independently of Christianity. In many cases, the Christian elements are not integral to the basic thought and were probably added on to a previously developed system. It is also clear that Gnostic ideas were in the air before the development of the great second-century systems, because they influenced some first-century writers such as Paul and John. There is no unanimity, however, on the precise origin of pre-Christian Gnosticism, for it appears to be a combination of Jewish, Greek, Hellenistic, and oriental elements. Its use of the Old Testament has produced the interesting hypothesis that it arose among heretical Jews. But it is strongly anti-Semitic, and it turns traditional Jewish ideas upside down. In contrast to it, protocatholic Christianity looks like an orthodox Jewish sect. It has affinities with the Jewish apocalyptic tradition, and it has been suggested that it originated from the disillusionment of hopes expressed in that tradition.[24] But it also has affinities with Greek philosophy and oriental mythology, and its use of these elements is more positive. Whatever the origin, Gnostics found Christianity particularly attractive and allied with it to produce a number of second-century sects. We know almost nothing of the precise organization of these groups. The Marcionites developed something in the form of a church, but most of the others probably took the model of the school. Even so, other Christian groups looked upon them as competitors.

The name is a form of the Greek word *Gnosis,* which we translate as knowledge. The Gnostic feels that he has been granted knowledge, which is a means of salvation. But *Gnosis* is not to be confused with learning. It

[24] See R. M. Grant, *Gnosticism and Early Christianity*, 2nd ed. (New York: Columbia University Press, 1966).

does not result from a long process of study, gradually built up by reading books, listening to lectures, and discussing with scholars. Knowledge in this sense rests on the assumption that human beings have within themselves the ability to arrive at understanding. For reasons that will soon become apparent, Gnostic Christians were convinced that man could not achieve knowledge without divine aid. *Gnosis* comes to him from outside and is the content of revelation. It cannot be taught but must be revealed. For this reason, *Gnosis* is secret and contained within the community of Gnostics.

In the second century, there was a bewildering array of Gnostic Christian groups, and it is difficult to generalize about them. They are so diverse that some do not use the concept of *Gnosis*. Irenaeus bemoaned the fact that each day one of them came up with something new.[25] Most of our information comes from non-Gnostics, although we now have a good bit of Coptic Gnostic material from Nag Hammadi, among them the Gospel of Thomas. Since it would be impossible to give an adequate description of each group, we shall first describe some of the more common characteristics and then examine two influential, but quite different, groups—the Valentinian and the Marcionite.

Fundamental to almost all Gnostic religion is a metaphysical dualism, which may be expressed in a contrast between light and darkness, truth and falsehood, good and evil, or spirit and matter. It means that there is something that is of God, the divine, and something that is not, the demonic. The demonic is hostile to God and to all who belong to him. God is absolutely transcendent to the world and unknowable through nature. There is no trace of him in the world, for he is not the creator. The world is the sphere of the demonic, and God is alien to it.

The universe is the creation of the demonic being, usually called the *Demiurge,* and he rules over it. The universe is structured in such a way that man is imprisoned within it. The earth is surrounded by seven planetary spheres and one made up of the fixed stars. The *Demiurge* has placed rulers (called *archons*) over each of the spheres, and they serve to separate the universe and men from God. The rule of the *Demiurge* and the *archons* is called Fate, a force that alienates man from a freedom which is rightly his.[26] Hans Jonas describes the Gnostic universe as "a vast prison whose innermost dungeon is the earth, the scene of man's life."[27]

Man finds himself a resident in this world and subject to Fate, but he is really a stranger to it. Strictly speaking, man is composed of three parts

[25] Irenaeus, *Against Heresies* I, 18:1.
[26] On the rule of Fate, see pp. 69 ff., on Stoic thought, and p. 76, on astrology.
[27] *The Gnostic Religion*, 2nd ed. (Boston: Beacon Press, 1963), p. 43.

—body, soul, and spirit. Spirit is a portion of the divine that fell from the upper world. In order to imprison it, the *archons* created bodies and souls and made them subject to the rule of Fate. The usual state of the imprisoned spirit is sleep, but it may be awakened through *Gnosis* and apprised of its condition. Man, thus, is a mixture of the divine and the demonic. When the awakened spirit discovers that it does not belong here, it causes in man a deep dissatisfaction. He is lonely and alienated and frustrated in his imprisonment.

Salvation comes by way of a messenger from the divine region, who breaks through the stellar and planetary spheres to bring *Gnosis* to man. After death, the Gnostic, having received *Gnosis* and now being free of his body, begins his trek through the spheres. He is still a spirit surrounded by a soul. The soul is understood to be a seven-layered covering around the spirit, and at each sphere one layer is removed. At the end, the spirit is free and finally reunited with the divine substance. Salvation has a twofold significance for the Gnostic. It is release from demonic bondage and absorption into divinity.

When Jesus is regarded as the savior, he is described in a Docetic fashion. This Christology should be familiar by now, since we encountered traces of it in the Gospel of John and the Gospel of Peter and opposition to it in I John and Ignatius. For Gnostic Christians, the savior of mankind must be a pure spirit, otherwise he would be imprisoned in soul and body as we are, and a fellow prisoner could not execute our escape. If it seemed to the disciples that Jesus was human, this was the result either of intentional deception or of the disciples' inability to ascertain the presence of pure spirit. Whatever the disciples felt, Gnostics were sure that Jesus was not composed of soul and body, that he was not born of Mary, and that he did not die.

Ethics was a matter of secondary importance in Gnostic Christianity, because it involved man's relation to the created world. The Gnostic was able to adopt either of two opposing life styles—either ascetic or libertine. If man exists as a spirit imprisoned in a soul and a body, it stands to reason that he ought to have as little as possible to do with the prison. The spirit should practice a kind of dominance over the other components to prepare itself for its release. This way leads to asceticism, and the practicing Gnostic would avoid contact with the world as much as possible. He would be unmarried and celibate, and he would practice fasting and perhaps poverty. But, on the same premises, it is possible to regard the soul and body as irrelevant. Nothing is to be gained by disciplining the body and soul, for the spirit is to lose them anyway. This way leads to libertinism, which permits indulgence in sex, food, drink, and wealth with impunity. Both forms of this ethic are identified with Gnostic Christianity, according to its opponents. Both are altogether directed toward the individual, and neither one leads to the development of a social ethic. In general, Gnostics said nothing about political or economic structures, but neither did most of the other Christian groups.

To express their beliefs, Gnostic Christians frequently employed myth.[28] Modern readers are almost never inspired by this device and are often offended by it. We must remember, however, that mythology was part of the cultural equipment of the day and that men of the early centuries adopted an attitude quite different from ours. Myth to them was a narrative description of the nonhistorical world, and they would not look upon the nonhistorical as necessarily untrue. To the Gnostic, myth was also a way of accounting for man's presence in this foreign land. To be sure, Gnostics have no monopoly on myth. Not only was it fundamental to classical and Hellenistic religion, but it also played a role in the Old Testament and in other varieties of Christianity. In the case of the latter, we need only recall the prologue to the Gospel of John, which tells of the preincarnate *Logos,* and the hymn in Philippians, which has the Christ empty himself of divinity. The Gnostic myths differ from the other Christian myths only in their complexity. They consist of innumerable characters and a seemingly endless succession of events. In order to give just due to Gnostic Christianity, we must attempt to see beyond the myths to the human importance of their message. In focusing their attention upon man, who feels within himself a basic conflict, they were able to give expression to the depths of human life.[29] Man feels that he is part of the world in which he lives, but he does not always feel content in it. He is torn between desires of the material and guilt at succumbing to them. He has aspirations that are unfulfilled because of his physical and moral incapacities. He feels that the observable world must not be all there is and that somehow he is related to, but separated from, that other world beyond this one. The Gnostic is able to speak to frustrated men and tell them that they are aliens and prisoners and assure them that it is possible to return home. The Gnostic proclaims that man has a savior, who has come to release him and lead him back. He is able to say that frustration will finally disappear, because man will achieve his authentic selfhood and will become a pure spirit free of soul and body. But in order to confirm this message, it is necessary to objectify it,

[28] For definition of myth, see pp. 24 ff.
[29] The mystery religion also appealed to some of the same human needs; see pp. 77 ff.

to root it in the very structure of reality, to describe the process through which man became alienated and will return. Modern man may prefer a rational theology, philosophy, or psychology. The Gnostics and their contemporaries preferred myth.

It is necessary now to look in more detail at two groups of Gnostic Christians. The first is that of Valentinus, probably the most influential of the Gnostics. He probably came from Egypt, but he resided at Rome from c. A.D. 135–165. Some of his followers set up schools of their own, and we know of Valentinianism mainly through them. The Gospel of Truth, however, may be a work of Valentinus himself.

The Valentinian system is a complex description of creation and redemption.[30] The creation myth begins with the existence of a god named *Abyss*. The name indicates the importance of certain qualities of the divine—namely, depth, unknowability, eternality, and limitlessness. *Abyss*, as an unbounded depth, symbolizes deity in its most profound and inscrutable sense. But *Abyss* has other qualities, which are personified. He is paired with Silence, a further symbol of the incommunicable deity. *Abyss* and Silence give birth to two further qualities, Mind and Truth. These in turn produce *Logos* and Life. Altogether there are thirty personifications, the last one being *Sophia*, or Wisdom. These thirty *Aeons* make up what is called the *Pleroma*, or Fullness, the sum total of all divinity and goodness. Each pair in the *Pleroma* is composed of a male and a female. *Abyss*, Mind, and *Logos* are male, and the others are their female consorts. Together they give birth to the succeeding *Aeons*. Although Irenaeus and other opponents accused Valentinus of polytheism, it is not clear that the charge is fair. To be sure, the *Aeons* are thought of as to some degree independent of one another. Yet they are all born of *Abyss*-Silence. The figure of the family and birth is appropriate in calling attention to the tension between unity and independence. At conception, a mother and her son are so intimately connected that the son is a completely dependent and indistinct part of the mother. At birth, the son is distinct, and his independence begins and grows gradually. The developing family is a process of indistinct persons becoming distinct and dependent persons becoming independent. Throughout the process, the family exists in a state of tension between unity and independence. The same is the case in the Valentinian *Pleroma*. As the deity gives expression to one of his qualities, that quality becomes a distinct entity. It is true that there are thirty deities in the *Pleroma*, but they are all projections of the original God.

[30] See Jonas, op. cit., pp. 174–205, for a thorough and clear analysis of Valentinianism.

Within the *Pleroma,* there are certain gradations. The distance between *Abyss,* the highest, and *Sophia,* the lowest, is emphasized. Mind is the only one that can know *Abyss,* but all the others desired this knowledge. *Sophia* desired it to such an extent that she had to be restrained by a personification called Limit, a kind of guardian of *Abyss* and the *Pleroma.* Limit restored her to her proper place in the *Pleroma,* but the unfulfilled desire that she had expressed became independent of her. This personified desire was thrown out of the *Pleroma* and is afterward called the Lower *Sophia,* or *Achamoth.*[31] Disturbed by the crisis caused by *Sophia,* the other *Aeons* prayed to *Abyss,* who gave birth to two more—Christ and Holy Spirit. Their duties were to restore order in the *Pleroma* and to begin the recovery of the fallen *Achamoth.* When the original order of the *Pleroma* was established, all the *Aeons* together produced Jesus, who was not paired with a female.

The scene now shifts to the region outside the *Pleroma,* at present inhabited only by *Achamoth.* Christ stretches outside the *Pleroma* only long enough to acquaint *Achamoth* with her separation from deity and to awaken her desire for restoration. In her frustration she expresses grief, fear, shock, and ignorance. These negative expressions become independent of her and become sources of the four material elements: earth, air, fire, and water. But *Achamoth* expresses a fifth emotion, that of turning toward the *Pleroma,* a conversion. In response to her turning, Jesus comes to be her consort and grants to her *Gnosis,* which frees her from her negative passions. In her joy she produces spirit, which continues to exist in the lower world. She also produces soul and forms it into a being called the *Demiurge.* He is characterized by ignorance, which *Achamoth* can use to obtain her will. *Demiurge* then creates the seven planetary spheres and the earth. He also creates man by imprisoning spirit within soul and combining them with the material elements. Man, therefore, is the creation of *Demiurge,* but he preserves a spiritual element from the fallen but restored *Achamoth.*

The work of human salvation is largely carried out by Jesus and Christ, and for it the restoration of *Achamoth* serves as a model. Jesus and Christ descended upon the earthly Jesus at his baptism and left him before his passion. In this system the earthly Jesus is only the vehicle for the saving work of the divine Jesus and Christ. He was completely human, and he died, but his death is irrelevant to salvation. Salvation comes when Jesus and Christ impart *Gnosis* to men of spirit. Not all men will be saved, be-

---

[31] *Achamoth* is Hebrew for wisdom, so is the equivalent of the Greek *Sophia.*

cause in some the spiritual element is minimal or missing. When the work of Jesus and Christ has been completed, all spirits and *Achamoth* re-enter the *Pleroma*.

Amid all of this complexity, it is possible to see that Valentinian Gnosticism was struggling with a difficult problem. It is assumed that there is such a thing as the visible world, which could not have originated itself. But it is also known that there are elements within the world that are hostile to God. Creation myths must face this problem. The one in the first chapter of Genesis attempted to do so by affirming that nothing in the world was opposed to God. For each thing he created, God pronounced: "It is good." But in the story in Genesis 2, some evil, hostile element inexplicably appears. A serpent tempts Eve and Adam to disobey, but no explanation of the serpent's origin is offered. The Valentinian myth gives a full explanation: there was a primeval split within the Godhead itself, originally caused by desire for God, but resulting in the fallen state of the creation and a temporary dualism.

Marcion is a quite different kind of Gnostic, so different that many decline to classify him with the others. He was a wealthy shipowner from Pontus, in Asia Minor. Hippolytus reports that his father, a bishop, had excommunicated him because of his heretical views. He came to Rome about A.D. 140 and joined the Church there but was excommunicated a few years later. He spent the remaining years of his life (until c. A.D. 160) organizing churches all over the Empire. His success may be gauged by the attention he attracted from opponents. Irenaeus, for example, was afraid that his teaching would pull many away from the "true" faith. His writings have completely disappeared except for quotations and summaries from his opponents.

Marcion is unlike other Gnostic Christians in that he has no *Pleroma* and no emphasis on *Gnosis*. He is, however, Gnostic in his dualism, which is stricter than that of the Valentinians. Fundamental to his thought is the idea of two gods—one the creator, the other the savior. The two gods are totally unlike each other and hostile to each other. There is no genealogical relation between them as there is between *Abyss* and *Demiurge* in Valentinianism. The creator god is characterized by pettiness, and he rules the world by retributive, vindictive justice. He is known in nature and through the Old Testament. His creation of the world is described in Genesis, and he gave the Torah, which is recorded in the other Scriptures. The other god is one of saving love, revealed for the first time by Jesus. The god Jesus addressed as father has nothing to do with the Old Testament god, and his function is to save man from the creator's rule. He does so out of his freely given grace, for the men he saves are not fallen spirits who belonged to him. They really belong to their creator, the lesser god. The loving god saves them by adopting them as his own. Marcion's Christology was Docetic. The Christ was not a product of the creator god. He came directly from the loving god in the fifteenth year of Tiberius and assumed an apparently human body. His death was the price paid to the creator for man's salvation. Man receives his salvation in faith, not by *Gnosis*.

Marcion's inspiration came from Paul. He was deeply impressed with Paul's contrast of law and gospel, but he did not see the profound unity between them that Paul did. To him the gospel was completely new, in no way anticipated in the Old Testament.[32] Thus, he made Paul's letters (excluding the Pastorals) the basic canon for his churches and included with them the Gospel of Luke in a form lacking any suggestion of connection between Jesus and the creator god. The Old Testament was totally discarded as the work of the creator, and it gave expression to his pettiness and inconsistency. To our knowledge, Marcion's canon, consisting only of Luke and Paul, was the first attempt to form a body of Christian Scripture. His canon, his organizing ability, and his demand for strict asceticism created a strong group of churches parallel to and distinct from the protocatholic churches.

Inconsistencies are apparent in Marcion's thought. How, for example, can the death of Jesus have significance within a Docetic Christology? But Marcion was more of a religious man than a theologian. Adolf Harnack's estimate rings true:

> [Marcion] had in general nothing to do with principles, but with living beings whose power he felt, and . . . what he ultimately saw in the Gospel was not an explanation of the world, but redemption from the world,— redemption from a world, which even in the best that it can offer, has nothing that can reach the height of the blessing bestowed in Christ.[33]

Marcion's effort to establish a religion, purified of its Jewish background, with its own Scripture, its own organization, and a rigid ethic, was appealing to many, but challenging and threatening to most Christian groups.

Marcion, Valentinus, and Gnostics in general pressed a distinct advantage. They were able to analyze and offer a cure for the human tragedy without being burdened by the necessity to make historical events significant.

---

[32] Marcion agreed that the Old Testament had predicted the coming of a Messiah, but he maintained that those predictions were not fulfilled in Jesus. That Messiah is yet to come from the creator god, but his coming is totally irrelevant to the god of love.

[33] Adolf Harnack, *History of Dogma*, trans. Neil Buchanan (New York: Peter Smith, 1958), Vol. 1, p. 269.

Their effort may still be applauded by those who prefer to make sense of the world by the use of ideas rather than the analysis of events. History has a way of being ambiguous and subject to diverse interpretations. Primitive, Pauline, and Jewish Christians felt the need to make sense of the past and found in the past the clue to all human life. Gnostics could work purely in the realm of theory. We may be assured that to many, then and now, their version of Christianity is by far the clearest and most compelling.

PROTOCATHOLIC CHRISTIANITY

In the third century, the variant Christian groups began to be either eliminated or assimilated into a single synthesis. The synthesis is known as catholic Christianity. But catholic Christianity did not simply burst on the scene as a novel phenomenon or even as an *ad hoc* attempt at elimination and assimilation. It had been prepared for by an earlier tradition, to which we may give the name protocatholic.

The apologetic and antiheretical literature illustrates this tradition, for in it the constituent elements are brought together in a visible way. In particular, the writing of Irenaeus exemplifies an attempt to create a single form for the Christian faith with definite and clear limits. To him, the church must rest upon the authority of the apostles and bishops, a definite creed, and a limited canon of sacred writings. These three formal elements became the building blocks for catholic Christianity, giving it a controlling organization and a means for distinguishing true and false faith. Irenaeus is our best guide to an understanding of protocatholic Christianity, for he was both a representative and a crucial figure. He represented a viewpoint that was probably dominant in his own region, and he stood at a point from which he could look back to diversity and ahead to unity.

What produced protocatholic Christianity? It is possible to point to three specific factors which played a part in its development. The first was the delay of Jesus' Parousia. The vivid expectation of primitive and early Pauline Christianity finally had to give way, and we have already seen the effects of the delay in the later letters of Paul. Jewish Christianity retained a belief in the second coming but did not expect an immediate fulfillment of it. Johannine and Gnostic Christianity substituted a belief in some form of eternal life for the individual in place of a cataclysmic end to history. Protocatholic Christians adapted to the delay by retaining in their creed a statement of the second coming but at the same time giving attention to the structure of a continuing Christian community. Certainly, they expected

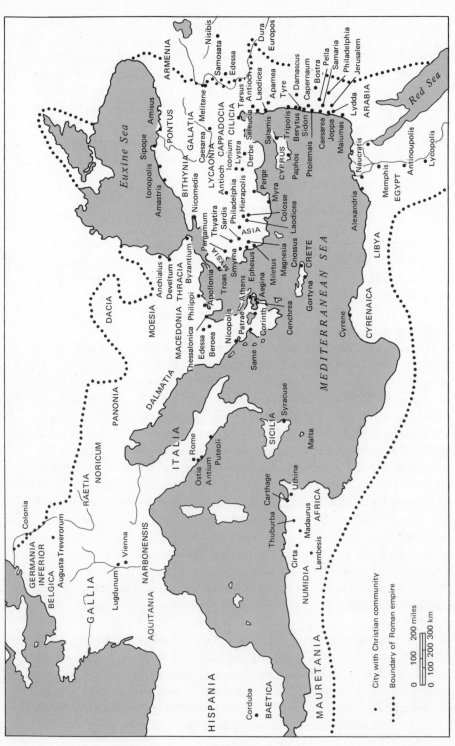

FIGURE 26 The Church in the Second Century. (Adapted with permission of The Macmillan Company from *The Macmillan Bible Atlas* by Y. Aharoni and Michael Avi-Yonah. Copyright © 1968 by Carta, Jerusalem. Copyright © 1964 by Carta, Jerusalem.

nothing to happen in the immediate future. The church finally came to speak of the immortality of individual Christians rather than the corporate resurrection on the last day. By the fourth century, Eusebius was able to characterize Papias as somewhat stupid for his materialistic eschatological expectations.[34]

A second obvious factor in the development of protocatholic Christianity was the very fact of diversity. A movement that had initially allowed a wide freedom in the expression of faith began to ask if such diversity were not dissolving the very meaning of the movement. Can Christianity mean anything if it includes both Jewish Christians and Gnostic Christians? The situation is complicated by the fact that the diverse groups were making religious claims. When a man proclaims a religious doctrine, he is not simply giving his opinion, which may be discussed, analyzed, and finally accepted or rejected. He believes that he is uttering an absolute truth, and he is demanding acceptance and allegiance from his hearers. When two competing claims are made in the name of one religion, mutual rejection is more likely to result than mutual toleration. To solve the problem, one may call for a dissolution of the movement into independent groups or plead for unity amid a tolerable diversity. Protocatholic Christianity did neither. It intended to create a united church, but it did so by attempting to discover the heart of Christianity and by proclaiming it over against the diverse claims of all other groups. Its proponents did this not simply in order to preserve meaningfulness for the word *Christian,* but in order to remain faithful to what they had found in Jesus the Christ.

A third factor influencing protocatholic Christianity was the threat from outside. The Apologists, who attempted to answer the challenges of Roman authority, knew that they had to produce a definition of Christianity that was acceptable to the government officials. A definition is both positive and negative. It states what a thing means and, in so doing, limits the meaning. Christianity had to be understood as excluding some people who claimed to be Christians. Justin deplored the fact that Christians did not all believe the same things and live the same way. He called upon Rome to differentiate between various Christians and to punish only those who committed actual crimes. In affirming that Christianity is not a crime, he implies that the true Christian is not a criminal, an implication that Athenagoras makes explicit. This means that not all who claim the name are really Christians. The long and short of it is that oppression taught the church that it needed

[34]Eusebius, *Church History* III, 39:12.

a visible unity, for it was recognized that a divided church could not long stand.

Irenaeus has made clear the formal elements in protocatholic Christianity. In insisting on a particular form, he also had in mind the preservation of certain emphases and beliefs, for a form without a content is meaningless. A further analysis of Irenaeus' forms should give us some insight into the interests and beliefs of protocatholic Christianity. We therefore ask: Why did protocatholic Christianity, as illustrated by Irenaeus, insist on apostolic succession, a particular canon, and a certain creed?

The doctrine of apostolic succession was for Irenaeus a particularly important safeguard for faith. It guards the episcopacy against false claimants, for the bishop must stand in a line of succession from the apostles. The form implies two major emphases in protocatholic thought. In the first place, there is an implicit emphasis on historical continuity. Irenaeus believes that the faith he holds is in conformity with that of the apostles and of primitive Christianity. Whether or not he is correct is debatable, but the fact that he makes the claim indicates that he is interested in the historical manifestation of faith. On this point he may be contrasted with Marcion and the Gnostics. Gnostics said that it really did not matter what the apostles taught or what primitive Christians believed. *Gnosis* comes to a man quite independently of these previous and particular occurrences. Marcion revered Paul, but he was quite sure that the other apostles understood nothing of the message that Jesus taught. Irenaeus, in his argument against the secret doctrines of the Gnostics, insisted on the historical visibility of the revelation in the Christ and the continuity in the transmission of the revelation. It was primarily in reaction against Gnostic disparagement and esoteric claims that Irenaeus developed the doctrine of apostolic succession, and it is apparent that historical continuity is important to him. In the second place, apostolic succession implies an emphasis on the historical Jesus. What gives authority to the apostles is the fact that they had been with Jesus. Irenaeus makes his own stand clear in his polemic against Docetism. Those who accepted a Docetic Christology found it necessary to say that the apostles were deceived and that their testimony should be dismissed. Irenaeus correspondingly emphasized the disciples' contact with a genuinely human, flesh-and-blood Jesus, who is nonetheless the Son of God. In both of these emphases the protocatholic respect for history is apparent.

The canon of sacred writings was for Irenaeus a second guarantee of the faith. It is probable that protocatholic Christians saw the strength that a canon provided for the Marcionites and the danger of the particular one they had. Thus, they accepted the Marcionite idea of the canon, but they enlarged it to include about the same books contained in the modern Old and New Testaments. Why did they accept these particular books and not others? Some, of course, were excluded because they were too closely identified with rejected groups.[35] The four gospels were included because they presented a historical Jesus, and the other New Testament books were acceptable because they were thought to have been written by apostles. There seem to be three reasons for the inclusion of the Old Testament. In the first place, it taught monotheism. Irenaeus was rightly convinced that primitive Christianity was monotheistic. He may not have been fair in his appraisal of Valentinian Gnosticism, but he thought it taught polytheism, because it spoke of gods in the plural. He also felt that true Christianity was opposed to the Marcionite belief in two gods and that the Old Testament provided a means to counter this teaching. In the second place, the Old Testament taught that the world was created by the one God. Monotheism and a positive attitude toward creation go together. It is only against the background of some form of dualism that one can be wholly negative about the world. Irenaeus knew that the Old Testament would counter Gnostics and Marcionites on this score. The third reason for the retention of the Old Testament was the belief that the prophets had foretold the coming of Christ. This too is an anti-Marcionite reaction, for Marcion said that the prophets were inspired by the creator god, not by the father of Jesus Christ. Irenaeus' interest in history is again visible. For him, the Christ did not suddenly appear on the scene; he was anticipated and announced ahead of time, and he fulfilled the expectations of the men of the past who devoted themselves to the one God.

The creed cited by Irenaeus gives explicit notice of the things he feels Christians must hold to.[36] To him it is the faith of the apostles and the universal church. The claim to universality must not be taken lightly. It is probable that the creed was recited in a significant number of churches, and, if so, we can say that protocatholic Christianity had achieved a degree of unity even before Irenaeus. The creed expresses belief in one God, who is the creator, one Jesus Christ, the Son of God, who was made flesh, and the Holy Spirit, who inspired the prophets to foretell every event of Jesus'

---

[35] Although the Gospel of Matthew was treasured by Jewish Christians, it seems to have been widely used by other groups. It came to play an important role in catholic Christianity because of the support it gave to the power and primacy of Peter, particularly in 16:18 ff. The Jewish Christians revered Peter over against Paul; catholic Christians looked upon him as the first bishop of the Roman Church. In Matthew, Jesus gives him the keys of the kingdom and confers on him the right to forgive sins.

[36] *Against Heresies* I, 10:1; see p. 266 f.

The Madonna and the Prophet, third-century fresco from the Catacomb of Priscilla, Rome. (*Courtesy* Pontifical Commission for Sacred Archives, Rome.)

life; the creed concludes with a recitation of the events. It, therefore, continues emphasis on the same points of importance we found earlier—monotheism, the historicity and humanity of Jesus, creation as the work of one God, and the inspiration of the prophets.

This brief analysis of Irenaeus' formal elements has enabled us to discover some of the beliefs that protocatholic Christianity insisted on preserving. These are: the historicity and continuity of Christian faith; the historicity and humanity of Jesus; the unity of God; the historical value of the prophets; the universality and unity of the church; and the creation of the world by God. The most notable characteristic of this form of Christianity is its historical awareness. It adopts a history of salvation—a message predicted by the prophets, proclaimed by Jesus, preserved by the apostles and their successors. In relation to other contemporary varieties of Christianity, protocatholicism is a product of exclusion and assimilation. It accepts the Jewish Christian feeling for historical continuity but rejects its ethnic identity. It accepts from Gnosticism the basic human desire for salvation but rejects the entire Gnostic structure of divine and human. It also picks up and formalizes elements from earlier Christian traditions. It claims to be continuous with primitive Christianity but rejects its eschatological expectation. With Paul, it rejects the demands of Torah but suppresses his emphasis on freedom in the Christian life and virtually ignores the more subtle aspects of his legal theory. In large measure, it accepts the Johannine Christology and sacramentalism, but it rejects the semi-Docetic and ahistorical tendency and de-emphasizes those points that were conducive to Gnostic interpretations.

Protocatholic Christianity is a synthetic form made necessary by the historical contingencies of the second century. It was chiefly a reaction and response to the Gnostic crisis. But it had also been growing alongside other forms. It is not simply a synthesis but a retention and elaboration of older views. Once we have seen what this form of thought meant to a man such as Irenaeus, it is possible to look back and see certain similarities, which in other contexts served as anticipations for the more developed thought. The pseudo-Pauline letters had drawn from Paul but moved surely in the direction of protocatholic thought. The epistle to the Ephesians put a great deal of stress on the unity of the church, and the Pastoral epistles underscored the authority of church officials. I Clement called for obedience to the constituted officers of the church, and Ignatius made the bishop the visible and present representative of Jesus Christ. The author of II and III John, who called himself a presbyter, felt no reluctance about interfering in distant churches and expecting them to respect his authority. The author of Luke-Acts, in presenting a history of salvation, paved the way for an understanding of historical continuity and for a doctrine of the church as part of the work of God. Luke took special pains to relate all of the early apostles to one another, so that even an independent Paul receives authorization from the Jerusalem apostles. His narrative of the apostles easily led to the doctrine of apostolic succession. Documents such as Jude, II Peter, and I John show as much concern for the danger of Docetic-Gnostic thought as does Irenaeus. Finally, we must call attention to the contribution of the Synoptic writers. They do not seem to react in any conscious way against

Docetism, but it is significant that they found it appropriate, even necessary, to present their faith in terms of the deeds and sayings of the historical Jesus. Since Christians of all stripes were able to proclaim their faith without any detailed information on the historical Jesus, the effort of the Synoptic writers (and to a lesser extent John) stands out in bold relief. In so doing they gave to protocatholic Christianity a heritage of preserved tradition that forced it to renounce Docetism and provided the wherewithal for the task.

A historical judgment to the effect that the dominance of protocatholic Christianity was inevitable is unwarranted. Since the church moved in this direction, it is possible to see that it made explicit a number of implicit ideas and forms. It is true that it claimed to be in perfect harmony with the religion of primitive Christianity, and there is a good deal of merit in the claim. But primitive Christianity had the seeds of a number of developments, and Jewish Christianity made the same claim with perhaps better justification. The dominance of protocatholic and later catholic Christianity brought to an end the period of uncontrolled diversity in early Christianity. But that earlier freedom of thought did not completely disappear. The church retained such writings as the letters of Paul and the Gospel of John, in which from time to time men were able to find grounds for freedom in faith. People will remember that the Johannine Jesus said, "The truth will set you free."[37] People will remember the battles of Paul against Judaizers and draw analogies to their own battles against a dominating and oppressive church. Ernst Käsemann has dramatically expressed the paradox that in preserving the letters of Paul the church preserved the seeds of "her own permanent crisis." "She cannot get away from him who for the most part only disturbs her. For he remains even for her the Apostle to the heathen; the pious still hardly know what to make of him."[38]

DIVERSITY AND UNITY

Now that we have looked at examples of the diversity in early Christianity, it is necessary to see if some answer can be given to the question: What was the nature of early Christianity? The question should allow for a reasonable distinction between basic issues and particular approaches.

[37] John 8 : 32.
[38] Ernst Käsemann, "Paul and Nascent Catholicism," in *Distinctive Protestant and Catholic Themes Reconsidered* (New York: Harper-Row, 1967), p. 26.

If we concentrate on the particular approaches, it is clear that early Christianity was a changeable and diverse phenomenon. It was certainly no one thing, as we have seen. So it is impossible to give a simple answer to the question, What was it like to be a Christian in the early days? The character of one's religion would depend in part on the precise time and place

The Enthroned Christ, mosaic dating from before A.D. 547, San Vitale, Ravenna. (*Courtesy* Alinari-Art Reference Bureau.)

in which he lived, for the Christianity in Palestine during the primitive period was not the same as that in Gaul toward the end of the second century. Furthermore, the movement was vitally affected by the culture of those who embraced it. It mattered a great deal whether one had been a Jew or a Gentile before he became a Christian, or whether he had been exposed to a body of Gnostic thought forms. It also mattered a great deal that certain creative thinkers had left the impress of their own personality and thought on the religion. Christianity would have been far poorer without the writing of Paul, or John, or the anonymous author of Hebrews, or the Synoptic writers. These observations are important, because it is usually assumed that an analysis of the movement will produce a unified body of ideas which can serve as a means of distinguishing between Christian and non-Christian ideas. But such is not the case, for the ideas must always be classified as Johannine, Pauline, Gnostic, or one of the others. This fact itself reveals a great deal about the character of early Christianity. It was the kind of religion that was subject to change. If our analysis of early Christianity can point to any one thing as characteristic of the movement it is that of adaptability. It showed itself to be responsive to the challenges of *changing times, diverse thinkers,* and *cultural differences.* To be sure, early Christianity passed over into catholic Christianity, a further response to these stimuli, but a response that insisted on the perpetuation of a particular content. But this was not the whole, as we have seen.

If adaptability is accepted as the chief characteristic of the particular approaches in early Christianity, we must yet ask about the basic issues in the movement. The character of a movement is illuminated by the issues to which it addresses itself. Although early Christianity produced a variety of answers to the questions, there is yet a kind of unity in the questions themselves. The importance of the questions lies in the fact that they reveal certain underlying concerns. It is these concerns that give unity to early Christianity. The concerns are two in number: a concern for the relationship between God and man, and a concern for the centrality of Christ.

From earliest days, Christians addressed themselves to the problem of the relationship between God and man. Primitive Judaean Christians came out of a background which assumed that the relationship had been once and for all proclaimed in terms of Torah, but they came to feel that something more had to be said about the relationship. Other Christians differed widely in their definition of the divine-human relationship, but they agreed that it had suffered some disruption. Paul felt that man was in slavery to Sin and that Torah could not liberate him. Gnostic Christians also talked about man's slavery, but they expressed it in a more metaphysical and less historical sense.

Amid the diversity, early Christianity showed itself to be concerned with the problem of man.

Christians also saw in Christ the solution to the human problem. All varieties accepted the belief that in Jesus something salvatory was either beginning or had in fact been accomplished. It is true that here we come upon an amazing variety of interpretations. Primitive Judaean Christians looked to the future for the decisive saving event. Paul looked to the future also, but he felt that the death of Jesus was the central event in which God's justification, reconciliation, and redemption took place. Later Jewish Christians saw the chief significance of Jesus in his abolition of the sacrificial practices of the Jews. Johannine Christianity saw the solution to the human problem in the revelation of the Father granted by the divine-human Jesus, who had been with the Father from the beginning. Gnostic Christians tended to see the solution as a release from the creator God accomplished by Christ. Although their portraits were materially different in content, the variant Christian groups tended to unite around the proposition that Christ is the solution to the problematic relationship between man and God.

These issues seem to form the framework within which early Christianity operated: a dissatisfaction with human life and a confidence that in Christ God was solving the problem. These issues force us now to look in greater detail at one of the most baffling of all historical mysteries—the life of Jesus himself. Since it is the case that Christians, explicitly or implicitly, saw in him the cornerstone of their faith, it is appropriate to attempt a reconstruction of the church's memory of Jesus, the task of the concluding section of this book.

Part Four

Jesus and Early Christianity

Gero's crucifix, c. 970 in the cathedral at Cologne. (*Courtesy* Dr. W. Schulten, Cologne.)

The reader may reasonably ask why the study of Jesus comes at the end of a book on early Christianity. After all, he came first chronologically, so why not treat him first? Since he was the initial factor in the development of the Christian movement, how can we defer attention to him until the end? Is it not illogical to pursue an unchronological order?

Although many studies of early Christianity have followed a chronological approach, there are two good reasons for treating Jesus at this later point. The first is that it gives us better insight into the perspective of early Christianity. A fundamental fact, which has been notable in our survey of the literature, is that Christians did not immediately turn their attention to the historical Jesus. The earliest written materials were concerned with problems of theology, Christology, eschatology, and practical church matters. Historical material about Jesus is alluded to incidentally and indirectly in this material, but the authors were more interested in Jesus' present position and future appearance than in his past deeds. Even when those writings that contain substantial historical material appear, they present themselves not as historical records but as gospels—that is, forms for proclaiming the Christian message. After the appearance of the gospel form, Christians continued their reflection upon theological and ecclesiological matters in their sermons, letters, apologies, and antiheretical writings. This habit of early Christians may appear strange to the modern interpreter, who assumes that the Christian movement is chiefly a response to the historical Jesus. Our tendency is to see Jesus as the founder of a movement, which must, in the course of its development, work out the implications of his words and deeds. But this modern assumption is only a partial truth, and its deficiency is demonstrated by the fact that Paul could preach the gospel without dependence on Matthew or Mark or Luke and with negligible reference to the historical Jesus. While it is true that Jesus came first, it is not true that Christianity simply worked out the implications of his words and deeds. A study in which the historical Jesus precedes the development of the institution and its theology does not accurately represent the perspective of the movement itself.

A second reason for deferring the study of Jesus until now is dictated by the materials with which we must deal. Almost all of the information relating to the historical Jesus is found in documents that come out of the life of the church. This is a fact of fundamental importance. If we find that the Synoptic Gospels provide a basic corpus of source material for Jesus, we are obliged to treat them as evidence. To do so, we must know why the authors are telling what they tell; and to discover this we must know all we can about them and about their historical context. Now, this context is partly determined by the early Christian movement itself. The authors of the gospels were Christians, and they were writing, so to speak, in midstream. Because they are the only ones who provide evidence for the life of Jesus, it is essential for us to understand their historical context in order to use them. As a result, a study of Jesus must work backward, from the Christian movement to the historical person. Although he came first chronologically, our study cannot take a strictly chronological approach. So the study of Jesus comes at the end rather than at the beginning.

Chapter Eleven

Problems and Possibilities in the Study of Jesus

A genuinely biographical interest in Jesus is a peculiarly modern one. Prior to the middle of the eighteenth century, the Christian either accepted the four canonical gospels as strictly accurate historical records or else neglected history altogether. For him, a critical biography of Jesus was simply not an alternative. In the post-Enlightenment era, the study of history, along with the study of nature, became an absorbing human enterprise. Since then there has been a flood of books on the life of Jesus. The enterprise has had its glories and frustrations, but the history of the study has succeeded in demonstrating its problems.

PROBLEMS

One of the chief problems has been the perspective of the modern scholar. Although this is a major problem in any historical writing, the study of the life of Jesus has been particularly plagued by it. Henry Cadbury, in *The Peril of Modernizing Jesus*,[1] pointed to the large number of anachronisms in biographies of Jesus. Many of them intrude into the story in inoffensive ways, but they display an amazing degree of scholarly carelessness. Cadbury cites some authors who wrote of "doctors' offices and a morgue in Jerusalem, or of a first century house in Nazareth with a separate kitchen and private upstairs bedrooms for a family of eight or more persons."[2] He observes that those who perpetrate such gross anachronisms in reference to minor points are likely to include more subtle modernizations of major points. If they assume that Jesus' house was modern and Western, they are likely to present his words and message as agreeably modern.

[1] Naperville, Ill.: Allenson, 1962.
[2] Ibid., p. 10.

The modernization of Jesus becomes an acute danger in the ideological sphere. In *The Quest of the Historical Jesus,* first published in German in 1906,[3] Albert Schweitzer made a thorough analysis of the lives of Jesus written in the eighteenth and nineteenth centuries. The reader of the *Quest* is impressed not only with the quantity of published material and the variety of approaches, but also with the modern character of Jesus discovered by the scholars. He appears in some as a social theorist, in others as a lover of nature, or a romantic, or a revolutionary. In one biography, not dealt with by Schweitzer, Jesus is a top management executive.[4] Schweitzer was highly critical of research on the life of Jesus, because he felt that scholars were unable to break through their own assumptions about man, nature, and history, and because they tended to attribute their assumptions to Jesus. He suspected that each writer intended to show that Jesus was relevant to modern times and shared the world view and social concerns of the author's day. The basic methodological fault in the movement was its failure to take seriously the historical context in which Jesus lived. Each author tended to treat him as his own contemporary. Such a tendency reveals that the eighteenth- and nineteenth-century biographers were not primarily interested in history but in relevance. Presumably, if they had found Jesus to be thoroughly and unequivocally a man of his own time, they would have lost interest in him. They would conclude that he had nothing to say to us, and they would have found no value in historical study.

Schweitzer insisted that Jesus belonged to his own day, not to ours. He is a stranger to us, and he will always remain so. To Schweitzer, Jesus held a vivid expectation about the end of history and about his own place in the events of the end time. He expected God to bring the world to an end and even attempted to force God to action. Schweitzer wrote:

> In the knowledge that He is the coming Son of Man [Jesus] lays hold of the wheel of the world to set it moving on that last revolution, which is to bring all ordinary history to a close. It refuses to turn, and He throws Himself upon it. Then it does turn; and crushes Him. Instead of bringing in the eschatological conditions, He has destroyed them. The wheel rolls onward, and the mangled body of the one immeasurably great man, who was strong enough to think of Himself as the spiritual ruler of mankind and to bend history to His purpose, is hanging upon it still. That is His victory and His reign.[5]

---

[3] English translation by W. Montgomery (New York: The Macmillan Company, 1910).

[4] Bruce Barton, *The Man Nobody Knows* (Indianapolis, Ind.: Bobbs-Merrill, 1925).

[5] Schweitzer, op. cit., p. 370 f.

Schweitzer portrayed Jesus as a stranger to our day, as one whose convictions were quite contrary to our most cherished beliefs. A deluded prophet cannot be a continually relevant leader. Jesus, therefore, "comes to us as One unknown."[6]

The tendency to modernize relates to the very purpose for which the study of Jesus may be undertaken. Schweitzer suggests that a major motivation for the study has been that of demonstrating the relevance of Jesus. Most of those associated with the endeavor were convinced that Jesus had something important to say to their generation, and they set out to make his relevance explicit. It is probable that some such attitude is present in any kind of historical study, for one studies the past partly in order to illuminate the present. We rarely find a historian who operates from a purely antiquarian interest and produces a thoroughly irrelevant work. Surely the study of history need not be the study of the past for its own sake, but neither does it bring the past into the present in a simple and immediate way. There is a kind of continuum in human affairs, a process of temporal relationships whereby a generation leaves its mark on succeeding generations. Within the continuum there are institutions that have crossed the generations, and Christianity is one of them. Anyone interested in the present age may reasonably devote attention to the contribution that Christianity has made to it. Christianity has a history that leads back to Jesus, so the study of Jesus is a significant effort to understand the institution and its contribution to our world. Such study must respect the boundaries of time and must not expect Jesus to embrace the best thought of our day. But neither does it engage in the effort out of idle curiosity.

The problems of the historian's purpose and perspective are fundamental to the study of Jesus. Not only must the historian uncover his own assumptions and clarify his purpose, but he must also be aware of a world view that is foreign to his own. The chief problem he encounters is the mythological thought of the ancient world, that tendency to objectify other-worldly things in terms of this world. The historian can neither adopt the mythology of the ancient world nor discard it. He must, rather, demythologize; that is, he must attempt to see what kind of anthropological or existential understanding is enveloped within the mythology.[7]

Another problem with which historians of all periods must deal relates to the nature of human memory. Memory is the original source for any historian, for it precedes the writing of documents and the carving of in-

[6] Ibid., p. 403.
[7] See pp. 24 ff.

scriptions. The nature of human memory has been previously discussed, and the reader may wish to refresh his own memory, specifically in connection with four major observations:

1. Not everything is remembered.
2. What is remembered is remembered as having meaning.
3. The memory of meaning tends to obliterate the memory of event.
4. Traditional significance comes to be attached to events of a public nature lying deep in the past.[8]

The problem of human memory is compounded, in the case of Jesus, by the fact that his words and deeds were retained only in oral form for several decades. This fact has produced several additional difficulties, which were previously discussed.

1. A great deal of factual material about Jesus did not enter the oral tradition.
2. The material that came into the oral tradition did so because it had been interpreted as significant.
3. The oral tradition contained diverse interpretations.
4. The oral tradition confused the original words of Jesus and the interpretations.
5. The oral tradition was carried on through preaching, teaching, debates, worship, and prophecy.
6. No connected account of the life of Jesus was preserved.
7. The context in which the material was used determined its meaning.
8. Sayings and stories used in the oral tradition may have had sources other than Jesus.
9. The Aramaic context of the oral tradition was modified and expanded by the Hellenistic.
10. The oral tradition used a limited number of forms.[9]

Even when we get to the period of written material, our problems are not over. For one thing, we suffer from a lack of neutral or unsympathetic sources. We are unable to achieve any balance, for unsympathetic material is all but nonexistent. The Roman Suetonius refers to the Christian movement but betrays no real knowledge of Jesus.[10] Tacitus states that "Christus" was sentenced to death by the procurator, Pontius Pilate.[11] The Jewish

[8] See p. 6 f.
[9] See pp. 164 ff.
[10] *Life of Claudius* 25:4.
[11] *Annals* 15:4.

historian Josephus has one incidental note in connection with the execution of James. He identifies James as "the brother of Jesus, who is called Christ."[12] References in the Jewish Talmud appear to be dependent on the Christian gospels. Only two points may be inferred from these sources: that Jesus and James were brothers, and that Jesus was executed by Pilate.

Even among the Christian writings we do not have as much relevant material as we should like. A few details about the historical Jesus may be found in incidental remarks in the letters, but there is almost nothing in the sermons, apocalypses, apologies, or in the antiheretical literature. Gospels, therefore, constitute the major source of information about Jesus. Among them, some, such as the Gospel of John, have only a secondary interest in history, and others, such as the Infancy Gospel of Thomas, the Book of James, and the Gospel of Peter, are dependent upon earlier gospels and add little of historical value. This leaves the Synoptic Gospels and possibly the Gospel of Thomas as the prime sources of information on Jesus. The large amount of common material in the Synoptics (and Thomas) further reduces the quantity of material. When all is said and done, the historian must rely on a relatively small amount of written material, all of it from sympathetic sources.

We have previously observed that it is necessary to know several things about a document in order to judge its evidential value. We should know the provenance, date, and authorship of the document, the occasion that lies behind it, the purpose of the author, the history of its textual transmission, and the language in which it was written.[13] Such information as we have about the gospels was analyzed in chapters six and seven. This analysis called attention to a further problem with our sources—namely, that we do not know enough about them. Ideally, we should be in possession of firm information about the sources in order to make appropriate inferences from the evidence they offer, but in the case of our gospels there are few certainties. Their provenance is almost never a matter of record. The dating can be established only within broad limits. The authors are anonymous. The occasions and purposes are variously conceived. Add to this the facts that the original manuscripts are missing and that the gospels were written in an archaic language, and the historian has nearly insuperable odds against him.

If some kind of satisfactory assessment can be made on the above matters, the historian will encounter still another difficulty. The source material does not easily lend itself to historical investigation. Insofar as we are able to dis-

[12] *Antiquities* XX, 9:1.
[13] See pp. 13 ff.

cover it, the purpose of the gospel writers was not to relay historical information. The gospels are kerygmatic rather than historical, for they intend to present the preaching of the church rather than the history of Jesus.[14] The authors were religious writers, and they wrote in the belief that the one who was once among men in a historical situation has now become the Lord of the church. Although they affirm that this Jesus was a historical entity, a human being, their interest is not in what he once did but in what he is doing now. They care less for his past deeds than for his present significance. To them his words are not of the past to others, but addressed to the present-day church. In short, the interest of the gospel writers is not primarily in preserving those things that impressed the people who met Jesus but in demonstrating his contemporary significance. It may not be untrue to say that the evangelists did just what eighteenth- and nineteenth-century biographers did: they presented Jesus as their own contemporary.

Not only do the gospel writers generally display an annoying lack of interest in historical matters, but they are also particularly uninterested in the psychology of Jesus. This fact should cause no surprise, because the study of psychology is a fairly recent one. But psychological questions usually stand at the center of modern biography, and the lack of psychologically sophisticated sources is a serious deterrent to the study of Jesus' life. We should like to know why he did certain things, what he understood about the actions of others, what he meant by what he said, and how he understood himself. But his inner consciousness is nowhere revealed in our sources. In view of the fact that the primitive church regarded him as Messiah, the question of Jesus' own Messianic consciousness is a central one. Did he believe himself to be Messiah, and, if so, how did he understand the term and what did he intend for himself? Eighteenth-, nineteenth-, and even some twentieth-century studies of Jesus do not hesitate to tackle the question of Jesus' Messianic consciousness, and they frequently offer definite, usually affirmative, answers. But they do not recognize that they are going far beyond the source material and are entering areas for which no evidence can be cited. Jesus has also been an attractive figure for professionally trained psychologists and psychiatrists. Some have found him to be paranoid, because he often spoke about his opponents. Some have called attention to his hallucinations. He heard a voice from heaven at his baptism, and he imagined that he was talking with the devil in his temptations. He had an exaggerated self-consciousness, which displayed itself at the age of twelve

---

[14] It is true that Luke is more historically oriented than are the other writers, but he is dominated by a particular conception of salvation history. See pp. 208 ff.

when he interviewed the priests at the Temple. He had delusions of grandeur, which led him to claim an identity with God; his speech was characterized by a high degree of egocentrism; and his actions were often irrational; for example, he cursed a fig tree for not bearing fruit out of season.[15] These psychiatric studies fail precisely at the point of sources. They treat the gospel writers as historians and biographers, and they fail to take into account the possible mixing of authentic statements of Jesus with statements arising from other sources. Moreover, they should have known that a psychological diagnosis of Jesus is impossible. Direct observation by a professionally competent or, at least, a psychologically sophisticated observer is essential to any diagnosis, and neither was available in the case of Jesus.

POSSIBILITIES

These problems should make it perfectly clear that a biography of Jesus is impossible. But is it altogether impossible to infer historical information about Jesus?

Several considerations enable us to answer this question negatively. For one thing, we can be confident that Jesus was a character of history. A generation ago, some scholars were denying his existence. They were impressed with the fact that interest in the earthly life of Jesus arose at a relatively late date in the history of Christianity, and they concluded that the movement started with a theology of a divine Christ and moved toward a history of a fictitious Jesus. Their case was bolstered by citing the use of miracle stories in telling the life of Jesus and the parallels with Hellenistic hero cults. The heroes allegedly had one divine parent but lived a historical life and ascended to divinity. It was felt that Christians intended to present their God in much the same way. Although scholars today give full weight to the problems of historical study, they recognize a basic fault in the denial of Jesus' existence, namely a failure to account for Christian motivation. To be sure, there are parallels between the hero cults and Christianity, but the former were largely cults of healing. Christianity, on the other hand, was basically an eschatological faith in its primitive period, and the form of the hero cult would hardly have seemed an appropriate vehicle for its message. If Christians, for whatever reasons, believed in a deity who was to come at the end of time, why would they invent for him a human history and

---

[15] For an analysis of several psychological studies of Jesus, see Walter E. Bundy, *The Psychic Health of Jesus* (New York: The Macmillan Company, 1922).

project it into the recent past? The tendencies of the world in which Christianity moved were largely against such a process. Jews knew of no humanized deity, and adherents of Graeco-Roman religions felt no need to historicize their gods. Even in the case of the hero cults, there is no evidence that belief started with a nonhistorical deity and moved toward the historical. The general tendency is, in fact, away from history. Adherents of mystery religions and of Christian Gnosticism sought to escape from the bounds of time and space, and they saw no value in the historical realm. If one should argue that the fiction of Jesus' historical existence was invented in order to counteract Docetism, we should reply that the evidence points in the other direction. Docetists seem to be the inventors in this case, since they go to great lengths to deny the humanity of Jesus. Why should anyone claim that Jesus only appeared to be human unless people had generally assumed the humanity as a fact? Docetism has no meaning except as a reactionary movement against claims about the historical existence of Jesus. The fact is that the existence of Jesus was no great asset to Christian preaching, and belief in an incarnate deity was a stumbling block to many Hellenistic people who might otherwise have put credence in the Christian proclamation. Motivation for the invention of a historical Jesus has not been explained: if there had been no historical Jesus, there would be no need to invent one.

In addition, there are positive reasons for accepting the historicity of Jesus. The earliest Christian writer, Paul, assumed that Jesus was a historical reality and that he was a descendant of David.[16] He knew of some historical events such as the last supper and the crucifixion, but he cautioned against an overemphasis on a fleshly Jesus.[17] We have also seen that belief in the resurrection of Jesus was at the originating point of the Christian movement. Although historical method is not equipped to analyze the resurrection as an event, belief in it is surely a fact of history. What early Christians believed in was the resurrection of a human being, for it is meaningless to speak of resurrection unless you are referring to a mortal being who was known to be previously alive. Thus, we may be confident that there was a Jesus.

Our documents also speak of Jesus as having a certain location in space and time. They claim that he was a Palestinian Jew, who had some connection with Galilee and Jerusalem, that he had a family, including a brother who survived to head the church, and that he was executed under Pontius Pilate. In addition to these fundamental points, the written material tells of his birth at the time of Herod the Great or Augustus, his ministry at the time of

[16] Romans 1:3.
[17] See I Corinthians 11:23–26; Galatians 3:1; I Corinthians 2:2; Philippians 2:8; II Corinthians 5:16.

Tiberius, and about his contacts with Herod Antipas. The historical accuracy of these details may be questioned, but their presence within the materials presents a consistent picture of Jesus as a figure of the first half of the first century. This fundamental context that appears in the gospels must not have been a matter of the authors' choice. As citizens of the wider world of Roman Hellenism, they probably would not have chosen to present Jesus as a Jew, for a more universal figure would be more attractive. In their world a Jew was generally regarded as a narrow, legalistic, antisocial man with less than universal appeal. Neither is the location of Jesus in the recent past a product of invention. Christianity was, as we have seen, disparaged in some quarters for its newness, and the movement might have fared better if Christians could have put Jesus several centuries earlier. In this light, it is interesting to see that the author of the Gospel of John was sensitive to this issue and presented a Christ who was as old as creation and who could say, "Before Abraham was, I am."[18] The earlier authors, however, made no effort to predate Jesus. The overwhelming evidence indicates that Christians knew they were not dealing with a mythological figure who was eternal and nonhistorical. They pointed to a historical human being, whom they knew to have existed within a certain geographic space at a particular time. This general historical nexus must be correct: Jesus was a Palestinian Jew of the first century.

We have observed that the interest of Christians in the historical Jesus was relatively late in making an appearance. This point must now be qualified. It is true that some basic theological and Christological reflection had occurred before the written gospels appeared, and it is true that the gospels are the first documents to use historical incidents as vehicles for Christian proclamation. Yet it is also true that behind these documents lies a period during which Christians circulated material about Jesus in oral form. They were not primarily interested in accurate preservation of the material, but they surely felt that their proclamation had an intimate connection with the words and deeds of Jesus. They preserved those things that they felt were significant, yet they understood them in connection with the particular historical phenomenon of Jesus. In the process, they probably used material from other sources and modified everything. Nevertheless, the fact that they circulated words and deeds as *his* words and deeds means that they were not devoid of interest in the historical Jesus.

We must agree that it is manifestly impossible to write a biography of Jesus that is faithful to the sources and acceptable to modern historiography.

[18] John 8:58.

Nevertheless, we must affirm that certain facts can be established beyond a reasonable doubt; namely, the historical existence of Jesus and his context as a first-century Palestinian Jew. In addition, we may assume that the early Christians were interested in Jesus as a historical person and in what he did and said. These recognitions do not solve the problem of studying the life of Jesus, but they enable us to approach the possibility of doing so. Two tasks are essential in pursuing this possibility. We must, first, work through the written material to find the earliest traditions bearing on the life of Jesus. Second, we must examine the earliest traditions to see what inferences may be drawn from them. To these tasks we turn in the following chapters.

Chapter Twelve

The Tradition about Jesus

Fortunately, it is possible to identify with some assurance certain traditions about Jesus that lie behind the written documents and some that originated in the earliest period. The primitive Christian *kerygma,* isolated by C. H. Dodd, provides one base from which our study may proceed.[1] This *kerygma* proclaimed that in Jesus the last day had dawned and that, at his resurrection, Jesus had become the Messianic head of the new Israel. It pointed to the Holy Spirit in the church as the sign of Christ's present power and glory and proclaimed his imminent return. It included a brief mention of the ministry of Jesus, his Davidic descent, his death, and his resurrection. It closed with an appeal for repentance. The fullest account of the ministry is given in a speech of Peter in Acts 10:35–38, which Dodd takes to be close to the original form of the Jerusalem (in distinction from the Pauline) *kerygma.* Here we are told that the ministry of Jesus began in Galilee after that of John the Baptist, that Jesus went about doing good and healing, and that he was hanged on a tree and raised on the third day.

A second base for our study is provided by the method of form criticism, which makes it possible to distinguish between the earliest kernel of a saying or story, its embellishments, and the contributions of the gospel writers. Form criticism is an art, not a science, so one must not expect universal agreement among those who practice it. Nor will an unassailable account of the earliest traditions emerge. Nevertheless, it partially succeeds in pushing aside the curtain that separates us from those traditions.

At the outset, we must recall a certain limitation of an oral tradition; namely, that it does not provide a chronological framework for the life of Jesus. The primitive Jerusalem *kerygma* recited the broad outline: Jesus' Davidic birth, his ministry starting in Galilee after John, his miracles, his death, and his resurrection. Other than that, we have no genuine indication

---

[1] *The Apostolic Preaching and Its Developments* (New York: Harper & Row, 1939). See also p. 167 f.

[351]

Madonna and Child, third-century fresco from the Catacomb of Priscilla, Rome. (*Courtesy* Pontifical Commission for Sacred Archives, Rome.)

of the sequence of events. The Synoptic authors used the kerygmatic outline and expanded it into a framework, which they filled in with deposits from the oral tradition. For this reason we must be on our guard against an improper use of sequences in the gospels and must admit that the earliest traditions were not sequential.

With this caveat in mind, we may turn now to an analysis of selected topics. This procedure is not intended to cover every segment of the tradition and certainly not every verse of the gospels. The student who desires a more comprehensive treatment of a particular item may refer to the commentaries and monographs listed in the Bibliography. Here we can only be suggestive of the main lines of scholarly interpretation on a few selected topics, chosen as illustrative of a method by which the earliest traditions can be identified. The topics are: the birth, the baptism, the teaching, the miracles, the trial, the death, and the resurrection of Jesus.

THE BIRTH OF JESUS

Accurate information about the birth of an ancient man is generally very difficult to obtain. It was not considered important unless the man achieved notoriety, and by then it was usually too late to rescue the information. As a general rule, the ancient world celebrated the death day of an esteemed leader, because the birth date was unknown. In this light, it is surprising that we have stories of the birth of Jesus.

The primitive *kerygma* contained a belief in Jesus' Davidic ancestry. It is found both in the Jerusalem form of the *kerygma* (Acts 2:30–31) and the Pauline (Romans 1:3). Dodd observes that this belief was not a matter of vital importance for Paul.[2] It formed, rather, a part of the pre-Pauline tradition about Jesus and served to authenticate the belief in his Messiahship. Here, then, is a firm point in the early tradition: the belief that Jesus was a descendant of David.

The Gospel of Mark has no explicit material on the birth of Jesus, but its author accepts the early tradition, as he allows various characters in the Gospel to call Jesus son of David. In one passage, however, a question is raised about the relationship between Messiah and Davidic descent. In Mark 12:35–37, Jesus asks: "How can the teachers of the law maintain that the Messiah is 'son of David'?" Then, after quoting Psalm 110:1, he says: "David himself calls him 'Lord'; how can he also be David's son?" Bultmann classifies this as a legal saying. He suggests that it may have arisen at a time when there was some tension between belief in Jesus as Lord and belief in him as son of David. Alternatively he suggests that it may have been used by Gentile Christians, who were uninterested in Davidic descent because of its ties with Judaism.[3] In either case, the saying did not form a part of the earliest tradition. Because it questions the belief in Jesus' Davidic

[2] Ibid., pp. 21 f.

[3] Rudolf Bultmann, *The History of the Synoptic Tradition*, trans. John Marsh (New York: Harper & Row, 1963), pp. 136 f.

descent, the belief must have arisen first. The saying represents a later stage of reflection upon the Davidic sonship and a tendency to de-emphasize or even reject it.

Matthew and Luke provide us with detailed information on the birth of Jesus. The opening chapters of both gospels are devoted entirely to nativity material, most of it quite familiar. What many casual readers fail to notice, however, is that the two gospels draw on different materials in their treatment of the birth. Each author had his own private source or sources for the opening chapters, and the sources were independent of one another. Matthew's material is usually classified as M, and Luke's as L.

Matthew begins with a genealogy that shows Jesus' descent from David. He starts with Abraham, includes David and the kings of Judah, and concludes with Jacob, the father of Joseph, "the husband of Mary, who gave birth to Jesus called Messiah."[4] Then Matthew narrates the circumstances preceding and surrounding the birth. Joseph has discovered that his fiancée is pregnant and has decided not to go through with the marriage. But an angel appears to him in a dream and tells him that Mary has conceived by the Holy Spirit and will give birth to a son who is to be named Jesus.[5] The angel further explains that the birth will fulfill the prophecy of Isaiah 7 : 14, which Matthew quotes. Joseph is obedient to the angelic message, and Jesus is born in Bethlehem during the reign of Herod the Great. Later on, astrologers from the east observe a star, and they come to search out the one they believe to be the new-born king of the Jews. They find the child in a house, presumably in Bethlehem, and present him with gifts of gold, frankincense, and myrrh. Afterward, Joseph has another angelic visitation, in which he is warned to take the family to Egypt in order to protect Jesus from the wrath of Herod, who orders the death of all children born in Bethlehem within the past two years. When Herod dies, Joseph receives a third vision, in which he is told to return, but to Galilee rather than Judaea for fear of Herod's son, Archelaus.

Luke precedes the story of Jesus' birth with one about the birth of John the Baptist to Zechariah and Elizabeth, both of priestly descent. The angel Gabriel announces the birth of John to Zechariah even before conception takes place. Zechariah is dubious, because he and his wife are very old, so as punishment he is stricken with dumbness. When Elizabeth is six months pregnant, Gabriel visits Elizabeth's kinswoman, Mary, in Galilee and announces that she will conceive and give birth to a son by the Holy Spirit.

[4] Matthew 1 : 16. Note the textual variants listed in the Revised Standard Version and the New English Bible.

[5] The name is a variant of the Hebrew Joshua, and means savior.

At the time, Mary is engaged to Joseph. Luke next tells of the birth of John and his naming, which releases Zechariah from the spell of dumbness. During the latter days of Mary's pregnancy, it becomes necessary for her to go with Joseph to Bethlehem, to be counted in the census decreed by Augustus. Luke specifies that this survey was made while Quirinius was governor of Syria. So Mary gives birth to Jesus in Bethlehem and lays him in a manger. Nearby shepherds are sent by an angel to visit the new-born child. Luke concludes the nativity story with the circumcision and naming of Jesus, his presentation in the Temple, the testimony of Simeon and Anna, and the return of the family to Nazareth. After the story of Jesus in the Temple at the age of twelve, the recounting of the preaching of John the Baptist, and the narrative about Jesus' baptism, Lukes gives the genealogy of Jesus. His ancestry is traced through Joseph, son of Heli, back through David and Abraham to "Adam, son of God."

That the Matthaean and Lukan narratives are from independent sources is shown by the different assumptions that they make on such matters as the date of Jesus' birth, his ancestry, and the circumstances surrounding the birth. Neither one gives a precise statement about the date of the birth, but Matthew places it during the reign of Herod the Great, who died in 4 B.C. His chronology allows for no precision, but there are two extreme points that may be cited. Joseph brings the family back from Egypt when Herod dies, and at that point Matthew refers to Jesus as a child.[6] It is not likely that an author would call anyone past the age of twelve a child. If Matthew thinks of Jesus as no older than twelve in 4 B.C., then he could not have been born before 16 B.C. The massacre of the children is relevant for the other extreme point. This event supposedly occurred when Jesus was two or less, for Herod calculated the date of birth in accordance with the visit of the astrologers. Matthew does not say when the massacre took place within the reign of Herod, but it could not have happened after 4 B.C. This means that Jesus was two years old sometime before 4 B.C., and so 6 B.C. could be about the latest possible date for the birth of Jesus. Thus, according to Matthew or his source, Jesus was born between 16 B.C. and 6 B.C. Luke, however, dates the birth specifically to coincide with a census ordered by Augustus during the governorship of Quirinius. Such a census is reported by Josephus and dated in A.D. 6. The taxation that followed from it resulted in a rebellion led by one Judas of Galilee.[7] Matthew and Luke are at least twelve years apart in their dating of the birth.

[6] Matthew 2:21. See Mishnah, Pirqe Aboth 5:21.

[7] Josephus, *Antiquities* XVII, 13:5; XVIII, 1:1; 2:1; *War* II, 8:1; VII, 8:1. Luke 1:5 places the priesthood of Zechariah during the reign of "Herod king of Judaea."

The two genealogies are remarkably dissimilar and must have originated quite independently. They both trace the ancestry through Joseph to David and thence to Abraham (to Adam in Luke). In the generations between Abraham and David, several names, familiar from Old Testament genealogies, appear in both lists. But between David and Joseph there is no possibility of harmonization. Two or three names appear in both but in different locations. Zerubbabel is the eleventh generation from Jesus in Matthew and the twentieth in Luke. Shealtiel is the twelfth in Matthew and the twenty-first in Luke. Luke's Matthat may be the same as Matthew's Matthan. From David to Joseph no other names appear in both.

In addition, the circumstances surrounding the birth are different. Matthew features a series of angelic visitations and a visit of astrologers. Luke concentrates on a manger birth and a visit of shepherds. The only conclusion possible is that each writer had distinct sources for the birth narratives and genealogies.

Perhaps the basic material behind the gospels can be discovered by recognizing the editorial material in the two gospels. Matthew has arranged his material in line with his motif of Jesus as the new Moses. The motif is suggested by the flight to Egypt and the return, which calls to mind the sojourn of Israelites in Egypt and the Exodus. Matthew makes the theme explicit by quoting Hosea 11:1, "I have called my son out of Egypt."[8] The massacre of the children also calls to mind the killing of first-born Egyptians at the time of Moses. Subsidiary themes in Matthew are the angelic visits to Joseph and the fulfillment of prophecy. Luke's story is characterized by a parallelism between the births of John the Baptist and Jesus and by his citation of the testimony of human witnesses. He includes two hymns, which were probably of Jewish origin.[9]

When the editorial material has been stripped away, we are left with two legends, both of which state that Jesus was born of the virgin Mary, and two genealogies, both of which claim that Jesus was descended from David. Herein, of course, lies a basic problem. If Joseph was not the father of Jesus, as the legends suggest, then the genealogies are meaningless. Or, if Jesus was a descendant of David, as the genealogies claim, then he was

He may have committed an anachronism at this point, but his time span is not sharply defined and he may have intended to designate Herod Archelaus in 1:5. Although Archelaus was not granted the title king, the tetrarchy of Judaea was his. Luke is not careful to distinguish the various Herods. In 3:1, for example, he refers to a Herod as tetrarch of Galilee, when he obviously means Antipas.

[8] Matthew 2:16.

[9] Luke 1:46–55, 68–79. See Bultmann, op. cit., p. 296.

not born of a virgin mother. In both genealogies, Jesus' relationship to David is drawn through Joseph, not Mary. Indeed, Luke implies that Mary is a member of the priestly tribe of Levi rather than of the Davidic tribe of Judah. So the only way Jesus could have had Davidic blood is through Joseph. To be sure, the evangelists are not blind to the problem. Matthew does not say that Joseph is the father of Jesus but the husband of Mary. Luke calls Jesus, "the son, as people thought, of Joseph."[10] These statements do not relieve the problem, but they show that the authors were aware of it.

The legends and genealogies suggest the prior existence of two traditions: one that Jesus was son of David, and one that he was Son of God. The traditions probably existed for some time before the genealogies and legends arose. Between the two traditions, it is not difficult to decide which is the earlier. The primitive *kerygma,* as it is found in Acts and Paul, affirmed belief in the Davidic ancestry of Jesus. This was surely cited as evidence for Jesus' Messiahship, and it would have been understood by both Jews and primitive Palestinian Christians. In time, genealogies came to be used as documentation for the tradition. But, because there was no control, more than one genealogy came into being. Gentile Christians inherited belief in Jesus as Messiah, but they lacked the background for fully comprehending its meaning. So they began to speak of Jesus as Lord or Son of God.[11] The idea of virgin birth was familiar to them from the stories of heroes, so it would be natural for them to think of Jesus as son of the virgin. In time, various legends gave concrete expression to the tradition.[12]

We conclude that the earliest tradition about the birth of Jesus was that he was a descendant of David. But this was not meant as a simple fact of history; it was a religious statement. It was a way of affirming belief in Jesus as Messiah. Although the legends of virgin birth entered the tradition at a later point, they were offered as attempts to make a religious assertion of the same value. The writers of Matthew and Luke brought together the old and the new, and the durability and attractiveness of their narratives point to their success. Nevertheless, they do not succeed in veiling a point of trouble in early Christianity, a point uncovered in Mark 12:35-37. It was first introduced when some asked if the confession of Jesus as son of David is really a sufficient expression of his meaning?

[10] Luke 3:23.
[11] See pp. 282 ff.
[12] The Book of James, for example, is a development of the legends. It focuses attention on the life of Mary and Joseph prior to the birth of Jesus. See pp. 223 ff.

THE BAPTISM OF JESUS

We have seen that baptism was used as a rite of initiation in primitive Christianity, where it signified repentance of one's sins. It was also referred to by Paul, to whom it signified a dying and rising of the Christian.[13] The Qumran community used a daily baptism as a ritualistic cleansing. John the Baptist is portrayed as an eschatological figure, who is known chiefly for his practice of baptism. The primitive Christian *kerygma* did not contain a statement about Jesus' baptism, but all three Synoptic Gospels reported it, the Gospel of John alluded to it, and the Gospel of the Ebionites treated it as the birth of the Messiah.

In all three Synoptic Gospels the baptism is reported in the form of a legend, in which there are three parts: the baptism itself, the descent of the spirit, and the voice from heaven. Mark puts it simply. After he had been baptized in the Jordan by John, Jesus saw the heavens open and the spirit descend in the shape of a dove. A voice from heaven addressed him: "Thou art my Son, my beloved; on thee my favour rests."[14] The descent of the spirit is described as an experience of Jesus, and the words are addressed to him, although Mark may have understood that others heard them. Luke varies from Mark chiefly in describing the spirit's descent as an objective happening rather than a private experience of Jesus. Matthew makes the words from heaven a public proclamation: *"This is* my Son."[15] He also adds a conversation between John the Baptist and Jesus, in which John attempts to dissuade Jesus from being baptized. He says, "I need rather to be baptized by you."[16] Jesus insists, however, on the ground that he should conform to all that God requires. The Gospel of John omits a specific report of the baptism but has the Baptist describe the spirit's descent as his own experience. The Gospel of the Ebionites has the objection of John the Baptist as in Matthew, and to the heavenly words adds the sentence, "This day I have begotten thee."[17]

Matthew and John exhibit a certain embarrassment with the baptism story. In Matthew, Jesus' reply to the Baptist is flimsy and suggests that he is acting for effect only. John omits the narrative altogether. The problem

---

[13] Especially in Romans 6:1–4.
[14] A quotation from Psalm 2:7.
[15] Matthew 3:17.
[16] Matthew 3:14.
[17] A continuation of the quotation from Psalm 2:7, found in Epiphanius, *Refutation of All Heresies* XXX, 13:7 f.

they recognize is that baptism was associated with repentance but that Jesus had no sin of which he should repent. The problem, however, must be considered secondary, for Mark seems totally unaware of it. It arose at a later stage of reflection, possibly during the interval between the publication of Mark and the writing of Matthew. Mark's report of the baptism precedes the reflection on it. If we ask why Mark included the narrative, the probable answer is that it formed part of the tradition on which he drew. But did this tradition go back to the earliest days? Bultmann feels that it did not but rather originated in the Gentile churches, which associated baptism with a conferral of the spirit.[18] If one understands that the spirit descends upon the Christian at his baptism, he might feel that Jesus received the spirit in the same way. For this reason the story of Jesus' baptism included the story of the spirit's descent. In this way, Jesus' baptism becomes a kind of prefiguring of Christian baptism. Other scholars take the point of view that the earliest tradition included the baptism narrative as the story of Jesus' consecration as Messiah. This point of view is difficult to maintain, because the earliest *kerygma* seems to omit it and because primitive Christianity identified the public proclamation of Jesus' Messiahship with the resurrection. On the other hand, the earliest tradition cited Jesus' Davidic descent as a sign of Messiahship, so an interpretation of the baptism as a second sign should present no difficulty. In both cases, the sign would point forward to the resurrection. Moreover, Mark's report suggests that, in the legend on which he drew, the dove and the voice were not public signs. In this case there is no conflict with the primitive tradition about the resurrection. When taken together, the evidence strongly suggests that early tradition included a belief that Jesus had been baptized. If the tradition is early, it is easy to see how later reflection would smoke out the problems. If it is not, it is difficult to see how it could have entered the tradition at all. Thus, at a very early date Christians proclaimed the baptism of Jesus. But, as with Davidic descent, they did not proclaim it as a simple fact of history. It was a religious proclamation of Jesus' future Messiahship: the baptism was the sign of his adoption by God. Even in the earliest days the religious meaning was primary.

THE TEACHING OF JESUS

The primitive *kerygma* did not include a specific statement about Jesus' teachings, but the Synoptic Gospels, John, and Thomas present abundant

---

[18] Bultmann, op. cit. pp. 247–253.

illustrations of it. It is contained in apophthegms, dominical sayings, and similitudes, found in all three Synoptic Gospels and in the Gospel of Thomas. Some are logia which contain typical wisdom sayings and probably circulated widely but were not originally connected with Jesus. Some are prophetic sayings, which came into the tradition as revealed sayings of the risen Lord. A number of the apophthegms probably arose in the context of debates between Christians and Jews over the Torah or over some legal point. Still others represent attempted solutions to ecclesiastical problems. As a consequence, not all of the teaching material in the gospels was contained in the earliest oral tradition.

The teaching to which the Synoptic Gospels attach the greatest weight is that about the kingdom of God. In terms of quantity, this material preponderates. It occurs in the form of apophthegms, dominical sayings, and similitudes, so it is not limited to any one form of transmission. The teaching is probably part of the early tradition for several reasons.

For one thing, primitive Christianity had a strong eschatological orientation, and the kingdom of God is presented as an eschatological phenomenon. In those early days, Christians expected the coming of Jesus as Messiah-Son of man; and a basis for this belief is found in the teachings about the kingdom. Their Messianic expectation is intimately related to the kingdom tradition. Their affirmation that Jesus proclaimed the kingdom, together with their resurrection faith, may have served as the basis for their Messianic beliefs. The fact of the church's Messianic expectation points to an early tradition about Jesus as proclaimer of the kingdom.

Secondly, the teaching about the kingdom of God is similar to current Jewish Messianic expectations. To be sure, Jews were not in agreement on Messianism, nor did they all regard it as important. Yet there is nothing in the teaching on the kingdom that would clash with basic Jewish expectation. The age of the Messiah is the age in which God manifests his righteousness, and the phrase *kingdom of God* rightly reflects the meaning of it. The imminence of its coming and its initiation by the Son of man is consistent with Jewish thought, and the concept of history that is embedded within it is basically Jewish. Since the earliest traditions about Jesus were linked with people of a Jewish background, and since the teaching about the kingdom is consistent with that background, it is probable that the earliest Christian tradition included sayings on the kingdom.

Thirdly, the teaching on the kingdom is central to the other teachings in the gospels. In an editorial sentence, Mark summarizes Jesus' teaching as a proclamation of the kingdom: "After John had been arrested, Jesus came into Galilee proclaiming the Gospel of God: 'The time has come;

the kingdom of God is upon you; repent, and believe the Gospel.' "[19] But this does not seem to be simply Mark's idea, for the kingdom teaching is vitally related to the ethical teaching and the teaching on Torah. The ethical teachings tell what the present situation demands in terms of getting ready for the kingdom. The teaching on Torah shows that the imminence of the kingdom demands a different understanding of the Jewish law. For these reasons, the kingdom teaching appears to belong to the oldest Christian tradition.

It is, therefore, probable that primitive Christians presented Jesus as the one who proclaimed the kingdom and that this was the major thrust of their message. Two further questions, however, need to be faced. The first is, Did the early traditions contain any indication about the time at which the kingdom would come? The second is, Did the traditions say that Jesus' proclamation involved a particular demand on the part of his hearers?

As for the first question, it is clear that the kingdom was presented as a future event. The futuristic aspect of the kingdom is represented in a number of sayings about the Son of man:

Like lightning from the east, flashing as far as the west, will be the coming of the Son of Man.[20]

I tell you this: before you have gone through all the towns of Israel the Son of Man will have come.[21]

If anyone is ashamed of me and mine in this wicked and godless age, the Son of Man will be ashamed of him, when he comes in the glory of his Father and of the holy angels.[22]

There are some of those standing here who will not taste death before they have seen the Son of Man coming in his kingdom.[23]

Never again shall I drink from the fruit of the vine until that day when I drink it new in the kingdom of God.[24]

Although the traditional understanding of the future coming of the Son of man, which was held in primitive Christianity, is here attributed to Jesus, the identification of Jesus with the Son of man is not made. Here the

[19] Mark 1:14-15.
[20] Matthew 24:27; see Luke 17:24.
[21] Matthew 10:23.
[22] Mark 8:38; Luke 9:26.
[23] Matthew 16:28; Mark 9:1; Luke 9:27.
[24] Mark 14:25; Matthew 26:29; Luke 22:18.

Son of man appears to be a figure quite independent of Jesus, and the sayings reflect a belief that Jesus himself expected the future appearance of the Son of man. In the parables in which Jesus is ostensibly describing the kingdom, he does so in terms of a time of imminent judgment. A good example is the parable of the wheat and weeds in Matthew 13:24–30. A man planted wheat, but his enemy came along and sowed weeds among the wheat. When the workers asked the owner if the weeds should be pulled up, he replied that they should wait until harvest time. In the parable, the harvest is the kingdom, for that is the time of judgment, the time when God will separate the worthy from the unworthy. Several similar sayings point to the kingdom as a future event.

Some sayings in the gospels suggest that the kingdom is not simply expected as a future event but is experienced as a present phenomenon. One such saying is found in Matthew 13:16–17 and Luke 10:24, probably drawn from the Q source. It is a dominical saying, in which Jesus blesses those who hear what men of the past had longed to hear. It may belong to the earliest tradition, but even if it does, it does not imply that Jesus' hearers have experienced the kingdom itself.

In another saying, probably drawn from Q, we have a clearer allusion to the kingdom as present. Luke 11:20 has, "If it is by the finger of God that I drive out the devils, then be sure that the kingdom of God has already come upon you." The parallel in Matthew 12:28 reads, "If it is by the Spirit of God that I drive out the devils, then be sure the kingdom of God has already come upon you." In both, it is found in an apophthegm that describes a controversy between Jesus and some people who thought he had used the power of Beelzebub to cast out demons. Jesus counters their argument by offering two alternatives. If he is using the power of Beelzebub, he is using it against that prince of demons, and his divided kingdom is soon to fall. If, on the other hand, he is using the power of God, then God's kingdom has come. A subsidiary question is also raised about exorcisms performed by other Jews. Mark has something similar, but his is a purer apophthegm.[25] Here Jesus answers the accusation of his opponents by pointing to a ridiculous implication in their argument; namely, that it makes Satan a rebel against himself. The Q form of the apophthegm, in Matthew and Luke, shows signs of development from something like the Markan form. It introduces an irrelevant question and presents the alternative of Jesus' using the power of God, which is not essential to the original objection. Mark's narrative raises and meets the objection forcefully, simply, and directly, whereas the Q form serves only to confuse the issue. Thus, on

[25] Mark 3:23–26.

form critical grounds, it appears that the Q statement about the presence of the kingdom is secondary and did not belong to the earliest level of Christian tradition.

Luke 17:21 is a direct statement about the presence of the kingdom: "The kingdom of God is among you."[26] Luke uses this saying in the context of a larger section that is designed to de-emphasize eschatological expectation. It serves as a warning against expecting visible signs of the kingdom. In the following verses, Jesus goes on to say that the disciples must not be misled when people call them to see signs of the kingdom. The Son of man will indeed come, and his coming will be as visible as a flash of lightning. But first the Son of man must endure suffering and be rejected by the current generation. The passage appears to come from a relatively late period. It reflects a time when people were citing visible signs for the kingdom. The reference to rejection by the current generation reflects the church's experience some years after the time of Jesus.[27] The use of the phrase *Son of man* to express both the experience of Jesus' suffering and the expected eschatological appearance makes for some confusion. And the conflict between the idea of the kingdom as present, in 17:21, and as future, in 17:24 f., suggests that we do not have a pure saying in this passage. These verses did not belong to the earliest tradition but arose later on and were used by Luke to play down eschatological expectation.

There remain a few sayings in the Gospel of Thomas in which the kingdom is interpreted as a present experience; for example:

The Kingdom is within you, and it is outside of you.[28]

His disciples said to him: On what day will the rest of the dead come into being? And on what day will the new world come? He said to them: That which ye await has come, but ye knew it not.[29]

These sayings actually do not treat the kingdom as an event at all. It is rather the reality in which the man with *Gnosis* stands, and the concept is heavily individualized. The futurity of the kingdom is rejected, to be sure, but it is no longer thought of as an age, present or future. The gnosticizing tendency has removed both the societal and temporal aspects of the kingdom. These sayings could not have been part of the earliest Christian tradition.

[26] Note the variant translations of Luke 17:21 in the New English Bible.

[27] There is also an apparent conflict with a saying in Matthew 16:28; Mark 9:1; and Luke 9:27, which proclaims the advent of the kingdom within the present generation.

[28] Gospel of Thomas, Saying 3.

[29] Gospel of Thomas, Saying 51.

It is probable that the earliest tradition did not present the kingdom as a present phenomenon. It spoke of it entirely as a future event, but it made no effort to define the time with any precision. The best we can say is that it proclaimed the kingdom as an event of the very near future and probably expected it within a generation.[30] Jesus was understood as the one who proclaimed the kingdom, so he might have been compared with those prophets who predicted an eschatological event. But he was distinguished from them by the understanding that his appearance was not the prediction of the kingdom, but the announcement that the kingdom was beginning to appear. The kingdom of God is an event of the future, but it is a future that is virtually present. The relation of dawn to sunrise is analogous to this conception. At dawn we may say that sunrise is yet to come, but dawn is an assurance that it is close at hand. So Jesus announces the kingdom in the way that dawn announces sunrise. The kingdom was, in the early tradition, proclaimed as an event belonging to the near and assured future.

A second- or third-century sarcophagus showing the figure of the good shepherd in the center. (*Courtesy* Vatican Museum.)

The second question we need to pose is this. Did the early traditions say that Jesus' proclamation involved a particular demand to be met by his hearers? Several possibilities present themselves, and the demands of the kingdom have been interpreted by scholars in various ways. If the kingdom is coming, perhaps men ought to pitch in and help construct those conditions that will hasten its arrival. This might include a certain kind of social action, which arranges political conditions in such a way as to exhibit the principles of the kingdom. Or it may mean that men should begin to live by the rules of the kingdom and that when enough people begin so to live,

[30] Matthew 16:28; Mark 9:1; Luke 9:27.

the kingdom will be here. But these ideas are not even suggested by the texts preserved in the gospels. On the contrary, we have an implied condemnation of human effort in Matthew 11:12 and an assurance that the kingdom is God's gift in Luke 12:32.

The texts do present Jesus as making certain demands, although they may not be obvious to the modern intellect. Mark's summary statement says that Jesus' proclamation of the kingdom was followed by a demand for repentance.[31] This demand is part of the fabric of the Synoptic presentation of Jesus' teachings. It is intimately related to the proclamation of the kingdom, for if the kingdom means judgment, the proclamation implies a demand for repentance. We must be careful to note that repentance does not affect the coming of the end. One does not hasten the coming of the kingdom by repenting or delay it by refusing to repent. The kingdom simply comes automatically, just as a seed planted in the ground grows into a plant.[32] The coming of the kingdom is proclaimed as a fact, and repentance is presented as the appropriate response to the impending fact. The urgency of the need for repentance is sounded in a number of sayings. There is neither time to regret what is past or to dispose of it in the usual way. "No one who sets his hand to the plough and then keeps looking back is fit for the kingdom of God."[33] "Leave the dead to bury their dead."[34] The intimate connection of the demand for repentance with the proclamation of the kingdom suggests that both are to be found in the early tradition.

The repentance demanded by the impending kingdom involves a radical decision on man's part. The kingdom means the end of all usual values, so one must decide between the values of the present and those of the future. Present values are generally understood in terms of material possessions. So the demand means that one must not store up earthly treasures or try to hold on to his wealth.[35] A camel can go through a needle's eye with greater ease than a rich man can go into the kingdom.[36] On any scale of values, however, the kingdom is worth the sacrifice. A merchant, dealing in fine pearls, who finds one of very special value sells everything he owns

---

[31] Mark 1:14–15. The language of Mark 1:15 suggests that the phrase, "and believe the Gospel," is secondary or editorial. *Gospel* is the technical term that Christian preachers used to designate their message.

[32] See Mark 4:26–29.

[33] Luke 9:62.

[34] Luke 9:60; Matthew 8:22.

[35] See Matthew 6:19–21.

[36] See Mark 10:25 and parallels. The interpretation that "needle's eye" is the name of a Jerusalem gate is without foundation.

in order to purchase it.[37] A man who finds a treasure in a field sacrifices everything in order to purchase the field.[38] The point in these sayings is not that one makes a prudential calculation of values and tries to obtain a good bargain but that the kingdom is worth any sacrifice. Repentance, therefore, means a rejection of those things associated with life as usual and an acceptance of the kingdom. It is not simply material possessions that must be rejected but anything that hinders a full acceptance of the kingdom. It may be necessary for some to cut off a hand or pluck out an eye.[39]

Repentance does not mean simply turning away from something, it means also a turning toward something; in this case it means obedience to the demand of God. The gospels include a number of teachings on this subject. Many of them are found in apophthegms that tell of conflicts between Jesus and representatives of Judaism. They deal with questions about law or about the basic meaning of Torah. There is, however, a problem in these narratives, because in some Jesus is shown to uphold the Pharisaic understanding of Torah, and in others he seriously questions it.

Matthew has most of the former type, such as:

> Do not suppose that I have come to abolish the Law and the prophets; I did not come to abolish, but to complete. I tell you this: so long as heaven and earth endure, not a letter, not a stroke, will disappear from the Law until all that must happen has happened. If any man therefore sets aside even the least of the Law's demands, and teaches others to do the same, he will have the lowest place in the kingdom of Heaven, whereas anyone who keeps the Law, and teaches others so, will stand high in the kingdom of Heaven.[40]

The tone of these sayings reflects a community that has begun to settle down in the world. The urgency of eschatological expectation is blunted in the clauses, "so long as heaven and earth endure" and "until all that must happen has happened." The ranking of people within the kingdom is inconsistent with the sayings we have just examined, where the demand for repentance would exclude talk about the lowest and the highest in the kingdom. In addition, there is a reactionary tone in the passage, which condemns the man who sets aside the law's demands and teaches others to do the same. It seems clear that some Christian group is being censured in this saying. If so, it may have originated in a group that reacted against the

---

[37] See Matthew 13:45 f.
[38] See Matthew 13:44.
[39] See Mark 9:43, 47.
[40] Matthew 5:17-19.

position of the liberal Jewish Christians led by Stephen or against Pauline Christianity. It would have been used by the more conservative Jewish Christians, but only after the split described in Acts 6. These sayings, therefore, cannot be part of the very earliest tradition.

In addition to the sayings that uphold Torah, Matthew has sayings of the opposite character. In chapter 5, he presents Jesus' commentary on some basic Old Testament regulations. The Old Testament said, Do not murder; Jesus says, Do not be angry. The Old Testament said, Do not commit adultery, but Jesus says, Do not be lustful. The Old Testament said, Do not commit perjury, but Jesus says, Do not be insincere.[41] In each case the authority of Jesus is invoked against that of Moses, and Matthew uses these words as part of his theme of Jesus as the new Moses. Notice also that, in these cases, the Mosaic words are those in the Ten Commandments, the heart of the Torah. Matthew has edited the sayings, but the original content is probably summarized in these three antitheses. The point of the antitheses is that the will of God cannot be restricted to the prohibition of specified acts. Prohibitions against murder, adultery, and perjury allow a man to interpret his duty toward God in a restricted sense. He may say: This is what I owe, and not a cent more. But in the antitheses the demand of God is interpreted in the most inclusive sense; it prohibits the inward attitudes that lead to external acts of disobedience. God demands nothing less than the entire man, in his attitudes and actions. This interpretation involves a radical criticism of law, for it understands God's demand in terms with which law cannot deal. Law and courts can control murder, adultery, and perjury, but not anger, lust, and insincerity. Not only in Matthew, but in other strata of Synoptic material as well, the attitude of Jesus toward Torah is represented as critical. Jesus attacks Pharisees for failing to distinguish between the more and the less important elements in Torah, for "straining gnats and swallowing camels."[42] He attacks the hypocrisy of Pharisees in particular and of Jews in general.[43] And he treats the regulations on Sabbath as secondary to considerations of human need.[44] These sayings probably represent the position of the liberal Jewish Christians such as Stephen, and they are earlier than the pro-Torah sayings. They did not, however, belong to the period of the earliest traditions, for that period was dominated by a more conservative group, which could hardly have circulated such anti-Torah sayings.

[41] See Matthew 5:21 f., 27 f., 33 f.
[42] Matthew 23:24.
[43] Matthew 23:25; see Luke 11:39 f.; Mark 7:6 f.
[44] See, e.g., Mark 2:27.

That Jesus was critical of Torah probably came in by implication, for there are similar sayings that are not related to questions of law. In these, Jesus' teaching is not presented as a protest against Torah but as a positive demand of God for love. One must love his neighbor as himself.[45] He must love his enemy and forgive without limit.[46] The demand for love concentrates on one's attitude and intention, but the matter cannot be left there. The parable of the Good Samaritan defines the working of love as the unlimited helpful response to a fellow human being in need.[47] The teaching makes no effort to list precisely appropriate responses to particular situations, but it gives examples of such responses. The notable characteristic in the examples is the lack of measurement. A Samaritan does what he thinks is helpful but stands ready to do more if needed. A father of a derelict but returned son greets him with a celebration without worrying about punishment or equal treatment for a son who caused no trouble.[48] One who is asked for a coat gives two, and one who is asked to go one mile goes two.[49] Even here the point is not simply a demand for doing something extra. The teachings do not call for a simply literal performance of the demand after which one can grudgingly say, "I have gone the second mile." The point is that the response is not to be measured. Love simply has no limit.

These sayings, and others like them, came into the tradition unconnected with problems of law. Yet they present the same attitude as those critical sayings preserved by the liberal Jewish Christians. We may reconstruct the history of the tradition as follows: In the very earliest days the church affirmed that Jesus had proclaimed love as the means of fully responding to the demand of God. The liberal branch, as exemplified by Stephen, felt that this teaching implied a criticism of the Torah, because Torah limited man's loving response. This group began to circulate anti-Torah sayings. The conservative branch attacked this point of view and maintained that Jesus had not pitted himself against Torah. Their debates with the liberal group produced a number of pro-Torah sayings. This latter group of sayings found their way into the source peculiar to Matthew, M. The anti-Torah statements and the sayings on love, however, found their way into the other Synoptic sources. The resultant gospels include sayings, apophthegms, and similitudes of different character and of various ages.

A summary of the earliest traditions about Jesus' teaching should show,

---

[45] See Mark 12:31 and parallels.
[46] See Matthew 18:21 f.
[47] See Luke 10:30–37.
[48] See Luke 5:11–32.
[49] See Matthew 5:40 f.; Luke 6:29.

if possible, the inner connection among its component parts. This may be done in the following way: Jesus was presented as proclaimer of the imminent kingdom of God, which would be ushered in by the Son of man. The proclamation was understood as the very dawning of the great day. It demanded repentance, which meant a renunciation of life as usual and radical obedience to the will of God—that is, love of one's neighbor. Love was understood as an unmeasured response to a human being in need and a renunciation of such things as anger, lust, and insincerity. In the earliest days the question of Torah appears not to have been raised. The earliest tradition is well summarized in Mark 1:15: "The time has come; the kingdom of God is upon you; repent [and believe the Gospel]."

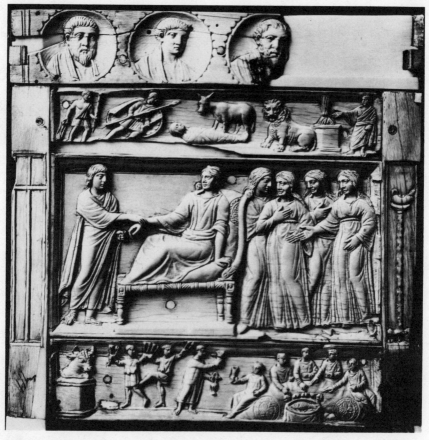

The raising of Jairus' daughter, fourth-century ivory casket from the Church of Santa Giulia, Brescia, Italy. (*Courtesy* Christian Museum, Brescia.)

THE MIRACLES OF JESUS

Miracle stories are found in all three Synoptic Gospels, the Gospel of John, and the Infancy Gospel of Thomas. But they are not found in all layers of Synoptic material, for the Q source shows no evidence of containing miracle stories.[50] Mark is the source for most of the miracle stories in Matthew and Luke, each of whom have only one or two that are not derived from Mark. But John and the Infancy Gospel of Thomas continue the tradition with non-Markan stories. They are in the form of nature miracles, healings, exorcisms, and resuscitations.

In the study of miracle stories, form critics have shown that we must work back from the written narrative to the earliest form of the story. The way in which this analysis works may be illustrated by reference to one miracle story—for example, Mark 5:1-20, the exorcism at Gerasa. The first step is to discover the editorial materials in the narrative—namely, the additions that Mark made to a story he found elsewhere. In this narrative, we can spot editorial work in the geographical note in verse 1 and in the explanatory note in verse 8. The second step is to discover embellishments and secondary additions. These elements made their way into the narrative in the course of tradition but did not originally belong to it. The form critic will be on the lookout for a number of things. He will look for a description of action that detracts from the main action. He will look for novelistic treatments, which show a particular interest in some character. He will look for details that might pose an inconsistency with the main line of action. And he will look for material of an expository nature—material, that is, that makes some application of the story to a more general situation or tries to draw a moral out of it. Study of the development of oral traditions in general shows that these kinds of things are added to a miracle story in the course of its oral transmission. In the example in Mark 5, the transfer of the demons to the swine in 10-13 detracts from the main action, so it is probably secondary.[51] The reaction of the crowd in 14-17 also adds to the action and is partly secondary. The follow-up in 18-20 is novelistic and comes out of an interest in the subsequent history of the cured demoniac. When these secondary elements have been

[50] Except perhaps the exorcism of a demon from a dumb man in Matthew 9:32-34 and Luke 11:14.

[51] Bultmann, however, accepts these verses as part of the original narrative. See Bultmann, op. cit., pp. 210 f.

bracketed, we are left with the original form of the miracle story.[52] The accompanying text demonstrates the results of this analysis.

(So they came to the other side of the lake, into the country of the Gerasenes. As he stepped ashore,) a man possessed by an unclean spirit came up to him from among the tombs where he had his dwelling. He could no longer be controlled; even chains were useless; he had often been fettered and chained up, but he had snapped his chains and broken the fetters. No one was strong enough to master him. And so, unceasingly, night and day, he would cry aloud among the tombs and on the hill-sides and cut himself with stones. When he saw Jesus in the distance, he ran and flung himself down before him, shouting loudly, "What do you want with me, Jesus, son of the Most High God? In God's name do not torment me." (For Jesus was already saying to him, "Out, unclean spirit, come out of this man.") Jesus asked him, "What is your name?" "My name is Legion," he said, "there are so many of us." [And he begged hard that Jesus would not send them out of the country.

Now there happened to be a large herd of pigs feeding on the hill-side, and the spirits begged him, "Send us among the pigs and let us go into them." He gave them leave;] and the unclean spirits came out [and went into the pigs; and the herd, of about two thousand, rushed over the edge into the lake and were drowned.

The men in charge of them took to their heels and carried the news to the town and country-side; and the people came out to see what had happened.] They came to Jesus and saw the madman who had been possessed by the legion of devils, sitting there clothed and in his right mind; and they were afraid. [The spectators told them how the madman had been cured and what had happened to the pigs. Then they begged Jesus to leave the district.

As he was stepping into the boat, the man who had been possessed begged to go with him. Jesus would not allow it, but said to him, "Go home to your own folk and tell them what the Lord in his mercy has done for you." The man went off and spread the news in the Ten Towns of all that Jesus had done for him; and they were all amazed.]

( ) = Editorial material
[ ] = Secondary material

---

[52] On the other hand, Bultmann believes that Mark reported the story essentially intact in its original form. He says: "It also exhibits the typical features of exorcism of demons, and in their characteristic order: (1) meeting with the demons; (2) description of the dangerous character of such sickness; (3) the demon recognises the exorcist; (4) the exorcism; (5) the demonstrative departure of the demon; the impression on the spectator." Op. cit., p. 210.

The next step in the analysis of a miracle story is to discover the situation that may have given rise to the original form. Clues may be supplied by similar stories from the same period. It is possible that stories from Hellenistic or Jewish sources were modified and used in the Christian tradition. We do know, for example, that stories of exorcisms by Apollonius circulated in the Hellenistic world.[53] There are also stories of healings at a distance, healings of lame persons, of the blind and paralyzed, and raisings from the dead. Bultmann cites a probable parallel to the stilling of the storm (Mark 4:35–41) in Rabbinic literature from about A.D. 350:

> A Jewish child went on a voyage in a heathen ship. When a storm brought the ship into danger, all the heathen called on their gods and when that proved useless, finally urged the Jewish child to call on his God. When the child prayed, the storm ceased and the heathen paid respectful admiration.[54]

The parallels may show that Christians imported miracle stories from other traditions. But in a more important way they illustrate the kind of world in which the stories were circulating, and they give us some insight into the general situation that prompted them. After all, why did Christians tell miracles stories about Jesus? (To answer that they told the stories because they happened begs the question.) Since similar stories are told of Apollonius, the Rabbis, and even the emperor Vespasian, the answer must be that they thought of Jesus as somehow comparable with the great men of the age. It seems that miracle stories were told in order to demonstrate a person's value. Each age has its own measure of value. Among early Semites it was expressed in terms of a long life. In some cultures, ancestry or intelligence are expressions of value. Political power is nearly always a measurement of value. In our age, wealth is the chief demonstration of value. In the Hellenistic period it was the ability to work miracles. We must keep in mind the fact that Hellenistic people had neither the ability nor the inclination to make sharp distinctions between the possible and the impossible. To them, healings, exorcisms, and resuscitations were not, strictly speaking, impossible.[55] They were, of course, extraordinary, and so were used as indications of a person's extraordinary value. When Christians told miracle stories of Jesus, they were affirming his value.

But did the earliest traditions claim that Jesus worked miracles? The *kerygma*, as found in Acts 10:38, says that he "healed all who were oppressed by the devil." This may refer to general healings or exorcisms or

---

[53] See, e.g., Philostratus, *Life of Apollonius* IV, 20.
[54] Bultmann, op. cit., p. 234 f.
[55] See pp. 24 ff.

both, for oppression by the devil may designate either demon possession or illness, since it was generally understood that evil and illness were connected. On the other hand, form criticism concludes that most of the miracle stories originated in Gentile Christianity and so were not part of the very earliest tradition. Bultmann is convinced, however, that some miracle stories were told in the earliest days. He finds two groups. One is a group of miracle stories that were actually transmitted in the form of apophthegms. The fact that the stories were not told as miracle stories but were embedded in a form used to transmit the words of Jesus argues for their early origin. This group includes: two exorcisms in Matthew 12:22 ff. and Mark 3:12 ff., a Sabbath healing in Mark 3:1-5, the exorcism of a Syro-Phoenician woman's daughter in Mark 7:24-30, and the healing of the paralytic boy in Capernaum in Matthew 8:5-13.[56] The second group consists of three miracle stories that have parallels in Rabbinic literature or contain clear Palestinian traces. The three are: the stilling of the storm in Mark 4:35-41, the feeding stories in Mark 6:34-44 and 8:1-9, and the healing of the leper in Mark 1:40-45.[57] To be sure, this is a relatively small number, for most of the miracle stories betray a Hellenistic background and come out of Gentile Christianity. Yet they are sufficient to show that the earliest tradition looked upon Jesus as healer and exorcist. This claim was not, however, a report of a simple historical fact, but a designation of value. The intention of the tradition was to say something about Jesus as Messiah. His Messianic value was expressed in terms of miracles.

THE TRIAL AND DEATH OF JESUS

Our written sources unanimously agree that Jesus' death was the result of a judicial verdict and that he was crucified. Paul reflects the tradition at a number of points, and the non-Christian Tacitus refers to it.[58] The Synoptic Gospels present detailed narratives of the trial and death; the Gospel of John has a long section on it; and the Gospel of Peter has a few verses. The contents of these narratives should be kept in mind.

In Mark, Jesus is arrested at night and taken before the Jewish Sanhedrin. The court hears testimony that Jesus once threatened to destroy

---

[56] See Bultmann, op. cit., p. 239.

[57] See ibid., p. 240. Relevant parallels in Matthew and Luke are included in each case.

[58] See Galatians 3:1; I Corinthians 2:2; Philippians 2:8; Tacitus, *Annals* 15:4.

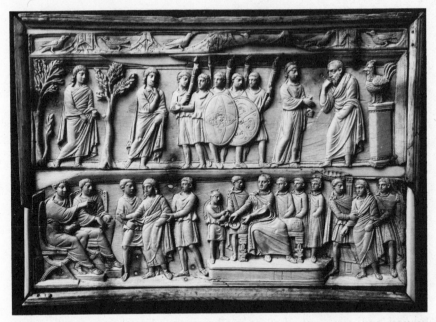

Scenes from the passion of Jesus, fourth-century ivory casket from the Church of Santa Giulia, Brescia, Italy. (*Courtesy* Christian Museum, Brescia.)

and rebuild the Temple, but Mark says that the witnesses did not agree, and he calls the testimony false. The high priest then questions Jesus directly: "Are you the Messiah, the Son of the Blessed One?" Jesus answers: "I am, and you will see the Son of Man seated at the right hand of God and coming with the clouds of heaven." [59] The high priest regards this as a self-incriminating confession and charges Jesus with blasphemy. The other members of the Sanhedrin agree, and they unanimously call for Jesus' execution. The following morning Jesus is taken before the procurator, Pontius Pilate, who asks him: "Are you the king of the Jews?" Jesus replies, "The words are yours," but he makes no defense. [60] Mark then tells of a customary Passover amnesty, in which the procurator releases one prisoner. Pilate offers to release either Jesus or Barabbas, a rebel and murderer. The crowd chooses Barabbas and insists on the crucifixion of Jesus. After being beaten and mocked by Pilate's soldiers, Jesus is crucified.

Matthew virtually duplicates Mark's account, but he adds three independent narratives: the death of Judas, the dream of Pilate's wife, and Pilate's

[59] Mark 14:61 f.
[60] Mark 15:2.

[374]

hand washing. Luke uses Mark's framework for his trial narrative, but he makes significant changes within it. He has no night meeting of the Sanhedrin but one the morning following Jesus' arrest. The court examines no witnesses but questions Jesus directly. He is asked if he is Messiah and Son of God, and he gives evasive answers to both questions. Afterward, the Sanhedrin takes Jesus to Pilate and brings three charges against him: subverting the nation, opposing the payment of Roman taxes, and claiming to be a king. Pilate is initially reluctant to hear the case, and he sends Jesus to be examined by Herod Antipas, when he finds him to be a Galilean. The examination seems inconclusive, and Jesus is returned to Pilate, who reaffirms his innocence. At this point Luke rejoins Mark's narrative and tells of the crowd's demand for the release of Barabbas and the crucifixion of Jesus and of Pilate's capitulation to the demand.

The account in the Gospel of John presents interesting similarities and differences. Here Judas procures a band of soldiers and officers from the priests and Pharisees. Jesus surrenders to them, saying, "I am he," to which all fall to the ground. He is taken to the high priest's father-in-law, Annas, who questions him about his disciples and his teaching and sends him to the high priest, Caiaphas, who sends him on to Pilate. Pilate calls for the accusation, to which the Jews reply that Jesus is an evildoer. Pilate tells them to judge him by their own law, but they answer that they are calling for the death penalty but cannot execute such a punishment. Pilate then questions Jesus directly, and we have the following dialogue:

Pilate: Are you the king of the Jews?

Jesus: Do you say this of your own accord or is this my accusation?

Pilate: Am I a Jew? This is the charge against you drawn up by your own people. What have you done?

Jesus: You say that I am a king. This is my purpose. Everyone who is of the truth hears my voice.

Pilate: What is truth?

Pilate then goes out to the Jews, declares Jesus innocent, and offers to release him in accordance with the Passover amnesty. But the crowd calls for the robber Barabbas. After he allows Jesus to be beaten, dressed in purple, and crowned with thorns, Pilate repeats his declaration of innocence. The chief priests and officers call for crucifixion, and Pilate offers to turn Jesus over to them, but the Jews tell him that their law demands capital punishment. Pilate again questions Jesus and again tries to release him, but the Jews insist that it would be disloyal to Caesar to release one who claims to be a king. Finally, Pilate orders Jesus to be crucified.

[375]

The surviving fragment of the Gospel of Peter begins with the statement that none of the Jews washed their hands, nor did Herod or any of his judges. There must have been a story, borrowed from Matthew, about Pilate's hand washing, which immediately preceded this. The fragment goes on to say that Herod gave the order for Jesus' execution.

In order to work back from these accounts to the earliest tradition, we must first identify the editorial additions, then isolate the sources on which the gospels depended, and finally infer the contents of the earliest tradition. The editorial additions are not difficult to find, for they generally form part of certain motifs to be found in the gospels. The first is a tendency to place responsibility for Jesus' execution on Jews rather than Romans. All the gospels have this tendency. In Mark and Matthew, the Jewish San- hedrin conducts the initial trial and acts as prosecutor before Pilate. Al- though Luke does not describe a Sanhedrin trial, he does have that body initiate the proceedings. When Jews are given a chance to release Jesus, they call for Barabbas. In Matthew, Pilate washes his hands as a symbolic act, declaring that he has no responsibility in the proceedings. To make the point clear, Matthew has the Jews shout: "His blood be on us and on our children."[61] The Gospel of John goes to great lengths to show the guilt of the Jews. Pilate repeatedly declares Jesus' innocence and attempts to release him. The Jews, however, insist that their law requires Jesus' execution and threaten to charge Pilate with insubordination if he refuses to crucify him. The Gospel of Peter has Pilate wash his hands and claims that it was Herod who ordered the crucifixion.

The other tendency of the gospels is to insist on the innocence of Jesus. Mark calls attention to disagreement among the witnesses and expressly declares their testimony false. In addition, he may intentionally describe an illegal Sanhedrin trial. This point is difficult to evaluate, because the rules of procedure are found in a Mishnaic tractate (A.D. 200) and may not have been known to Mark. At any rate, there are some sixteen points at which Mark's account varies from the Mishnaic rules.[62] The Mishnah, for example, forbade a night meeting of the Sanhedrin. It did not allow the court to seek a self-incriminating confession, and it did not allow a verdict of guilt to be given on the day a trial began.[63] If Mark knew these rules, he intentionally described an illegal trial. Matthew, of course, includes

[61] Matthew 27 : 25.
[62] An analysis of the Mishnaic rules and their application to Mark's Gospel is found in Herbert Danby, "The Bearing of the Rabbinical Criminal Codes on the Jewish Trial Narratives in the Gospels," *Journal of Theological Studies* 21: 51–76 (1920).
[63] Mishnah, Sanhedrin IV, 1.

these Markan materials but adds some of his own. He describes Judas' suicide as an act of remorse at the realization that he had betrayed an innocent man. In the midst of the Roman trial, Pilate's wife warns him to have nothing to do with this innocent man. In Luke, Pilate and Antipas both declare Jesus to be innocent, and in John Pilate makes repeated declarations to this effect.

The presence of these motifs in the gospels has produced many of the difficulties in the various narratives. In Mark, for example, the Jewish court convicts Jesus of blasphemy but makes no effort to carry out the penalty for blasphemy, namely stoning. Instead, they take him to Pilate and charge him with the Roman crime of sedition, the usual penalty for which is crucifixion. In John, the Jews demand Jesus' execution on the basis of Jewish law, then later on the basis of Roman law. The fact of a Passover amnesty cannot be verified in contemporary non-Christian records and is brought into the narratives in a peculiar way.[64] Although Pilate tries to use it as a device for securing Jesus' release, he presents as an alternative a man already convicted of sedition, that is, a man on an entirely different legal footing. Add to this the picture of Pilate acting totally under pressure from subject peoples. He is presented at one and the same time as convinced of Jesus' innocence and anxious for his release, as holding the powers of life and death in his hands, and as succumbing to the insistence of the people he governed, even though they offered no evidence for their charges.

The gospel writers surely viewed the execution of Jesus as a legal error and put the blame on the Jews. On what sources did they draw for the trial? Of course, Luke and Matthew drew on Mark.[65] The material in the Gospel of John does not appear to be based on a source independent of Mark; it is, rather, a free development of Mark (or a source like Mark). The Gospel of Peter is an elaboration and conflation of Matthew and Luke. Some scholars feel that Luke had a second trial source. He used Mark but altered it in the direction of his other source. Evidence for a second source is found in Luke's change from a night meeting of the Sanhedrin to a morning session and in his addition of a hearing under Antipas. Moreover, Luke alone omits the charge of blasphemy and records specific charges of treason brought before Pilate. If Luke had a second source, it went as follows: Jesus is arrested and held until

---

[64] A defense of the amnesty narrative is given by Charles B. Chavel, "The Releasing of a Prisoner on the Eve of Passover in Ancient Jerusalem," *Journal of Biblical Literature* 60: 273–275 (1941).

[65] In this case it is not impossible to assume the priority of Matthew. Mark and Matthew are nearly identical, and Luke could have used either as the basis of his narrative.

the next morning, when the Sanhedrin examines him. At the conclusion of the examination, he is taken to Pilate and charged with sedition. Pilate then sends Jesus to Antipas, who questions him and returns him to the procurator. It is not clear whether or not the source contained Antipas's verdict.[66] Other scholars are not convinced that Luke had a separate source for the trial. Bultmann, for example, believes that the other writers used Mark but felt free to add, delete, and modify items at will. He believes, however, that Mark had a *"primitive narrative* which told very briefly of the arrest, the condemnation by the Sanhedrin and Pilate, the journey to the cross, the crucifixion and death."[67] This brief narrative of Jesus' *condemnation* was enlarged by the addition of separate stories which told of the *proceedings* before the Sanhedrin and Pilate.

Whether or not Luke had a separate source, Bultman is probably right in suggesting that the earliest tradition contained no detailed narratives of the trial. Nevertheless, it is possible, by inference, to establish the existence of certain elements in the earliest tradition. For one thing, it seems clear that it contained a statement about Jesus' crucifixion under Pilate. The likelihood of such a tradition can hardly be doubted, since it is reflected in the early kerygmatic formulation, the letters of Paul, and one non-Christian writer.[68] Even without these references, it would be necessary to infer the tradition. For if there had been no claim that Jesus died at the hands of Romans and as a victim of Roman law, how could we account for the gospels' tendency to exonerate Rome? This motif, which produced so many difficulties in the gospel narratives, would have been totally unnecessary in the absence of a tradition of Roman responsibility. Without it, the evangelists could simply say that the Sanhedrin put Jesus to death for an alleged violation of Jewish law. Instead, they present a complex, even incomprehensible, picture of a Jewish trial that issued in a Roman execution over the protests of the chief Roman authority. The fact must be that the earliest traditions pointed to Rome as the party responsible for the death of Jesus.

A second element in the early tradition must have been a statement to the effect that Jesus was accused of royal pretension. The charge appears implicitly in all the gospels and explicitly in Luke. The gospels also indicate that the reason for the charge was a confusion of Messianship with royal power. The tradition may, indeed, represent a kind of confusion to which

[66] For a defense of this theory, see Joseph B. Tyson, "The Lukan Version of the Trial of Jesus," *Novum Testamentum* 3: 249–258 (1959).

[67] Bultmann, op. cit., p. 279.

[68] See Acts 2:23; 10:39; Galatians 3:1; I Corinthians 2:2; Philippians 2:8; Tacitus, *Annals* 15:4.

Christians themselves were victim. Opponents of Christianity, at certain times, claimed that their belief in Messiahship amounted to belief in a counter-king, and so Christians were charged with sedition. Under Roman law Christian Messianism and expectation of the kingdom of God was the object of suspicion. Their own experience may have led Christians to believe that Jesus himself was accused as a royal pretender.

A third element in the early tradition is the claim of Jewish responsibility in the death of Jesus. Such a motif is emphasized in the gospels, but it is also found in earlier material. In the Pentecost speech in Acts, Peter charges that the Jews "used heathen men to crucify and kill him."[69] More important is Paul's charge in I Thessalonians 2:14. He claims that the Jews killed Jesus and the prophets. He is able to say this in spite of the fact that he knows Jesus to have been crucified.

Earliest Tradition, A.D. 30-40
  Rome is responsible for Jesus' execution.

Secondary Traditions, A.D. 40-65
  Jesus was charged with royal pretension.
  Jews and Romans share responsibility for
  Jesus' execution.

Gospel Accounts, A.D. 65-150
  Rome was not responsible for Jesus'
  execution.
  Jesus was innocent of any crime.

FIGURE 27

It is impossible to be precise on the relative ages of these traditions. It seems reasonable to believe, however, that the earliest traditions affirmed that Jesus was crucified by the Romans. The tradition about the charge came somewhat later and resulted as an implication of Christian experience with Roman law. The tradition that blamed the Jews is later still. It probably originated among Gentile Christians, who felt a keen embarrassment about the tendency to blame the Roman government. Although this element is later, it found its way into the tradition prior to the time of Paul. Still, no detailed narrative of the trial was developed until Mark and perhaps the author of Luke's special source came along. Mark edited the primitive materials, which by now put a joint responsibility on Jews and Romans, and added comments which were intended to exonerate the Romans and estab-

[69] Acts 2:23.

lish the innocence of Jesus. The later gospels continued the same effort but freely edited the Markan material. If this analysis is correct, the earliest tradition put responsibility squarely on Rome.

Figure 27 summarizes the history of the tradition.

THE RESURRECTION OF JESUS

No serious scholar has raised a doubt about the place of the resurrection faith in early Christianity. It appears to be at the heart of the movement in its earliest days. Belief in it is reflected in the earliest identifiable forms of the *kerygma* and in nearly every Christian document of the first two centuries. It is not absolutely clear, however, what the earliest tradition about the resurrection was. In the treatment of primitive Christianity in chapter nine, it was maintained that the general conviction about Jesus' resurrection rested on certain reports of appearances, which occurred within the context of vivid eschatological expectation.[70] Although there is no need to question that hypothesis, it is necessary to test it by an examination of certain narratives that deal with the resurrection. Do the narratives actually point back to an early tradition, and can we define the contents of that early tradition? Although most of the Christian documents express the resurrection faith, five of the gospels contain narratives that call for examination: Mark, Matthew, Luke, John, and Peter.

The Gospel of Mark tells of the visit of Mary Magdalene, Mary the mother of James, and Salome to the tomb of Jesus on the Sunday after the crucifixion. On their arrival at the tomb, they found it unsealed. Inside there was a young man in a white robe, who proclaimed that Jesus had risen and was to meet the disciples in Galilee. At the end of the Gospel, the women fled from the tomb in terror.[71]

Matthew based his account on Mark's, but he included some alterations and some additional material. Here Mary Magdalene and one other woman, called the other Mary, go to the tomb. They find it unsealed as a result of an earthquake, and they meet an angel sitting outside the tomb. The angel proclaims Jesus' resurrection, invites the women to see the empty tomb, and announces a coming appearance of Jesus in Galilee. As the women leave, Jesus himself appears and repeats the angel's message. Matthew then includes a paragraph explaining the unbelief of the Jews. He claims that the Jewish priests bribed the tomb guards to say that Jesus' disciples had stolen

[70] See pp. 275 ff.
[71] Note that, in the earliest extant texts, Mark ends at 16:8.

the body. In Matthew's final scene, Jesus appears to the disciples on a mountain in Galilee and commissions them to baptize and teach.

Luke's account of the empty tomb is also based on Mark's. Mary Magdalene, Joanna, Mary the mother of James, and other women go to the tomb to find it open and empty except for two men, who announce Jesus' resurrection. They hasten to return to the city to report the news to the disciples. Then follows a narrative about Cleopas and another disciple, who are traveling from Jerusalem to Emmaus. Along the way Jesus joins them, but they do not recognize him until he sits down to eat with them. The two return immediately to Jerusalem and meet the other disciples, who proclaim that Jesus has appeared to Simon. Jesus himself then appears to all of them and demonstrates his corporal reality by inviting them to touch him and by eating a piece of fish. He gives the disciples a missionary command and orders them to remain in Jerusalem until they have received power from the spirit. He finally departs from them at Bethany.

In the Gospel of John, it is Mary Magdalene alone who discovers the empty tomb. Instead of entering, however, she reports the discovery to Peter and the beloved disciple. After a race to the tomb, won by the beloved disciple, Peter first enters to find only the grave clothes. After their departure, Mary Magdalene looks inside the tomb to see two angels, and subsequently Jesus himself appears to her. Later the same day he appears to the disciples, and a week later, to the whole group, including Thomas. Thomas's faith arises only when he touches the wounded body of Jesus.

In John 21, which was not originally a part of that Gospel, we have another appearance of Jesus, this time in Galilee.[72] Seven disciples are present: Simon Peter, Thomas, Nathaniel, the sons of Zebedee, and two others. Jesus appears to them as they are fishing on the sea of Galilee and directs them to a large catch.[73] When they come ashore, he and they eat breakfast together, and Jesus gives a missionary charge to Simon Peter. The chapter closes with an attempt to identify the author of the Gospel of John.

Only in the Gospel of Peter do we have a description of the actual resurrection, and even here the scene is set outside the tomb. Two men come down from heaven, enter the tomb, and escort Jesus outside. Its relatively late date, and its dependence on the Synoptics invalidates the Gospel of Peter as a witness to the earliest resurrection tradition.[74]

We may classify the resurrection narratives into two kinds: those dealing

[72] See p. 221.
[73] It is probable that John 21:1–8 is a variant of the narrative contained in Luke 5:1–11.
[74] See pp. 226 ff.

with an empty tomb, and those dealing with appearances. With both types there are serious problems. In all the reports of the empty tomb, the time of discovery is the same: the morning after the Sabbath, something over thirty-six hours after the burial. In all cases the discovery is made by women, and Mary Magdalene is always among them. But there the resemblance ends. The number and names of the other women are not the same, and their reaction is different. In Mark they flee; in the others they report to the disciples. Moreover, the contents of the tomb vary: in Mark, a young man sits inside; in Matthew, an angel sits outside; in Luke, two young men are inside; in John, the male disciples see the grave clothes, but Mary Magdalene later sees two angels. In the accounts of appearances, there are variations in regard to their number, their duration, their location, and the actual witnesses. In the matter of location, Luke and John set all the appearances in Jerusalem; Matthew and John 21 have them in Galilee.[75] Mark projects, but does not describe, an appearance in Galilee. A particular problem revolves around the nature of the appearances, especially in Luke, John, and John 21. In all three he appears and disappears suddenly as if out of nowhere. In John 20 he appears within a locked room. But in all cases the corporal nature of the appearance is emphasized. In Luke and John 20, disciples are invited to touch him, and in Luke and John 21 he eats fish to demonstrate his bodily resurrection. In these cases it is as if Jesus had come back to life in the very same body but with the added ability to materialize and dematerialize. A still more serious question is that about the witnesses to the appearances. In Mark, of course, there are none. In Matthew, Jesus appears briefly to the women at the tomb, then to the disciples in Galilee. In Luke, the two disciples going to Emmaus are accompanied by Jesus, but they do not recognize him until he departs. When they report to the other disciples, they are told that Jesus has appeared to Peter, and then he appears to all of them. In John 20, there are appearances to Mary Magdalene, to all the disciples except Thomas, then to all of them with Thomas. In John 21, the appearance is to seven of the disciples. On the matter of duration, Matthew gives no indication of time, but enough time has to elapse for the disciples to travel from Jerusalem to Galilee. Luke's major appearances occur on one day, except perhaps the one at Bethany. If that narrative is a duplicate of the ascension story in Acts 1, Luke must place it some forty days after Easter.[76] John 20 has the appearances extend over a period of one week.

Among the narratives about the empty tomb, that in Mark is surely basic to

[75] Matthew has an appearance to the women at the tomb in 28:9 f., but in it Jesus points to Galilee.

[76] See Acts 1:3.

the others. Matthew and Luke probably saw Mark's account in 16: 1–8, and John must have known a story that followed the same lines. Many of the variations in the accounts are those which form critics would call secondary additions. In the period of oral transmission, such things as names of witnesses and the contents of the tomb would be added. The fact that Matthew, Luke, and John alter Mark in these respects probably indicates that they were in contact with versions (probably oral) other than that of Mark. In the reaction of the witnesses, we are probably dealing with editorial alterations of the Markan narrative. Mark's ending could not be used by the others, because they added appearance narratives and felt it necessary to relate the experience of the women with that of the disciples. The earliest form of the empty tomb story would be very close to that in Mark, without the names or the description of the tomb's contents. It would simply tell that some women went to Jesus' tomb, found it empty, and fled in terror.

Most of the variations in the appearance narratives are due to editorial alterations. The location of the appearances is largely due to individual motifs of the gospel writers. Luke's use of Jerusalem in the history of salvation probably accounts for his setting of the appearances in and around that city. John's motive is not so clear, but he has tended to emphasize Jesus' connection with Jerusalem all along. Mark projected an appearance in Galilee, largely because of his feeling for the importance of that area vis-à-vis Jerusalem, and Matthew and John 21 probably shared that motif. The nature of the resurrection also follows the lines of the evangelists' theology. The duration and sequence of the appearances are the work of the editors. The names of the witnesses would be supplied in the secondary stage of oral transmission. If we may move back behind the editorial and secondary additions and alterations, we find a simple affirmation: Jesus appeared to his disciples.

We therefore find that there were two basic traditions about the resurrection of Jesus and that both circulated in the pregospel period. In their simplest form the two traditions went as follows: some women discovered Jesus' tomb empty and fled in terror; Jesus appeared to his disciples. Is it possible to discover which of these traditions is the earlier? In order to answer this question, it is necessary to come back to another piece of evidence about the resurrection. It is a matter of some significance that we have a written account of the appearance tradition that antedates the earliest written account about the empty tomb by several years. The fact that Paul has a catalogue of appearances in I Corinthians 15: 3–8 led us to the original hypothesis that reports of appearances gave rise to the resurrection faith. The fact that he includes these verses as part of the tradition that he received means that it dates back to a very early time. Our question now is: Does it antedate the earliest tradition about the empty tomb? Although no one can claim certainty in answering this question, an affirmative answer appears probable. In the first place, the fact that Paul knows nothing of an empty tomb carries some weight. More important, Paul's presentation in I Corinthians makes the disappearance of Jesus' body from the tomb a completely irrelevant matter. The catalogue that he cites occurs within the context of a discussion about the prospects for the resurrection of Christians. Some Corinthians doubted the resurrection because they knew that bodies decay in the ground. Paul, however, affirmed that the fate of the earthly body has no effect on one's resurrection, because it occurs with a spiritual body. Because he knew the earthly body to be destructible, he could understand its resuscitation to mean only a temporary extension of one's life. He believed, however, that the Christian rises with an imperishable body. The same is necessarily true of Jesus, "the first fruits of the harvest of the dead."[77] This entire line of thought would make nonsense out of the discovery of Jesus' empty tomb, and if Paul had known any tradition about it he could not have argued as he did. The fact that Paul could not have been aware of an empty tomb tradition does not rule out the possibility of one at such an early date, but it makes it improbable. A final bit of evidence for the priority of the appearance tradition is found in the primitive *kerygma* in Acts 10:35 ff.[78] The *kerygma*, here attributed to Peter, not only affirms the resurrection of Jesus but also cites appearances as evidence. "God raised him to life on the third day, and allowed him to appear, not to the whole people, but to witnesses whom God had chosen in advance—to us, who ate and drank with him after he rose from the dead."[79] Although Luke knows the empty tomb tradition, he does not use it in presenting the preaching of Peter.

We began this section with the observation that a conviction about the resurrection of Jesus on the part of early Christians is not subject to doubt. We also stated the hypothesis that the earliest Christians expressed their conviction in terms of an assertion that he had appeared to his disciples. Our investigation of the resurrection narratives has shown that two traditions lay behind the gospels: one saying that some women discovered the empty tomb, and the other that Jesus appeared to his disciples. Our conclusion is that the hypothesis is probably correct: the tradition about an appearance is earlier than that about an empty tomb.

[77] I Corinthians 15:20.
[78] See p. 167 f.
[79] Acts 10:40 f.

Chapter Thirteen

The Tradition and Jesus

The analysis in the preceding chapter has shown that there are at least six relatively firm points where we are able to identify early traditions about Jesus:

1. He was a descendant of David.
2. He was baptized by John.
3. He proclaimed the coming of the kingdom and demanded repentance.
4. He performed exorcisms and healings.
5. He was crucified by Pontius Pilate.
6. He appeared to his disciples after the crucifixion.

This is not an exhaustive list of early traditions, but it is representative of the main lines that bear upon the historical Jesus.

We must now ask if any of these traditions reflect an authentically historical memory. At first glance, there seems to be a heavy presumption in favor of the historical value of early traditions. For when we have identified them, we have come into contact with a time when the eyewitnesses of Jesus' life were still alive and were active in the movement. On the other hand, we have seen that the tradition did not arise as a way of preserving historical facts but of expressing religious conviction. When we attempt to make inferences from the tradition, we learn as much about the people who formed it as about Jesus.

The way in which inferences are drawn from traditional material is crucial to any historical work. One acceptable method was analyzed in our introduction, under the heading, "The Historical Argument."[1] The reader is invited to review that material and to be on the lookout for data, conclusions, qualifiers, warrants, rebuttals, and backings in the arguments that follow.

[1] See pp. 9 ff.

The youthful Christ, fourth-century statuette, Museo Nazionale delle Terme, Rome. (*Courtesy* Anderson-Art Reference Bureau.)

JESUS' ANCESTRY

The only data relevant for Jesus' ancestry is the early tradition itself. The fact that primitive Christians believed Jesus to be son of David probably means that he was in fact a son of David. The conclusion is probable unless one is convinced that Christians' belief in Jesus' Messiahship led them to claim Davidic ancestry for him. This rebuttal cannot be answered by saying that knowledge of Jesus' ancestry led to the conviction of his Messiahship. If that had been possible, then Jews must have raised the Messianic question every time a member of the Davidic family was born. In addition, it is clear that Christian Messianism did not arise out of speculation about or investigation into the circumstances of Jesus' birth. It arose out of the resurrection faith. Thus, the tradition of Jesus' ancestry might have come as a "reasonable" conclusion of faith or it might have been a fact that tended to confirm the prior faith. The latter alternative seems more probable, because Christian Messianism was oriented toward the future rather than the past. Primitive Christians did not claim that Jesus exercised Messianic functions in his lifetime, but they very early looked upon him as the future Messiah-Son of man. In this context Davidic descent was a secondary matter, perhaps useful in confirming the faith but not integral to it. Paul seems to represent the attitude in accepting the Davidic ancestry of Jesus as a traditional item, but not a matter essential for faith.

JESUS' BAPTISM

Primitive Christians affirmed that Jesus had been baptized. This datum could lead to three possible conclusions. The tradition may have arisen out of a conviction that Jesus received the confirmation of his Sonship in baptism. Because some kind of confirmation seemed necessary, baptism could serve as the vehicle for it. But why should Christians have settled upon baptism by John as the mode and moment of confirmation? There were problems with it to which they must not have been blind. It implied the superiority of John and Jesus' need of repentance. If the primitive community intended to say that Jesus received a commission from God, this conviction would more easily express itself in a narrative that avoided the problems. It is difficult to assume that the church would have created unnecessary problems for itself.

The tradition may have arisen as a cultic story. Baptism was a rite of initiation in the early days, and Christians may have felt inclined to connect the institution of their ritual with Jesus. They appear to have done this with the Eucharist, in which Jesus' last meal with his disciples was portrayed as the institution of a ritualistic act.[2] But there is a significant difference between the two. In the case of the supper, Jesus himself presides and commands the repeated practice of a meal. In the case of the baptism, however, Jesus is the object of the action rather than the subject. There is no command to continue the practice, and Jesus does not baptize his disciples.[3] If the last supper is a model for a cultic story, the baptism does not fit the model.

If the belief in Jesus' baptism did not arise out of the church's faith either as an expression of Jesus' confirmation or as a cultic story, there is a strong probability that it rests upon an authentic memory that Jesus was in fact baptized by John.

JESUS' TEACHINGS

The earliest traditions presented Jesus as the one who proclaimed the advent of the kingdom and demanded a repentance that involved the obedience of love. Primitive Christians lived in an eschatological climate that was pervaded by an expectation of the kingdom. They also practiced a kind of sharing of possessions, which exemplifies a tendency to de-emphasize life as usual. Their very activity points to something or someone who gave impetus to this way of living. We could not explain the tradition or the life of early Christians without pointing to an authoritative figure who did in fact proclaim the kingdom. The resurrection faith does not explain it, because it appears to arise within that same eschatological climate. We may say bluntly that, if Jesus did not proclaim the kingdom, someone else did, and the burden of proof is on the one who claims that it was not Jesus.

In addition, there is a point at which the early tradition goes against the church's theology. In the tradition, Jesus' teaching included his expectation of the Son of man. In it, the Son of man is the initiator of the kingdom and his advent is still future. Now, although Christians identified Jesus with the Son of man, the tradition does not make this identification. The separation between the two is preserved right down to the time of the Synoptics. In them, the term *Son of man* is frequently and only found on Jesus' lips, but

[2] Paul reflects this tradition in I Corinthians 11:23–26. The Synoptics also contain a narrative about Jesus' last meal. See Mark 14:17 ff.; Matthew 26:20 ff.; Luke 22:14 ff.

[3] The Gospel of John has a confused statement about Jesus' baptizing in 4:1 f. and substitutes a foot baptism for the eucharistic meal in 13:2 ff.

The Sermon on the Mount, third-century fresco from the Tomb of the Aurelii, Rome. (*Courtesy* Alinari-Art Reference Bureau.)

in no case where the eschatological emphasis is present is there an equation of Jesus with the Son of man.[4] This is a striking phenomenon. That the church attributed to Jesus a point of view in opposition to its own theology argues for the accuracy of the tradition at this point.

We conclude that Jesus probably proclaimed the kingdom and demanded repentance, as the tradition claimed. The memory of his teaching produced the eschatological climate of primitive Christianity. The kingdom teaching does not appear to be the product of faith, because it is partly inconsistent with the faith.

[4] In a number of passages, the phrase *Son of man* is used in a noneschatological context. In them, the meaning is probably "I" or "man." In Aramaic, the phrase is customarily employed in these ways.

A possible implication following from this conclusion must now be examined. Proclamation and demand imply a high degree of authority. The tradition, of course, grants this authority to Jesus, but is it possible that he claimed it for himself? If so, it is strange that the Synoptic Gospels display a reluctance to establish it directly. Mark's motif of the Messianic secret is a case in point. If the tradition had contained a memory that Jesus made a direct claim of authority, or, more specifically, clearly presented himself as Messiah, such a claim could hardly have disappeared from the tradition. But in Mark Jesus does not claim Messiahship until his trial, when he responds positively to the question of the high priest. The priest asks, "Are you the Messiah?"; and Jesus answers, "I am; and you will see the Son of Man. . ."[5] Even here the distinction between Jesus and the Son of man is maintained. The pattern in Mark points to the author's intention to use the trial narrative as the climactic point at which the hidden Messiah is finally revealed. Neither Matthew nor Luke reports Jesus' answer in quite this way. Matthew follows Mark's outline of the trial faithfully, but, instead of the clear acceptance of Messiahship, Matthew has Jesus reply ambiguously: "The words are yours."[6] Luke has: "If I tell you, you will not believe me; and if I ask questions, you will not answer."[7] Neither Matthew nor Luke consistently follows Mark's motif of the Messianic secret, but both change an unambiguous answer into an ambiguous one. This produces an overwhelming impression that Jesus was not remembered as having made direct Messianic claims. The early Christians were sure, however, that he presented himself with authority. That he actually did is implied by his proclamation and demand. He presents no evidence for his conviction, nor does he claim a special knowledge in the Gnostic sense. It is simply: "I say to you." The effect of this forceful authority is summarized in an editorial comment in Mark 1:22: "The people were astounded at his teaching, for, unlike the doctors of the law, he taught with a note of authority." It is also present in the antitheses in Matthew, in which Jesus' authority is set over against that of Moses. It is represented in a characteristic word that precedes a number of his sayings. This is the word, *Amen,* which is translated as "verily" or "truly" or (in the New English Bible) "I tell you this." Many modern scholars feel that *Amen* was a characteristic word that Jesus used to preface his teachings. It is a Semitic word frequently found at the conclusion of a clause, where it serves to indicate one's agreement with a proposition. There are no parallels

[5] Mark 14:62.
[6] Matthew 26:64.
[7] Luke 22:68.

in Rabbinic or later Christian literature to the use of the word at the beginning of a saying. So perhaps Jesus himself used the word in such a way that it would constitute an indirect claim of authority.[8] It is not possible to make legitimate inferences about Jesus' personal feeling of authority, but it is appropriate to suggest that he impressed his contemporaries with a high degree of authority. These impressions may be at the root of the veneration of Jesus by primitive Christians.

JESUS' MIRACLES

The earliest traditions affirm that Jesus performed exorcisms and healings. We, as twentieth-century people, cannot easily conclude from the early tradition that Jesus in fact performed miracles. Too much stands in the way of such an inference. We cannot approach the question of miracles without facing a number of problems. To be sure, we are in no position to say that we know all the rules whereby changes in nature and human beings take place. But we do know some things. We may be called upon at any time to revise our understanding of natural regularities, but we are cautious to do so and demand documented evidence provided under controlled situations. We have nothing like this in the early Christian traditions. Instead, we have unscientific reports preserved by pre-Enlightenment people. People who are not disposed to see nature as regular do not require what scientists require. The skeptical attitude was simply not present among early Christians, so they never produced anything resembling documented proof. In view of this situation, we cannot simply conclude that the tradition about miracles is historically accurate.

A rebuttal to this position is sometimes entered, that questions the relevancy of the warrant cited above. It is said that the demands of proof should not be placed upon Christian reports of miracles, because they are reports of the actions of Jesus. Implicit in the rebuttal is the assumption that

---

[8] Ernst Käsemann is largely responsible for reopening the historical study of Jesus after a hiatus caused largely by the publication of Schweitzer's *Quest* in 1906. (See p. 342 f.) Käsemann believes that Jesus' feeling of authority is one of the least dubious parts of the entire early Christian tradition. See his article, "The Problem of the Historical Jesus," in *Essays on New Testament Themes* (Naperville, Ill.: Allenson, 1964), pp. 15–47. The article was originally a lecture delivered in 1953. Käsemann wrote that Jesus' use of *Amen* and his claim to operate by the spirit mean that he looked upon himself as "the instrument of the living Spirit of God, which Judaism expected to be the gift of the End" (p. 42).

Jesus was not subject to the rules that bind human beings. But that assumption flies in the face of early Christian tradition, which affirmed that Jesus, *as a man,* performed these feats and which recognized that he was not unique in doing so. The idea that Jesus could do things no one else could do is foreign to the earliest tradition.

The necessary conclusion seems to be that the miracle tradition has no historical basis. But before we come to this conclusion, it is necessary to consider another rebuttal. In the ancient world, ill health and demon possession were frequently related to evil. If Jesus proclaimed the kingdom and authoritatively demanded repentance and if his demand was met by a positive response, as it must frequently have been, the ancient mind would have understood Jesus' effect as an overcoming of evil. We are in no position to deny that these positive responses might have shown themselves visibly. A mentally ill person who made a positive response to Jesus might very well have found a reorientation for his life that would result in a kind of mental peace. This possibility is most easily demonstrated by reference to the exorcisms. Although we do not talk about demon possession, we must not assume that there is no reality reflected in the term. We are familiar with those symptoms associated by the ancient world with demon possession, and in most cases demoniacs display symptoms with which modern psychology is familiar. Witness, for example, Mark's description of the demoniac at Gerasa.[9] He lived alone among the tombs. People had tried to bring him under control but had failed. He cried out and cut himself with stones. The information that Mark gives is not sufficient to provide the basis of a full diagnosis, but it is enough to suggest that some kind of mental illness was involved. The tradition of exorcism might well reflect the fact that Jesus' proclamation met a positive response. Since the ancient mind made no sharp distinction between mental and physical illness, the positive effect of Jesus could be described in terms both of healing and exorcism. The relation between Jesus' battle against evil and his healings is beautifully expressed in the kerygmatic formula: Jesus "went about doing good and healing all who were oppressed by the devil."[10]

Here we can only assent to a conclusion as possible. It is historically possible that Jesus had a positive effect on people that resulted in a visible improvement of their psychological or physical states. A fact such as this may account for the tradition of Jesus as healer and exorcist.

[9] Mark 5 : 1–20.
[10] Acts 10 : 38.

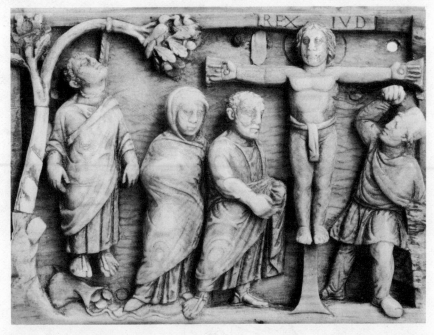

An ivory casket from c. 420, showing the death of Judas by hanging and Jesus on the cross. (*Courtesy* the Trustees of the British Museum, London.)

Jesus' Trial

That Jesus was crucified is one of the better-attested facts of early Christian history. It is affirmed in the *kerygma,* by Paul, and by Tacitus; it is never questioned by any writers, except the Gnostics, who generally have problems with a historical Jesus. It is included in the early traditions, which blame the Romans for the death of Jesus. Little question needs to be raised on this score, for it follows from the fact of crucifixion. Moreover, since crucifixion was generally used for political convicts, it is probable that Jesus was accused of a political crime, possibly sedition. The tradition that he was accused of royal pretension is probably the product of later Christian reflection. One suspects that the authority with which Jesus taught had something to do with the charge, for an authoritative proclamation of a kingdom would, in some quarters, seem politically dangerous. But we have no way to discover the evidence for the charge of sedition, nor can we verify or deny it. It is relevant to observe, however, that Roman procurators frequently dealt with Jewish revolutionists and that they dealt with them harshly. It is also relevant to note that Pontius Pilate had a reputation for tyrannical treatment of his subjects. Herod Agrippa I said that Pilate was recklessly arbitrary and that under him there were "continuous executions without even the form of a trial."[11] Josephus reports that, at the beginning of his rule, Pilate had his garrison soldiers enter Jerusalem by night, carrying staffs with the emperor's image. To protest the act, citizens stormed his citadel at Caesarea. Pilate kept them out for six days, and when they

FIGURE 28   A sketch of crucifixion position based on analysis of a skeleton found in the ancient cemetery at Givat Hamivtan in N. E. Jerusalem. The skeleton is about 2,000 years old. (*Courtesy* Time Magazine. © 1971 Time Inc.)

were finally admitted, they found themselves surrounded by soldiers with drawn swords. It was only when the people daringly bared their necks that Pilate relented.[12] Josephus also reports that Pilate misdirected Temple funds in order to build an aqueduct and that he violently crushed all opposition to his plans.[13] These facts do not argue either for Jesus' guilt or innocence,

[11] Quoted by Philo, *Embassy to Gaius*, 38; see also p. 55 f.
[12] Josephus, *Antiquities* XVIII, 3:1; *War* II, 9:2–3.
[13] *Antiquities* XVIII, 3:2; *War* II, 9:4.

but they enlighten us on the general climate and on the reputation of Jesus' judge.

The part that Jews may have played in the execution of Jesus is more difficult to determine. They may have had nothing to do with it, but in that case it is difficult to account for the early rise of the tradition about their complicity. Christian hostility toward Jews might have produced it, but hostility was not acute in the early days, except among the more liberal Jewish Christians such as Stephen. It is more likely that the tradition embodies a genuine historical memory. We can only guess at the possible form of their cooperation with Rome. In some places a Roman governor or procurator used an existing native court in his administration of justice. In Egypt, for example, native courts were allowed to judge minor civil cases involving such things as loans and contracts. In major criminal cases, especially in cases of political crimes, the native court was charged with gathering evidence against the accused and preparing a case for the procurator's judgment. In the presentation of the case, the native court, or its presiding officer, acted in the capacity of a prosecuting attorney.[14] If the judicial structure in Judaea was analogous to that in Egypt, we have a description of the part that the Sanhedrin may have played in Jesus' case. In addition, the Sanhedrin was made up largely of Sadducees, who were interested in a coexistence with Rome and in political order. Under these circumstances, it is not unreasonable to conclude that the Sanhedrin had some part to play in Jesus' trial, perhaps in preparing the case for Pilate. In any event, we must be careful to see things in the proper perspective. Roman responsibility for Jesus' death is clear and unquestionable. He was convicted of violating Roman law, and he was crucified. Jewish complicity in the execution is questionable and at best secondary.

JESUS' APPEARANCES

The resurrection of Jesus cannot be treated as an object of historical investigation. The resurrection of the dead to everlasting life is not, after all, a matter of history. Although belief in it is a historical phenomenon, such belief always points beyond history. The resurrection of Jesus can no more be proven by historical method than can the existence of God. Moreover, the material on which we must depend presents the resurrection of Jesus

[14] Evidence is found in the Oxyrynchus papyri. See A. S. Hunt and C. C. Edgar, *Select Papyri*, Loeb Classical Library (Cambridge, Mass.: Harvard University Press, 1934), Vol. II, pp. 172–225.

only as an inference. Except for the scanty narrative in the Gospel of Peter, nowhere can we find an attempt to describe the resurrection as an event. No character in any narrative is able to offer eyewitness testimony about it, to convey the process by which Jesus came back to life, and thus to verify the historical facticity of the resurrection. It is always and only an inference based upon the experience of an appearance of Jesus or the discovery of an empty tomb or the hearing of a message of angels. Thus, historical method cannot embrace the resurrection of Jesus.

These recognitions do not relieve a historian from a responsibility to attempt some explanation of the meaning of the resurrection faith. As we have seen, the earliest tradition in this matter was probably a statement that Jesus appeared to his disciples after the crucifixion. The historian cannot verify an inference based on this tradition, but he should make clear what it means. We therefore ask: What did Christians mean when they transmitted the tradition about Jesus' appearances?

Of central importance are the verbs used in the variants of the early tradition. The most frequently used verb in the gospel narratives is a form of the Greek *horaō*. This is only one of several verbs which express visual perception. But *horaō* can also refer to an intellectual exercise or to a spiritual perception. It is similar to the English *to see,* which has the same kind of ambiguity. If I say that I saw my friend this morning, it is clear that I am referring to a visual experience. But if I say that I see what you mean, I intend to express the fact that I understand. In addition, the verb *horaō* is used in the Greek translation of the Old Testament as a technical term to express the receiving of a revelation. When we read in Isaiah 40:5 that men shall see the glory of God, we do not think of a visual perception but rather of receiving a revelation from God. The variable meaning of the verb should guard us against a hasty decision to understand the resurrection narratives as pointing to visual experiences. They may signify something closer to spiritual perception or the receiving of a revelation.

A close study of the earliest written account of the appearance tradition should help to clarify its meaning. I Corinthians 15:3–8 is such an account, and the key verb is *horaō*. It is used in the passive, and may be translated: "Jesus was seen," or "Jesus allowed himself to be seen," or "Jesus showed himself," or "Jesus was revealed."[15] To the traditional catalogue of appearances, Paul adds the one to himself, and he is careful to use the same verb to designate both his experience and that of Peter, James, and the others.

---

[15] See Willi Marxsen, *The Resurrection of Jesus of Nazareth,* trans. Margaret Kohl (Philadelphia, Pa.: Fortress Press, 1970), p. 98.

He believes that whatever happened to them also happened to him. In his own case, he points to his experience of conversion, which he also refers to in Galatians 1:13 ff. In the Galatians passage he reminds his readers that he once was a persecutor of the church but became a missionary to the Gentiles when God *revealed* his Son to him. The passages are parallel in substance, although the wording and context differ. The most notable point is the change of verbs, from *horaō* in I Corinthians 15:8 to *apokalyptō* (to reveal) in Galatians 1:16. The fact that Paul could use either verb to designate his conversion experience is of highest significance. It means that he could give an account of his conversion experience without calling attention to visual elements. Since the verb *horaō* had frequently been associated with revelation, it is fair to suppose that Paul intended to signify his reception of a revelation in I Corinthians. That passage then would say: Jesus was revealed to Peter, the twelve, the five hundred brethren, James, the apostles, and me. A revelation may or may not have visual content, and in Paul's accounts it probably does not. Paul believed that Jesus had been raised with a spiritual body, and he developed that concept in I Corinthians 15. Surely he would not think of visual perception in relation to a spiritual body. In all probability, when Paul said that Jesus appeared to him, he meant to refer to a revelation but not to an experience with visual content. With Paul's letters, we are as close as we can possibly get to the earliest appearance tradition, and the evidence is that the tradition did not emphasize a visual experience.

Another element in Paul's account is the association of the revelation of Jesus with a missionary command. He says in Galatians that, as a result of his experience, he became a missionary to the Gentiles. In I Corinthians 9:1, he produces his mission to the Corinthians as evidence that he has seen the Lord. The association of an appearance with a missionary function is not unique to Paul, for it appears in other versions of the tradition. In Matthew, Jesus' Galilean appearance issues in a command for the disciples to baptize and teach. The climactic appearance in Luke is accompanied by a command to proclaim forgiveness. In John 20, the risen Jesus sends out the disciples and gives them power to forgive sins. In John 21, the appearance is accompanied by the command to Peter to feed Jesus' sheep. The Petrine *kerygma* in Acts 10 also couples the appearance with Jesus' command to proclaim him as judge of living and dead. In almost all references to a postresurrection appearance of Jesus, there is a missionary command, the fulfillment of which serves as the outcome of the experience. This fact points to the basic meaning of the appearance tradition. If we should ask what the appearances meant to those who experienced them, the answer would be that they felt appointed to preach. The functional meaning of the appearance is a conviction about the significance of Jesus and his message. This is true of the Pauline *kerygma,* the Petrine *kerygma,* and the appearance narratives in the gospels.

In summary, we may say that the appearance tradition in its earliest form meant that certain people claimed to have received a revelation in which they became convinced of the ultimate significance of Jesus and his message. Their experience resulted in their missionary activity. The focus of attention on Jesus and his message calls attention to the fact that Jesus had, in his lifetime, impressed his disciples with a personal authority and that he had proclaimed the kingdom and demanded repentance. The tradition about appearances means that his followers (and Paul) became convinced that his authoritative proclamation did not die at the crucifixion. It, and consequently Jesus, was alive in the missionary activity that ensued. To say that Jesus is alive means that Jesus is meaningful for me, that his message is absolutely true and must be proclaimed.

The ultimate basis for the conviction is not within the purview of historical investigation. Surely belief in the resurrection came as a result of the rise of certain convictions. But perhaps something further lies behind the convictions. Here the historian must admit a lack of knowledge. Nevertheless, he can assert that Jesus himself had impressed his disciples with his own conviction of authority and that he had convinced them that the kingdom was coming. Whatever be their experience, whatever be the process that lies behind the rise of their conviction, they became certain that no one, Jewish priest or Roman procurator, could put an end to it.

The information we have gleaned from the early tradition is by no means exhaustive. Other conclusions may be added to these, and implications may be drawn from the meager information we have. For example, does the fact of Jesus' baptism imply anything about his relation with John the Baptist?[16] Did the Roman accusation of Jesus imply that he was associated with Zealots?[17] Whatever be the answer to these questions, we shall never have enough information to write a biography of Jesus. We shall always lack those vital pieces of data on his intention, on what he thought of himself, and on what he really meant by his words and deeds. At best we end up with a few impressions about him, impressions that are lacking in in-

[16] For an affirmative answer, see Joseph B. Tyson, "Jesus and Herod Antipas," *Journal of Biblical Literature* 79:239–246 (1960).

[17] For an affirmative answer, see S. G. F. Brandon, *Jesus and the Zealots* (New York: Scribner's, 1967).

ternal connection and rational consistency. This is the case, because, when we have reached back as far as we can, we have only begun to understand something about the effect that Jesus produced upon some of his compatriots. This should not disillusion the historically minded, for a man is never a part of history except as he affects other persons. History knows of no such thing as a man in total isolation from his fellows. In the third century, the Christian hermit, St. Anthony, lived alone and made every effort to avoid contact with other men. He was only partially successful, because other men were attracted to the very isolation that he embraced, and they copied his way of life. From him began a stream of ascetic monasticism which formed a significant tradition in the Western world. The irony of St. Anthony is that if he had been completely successful, we should never have heard of him. To say that history knows of no man totally in isolation from his fellows does not mean that the historian is interested only in a man's effect on others. In many cases, one's intention and his effect are two different things, so the historian is interested in both and in the relation between them. But he recognizes that in some cases the intention cannot be recovered. The life of Jesus is one of those cases. We do not know his intention. We know only that he impressed many of his contemporaries as the one who authoritatively proclaimed the coming of God's kingdom and, with like authority, demanded repentance.

Bibliography

The books listed below are suggested as additional reading for students who wish to probe more deeply into selected subjects. Many titles familiar to the specialist are omitted because their authors presume technical or linguistic skills that are not usually mastered by the college student.

INTRODUCTION

General Introductions

Enslin, M. S. *Christian Beginnings*. New York: Harper and Row, 1956. 2 volumes.

Feine, Paul, and J. Behm. *Introduction to the New Testament*. Rev. W. G. Kümmel. Trans. by A. J. Mattill, Jr. New York: Abingdon, 1966.

Goodspeed, Edgar J. *A History of Early Christian Literature*. Rev. R. M. Grant. Chicago: University of Chicago Press, 1966.

Kee, H. C., F. W. Young, and K. Froehlich. *Understanding the New Testament*. Rev. ed. Englewood Cliffs: Prentice-Hall, 1965.

Marxsen, Willi. *Introduction to the New Testament*. Trans. by G. Buswell. Oxford: Blackwell, 1968.

Price, James L. *Interpreting the New Testament*. 2nd ed. New York: Holt, Rinehart and Winston, 1971.

Robert, André, and André Feuillet. *Introduction to the New Testament*. Trans. by P. W. Skehan et al. New York: Desclee, 1965.

Selby, Donald J. *Introduction to the New Testament*. New York: The Macmillan Company, 1971.

Spivey, R. A., and D. M. Smith. *Anatomy of the New Testament*. New York: The Macmillan Company, 1969.

Weiss, Johannes. *Earliest Christianity*. Trans. by F. C. Grant. New York: Harper and Row, 1959. 2 volumes.

A general introduction treats questions of provenance, chronology, authorship, occasion, and purpose of the early Christian writings. Most deal only with the canonical material. The Feine-Behm-Kümmel volume is usually referred to under the name of Kümmel, who thoroughly revised and updated the older work. It contains material on the development of the New Testament canon and the history of the text, and it includes comprehensive bibliographies. The book by Goodspeed concentrates on noncanonical material. Weiss is older than the others, but it is still valuable. It integrates the canonical and noncanonical writings with the history of Christianity to A.D. 150, and it includes an excellent bibliography.

Translations

The New English Bible. Oxford and Cambridge University Presses, 1970.

The Revised Standard Version. New York: Nelson, 1952.

Grant, R. M. et al. *The Apostolic Fathers*. New York: Nelson, 1964–1967. 5 volumes.

Hennecke, Edgar. *New Testament Apocrypha*. Ed. W. Schneemelcher. Trans. by R. McL. Wilson. Philadelphia, Pa.: Westminster Press, 1963, 1965. 2 volumes.

Jones, Alexander, ed. *The Jerusalem Bible*. Garden City, N.Y.: Doubleday, 1966.

Lake, Kirsopp. *Apostolic Fathers*. Loeb Classical Library. Cambridge, Mass.: Harvard University Press, 1950, 1959. 2 volumes.

Richardson, Cyril C., ed. *Early Christian Fathers*. New York: The Macmillan Company, 1970.

The New English Bible (NEB) and *The Revised Standard Version* (RSV) are available in a number of editions, both in paperback and hardcover. The NEB edition cited above contains the Old Testament Apocrypha. The volumes by Grant, Hennecke, and Richardson contain helpful introductions to the various documents. The Richardson edition cited above is a paperback. It is also available in hardcover from The Westminster Press, Philadelphia (1953). In this edition, it is volume 1 of The Library of Christian Classics. The various volumes of the Loeb Classical Library contain both the Greek or Latin text and an English translation. The entire series forms a basic source for a study of our period.

Study Tools

Aharoni, Y., and M. Avi-Yonah. *The Macmillan Bible Atlas*. New York: The Macmillan Company, 1968.

Bibliography

Buttrick, George A., ed. *The Interpreter's Dictionary of the Bible*. New York: Abingdon, 1962. 4 volumes.

Cross, F. L., ed. *The Oxford Dictionary of the Christian Church*. London: Oxford University Press, 1957.

Ellison, J. W., ed. *Nelson's Complete Concordance of the Revised Standard Version*. New York: Nelson, 1957.

Kittel, G., and G. Friedrich, eds. *Theological Dictionary of the New Testament*. Trans. by G. W. Bromiley. Grand Rapids, Mich.: Eerdmans, 1964–1969. 6 volumes so far published.

Van der Meer, F., and Christine Mohrmann, *Atlas of the Early Christian World*. Trans. by Mary F. Hedlund and H. H. Rowley. New York: Nelson, 1958.

Wright, G. E., and F. V. Filson. *The Westminster Historical Atlas to the Bible*. Rev. ed. Philadelphia, Pa.: Westminster Press, 1956.

Young, Robert. *Analytical Concordance to the Bible*. New York: Funk and Wagnalls, 1936.

The dictionaries edited by Buttrick and Cross will supply quick information on almost any subject related to early Christianity and its background. Concordances will help in locating a passage in the Bible if only a word or two is remembered. Ellison's is based on the RSV text and Young's on the old King James Version. Young's does, however, break down each entry in terms of the actual Greek or Hebrew word used in the Bible. The volumes edited by Kittel are detailed studies of the most important words used in the Bible and are generally helpful in spite of their use of Greek and Hebrew. Atlases will help to clarify a number of otherwise difficult points and vague references. The one by F. van der Meer deals with Christianity through A.D. 600 and contains unique maps and excellent examples of Christian art during the period.

Canonization

Grant, R. M. *The Formation of the New Testament*. New York: Harper and Row, 1965.

Several of the general introductions and commentaries (see below) also contain chapters on the history of canonization.

Historiography

Bartsch, Hans W., ed. *Kerygma and Myth*. Trans. by R. H. Fuller. New York: Harper and Row, 1961.

Collingwood, R. G. *The Idea of History*. Oxford: Clarendon Press, 1946.

Fuller, Reginald H. *The New Testament in Current Study*. New York: Scribner's, 1962.

Grant, R. M. *A Short History of the Interpretation of the Bible*. Rev. ed. New York: The Macmillan Company, 1963.

Harvey, Van A. *The Historian and the Believer*. New York: The Macmillan Company, 1966.

Neill, Stephen. *The Interpretation of the New Testament, 1861–1961*. London: Oxford University Press, 1964.

Robinson, James M., and John B. Cobb, eds. *The New Hermeneutic*. New Frontiers in Theology, II. New York: Harper and Row, 1964.

Collingwood and Harvey deal with the problems of interpreting and writing history. The volume edited by Bartsch is headed by an essay by Rudolf Bultmann, entitled "New Testament and Mythology." It also contains several essays critical of Bultmann's position in regard to demythologization and Bultmann's replies to his critics. The book edited by Robinson contains a series of essays on problems of interpreting religious texts. Grant and Neill deal with the history of the interpretation of early Christianity, and Fuller pinpoints the major problems of interpretation confronting scholars today.

THE HERITAGE OF EARLY CHRISTIANITY

The Hellenistic Period

Brinton, Crane, John B. Christopher, and Robert L. Woolf. *A History of Civilization*. Englewood Cliffs, N.J.: Prentice-Hall, 1967.

Cook, S. A., F. E. Adcock, and M. P. Charlesworth, eds. *The Cambridge Ancient History*. New York: The Macmillan Company, 1924–1939. 12 volumes.

Robinson, Charles A., Jr. *Ancient History*. 2nd ed. Alan Boegehold. New York: The Macmillan Company, 1967.

Schürer, Emil. *A History of the Jewish People in the Time of Jesus Christ*. Trans. by John Macpherson et al. New York: Scribner's, 1885. 5 volumes.

Tarn, W. W., and G. T. Griffith. *Hellenistic Civilization*. 3rd edition. London: Edward Arnold, 1952.

Brinton, Christopher, and Woolf is a survey of Western civilization; Robinson begins with prehistoric man and goes to A.D. 565. *The Cambridge Ancient History* contains detailed studies of the Hellenistic and Imperial periods, especially in volumes 7, 9, and 10. Schürer's work, soon to appear in a new edition, has been the standard history of Judaea in the Hellenistic period. The book by Tarn and Griffith is an excellent study of Alexandrian Hellenism.

Social Conditions in Imperial Rome

Benko, Stephen, and John J. O'Rourke, eds. *The Catacombs and the Colosseum*. Valley Forge, Pa.: Judson Press, 1971.

Carcopino, Jerome. *Daily Life in Ancient Rome*. Ed. H. T. Rowell. Trans. by E. O. Lorimer. New Haven, Conn.: Yale University Press, 1940.

Charlesworth, M. P. *The Roman Empire*. London: Oxford University Press, 1951.

Dill, Samuel. *Roman Society from Nero to Marcus Aurelius*. New York: Meridian, 1956.

Foakes-Jackson, F. J., and Kirsopp Lake, eds. *The Beginnings of Christianity*. New York: The Macmillan Company, 1920–1933. 5 volumes.

Frank, Tenny, ed. *An Economic Survey of Ancient Rome*. Baltimore, Md.: Rowman and Littlefield, 1938. 6 volumes.

Grant, Frederick C. *The Economic Background of the Gospels*. London: Oxford University Press, 1926.

Hadas, Moses. *Hellenistic Culture*. New York: Columbia University Press, 1959.

Mattingly, Harold. *The Man in the Roman Street*. New York: Numismatic Review, 1947.

Benko and O'Rourke have collected an excellent group of sociological studies relating to our period. Each essay was written by a member of the Philadelphia Seminar on Christian Origins. The books by Carcopino and Mattingly are written with scholarly care but are not pedantic. The six-volume survey by Tenny Frank is a standard reference work. Charlesworth deals with political institutions, education, and trade in the Roman Empire up to the time of Constantine. Grant analyzes the economic impact of Roman taxation and of Jewish religious observance on the Jews. Several essays in volume 1 of Foakes-Jackson and Lake are still useful.

Hellenistic Philosophies

Earl, Donald. *The Moral and Political Tradition of Rome*. Ithaca, N.Y.: Cornell University Press, 1967.

Grant, Frederick C. *Roman Hellenism and the New Testament.* New York: Scribner's, 1962.

Oates, Whitney J., ed. *The Stoic and Epicurean Philosophers.* New York: Modern Library, 1940.

The book edited by Oates contains translations of the writings of Epicurus, Epictetus, Lucretius, and Marcus Aurelius, together with introductions to each writer.

Hellenistic Religions

Ferguson, John. *The Religions of the Roman Empire.* Ithaca, N.Y.: Cornell University Press, 1970.

Glover, T. R. *The Conflict of Religions in the Early Roman Empire.* London: Methuen, 1909.

Grant, Frederick C., ed. *Ancient Roman Religion.* New York: Liberal Arts Press, 1957.

———, ed. *Hellenistic Religions.* New York: Liberal Arts Press, 1953.

Murray, Gilbert. *Five Stages of Greek Religion.* 3rd ed. Boston: Beacon Press, 1951.

Nock, A. D. *Conversion.* Oxford: Clarendon Press, 1933.

Rose, H. J. *Religion in Greece and Rome.* New York: Harper and Row, 1959.

Willoughby, Harold R. *Pagan Regeneration.* (Chicago: University of Chicago Press, 1929.

The two volumes edited by Grant contain basic primary material for the study of Hellenistic religion. Ferguson's book contains a wealth of detail and makes abundant use of ancient inscriptions. Studies by Willoughby, Murray, and Rose are excellent and largely sympathetic. Nock deals with the effects of various religions, including Christianity, on ancient man. Glover describes religion from the point of view of the sophisticated Roman.

Judaism

Burrows, Millar. *The Dead Sea Scrolls.* New York: Viking Press, 1955.

———. *More Light on the Dead Sea Scrolls.* New York: Viking Press, 1958.

Davies, W. D. *Christian Origins and Judaism.* Philadelphia, Pa.: Westminster Press, 1962.

Farmer, William R. *Maccabees, Zealots, and Josephus.* New York: Columbia University Press, 1956.

Finkelstein, Louis. *The Pharisees: The Sociological Background of Their Faith.* 3rd ed. Philadelphia, Pa.: Jewish Publication Society of America, 1962. 2 volumes.

Gaster, T. H., ed. *The Dead Sea Scriptures in English Translation.* Garden City, N.Y.: Doubleday, 1956.

Herford, R. Travers. *The Pharisees.* New York: The Macmillan Company, 1924.

Klausner, Joseph. *The Messianic Idea in Israel.* Trans. by W. F. Stinespring. New York: The Macmillan Company, 1955.

Moore, George Foot. *Judaism in the First Centuries of the Christian Era.* Cambridge: Harvard University Press, 1927. 2 volumes plus index.

Mowinckel, Sigmund. *He That Cometh.* Trans. by G. W. Anderson. Oxford: Blackwell, 1956.

Ringgren, Helmer. *The Faith of Qumran.* Trans. by Emilie T. Sander. Philadelphia, Pa.: Fortress Press, 1963.

Schechter, Solomon. *Aspects of Rabbinic Theology.* New York: Schocken Books, 1961.

Simon, Marcel. *Jewish Sects at the Time of Jesus.* Trans. by James H. Farley. Philadelphia, Pa.: Fortress Press, 1967.

Stendahl, Krister, ed. *The Scrolls and the New Testament.* New York: Harper and Row, 1957.

Toombs, Lawrence E. *The Threshold of Christianity.* Philadelphia, Pa.: Westminster Press, 1960.

Although it needs correction at several points, Moore's work is a valuable, comprehensive study of Judaism. Davies and Simon provide some of the needed corrections. Toombs's book is a brief analysis of the intertestamental apocrypha and pseudepigrapha. Burrows has a vivid description of the initial Qumran discoveries and provides some translations of selected scrolls. Gaster has other translations. The relationship between the Dead Sea Scrolls and the rise of Christianity is dealt with in a series of essays in the book edited by Stendahl. Schechter, Herford, and Finkelstein have admirable, sympathetic studies of the Pharisees, and Simon deals with lesser-known sects. Farmer attempts to show that there was a line of continuity running from the Maccabees to the later Zealots. Klausner and Mowinckel deal with the meaning and function of Messianic expectation in Judaism.

Bibliography

The Literature of Early Christianity
Commentaries

The Anchor Bible. Garden City, N.Y.: Doubleday. 4 New Testament volumes to date.

Brown, R. E., J. A. Fitzmyer, and R. E. Murphy, eds. *The Jerome Biblical Commentary*. Englewood Cliffs, N.J.: Prentice Hall, 1968.

Buttrick, G. A., ed. *The Interpreter's Bible*. New York: Abingdon, 1951–1957. 12 volumes.

The Harper's New Testament Commentaries. New York: Harper and Row.

The Moffatt New Testament Commentary. New York: Harper and Row.

A commentary traditionally contains introductory material and detailed exegetical notes on each New Testament document. Most present a verse-by-verse analysis of the text and are valuable for detailed research. The oldest in the group above is the Moffatt series, based on the translation of the New Testament by James Moffatt. The Harper series, by a distinguished group of English and North American authors, is not yet complete. *The Interpreter's Bible* carries the King James and RSV texts in parallel columns and a running exegesis printed below. A homiletical commentary, for use by preachers, is printed below the exegesis. The volumes of the Anchor Bible now in print deal with the Gospel of John (Raymond E. Brown), the Book of Acts (Johannes Munck), James, I, II Peter, and Jude (Bo Reicke). It promises to be a distinguished series. *The Jerome Biblical Commentary* is an excellent one-volume introduction and commentary by a group of Roman Catholic scholars. In addition to these commentaries, a number of similar works, which do not form parts of a series, are available. Several of these will be noted below.

The Letters of Paul

Bornkamm, Günther. *Paul*. Trans. by D. M. G. Stalker. New York: Harper and Row, 1971.

Buck, Charles, and Greer Taylor. *Saint Paul: A Study in the Dev 'opment of His Thought*. New York: Scribner's, 1969.

Knox, John. *Chapters in a Life of Paul*. New York: Abingdon, 1950.

Knox was one of the first to attempt a life of Paul on the basis of the letters alone. Buck and Taylor carried the process a bit farther and attempted to solve the problem of Pauline chronology by analyzing the course of the apostle's thought. Bornkamm deals with both the life and thought of Paul and uses the letters as his chief source. Treatments of the individual Pauline letters, as well as the others, are included in the commentaries listed above.

Oral Traditions ·

Bultmann, Rudolf. *The History of the Synoptic Tradition*. Trans. by John Marsh. New York: Harper and Row, 1963.

Dibelius, Martin. *From Tradition to Gospel*. Trans. by B. L. Woolf. New York: Scribner's, 1935.

———. *The Message of Jesus Christ*. Trans. by F. C. Grant. New York: Scribner's, 1939.

Dodd, C. H. *The Apostolic Preaching and Its Developments*. New York: Harper and Row, 1939.

Koch, Klaus. *The Growth of the Biblical Tradition*. Trans. by S. M. Cupitt. New York: Scribner's, 1969.

Montgomery, R. M., and W. R. Stegner. *Auxiliary Studies in the Bible: Forms in the Gospels: I. The Pronouncement Story*. New York: Abingdon, 1970.

Taylor, Vincent. *The Formation of the Gospel Tradition*. London: Macmillan and Co., 1935.

The books by Dibelius and Bultmann are fundamental to the study of oral forms in early Christianity. Bultmann's book was first published in German in 1921. Taylor's is a good English adaptation of the principles of form criticism. The book by Dodd represents his effort to identify the primitive Christian *kerygma*. The publication of Montgomery and Stegner consists of programed instructional material on the apophthegm, or pronouncement story. Use of this material should help the student recognize the meaning of form critical study and should facilitate his ability to distinguish between primary and secondary elements in traditional material.

The Synoptic Gospels

Bornkamm, G., G. Barth, and H. J. Held. *Tradition and Interpretation in Matthew*. Trans. by Percy Scott. Philadelphia, Pa.: Westminster Press, 1963.

Burkill, T. A. *Mysterious Revelation*. Ithaca, N.Y.: Cornell University Press, 1963.

Butler, B. C. *The Originality of St. Matthew*. Cambridge: Cambridge University Press, 1951.

Cadbury, Henry. *The Making of Luke-Acts*. London: Society for the Promotion of Christian Knowledge, 1958.

Conzelmann, Hans. *The Theology of St. Luke*. Trans. by Geoffrey Buswell. New York: Harper and Row, 1960.

Davies, W. D. *The Sermon on the Mount*. Cambridge: Cambridge University Press, 1966.

Farmer, W. R. *The Synoptic Problem*. New York: The Macmillan Company, 1964.

Grant, Frederick C. *The Gospels: Their Origin and Growth*. New York: Harper and Row, 1957.

Marxsen, Willi. *Mark the Evangelist*. Trans. by James Boyce et al. New York: Abingdon, 1969.

Nineham, D. E. *The Gospel of St. Mark*. Pelican Gospel Commentaries. Baltimore, Md.: Penguin Books, 1963.

Parker, Pierson. *The Gospel Before Mark*. Chicago: University of Chicago Press, 1953.

Perrin, Norman. *What is Redaction Criticism?* Philadelphia, Pa.: Fortress Press, 1969.

Stendahl, Krister. *The School of St. Matthew and Its Use of the Old Testament*. Philadelphia, Pa.: Fortress Press, 1968.

Streeter, B. H. *The Four Gospels*. London: Macmillan and Co., 1924.

The most widely accepted solution to the problem of the literary relations among the Synoptic Gospels is presented by Streeter. Other solutions are offered by Butler, Farmer, and Parker. Grant combines an analysis of the Synoptic problem with studies of the oral tradition and introductions to each of the Synoptics. Perrin's book is an introduction to the study of the gospels as finished products, a form of study used by most of the remaining authors on our list. Burkill, Marxsen, and Nineham treat Mark. Nineham includes a helpful section on oral tradition. Marxsen's book consists of four essays that attempt to discover the intention and point of view of Mark. Stendahl looks at Matthew as a scholastic writing. Davies analyzes the various settings through which the material in Matthew's Sermon on the Mount passed. The volume by Bornkamm, Barth, and Held consists of a series of essays on Matthew's eschatology, legal theory, and interpretation of the miracle stories. Cadbury deals with the authorship and theology of Luke-Acts, whereas Conzelmann concentrates on the theology.

Other Gospels

Bultmann, Rudolf. *The Gospel of John.* Trans. by G. R. Beasley-Murray et al. Philadelphia, Pa.: Westminster Press, 1971.

Colwell, E. C. *John Defends the Gospel.* Chicago: Willett, Clark and Co., 1936.

Dodd, C. H. *The Interpretation of the Fourth Gospel.* Cambridge: Cambridge University Press, 1953.

Grant, R. M., and D. N. Freedman. *The Secret Sayings of Jesus.* Garden City, N.Y.: Doubleday, 1960.

Käsemann, Ernst. *The Testament of Jesus.* Trans. by Gerhard Krodel. Philadelphia, Pa.: Fortress Press, 1968.

Martyn, J. Louis. *History and Theology in the Fourth Gospel.* New York: Harper and Row, 1968.

Montefiore, Hugh, and H. E. W. Turner. *Thomas and the Evangelists.* Naperville, Ill.: Allenson, 1962.

Smith, D. M. *The Composition and Order of the Fourth Gospel.* New Haven, Conn.: Yale University Press, 1965.

Bultmann's commentary on John first appeared in 1941 in German. This is the first English translation. Smith's book is a critical analysis of Bultmann's treatment of the Fourth Gospel. The Dodd commentary is difficult for the student who does not read Greek, but the sections on the Hellenistic religious and philosophical background of John are invaluable. Colwell classifies the Fourth Gospel as an apology, while Martyn sees its background in the dialogues between the synagogue and the emerging church. Käsemann emphasizes the Gnostic qualities of the author in his analysis of John 17. The books listed under Grant and Montefiore are studies of the Gospel of Thomas. For material on the other noncanonical gospels, consult the edition of Hennecke, listed under Translations.

Other Writings

Barrett, C. K. *Luke the Historian in Recent Study.* London: Epworth Press, 1961.

Kelly, J. N. D. *Early Christian Doctrines.* New York: Harper and Row, 1958.

Manson, William. *The Epistle to the Hebrews.* London: Hodder and Stoughton, 1951.

O'Neill, J. C. *The Theology of Acts.* London: Society for the Promotion of Christian Knowledge, 1961.

Ramsay, W. M. *The Letters to the Seven Churches of Asia.* New York: Armstrong, 1905.

The commentary series and translations listed earlier have valuable material on most of the writings considered in this book. The Richardson volume, listed under Translations, has introductions to the Didache, II Clement, Justin, Athenagoras, and Irenaeus, and includes further bibliographical references. The Apocalypse of Peter is dealt with in Hennecke, listed under Translations. Barrett reviews the research on the author of Acts and classifies him as primitive catholic, or, in our terminology, protocatholic. O'Neill's book is an excellent study of Acts. Conzelmann (see under Synoptic Gospels) is concerned with the comprehensive plan that guided the author of Luke-Acts. Manson connects the Epistle to the Hebrews with the group headed by Stephen in Acts 6–7. The old book by Ramsay deals with the first three chapters of the Revelation of John. A good analysis of Irenaeus and his contribution is contained in the book by Kelly.

VARIETIES OF EARLY CHRISTIANITY
General Treatments

Bauer, Walter. *Orthodoxy and Heresy in Earliest Christianity.* Ed. R. A. Kraft and G. Krodel. Philadelphia, Pa.: Fortress Press, 1971.

Bousset, Wilhelm. *Kyrios Christos.* Trans. by John E. Steely. New York: Abingdon, 1970.

Bultmann, Rudolf. *Theology of the New Testament.* Trans. by K. Grobel. New York: Scribner's, 1954, 1955. 2 volumes.

Carrington, Philip. *The Early Christian Church.* Cambridge: Cambridge University Press, 1957. 2 volumes.

Case, Shirley Jackson. *The Evolution of Early Christianity.* Chicago: University of Chicago Press, 1914.

Conzelmann, Hans. *An Outline of the Theology of the New Testament.* Trans. by John Bowden. New York: Harper and Row, 1969.

Harnack, Adolf. *The Mission and Expansion of Christianity in the First Three Centuries.* Trans. by James Moffatt. New York: G. P. Putnam's Sons, 1908. 2 volumes.

Lietzmann, Hans. *The Beginnings of the Christian Church.* Trans. by B. L. Woolf. New York: Meridian Books, 1949.

———. *The Founding of the Church Universal.* Trans. by B. L. Woolf. New York: Meridian Books, 1949.

McGiffert, A. C. *A History of Christian Thought*. New York: Scribner's, 1960. 2 volumes.

These general treatments deal with the history and theology of various early Christian movements. The ones by Bousset, Bultmann, Conzelmann, and McGiffert concentrate on the theological aspects. Bauer emphasizes the varieties and organizes his material around the chief locations of Christian groups. Its recent translation into English should make this significant book available to a wider audience. Bousset's *Kyrios Christos* has been influential since its initial publication in German in 1913. It deals with Christian Christologies from the earliest days to Irenaeus.

Primitive Christianity

Caird, G. B. *The Apostolic Age*. London: Duckworth, 1955.

Cullmann, Oscar. *Peter: Disciple, Apostle, Martyr*. Trans. by F. V. Filson. New York: Living Age Books, 1958.

Nock, Arthur D. *Early Gentile Christianity and Its Hellenistic Background*. New York: Harper and Row, 1964.

Streeter, B. H. *The Primitive Church*. New York: The Macmillan Company, 1929.

In addition to these four books, the books by Bousset, Bultmann, and Conzelmann, listed under General Treatments, are particularly good on primitive Christianity. Cullmann's book is an interesting study of the traditions and history of Peter. Nock concentrates on the origin of Gentile Christianity. Caird and Streeter are more comprehensive.

Pauline Christianity

Enslin, Morton S. *The Ethics of Paul*. New York: Abingdon, 1957.

Furnish, Victor P. *Theology and Ethics in Paul*. New York: Abingdon, 1968.

Sandmel, Samuel. *The Genius of Paul*. New York: Farrar, Strauss and Cudahy, 1958.

Schoeps, H.-J. *Paul: the Theology of the Apostle in the Light of Jewish Religious History*. Trans. by Harold Knight. Philadelphia, Pa.: Westminster Press, 1959.

Wiles, M. F. *The Divine Apostle*. Cambridge: Cambridge University Press, 1967.

Sandmel's book is a study of Paul from the point of view of a modern Jewish scholar. Schoeps emphasizes a positive relation between Paul and his Jewish background. Enslin and Furnish treat Paul's ethics, and the latter attempts to set the ethical teaching within the context of Pauline theology. Wiles studies the influence and treament of Paul in the second and subsequent centuries. In addition, consult the entries under the Letters of Paul.

Johannine Christianity

Wiles, M. F. *The Spiritual Gospel*. Cambridge: Cambridge University Press, 1960.

This is a companion volume to Wiles's *Divine Apostle* and serves the same function. In addition, see the books by Bultmann, Colwell, Dodd, Käsemann, Martyn, and Smith, listed under Other Gospels.

Jewish Christianity

Brandon, S. G. F. *The Fall of Jerusalem and the Christian Church*. London: Society for the Promotion of Christian Knowledge, 1951.

Daniélou, Jean. *The Theology of Jewish Christianity*. Trans. by John A. Baker. London: Darton, Longman and Todd, 1964.

Schoeps, H.-J. *Jewish Christianity*. Trans. by D. R. A. Hare. Philadelphia, Pa.: Fortress Press, 1967.

Schonfield, Hugh J. *A History of Jewish Christianity*. London: Duckworth, 1936.

Brandon's book centers on a historical incident but contains a good deal of material on Jewish Christianity and on Paul. Schoeps is a helpful, nontechnical introduction to the subject. The most comprehensive study of Jewish Christian theology is that by Daniélou.

Gnostic Christianity

Grant, Robert M. *Gnosticism and Early Christianity*. 2nd ed. New York: Harper and Row, 1966.

Grobel, Kendrick. *The Gospel of Truth*. New York: Abingdon, 1960.

Jonas, Hans. *The Gnostic Religion*. 2nd ed. Boston: Beacon Press, 1963.

Wilson, R. McL. *Gnosis and the New Testament*. Philadelphia, Pa.: Fortress Press, 1968.

———. *The Gospel of Philip*. London: A. R. Mowbray, 1962.

Studies of Gnostic Christianity done prior to 1947 have been made less valuable by the Nag Hammadi discoveries. The more recent studies, such as those by Grant, Jonas, and Wilson, have benefited from these finds. Grobel's *Gospel of Truth* and Wilson's *Gospel of Philip* are translations and commentaries on two Gnostic documents not dealt with in our study.

Protocatholic Christianity

Protocatholic Christianity and Irenaeus are dealt with in the relevant sections of several general treatments, such as Bousset, Carrington, Harnack, and Lietzmann. See also Kelly's *Early Christian Doctrines*, listed under Other Writings.

JESUS AND EARLY CHRISTIANITY

Anderson, Hugh, ed. *Jesus*. Englewood Cliffs, N.J.: Prentice-Hall, 1967.

Barrett, C. K. *Jesus and the Gospel Tradition*. Philadelphia, Pa.: Fortress Press, 1968.

Bornkamm, Günther. *Jesus of Nazareth*. Trans. by Irene and Fraser McLuskey. New York: Harper and Row, 1960.

Brandon, S. G. F. *Jesus and the Zealots*. New York: Scribner's, 1967.

Bultmann, Rudolf. *Jesus Christ and Mythology*. New York: Scribner's, 1958.

———. *Jesus and the Word*. Trans. by Louise P. Smith and Ermine Huntress. New York: Scribner's, 1934.

Bundy, Walter E. *The Psychic Health of Jesus*. New York: The Macmillan Company, 1922.

Cadbury, Henry J. *The Eclipse of the Historical Jesus*. Haverford, Pa.: Pendle Hill, 1963.

———. *Jesus: What Manner of Man?* New York: The Macmillan Company, 1948.

———. *The Peril of Modernizing Jesus*. Naperville, Ill.: Allenson, 1962.

Cullmann, Oscar. *Jesus and the Revolutionaries*. Trans. by Gareth Putnam. New York: Harper and Row, 1970.

Daniélou, Jean. *The Infancy Narratives*. Trans. by Rosemary Sheed. New York: Herder and Herder, 1968.

Dodd, C. H. *The Parables of the Kingdom*. Rev. ed. London: Nisbet and Co., 1936.

Higgins, A. J. B. *Jesus and the Son of Man*. Philadelphia, Pa.: Fortress Press, 1964.

Jeremias, Joachim. *The Central Message of the New Testament*. New York: Scribner's, 1965.

———. *The Parables of Jesus*. Rev. ed. Trans. by S. H. Hooke. London: Student Christian Movement Press, 1963.

Käsemann, Ernst. *Essays on New Testament Themes*. Trans. by W. J. Montague. Naperville, Ill.: Allenson, 1964.

Kee, Howard C. *Jesus in History*. New York: Harcourt, Brace, Jovanovich, 1970.

Klausner, Joseph. *Jesus of Nazareth*. Trans. by Herbert Danby. New York: The Macmillan Company, 1925.

Manson, T. W. *The Teachings of Jesus*. Cambridge: Cambridge University Press, 1948.

Marxsen, Willi. *The Resurrection of Jesus of Nazareth*. Trans. by Margaret Kohl. Philadelphia, Pa.: Fortress Press, 1970.

Moule, C. F. D. *The Phenomenon of the New Testament*. London: Student Christian Movement Press, 1967.

Otto, Rudolf. *The Kingdom of God and the Son of Man*. Trans. by F. V. Filson and B. L. Woolf. Grand Rapids, Mich.: Zondervan, 1938.

Perrin, Norman. *The Kingdom of God in the Teachings of Jesus*. Philadelphia, Pa.: Westminster Press, 1963.

Robinson, James M. *A New Quest of the Historical Jesus*. London: Student Christian Movement Press, 1959.

Schweitzer, Albert. *The Quest of the Historical Jesus*. Trans. by W. Montgomery. New York: The Macmillan Company, 1955.

Tödt, H. E. *The Son of Man in the Synoptic Tradition*. Trans. by Dorothea M. Barton. Philadelphia, Pa.: Westminster Press, 1965.

Via, Dan O. *The Parables*. Philadelphia, Pa.: Fortress Press, 1967.

Wilder, Amos N. *Eschatology and Ethics in the Teaching of Jesus*. New York: Harper and Row, 1939.

Zahrnt, Heinz. *The Historical Jesus*. Trans. by J. S. Bowden. New York: Harper and Row, 1963.

The fundamental work on the historical Jesus is still that of Schweitzer. His *Quest* is a review of the most significant lives of Jesus written prior to 1910. All serious studies of Jesus since that time have been influenced by Schweitzer's work. Cadbury's books are well written and nontechnical attempts to say something positive about the historical Jesus. Bundy's book is a review of psychological studies of Jesus, a popular form of study in the early part of this century. Bultmann's works represent his own attempt to demythologize the gospels. After Bultmann, many scholars felt that it was unfruitful to pursue the study of the historical Jesus. Ernst Käsemann, however, felt that there were still possibilities, and his book contains his 1953 lecture, which reinitiated studies of Jesus. Robinson's book is the American counterpart to Käsemann's lecture. Bornkamm, Zahrnt, and Moule are working under the influence of Käsemann, though in quite different ways. The problem of finding the historical Jesus through the faith of the Christian evangelists is dealt with in Barrett, Kee, and in Jeremias' *Central Message*. The Roman Catholic scholar Daniélou makes an interesting attempt to discover the historical basis of the narratives about Jesus' birth. Hugh Anderson's book is a collection of readings that exemplify historical and contemporary positions in regard to the study of Jesus. Brandon's book has recently stirred up a controversy about the revolutionary aspects of Jesus' ministry. Cullmann attempts to counter Brandon's claims. On the teachings of Jesus, Manson and Wilder are still worthwhile. The parables are treated by Dodd, Jeremias, and Via. Jeremias is particularly strong in relating the parables to Palestinian customs and society, but the student without a knowledge of Greek will have difficulty with this book. Via feels that many of the parables are based on literary, rather than oral, forms. Otto's book is fundamental to the study of Jesus' teachings on the kingdom. Perrin's, Tödt's, and Higgins' books are more recent and are ably done. Marxsen's is a popular but highly competent study of the resurrection traditions.

References to
Primary Sources

OLD TESTAMENT

OTHER JEWISH LITERATURE

NEW TESTAMENT

OTHER EARLY CHRISTIAN LITERATURE

GREEK AND ROMAN LITERATURE

General Index

A

Aaron, 105, 109, 115
Abel, 250
Abraham, 94, 244, 314, 354ff.
Abyss, 321ff.
Achaean league, 36
Achamoth, 322f.
Acquila, 244
Actium, battle of, 36f., 49
Acts of the Apostles, 28*n.*, 112, 129,
    131, 140, 167, 204, 206, 210f.,
    233, 235–242, 273–275, 280–282,
    331, 357, 379
  ending of, 240–241
  geographical structure, 235–239, 238
    (*map*)
  "We" sections in, 206, 237
Adam, 94, 300, 314, 323, 355f.
Aeons, 321f.
Aetolian league, 36
Age to Come, 108f., 114
Agrippa I, 53, 56, 240, 394
Agrippa II, 237
Akiba, 57, 114f., 118
Albinus, 56
Alexander Balas, 45
Alexander the Great, 34, 42, 67, 77
Alexander Jannaeus, 46f.
Alexandra, 46
Alexandria, 28, 42, 64, 87, 89, 120, 160,
    208, 222

Alexandrian empire, 36
Allegory, 247, 254
Amen, 390
Anatolia, 81
Andronicus, 278
Anencletus, 153
Angelology, 91
Anicetus, 157
Anna (in Luke 2:36), 355
Anna, mother of Mary, 224
Annas, 375
Anthony, St., 399
Antigonid empire, 36
Antigonus I, 36
Antigonus, son of Aristobulus II,
    49
Antiheretical literature, 264–267, 325,
    345
Antioch, 28, 44f., 64f., 68, 154, 201, 208,
    236f., 278f.
Antiochus III, 36, 42
Antiochus IV, 42–45, 51, 99, 192
Antiochus V, 44
Antipas, son of Herod the Great, 52f.,
    63, 276, 349, 375–378
Antipas of Pergamum, 256
Antipater, 49
Antoninus Pius, 40, 60, 261
Antony, 36f., 48f., 51
Aphrodite, 57
Apocalypse, 192, 246, 253–259, 345
Apocalypse of John. *See* Revelation of
    John

B

F

G

N

O

Oates, Whitney J., 70n.

Occasion of a document, 16–17

Octavian, *See* Augustus

Olympian cult, 77

Olympus, Mount, 75

O'Neill, J. C., 235

Onesimus, bishop of Ephesus, 155

Onesimus, a slave, 140

Oral tradition

  Christian, 163–181, 183f., 188, 201, 216f., 222, 275, 349

    see also Jesus, oral tradition and forms, 172–181

    see also Form criticism

  Jewish, 97ff., 113, 119, 202

Oral transmission, consequences of, 164–172, 344

Oriental culture, 34, 36

Origen, 150

Orontes River, 34, 36

O'Rourke, John J., 62n.

Orphic religion, 81f.

Osiris, 79, 81f.

Oxyrynchus papyri, 230n.

P

Palestine, 13, 33, 42, 63f., 66, 111, 118f., 170, 196 (*map*), 271, 286f., 334

Papias, 151, 163f., 168, 183f., 190, 199f., 217, 327

Parables, 177–178, 194, 200, 209, 215, 231

  see also Similitudes

Paraclete, 308

Parousia, 150, 197f., 325

Parthia, 36f., 40, 49, 58

Passover, 52, 103, 213, 215, 249–250

Pastoral letters, 143–145, 303, 331

  see also I Timothy, II Timothy; Titus, Letter to

Patmos, 255f., 258

Paul, 2, 64, 236, 239ff.

  Acts of, 242

  apostleship of, 278–280, 282, 290, 302

  in the Book of Acts, 235–242

  conversion of, 236, 286 (*illus.*)

  death of, 153, 190, 197

  in Jewish Christianity, 314

  letters of, 18, 28n., 128–141, 130 (*illus*), 150, 154, 167, 207, 240, 267, 273–275, 324f., 332, 334, 378, 397

  life of, 286–287

  travels of, 236–237

  see also Pauline Christianity; Specific letters of Paul

Pauline Christianity, 2, 65, 143, 212, 248, 251, 271, 285, 286–304, 331, 334, 367

  Christology in, 294–295, 300–301, 306

  ecclesiology in, 301–303

  eschatology in, 287–290, 298

  ethics in, 295–300

  faith in, 295

  grace in, 287

  man in, 293–294

  resurrection of Christians in, 287–290

  sexual ethics in, 296–298

  sin in, 292–295

  spirit in, 295

    see also Holy Spirit

  spiritual gifts in, 298–300, 303

    see also Tongues, speaking in

  Torah in, 290–295

  universalism in, 287, 292

  see also Paul; Specific letters of Paul

Pax Romana, 58

Peake, A. S., 95n.

Pella, 64, 192, 313

Pentateuch, 89, 97, 112